Music, Pantomime and Freedom
in Enlightenment France

Music, Pantomime and Freedom in Enlightenment France

Hedy Law

THE BOYDELL PRESS

First published 2020
The Boydell Press, Woodbridge

ISBN 978 1 78327 560 1

The Boydell Press is an imprint of Boydell & Brewer Ltd
PO Box 9, Woodbridge, Suffolk IP12 3DF, UK
and of Boydell & Brewer Inc.
668 Mount Hope Ave, Rochester, NY 14620–2731, USA
website: www.boydellandbrewer.com

A catalogue record for this book is available
from the British Library

The publisher has no responsibility for the continued existence
or accuracy of URLs for external or third-party internet websites
referred to in this book, and does not guarantee that any content
on such websites is, or will remain, accurate or appropriate

This publication is printed on acid-free paper

For my family

Contents

List of Musical Examples

Preface

Music and dance share many properties – both are nonverbal, both are ephemeral – but one key difference between them is that western art music was more readily notated than dance. This fundamental difference bridges text and performance and presents, for composers who know their craft well, a challenge as much as an opportunity to think about how best to write dance music, or music that accompanies actors' movements. Some composers begin with simple mimicry, depicting a gesture through music by composing, for example, an ascending melody for a dancer who raises her arm; but other composers go beyond this basic level of mimicry and establish more sophisticated relationships between music and motion. This book is an examination of how composers came up with musical ideas based on movement. In more concrete terms, I examine how composers in eighteenth-century France – especially Paris – wrote music that accompanied motion. My argument contributes to a growing corpus of literature on music and the body, or what Elisabeth Le Guin calls "carnal musicology."[1]

Composers active in eighteenth-century France were fascinated by foreign dancers – those from England and Italy, in particular – who incorporated the element of pantomime in their performances, and they processed this fascination by composing music that captured the effects of these dances. Many did not try to *translate* dancers' movements into music, but many recreated the most salient properties of these performances – precision, agility, sentimentality – through music. The kind of thinking across the mediums of music, gesture, and language was not new, for French composers had, since the early eighteenth century, created instrumental character pieces, some with suggestive titles, that portrayed all sorts of subjects: individuals, objects, animals, or natural phenomena.[2] What was new around the second half of the eighteenth century was that composers deliberately represented performers' ephemeral bodily movements through the more durable medium of notated music. In this book I argue that they used their agency – known generally as "moral liberty" in the Enlightenment – in three major ways: 1) they composed music for pantomime without following existing dance conventions; 2) their music heightened performers' awareness of their moral liberty during performances; 3) pantomime performances stimulated spectators to recognize themselves as thinkers of liberty.

I do not intend to supply practical tips for historical reconstruction of individual pantomimes, but those interested in historically informed performances – whether they are "reconstructions," narrowly defined, or productions inspired by historical sources – may find various aspects of the book useful, for I explain the meanings of

1   Elisabeth Le Guin, *Boccherini's Body: An Essay in Carnal Musicology* (Berkeley, CA: University of California Press, 2005); see also, for example, J. Q. Davies, *Romantic Anatomies of Performance* (Berkeley, CA: University of California Press, 2014); Ellen Lockhart, Animation, *Plasticity, and Music in Italy, 1770–1830* (Berkeley, CA: University of California Press, 2017).

2   See David Fuller, "Of Portraits, 'Sapho,' and Couperin: Titles and Characters in French Instrumental Music of the High Baroque," *Music and Letters* 78, no.2 (1997), 149–74.

every pantomime in its context, informed by printed sources and unpublished archival materials. My discussion is by no means confined to the element of pantomime within a larger work, such as an opera or a ballet, for I discuss how the component of pantomime serves the composition in which it appears. Nor am I interested in simply describing technical aspects of the music. Instead, I aim at understanding a composer's *thinking* whenever he explicitly employed the designation of pantomime.[3]

Ultimately, my examination of these musical settings of pantomime contributes to a history of universal language. Most eighteenth-century composers were not too interested in the abstract concept of "instrumental music"; rather, they followed seventeenth- and eighteenth-century classical scholars, who marveled at accounts of ancient Roman pantomime performers who could metaphorically *tell* histories to spectators through dance and gestures. They became interested in perceptible (or *sensible*, in French and in English) relationships between music and bodily movement. Implicit in their sense of wonder was an awareness that the art of pantomime was a tried-and-true universal language in antiquity.

How could one find this lost universal language in the "modern" time, in the seventeenth and eighteenth centuries? Novelist Charles Sorel mentioned in his book, *La Bibliothèque française* (1664), that a Jesuit priest called Philippe Labbé who had mastered Greek, Latin, German, and French devised a grammar for a universal language.[4] The idea of creating a universal language from scratch had lost appeal during the final decades of the seventeenth century and the early eighteenth century, but the search for such a language returned in a cluster of mid-century writings that shaped the Enlightenment. In his *Discours préliminaire des éditeurs* to the *Encyclopédie, ou Dictionnaire raisonné des sciences, des arts et des métiers* of 1751, Jean Le Rond d'Alembert remarked that a universal and conventional language was needed to replace Latin, although it was a language with a high degree of clarity and precision. Soon afterwards, the search for a universal language took a sharp turn. In *Discours sur l'origine et les fondements de l'inégalité parmi les hommes* (or the *Second Discourse*) of 1755, Jean-Jacques Rousseau made a decisive claim that inarticulate cries, gestures, and imitative noises had long constituted a kind of universal language. The attributed author Charles Pinot-Duclos claimed in his article "Declamation of the ancients" in the *Encyclopédie* that it was nonverbal signs – not any single language – that could transcend linguistic barriers and become intelligible to people of *all* nations. Friedrich Melchior Grimm declared in the article "Lyric Poem" in the *Encyclopédie* that "every universal language is vague by its nature."[5]

---

3   I use the pronoun "he" because I have not identified any female composer active in seventeenth- and eighteenth-century France who used the designation of "pantomime" in her compositions in this period.

4   Charles Sorel, *La Bibliothèque française* (Paris: Compagnie des Libraries du Palais, 1664), 5–6. [ARTFL]

5   "Toute langue universelle est vague par sa nature." Friedrich Melchior Grimm, *Encyclopédie, ou Dictionnaire raisonné des sciences, des arts et des métiers, etc.*, ed. Denis Diderot and Jean Le Rond d'Alembert, 17 vols. (Paris: Briasson and others, 1751–65); University of Chicago: ARTFL Encyclopédie Project (Autumn 2017 Edition), ed. Robert Morrissey and Glenn Roe, http://encyclopedie.uchicago.edu/, vol. 12, s.v. "Poème lyrique." [ARTFL] On universal language, see Jean Le Rond d'Alembert,

As nonverbal artistic mediums, music and pantomime impart semantic meanings that are inevitably vague. Yet, inspired by descriptions of ancient pantomime
performers and performances of modern Italian and English pantomime dancers,
composers believed they wrote music that was intelligible for *all* audiences, regardless of their level of literacy, linguistic background, cultural heritage, or nationality.
They found in the art of pantomime a tool in their compositional toolbox, a tool that
helped them to *explore* the relationships between music and movement, not one that
prescribed how or what they should compose. This is of course not to say that composers became less creative when they composed something other than pantomime
(e.g., a menuet or an instrumental interlude), but that they relished the opportunities to create new effects by thinking musically through pantomime. In these pages
you will find a story of their discoveries.

Preliminary Discourse to the Encyclopedia of Diderot, trans. with intro. by Richard N.
Schwab (Chicago: The University of Chicago Press, 1995), 93; Jean-Jacques Rousseau,
The Collected Writings of Rousseau, ed. Roger D. Masters and Christopher Kelly, 13 vols.
(Hanover, NH: University Press of New England, 1990–2010), 3:45 [*CWR*]; Charles
Pinot-Duclos [attributed author], *Encyclopédie,* s.v. "Déclamation des anciens."

Acknowledgements

I would like to express my gratitude to the following individuals, institutions, and groups that have helped me publish this book.

I thank, above all, Martha Feldman for her strong belief in my ability to begin and finish this book project. I am also grateful to Elisabeth Le Guin for her ongoing moral and tangible support, and to Suzanne Cusick who moved it along at critical moments.

I thank Olivia Bloechl for reading drafts of chapters 1, 2, and 3 and offering helpful comments. I also thank her for sending me a manuscript of her book, *Opera and the Political Imaginary in Old Regime France*, before it was published.

Over the years, Jacqueline Waeber and I have had many stimulating conversations. She generously shared with me her profound knowledge on Rousseau, eighteenth-century French opera, pantomime, and melodrama. I thank her for friendship and unfaltering counsel. I am indebted to her for sending me a copy of her book chapter, "Rousseau on Music: A Case of Nature vs. Nurture," from *The Rousseauian Mind* (2019), edited by Eve Grace and Christopher Kelly, before it was published.

I thank Sylvie Bouissou for directing me to the four-volume *Dictionnaire de l'Opéra de Paris sous l'Ancien Régime (1669–1791)* (2019–20) and I thank Maria Gullstam for sending me bibliographic information.

More generally, I have benefitted from exchanges with David Charlton, Thomas Christensen, Georgia Cowart, Don Fader, Rebecca Geoffroy-Schwinden, the late Philip Gossett, Rebecca Harris-Warrick, Melinda Latour, Stephen Rumph, and Marian Smith. I thank Michael Beckerman, Bruce Alan Brown, Bonnie Gordon, Mitchell Morris, Pierpaolo Polzonetti, Raymond Knapp, Jann Pasler, Nancy Rao, John Rice, Elaine Sisman, Judy Tsou, and Emily Wilbourne for their words of encouragement.

I thank a number of administrators at the School of Music of the University of British Columbia – T. Patrick Carrebré (Director, 2019–), Alexander Fisher (Acting Director, 2018–19), Richard Kurth (Director, 2012–13, 2014–18), John Roeder (Acting Director, 2013–14) – for facilitating research leave and course release, and for protecting this project in ways I might never know.

The American Society for Eighteenth-Century Studies/The Andrew W. Mellon Foundation Short-Term Research Fellowship provided me with funding to conduct research at the Harry Ransom Center of the University of Texas at Austin. An American Society for Eighteenth-Century Studies Short-Term Fellowship brought me to the Newberry Library. The Early Career Scholar Award of Peter Wall Institute for Advanced Studies gave me funding and a course release to do research. A UBC Faculty of Arts Humanities and Social Sciences Research Fund provided resources to consult archival sources in Paris.

I am deeply grateful to the following librarians who helped me obtain materials for this project: Kevin Madill of the University of British Columbia, staff at branches of the Bibliothèque Nationale de France, the Bibliothèque-Musée de l'Opéra, the Regenstein Library of the University of Chicago, the Special Collections of the

University of Chicago, the Newberry Library, and the Harry Ransom Center of the University of Texas at Austin.

Linguist Dr Simone Ralalaharimanitra and Shawn Keener helped me translate some French passages into English. Claudio Vellutini and Shawn Keener helped me translate a few Italian passages.

During the final writing stage, I have profited hugely from Corinna Fales's editorial expertise. Shawn Keener and Lisa Slouffman also gave me sound editorial advice at earlier stages.

My sincere thanks to Dr Michael Middeke, Editorial Director at Boydell & Brewer Ltd, who acquired this book and offered crucial guidance along the way, and to Dr Elizabeth Howard, assistant editor, for her patience. I thank Ingalo Thomson for copyediting this manuscript and for her careful and precise work and I thank Nick Bingham, senior production editor, and his team. A special thank you to Suzanne Ryan who nudged me to broaden my research at an early phase, and I also thank Norm Hirschy and Marta Tonegutti for their guidance at subsequent phases of the project. I am very thankful for the substantive and sympathetic comments, questions, suggestions, and criticisms of anonymous readers.

I feel very fortunate to have been able to work with the following knowledgeable and congenial current and former colleagues at the University of British Columbia: Professor Emeritus Gregory Butler and Lynn Butler, Alan Dodson, Alexander Fisher, Brandon Kornaval, Richard Kurth, David Metzer, Professor Emerita Vera Micznik, Robert Taylor, Claudio Vellutini and Valerie Whitley. Colleagues from the composition, music theory, and ethnomusicology divisions – Dorothy Chang, Nathan Hesselink, Richard Kurth, Laurel Parsons, Ève Poudrier, Robert Pritchard, John Roeder, and Michael Tenzer – have also stimulated my thinking in ways I have yet to fully understand.

I feel very honored to have met Barbara Hill Moore, Meadows Foundation Distinguished Teaching Professor of Voice at Southern Methodist University, who has been an energizing cheerleader for this project.

Marta Hunter, my compassionate Alexander Technique teacher, has taught me for three years a considerable amount about bodily movement. Her expertise and wisdom have informed this book on many levels.

All published materials have been substantially rethought and revised for this book. Two of my published essays formed the basis for this book. Materials from my article "'*Tout, dans ses charmes, est dangereux*': Gesture and Seduction in Grétry's *Céphale et Procris* (1773)," published in *Cambridge Opera Journal* 20/3 (2010), were thoroughly revised for Chapters 1 and 2. An expanded and heavily revised version of my essay, "From Garrick's Dagger to Gluck's Dagger: The Dual Concept of Pantomime in Gluck's Paris Operas" (2009), published in *Musique et geste en France de Lully à la Révolution: Études sur la musique, le théâtre et la danse*, edited by Jacqueline Waeber, provides the foundation for Chapter 3. I thank Jacqueline Waeber, editor of the collection of essays, for the permission to revise this essay for this book. For Chapter 1 I also used some materials from my essay, "Harpocrates at Work: How the God of Silence Protected Eighteenth-Century French Iconoclasts" (2017), published in *Oxford Handbook of Music and Censorship*, edited by Patricia Hall (New

York: Oxford University Press, 2017). Some materials of my "Music, Bacchus, and Freedom," in *Oxford Handbook of Music and the Body*, edited by Youn Kim and Sander L. Gilman (New York: Oxford University Press, 2019), were revised for Chapter 4.

I thank God for putting me in touch with the loving and inquisitive friends at one of the Small Groups of the Kitsilano branch of Tenth Church. Current members of this group are Kenneth Chan and Madeleine Irving, Sarah and Joel Heng Hartse, Shijie Lu and Priti Sanghani, Maureen Mogambi, John and Naomi Pattison-Williams, and Romi Ranasinghe. In our regular group meetings, I have developed a deep conviction that musicology can and should be made intelligible to artists, conservationists, English professors, education and finance professionals, economists, engineers, epidemiologists, lawyers, and theologians.

Finally, I feel tremendously blessed to have some very good friends – Elise Botiveau, Betty So, and Sandra Yim – and an ever-supportive family.

Abbreviations

ARTFL   The ARTFL-FRANTEXT database, http://artfl-project.uchicago. edu.

CWR   Rousseau, Jean-Jacques, *The Collected Writings of Rousseau*, edited by Roger D. Masters and Christopher Kelly, 13 vols. (Hanover, NH: University Press of New England, 1990–2010).

EE   The Electronic Enlightenment database, http://www.e-enlighten-ment.com/.

F-Pn   Paris, Bibliothèque Nationale de France.

F-Po   Paris, Bibliothèque-Musée de l'Opéra.

Encyclopédie   *Encyclopédie, ou Dictionnaire raisonné des sciences, des arts et des métiers, etc.,* edited by Denis Diderot and Jean Le Rond d'Alembert. University of Chicago: ARTFL Encyclopédie Project (Autumn 2017 Edition), edited by Robert Morrissey and Glenn Roe, http://ency-clopedie.uchicago.edu/.

OC   Rousseau, Jean-Jacques, *Œuvres complètes*, edited by Bernard Gagnebin and Marcel Raymond, 5 vols. (Paris: Gallimard, 1959–95).

OOR   Rameau, Jean-Philippe, *Opera Omnia*, edited by the Société Jean-Philippe Rameau, general editor: Sylvie Bouissou (Paris: G. Billaudot, 1996–).

OCV   Voltaire, *Œuvres complètes de Voltaire,* edited by Theodore Besterman and others (Oxford: Voltaire Foundation, 1968–).

US-Cn   Chicago, Newberry Library.

Notes on Text

The original text of non-English sources is provided in the footnotes. All translations are my own unless otherwise noted. The orthography of quotes from French texts and titles has been modernized. The original titles of non-French text are preserved.

Introduction

Right after Louis XVI was guillotined at the Place de la Révolution, at about 10 a.m. on January 21, 1793, Louis XIV's confessor, the Irish-born priest abbé Henri Essex Edgeworth de Firmont, saw one of the executioners – a teenager no older than eighteen – grab the late king's severed head and walk it ceremonially around the scaffold, showing it to the spectators as he let out "the most dreadful cries" (*des cris les plus atroces*) and made "the most indecent gestures" (*des gestes les plus indécents*). The teenager did not say a word, let alone present a coherent speech. His expressions of enthusiasm contrasted sharply with the grandiloquence valued by the Immortals of the Académie française and violated codes of civility practiced in the Old Regime. But they worked. After a moment of gloomy silence, some spectators exclaimed: "*Vive la république!*" (Long Live the Republic!) Thousands of spectators joined in, throwing their hats in the air in celebration of the death of Louis XVI.[1]

The execution was much like a scene in a play. The young guard demonstrated his "moral liberty" (*la liberté morale*), defined in the *Encyclopédie* as a liberty that "resides in the power that an intelligent being has to do what he wants, according to his own determination" – when he expressed himself by nonverbal cries and gestures.[2] In this instance, his expression of moral liberty had political implications, for he exercised his natural right to express himself, a right articulated in Article 11 of the *Déclaration des droits de l'homme et du citoyen de 1789*. Here is Keith Michael Baker's 1987 English translation of it: "The free expression [*libre communication*] of thoughts and opinions is one of the most precious rights of man: thus every citizen may freely speak, write, and print, subject to accountability for abuse of this freedom in the cases determined by law."[3]

There was nothing special about an executioner getting excited after guillotining a notable criminal in public, but what made Louis XVI's death noteworthy was that the young guard's histrionics were grounded in Enlightenment ideas about the

---

1   Henry Essex Edgeworth de Firmont, *Mémoires de M. l'abbé Edgeworth de Firmont: dernier confesseur de Louis XVI*, compiled by C. Sneyd Edgeworth and trans. from English by Edmund Burke (Paris: Gide, 1815), 93–94.

2   "LIBERTÉ, s.f. (Morale.) La liberté réside dans le pouvoir qu'un être intelligent a de faire ce qu'il veut, conformément à sa propre détermination." Jacques-André Naigeon and abbé Claude Yvon [attributed], *Encyclopédie*, vol. 9, s.v. "Liberté [Morale]."

3   "La libre communication des pensées et opinions est un des droits les plus précieux de l'homme; tout citoyen peut donc parler, écrire, imprimer librement, sauf à répondre de l'abus de cette liberté dans les cas déterminés par la loi." https://www.legifrance.gouv.fr/Droit-francais/Constitution/Declaration-des-Droits-de-l-Homme-et-du-Citoyen-de-1789. Translation taken from Keith Michael Baker, John W. Boyer, and Julius Kirshner, eds, *The Old Regime and the French Revolution* (Chicago: The University of Chicago Press, 1987), 239.

origins of language. Screams exemplified the "cry of nature" (*le cri de la nature*), defined by Rousseau in the *Second Discourse* (1755) as "man's first language, the most universal, most energetic, and only language he needed before it was necessary to persuade assembled men." At the theater, bodily gestures were called "pantomime," defined by Jean-François Marmontel in the *Supplément à l'Encyclopédie* (1776–77) as "the language of action, the art of speaking to the eyes, [or] mute expression." However, the practice of pantomime was not confined to the theater. Painters and sculptors, as Claude-Henri Watelet mentioned in his article "Pantomime," in the *Encyclopédie méthodique* of 1788, also presented characters in their paintings and sculptures that were so expressive that they seemed to "*speak* an intelligible language to the spectators."[4]

Translating the French word "*communication*" into the English word "expression," Baker discloses in his 1987 translation the logocentric bias in the wording of *la libre communication*. According to the article "Communication (Grammar)" in the *Encyclopédie*, "communication" variously meant sharing or transferring rights, the connection between separate parts of a building, or the presentation of something to another person. "Expression," however, referred to voice (e.g., a moan), gesture (e.g., a hand signal), or speech (i.e., writing, utterance).[5] Given the diverse meanings of the word "communication," the term "freedom of communication" requires clarification and, indeed, the second sentence of Article 11 sharpens its meaning by defining "communication" specifically as the utterance, writing, and printing of thoughts and opinions. Thus the idea of "freedom of communication" carries with it a "logocentric" meaning (i.e., a meaning "centered on reason," according to *Oxford English Dictionary*).[6] By contrast, Baker's translation, "expression," mitigates this logocentric bias by designating verbal *and* nonverbal forms of human expression. Baker's translation of "free expression," therefore, offers a more inclusive interpretation than does the French phrase *la libre communication*. *La Constitution française* of 1791 retained the logocentric bias and extended its protection more explicitly to "free press": it guarantees "the liberty to every man to speak, write, print, and publish his opinions without having his writings subject to any censorship or inspection before their publication."[7] In both the *Déclaration* and the *Constitution*, the liberty to produce speech and to disseminate printed materials was guaranteed, while the

---

4   *CWR* 3:31; "Pantomime, s.f. (Art dramatique.) C'est le langage de l'action, l'art de parler aux yeux, [ou] l'expression muette." Marmontel, *Supplément à l'Encyclopédie*, vol. 4, s.v. "Pantomime"; "La connaissance de cet art [pantomime] est très-utile aux peintres, & aux sculpteurs, puisque les personnages qu'ils créent ou représentent sont privés de la parole, & doivent cependant parler aux spectateurs un langage intelligible." Claude-Henri Watelet, *Encyclopédie méthodique, ou par ordre de matières, sér. 11, Beaux-arts* (Paris: Panckoucke, 1788), vol. 1, s.v. "Pantomime."

5   On the definitions of these two words, see Denis Diderot, *Encyclopédie*, vol. 3, s.v. "Communication [Grammaire]," and Edme-François Mallet, *Encyclopédie*, vol. 6, s.v. "Expression [Belles-Lettres]."

6   "Logocentric, adj," *Oxford English Dictionary Online*, June 2019, Oxford University Press, accessed July 4, 2019.

7   "La liberté à tout homme de parler, d'écrire, d'imprimer et publier ses pensées, sans que l'écrits puissent être soumis à aucune censure ni inspection avant leur publication." https://www.conseil-constitutionnel.fr/les-constitutions-dans-l-histoire/

liberty to express oneself by means of gesture, silence, or other non-verbal medium was implied but not *expressly* protected.

By "liberty" (what is commonly called "freedom") I do not mean "civil" or "political" liberty – legal terms that accrued meanings within the political framework of eighteenth-century France – but primarily "moral" liberty and, to some extent, "natural" liberty.[8] My emphasis on "moral liberty" comes from the *Encyclopédie*, which includes sixteen articles that have the word *liberté* in their titles. Descriptions of four of them – civil liberty, moral liberty, natural liberty, and political liberty – were particularly substantial, but none of them provides a comprehensive overview of liberty. Taken together, these articles disclose a pluralistic understanding of liberty in the Enlightenment, providing an epistemological justification for keeping these terms thematically related yet conceptually distinct. On top of that, the *Système figuré des connaissances humaines* offers a schematic representation that illustrates all bodies of knowledge covered in the *Encyclopédie*, complete with explanations by Denis Diderot in the *Prospectus* (November 1750) and by d'Alembert in the *Discours préliminaire* (June 1751). These features established an epistemological infrastructure for me to navigate across different ideas of liberty in the Enlightenment.

In what follows, I explore examples of pantomime in eighteenth-century French music as vehicles for liberty. These vehicles for liberty function in a three-pronged way: first, composers understood that they had moral liberty during the act of composition, especially when they used their musical settings of pantomime as texts that explore the idea of moral liberty through music and movement. Next, their texts provided the foundation for performance, during which performers – especially highly affecting ones – supplied their idiosyncratic interpretations of the texts and contributed another layer of moral liberty to the compositions. Finally, spectators cultivated their own agency by reflecting upon the texts and performances that bespoke multiple layers of individual expressions.

Using this three-pronged model as my basis, I discuss the relationships between music, pantomime, and freedom in five chapters. In Chapter 1 I study the ways that the composers Jean-Joseph de Mondonville, François Couperin, and Jean-Philippe Rameau (also, to a lesser extent, Bernard de Bury) realized their moral liberty whenever they used the designation of pantomime in their musical compositions from the 1730s through 1760. In Chapter 2 I turn to Rousseau, who used pantomime in a play-within-a-play structure in *Le Devin du village* (1752–53) that encouraged spectators to become thinkers who could develop their own thoughts about theatrical performances and discuss them with other spectators. In Chapter 3 I demonstrate that Christoph Willibald Ritter von Gluck's pantomimes, in some of his Paris operas in the 1770s, helped to cultivate audiences' freedom to interpret signs. In Chapter 4 I examine the relationship between bodily movement and freedom. Using a cluster of settings of the story of the Danaids, including Antonio Salieri's *Les Danaïdes* (1784), I ask how types of action – dramatic action, physical action, and thoughtful inaction –

---

constitution-de-1791. Translation taken from Baker, Boyer, and Kirshner, eds, *The Old Regime*, 250.

8   On the political culture in the Old Regime, see David A. Bell, *Lawyers and Citizens: The Making of a Political Elite in Old Regime France* (New York: Oxford University Press, 1994), 4–6.

illustrate the idea of freedom of action from the late 1770s through 1784. In Chapter 5
I explain how Salieri and the librettist Pierre-Augustin Caron de Beaumarchais used
pantomime as a type of dance that imitated atoms' movement in nature, and I show
how their treatment of pantomime in their opera *Tarare* (1787) linked the idea of
moral liberty to that of natural liberty in pre-Revolutionary France. After examining all major compositions in French music from 1733–90 that include pantomime,
I argue that composers, writers, and thinkers in France created examples of "free
expression," illustrating facets of moral and natural liberties in compositions that
incorporated the component of pantomime, without directly making claims about
civil and political liberties.

I write this book to explain what it meant for Jean-Georges Noverre to call his
brand of *ballet-pantomime* "an offspring of liberty" (*un art enfant de la liberté*), and
this led me to the history of pantomime. In the seventeenth century, a pantomime
referred to a type of performer, not a theatrical practice. Molière's references to pantomimes in the *comédie-ballet Les Amants magnifiques* (1670, music by Lully) were
to *persons* who express everything through their steps, gestures, and movements
(V/iii). The word "pantomime" entered the French lexicon in Antoine Furetière's
Dictionnaire universel (1690): pantomimes, or buffoons at the ancient theaters, were
similar to the seventeenth-century comic dancers called *baladins* who acted out
many types of characters and actions while dancing.[9] In the eighteenth-century, the
baladins performed "base comedy" (*bas comique*) at the Opéra Comique. But this
definition – pantomimes as "buffoons" or *baladins* – was rejected by contemporary
writers who studied serious pantomimes in antiquity. Composers active in France
did not use the designation "pantomime" exclusively for comic situations. Among
about twenty-five pantomimes in operas and instrumental works that I have consulted, most refer to dances; some refer to actors' physical action; a few are comic,
and most are serious (*noble*). The choreographies of the dances are lost, but the
intended *effects* of many of them can be gleaned from printed or handwritten verbal
descriptions in scores, performance parts, libretti, performance reviews, parodies,
and relevant contemporary writings on dance, opera, and theater. In addition to
these primary sources, a body of literature from the disciplines of music, dance, and
theater created the foundation for examining this topic. Still, one question remains
unanswered: on what intellectual ground did Noverre relate the ballet-pantomime
to liberty?[10]

9   Jean-Georges Noverre, *Lettres sur la danse, et sur les ballets* (Lyon: Delaroche, 1760),
    253. Note that Noverre used the designation *danse en action* or *ballet en action*. For a
    definition of "Pantomime," see Antoine Furetière, *Dictionnaire universel*, 3 vols. (La Haye
    and Rotterdam: Arnout & Reinier Leers, 1690), vol. 3, s.v. "Pantomime." On the ballet-
    pantomime, see Marina Nodera, *Dictionnaire de l'Opéra de Paris sous l'Ancien Régime
    (1669–1791)*, ed. Sylvie Bouissou, Pascal Denécheau, and France Marchal-Ninosque, 3
    vols. (Paris: Classiques Garnier, 2019), vol. 1, s.v. "Ballet-Pantomime."

10 On music and pantomime, see, for example, Daniel Heartz, "Diderot and the Lyric
    Theater: 'The New Style' Proposed by *Le Neveu de Rameau*," in John A. Rice, ed.,
    From Garrick to Gluck: Essays on Opera in the Age of Enlightenment (Hillsdale, NY:
    Pendragon, 2004), 237–54; Jacqueline Waeber, ed., *Musique et geste en France de Lully*

Let us begin with dance – the basics of any ballet – including ballet-pantomime. Rebecca Harris-Warrick's *Dance and Drama in Baroque Opera: A History* (2016) offers a definitive account of the history of dance in French lyric repertories. This work provides the critical insight that theatrical dance was always integral to Baroque opera, although librettists such as Antoine Houdar de La Motte included what Harris-Warrick has called the "decorative dance sequence" that expanded the divertissement, making dances suspend the plot rather than driving it forward. Decorative dances function as a diversion, as they stimulate the senses of sight and hearing rather than the mind.[11] Yet, not *all* dances in French Baroque opera were decorative. The term "Decoration (Opera)," as Louis de Cahusac defined it in the *Encyclopédie*, meant stage design that should supply an illusion convincing enough to *transport* the audiences metaphorically from a real place to an imaginary place. An operatic decoration should stimulate rather than stifle imagination, which was theorized by French philosopher Étienne Bonnot de Condillac as an advanced mental operation that revives ideas in the absence of objects and, consequently, makes new combinations. In other words, while some dances play a "decorative" function, an operatic "decoration" should be anything but merely decorative.[12]

The distinction between "decoration" and the "decorative" raises a broader question about the cognitive operations required to experience an opera. In *Opera and Political Imaginary in Old Regime France* (2018), Olivia Bloechl proposes the concept of "inoperativity." First coined by philosopher Giorgio Agamben, this concept can be employed to mark the operatic places where the dramatic pace slows down, where one relaxes in response to an operatic element – a contemplative chorus, an instrumental interlude, or a graceful dance – that is less cognitively taxing than others.[13] By drawing attention to the experience of opera-watching rather than the components of French opera, Bloechl theorizes the *fluctuation* of audiences' attention during the performance. A change from listening to an ariette to watching a dance, for example, directs audiences' attention from the sung text to the visual text. To compose a French opera, then, was to manage spectators' attention.

In general, the term inoperativity is closely linked to logocentricity, since a sung number generally requires the audiences to follow the text closely, while an instrumental piece or a dance allows audiences to take a mental break. The concept of

à la Révolution: Études sur la musique, le théâtre et la danse (Bern: Peter Lang, 2009). On ballet-pantomime, see, for example, Edward Nye, *Mime, Music, and Drama on the Eighteenth-Century Stage: The Ballet d'action* (Cambridge: Cambridge University Press, 2012); Nathalie Rizzoni, "Le Geste éloquent: la pantomime en France au XVIIIᵉ siècle," in Waeber, ed., *Musique et geste*, 129–48.

11   On "decorative" dances, see Rebecca Harris-Warrick, *Dance and Drama in French Baroque Opera: A History* (New York: Cambridge University Press, 2016), 303, 353, 453; on La Motte and the decorative dance sequence, see Rebecca Harris-Warrick, "Ballet, Pantomime, and the Sung Word in the Operas of Rameau," in Cliff Eisen, ed., *Coll'astuzia, col giudizio: Essays in Honor of Neal Zaslaw* (Ann Arbor, MI: Steglein, 2009), 31.

12   Louis de Cahusac, *Encyclopédie*, vol. 4, s.v. "Décoration [Opéra]." On imagination, see Étienne Bonnot de Condillac, *Essay on the Origin of Human Knowledge*, trans. Hans Aarsleff (Cambridge: Cambridge University Press, 2001), 54 n.20.

13   Olivia Bloechl, *Opera and the Political Imaginary in Old Regime France* (Chicago: The University of Chicago Press, 2017), 26, 52.

inoperativity indicates a conceptual difference between dance and signs, a difference central to the theory of knowledge in the Enlightenment. It is best illustrated in *Système figuré*, where opera falls into the category of imagination, but signs belong to that of reason. Signs include two types: gesture and characters. While gesture is further subdivided into pantomime and declamation (i.e., the art of delivering speech with natural expression, including facial expressions, gesture, and voice), characters are either ideograms, hieroglyphics, or heraldic signs. This taxonomy broke new grounds. While Diderot and d'Alembert used Ephraim Chambers's *Cyclopaedia* (1728) as a model for the *Encyclopédie*, their *Système figuré* does not follow Chambers's "The View of Knowledge" (1728), which classifies words, figures, and fables as symbols and leaves no room for nonverbal signs such as gestures. Rather, Diderot and d'Alembert took their model from Francis Bacon, who grouped gestures and hieroglyphics into signs in *The Advancement of Learning* (1605). Based on Bacon's classification, Diderot and d'Alembert revised Chambers's logocentrism by conceiving of gestures as on a par with characters. As shown in *Système figuré*, gesture is a type of sign, which belongs first to grammar, then to the science of the instrument of discourse, and to the art of communication, to logic and, on the broadest level, to the domain of human science. In this design, Diderot and d'Alembert's Baconian conception separated rhetoric into its constituent components and postulated a gesture as a sign.[14]

What, then, is a sign? According to the article "Sign" in the *Encyclopédie*, a sign consists of two components: a signifier and a signified. The anonymous author of this article quoted (without attribution) Condillac's definitions of "accidental signs" (i.e., the objects that trigger the ideas they were once connected with), "natural signs" (i.e., the cries endowed by nature for expressing the emotions of joy, fear, etc.), and "instituted signs" (i.e., signs that have an arbitrary relation to our ideas) in his *Essai sur l'origine des connaissances humaines* (1746). Condillac invented the concept of "accidental" signs and borrowed the other two types from John Locke's "The Doctrine of Signs" in *An Essay Concerning Human Understanding* of 1690 (4.21.4) and abbé Jean-Baptiste Dubos's natural signs and instituted signs. Both men considered signs as elements of logic.[15]

Based on writings about ancient Greek rhetoric and ancient Roman pantomime (most notably by Lucian) and a pro-ancient cohort of writers (e.g., Claude-François Menestrier, Pierre Jean Burette, Jacques Bonnet) in the Quarrel of the Ancients and Moderns, Dubos envisioned pantomime as a type of a dance for the Enlightenment,

14   Ephraim Chambers, *Cyclopædia, or, an Universal Dictionary of Arts and Sciences*, 2 vols. (London: J. J. Knapton and others, 1728), 1: ii. Francis Bacon, *Advancement of Learning and Noveum Organum*, rev. edn (New York: Co-operative, 1900), 163. On Bacon's classification of signs, see d'Alembert, *Preliminary Discourse*, 163. On classifications of knowledge, see Richard Yeo, "Classifying the Sciences," in Roy Porter, ed., *The Cambridge History of Science, vol. 4: Eighteenth-Century Science* (Cambridge: Cambridge University Press, 2003), 249–63.

15   For a definition of "sign," see *Encyclopédie*, vol. 15, s.v. "Signe [Métaphysique]." On the natural and instituted signs, see Jean-Baptiste Dubos, *Réflexions critiques sur la poésie et sur la peinture*, 3 vols. (Paris: Mariette, 1733), 224. Unless otherwise noted, all mentions of Dubos's *Réflexions critiques* refer to the 1733 edition. On the three types of signs, see Condillac, *Essay*, 36.

and his *Réflexions critiques sur la poésie et sur la peinture* (2 vols., 1719; 3 vols., rev. edn 1733) provided materials for a discourse on pantomime in the eighteenth century. In response to Dubos, writers including Jean Nicolas Servandoni (1741), Condillac (1746), Johann Mattheson (1749), Claude-François-Félix Boulenger de Rivery (1751), Cahusac (1754), Gotthold Ephraim Lessing (1755), Diderot (1757–59), Noverre (1760), Ranieri de Calzabigi (1761 and 1765), Louis de Jaucourt (1765), Rousseau (1768, 1776–77), Pierre-Jean-Baptiste Nougaret (1769), William Cook (1775), Marmontel (1776–77), Michel Paul Guy de Chabanon (1779), Johann Jakob Engel (1785), Watelet (1788), and François-Henri-Stanislas de L'Aulnaye (1790) published at least forty-five writings on pantomime across Europe. These publications ranged from books (or sections of books) to journal articles to dance *dissertations* and prefaces to libretti, and to entries in the *Encyclopédie*, the *Supplément à l'Encyclopédie*, and the *Encyclopédie méthodique*. The discourse on pantomime did not overlap neatly with that of pantomime as a cultural practice, however. Dubos himself identified a handful of theatrical dances by Jean-Baptiste Lully as precursors of the type of pantomime he considered fitting for the Enlightenment, although the phenomenon was far more common than he admitted, and composers and their collaborators continued to employ pantomimes well into the nineteenth century and beyond. But it is this core body of writings from 1719 to 1790 that contained a discourse on pantomime as an intellectual topic of the Enlightenment.

The influence of Dubos's work has long been recognized, but we have seen a resurgence of scholarly interest in it. In *The Enlightenment: A Genealogy* (2010), Dan Edelstein argues that Dubos's *Réflexions critiques* concluded the Quarrel of Ancients and Moderns (1680s–1720s) and set the stage for the Enlightenment. In Edelstein's view, the Quarrel of the Ancients and Moderns developed an awareness shared by the *philosophes*, who considered antiquity the golden age and *their* epoch enlightened. Inspired by Edelstein's argument, I will argue in this book that pantomime was an Enlightenment phenomenon – an *intellectual* phenomenon rooted in the rediscovery of ancient Roman pantomime – that justified a *cultural* phenomenon across seventeenth- and eighteenth-century Europe.[16]

Yet, despite its pan-European circulation, Dubos's *Réflexions critiques* received mixed reviews. About twenty years after he published the three-volume edition, Cahusac extended Dubos's thinking on pantomime in his *La Danse ancienne et moderne* (1754) while criticizing Dubos's lack of knowledge on French dance and opera: "One cannot put more spirit or more erudition in a work than the abbé Dubos had spread through this part [vol. 3] of his [*Réflexions critiques*], but it [his work] lacks foundations."[17] Voltaire agreed with Cahusac and elaborated Cahusac's criticisms in *Le Siècle de Louis XIV* (1775): "All artists read his *Réflexions sur la poésie, la peinture et la musique* fruitfully. This is the most useful book ever written on these subjects

16 On Dubos's *Réflexions*, see Dan Edelstein, *The Enlightenment: A Genealogy* (Chicago: The University of Chicago Press, 2010), ch. 5.

17 "On ne peut mettre ni plus d'esprit, ni plus d'érudition dans un ouvrage que l'abbé Dubos en a répandu dans cette partie [vol. 3] du sien; mais elle manque par les fondements." Cahusac, *La Danse ancienne et moderne ou Traité historique de la danse*, ed. Nathalie Lecomte, Laura Naudeix, and Jean-Noël Laurenti (Paris: Éditions Desjonquères, 2004), 36.

in any of the nations in Europe ... He did not know music, though; he had never been able to write verse, and did not own a painting. But he had read, heard, and reflected a lot."[18]

Cahusac and Voltaire's criticisms suggest that there was a chasm between the culture of dance and the Enlightenment as an intellectual movement. Dubos had passed away in 1742, before Cahusac published his *La Danse ancienne et moderne* in 1754. Although Dubos had died, his influence lived on. Thus, it is important to understand why Cahusac disagreed with Dubos's points, and the reception of these two books molded the discourse on pantomime through the end of the Old Regime.

One of their most significant disagreements was about signs. In *La Danse*, Cahusac ignored Dubos's distinction between natural and instituted signs, a distinction that became a core idea in the Enlightenment conception of reason; instead, Cahusac preferred the theatrical term "action." Noverre understood the implication of their disagreement. In his *Lettres sur la danse* (1760), published the year after Cahusac's death, Noverre explained in the last letter that Dubos's notion of "sign" challenged dance as a primarily non-significative, non-imitative art: "How has the word 'pantomime' *not* shocked all those who dance the serious [style]?"[19]

The impact of Dubos's argument on pantomime can be measured by the reception of Dubos's and Cahusac's books. Dubos's ideas of signs and pantomime were cited numerous times after Cahusac's death; by contrast, *La Danse ancienne et moderne* was rarely cited among the *encyclopédists* and the *philosophes*, although Cahusac wrote 130 articles for the *Encyclopédie*, and Charles Compan found Cahusac's book an indispensable source for his *Dictionnaire de danse* (1787). This difference in reception might have had something to do with Cahusac's mental condition. Diderot told Grimm, in a letter dated May 1, 1759, that Cahusac had mental problems and was kept at the Charenton asylum in Saint-Maurice.[20] Cahusac died a few weeks later, on June 22. At around the same time, Diderot, who had been thinking about signs and physiognomy since his early work, *Essai sur le mérite et la vertu* (1745), wrote his most important contributions on pantomime – the domestic drama *Le Fils naturel* (1757), *Entretiens sur le fils naturel* (1757), *De la poésie dramatique* (1758), and the comedy *Le Père de famille* (Toulouse, 1759; Paris, Comédie-Française, 1761) – in which he demonstrated Dubos's point: actors should incorporate gestural and vocal signs in their acting (*jeu* or "pantomime") that could impart a dimension of truth (*vérité*). He asked, in *De la poésie dramatique*, "Accustomed as we are, to a mannered declamation, made symmetrical and very far from the truth, are there many people who

18 "Tous les artistes lisent avec fruit ses *Réflexions sur la poésie, la peinture et la musique*. C'est le livre le plus utile qu'on ait jamais écrit sur ces matières chez aucune des nations de l'Europe ... Il ne savait pourtant pas la musique; il n'avait jamais pu faire de vers, et n'avait pas un tableau. Mais il avait beaucoup lu, vu, entendu et réfléchi." Voltaire, *Œuvres complètes de Voltaire*, ed. Theodore Besterman and others (Oxford: Voltaire Foundation, 1968–), 12:64. [*OCV*]

19 "Combien le mot Pantomime n'a-t-il pas choqué tous ceux qui dansent le sérieux?" Noverre, *Lettres*, 470.

20 Diderot, *Œuvres*, ed. Laurent Versini, 5 vols. (Paris: Laffont, 1994–97), 5:93–95.

can do without it [pantomime]?"[21] Jaucourt cited Dubos's *Réflexions critiques* exten-sively and wrote the article "Pantomime" (1765). Following Jaucourt, Marmontel wrote about gestures as signs in a new article "Pantomime" for *Supplément à l'Ency-clopédie* (1776–77) and had it reprinted in his *Éléments de littérature* (1787). In these writings, the art of pantomime became dissociated from the *bas comique* tradition and was understood to be a vehicle for truth. While Dubos had limited practical knowledge of music, dance, and opera, his *ideas* about signs and his research into ancient Roman pantomimes influenced writers of the intellectual circle that shaped the Enlightenment.

That said, favorable reception of Dubos's discussion on pantomime does not mean that his ideas were readily accepted; in fact, it was the debates about Dubos's *Réflexions critiques* that *defined* the impact of this work. The pro-ancient and anti-modern Dubos acknowledged that there were English, Chinese, and Persian pantomimes in his time, but he did not find any of them comparable to the ancient Roman pantomimes he had in mind. Speaking of the English actor and ballet master Roger, who mimed so well that he could make himself intelligible without any words at the Parisian fairground theaters from 1729 to 1731, Dubos questioned his *knowl-edge* of ancient pantomime actors: "What apprenticeship had Roger had compared to that of pantomimes of the ancients? Did he even know that there had ever been a Pylade and a Bathyllus?"[22]Yet Dubos's elitist position was repudiated by the next generation of Enlightenment writers. In the article "Pantomime" in the *Encyclopédie*, Jaucourt accepted Dubos's summary of Roman pantomime, but he challenged his anti-modern bias, emphasizing the versatility of the English actor David Garrick, who excelled at "all sorts of tragic and comic subjects."[23]

On one level, the shift in the discourse from the past to the present made pan-tomime a re-emerging phenomenon, a theatrical practice that reigned supreme in ancient Roman theater, whose *spirit* – not style – returned to the eighteenth century. As mentioned above, pantomime was categorized as an art of communication in *Système figuré*, but it did not belong to any of the fifteen dance types – bourrée, rigau-don, gavotte, gaillarde, menuet, passepied, courante, sarabande, folie d'espagne, loure, forlane, gigue, canarie, chaconne, and passacaille – in the tradition of *la belle danse*. These facts help explain why the art of pantomime deserves special attention. Dance played a part in the "civilizing process" theorized by Norbert Elias in the 1930s, a social process emphasizing habituation of correct bodily movements, tech-nical refinement, and institutionalized self-control that contributed to what Bonnet

---

21 "Accoutumés comme nous le sommes, à une déclamation maniérée, symétrisée et si éloignée de la vérité, y a-t-il beaucoup de personnes qui puissent s'en passer?" Diderot, *Œuvres*, 4:1343.

22 "Quel apprentissage Roger avait-il fait en comparaison de celui que faisaient les pantomimes des anciens? Roger savait-il seulement qu'il y eut jamais eu un Pylade & un Bathylle?" Dubos, *Réflexions*, 3:289.

23 "Le fameux Garrick est un acteur d'autant plus merveilleux, qu'il exécute également toutes sortes de sujets tragiques & comiques." Jaucourt, *Encyclopédie*, vol. 11, s.v. "Pantomime."

called, in *Histoire générale de la danse* (1723), "the politeness [*politesse*] of civil life."[24] They were taught by dance masters, practiced regularly at public and private balls, performed at the theater in French opera. Unsurprisingly, none of the 539 dances recorded by the Beauchamp-Feuillet notation, in sources dated 1700–1790, includes the word "pantomime" in its title. This piece of evidence supports the view that pantomime was fundamentally distinct from dance, although choreographers adopted elements of pantomime for the development of ballet-pantomime.[25] To make clear this view, *Système figuré* offers a diagram that *visualizes* the epistemological distance and categorical boundaries that separate pantomime as an operatic component, from pantomime as a means of communication.

On another level, the narrative of re-emergence intersected with the recognition of an ongoing practice. Most choreographers and dancers had incorporated the element of pantomime in dances as amusement for the fairground theaters, the minor theaters at the boulevard, the Théâtre Italien, and the Comédie-Française, without explicitly intending to revitalize the ancient Roman practice – although some of them such as Burette, Bonnet, and Servandoni deployed the *rhetoric* of revival to justify their artistic visions.[26] One way to study pantomime as a phenomenon of Enlightenment France, I propose, is to use the *Système figuré* as an epistemological schema for elucidating a few historical strands: the genealogy of dance, the archaeology of human communication, the hierarchy of fine arts, and materialist ideas of movement.

In the years surrounding Cahusac's death, the *philosophes* thought about bridging the divide between dance and signs at the theater, although the view was still acute at times that pantomime was more of a threat to dance than an extension of it. In his *Entretiens sur le fils naturel*, Diderot went so far as to claim: "Dance is still waiting for a man of genius; it is bad everywhere because people hardly suspect that it is a genre of imitation. Dance is to pantomime, as poetry is to prose, or rather as natural declamation is to song. It is a measured pantomime."[27] One should not take Diderot's remarks as an accurate account of the status quo of dance in France, since superb pantomime dancers (e.g., the English choreographer Mainbray and

24   Norbert Elias, *The Civilizing Process: Sociogenetic and Psychogenetic Investigations*, trans. Edmund Jephcott with some notes and corrections by the author, rev. edn ed. by Eric Dunning, Johan Goudsblom, and Stephen Mennell (1994 ; Oxford: Blackwell, 2000), 119; Jacques Bonnet, *Histoire générale de la danse sacrée et profane* (Paris: D'Houry, 1723), xxii.

25   On this corpus, see Francine Lancelot, *La Belle Dance: catalogue raisonné fait en l'An 1995* (Paris: Van Dieren, 1996), xii. On the fifteen dance types, see ibid., xxxiv–lvii.

26   See Rebecca Harris-Warrick and Carol G. Marsh, "The French Connection," in Rebecca Harris-Warrick and Bruce Alan Brown, eds, *The Grotesque Dancer on the Eighteenth-Century Stage: Gennaro Magri and His World* (Madison, WI: The University of Wisconsin Press, 2005), 173–98.

27   "La danse attend encore un homme de génie; elle est mauvaise partout, parce qu'on soupçonne à peine que c'est un genre d'imitation. La danse est à la pantomime, comme la poésie est à la prose, ou plutôt comme la déclamation naturelle est au chant. C'est une pantomime mesurée." Diderot, *Œuvres*, 4:1182–83.

the Italian dancer Barbarina Camparini) had already generated widely reported bursts of excitement in Paris around 1740; rather, they should be understood in the context of Dubos's theory of signs. If anything, the chasm between discourse and practice indicates that the phenomenon of pantomime in Enlightenment France demands bilateral contextualization.

In my investigation I find Diderot's idea of "merging" (*réunir*) helpful. In *Entretiens sur le fils naturel* Diderot advised using pantomime as one of many constituent *elements* that supplemented and sometimes even substituted for speech in a play: "One feels no less the force of pantomime alone, and of pantomime united to the discourse."[28] Jacqueline Waeber has adopted his ideas, tracing the development of *récitatif obligé* and the beginning of *mélodrame* in Rousseau's *Pygmalion* (1770).[29] I, on the other hand, want to know how composers in France used the element of pantomime in their musical works. While the consensus is that pantomime became a major theatrical phenomenon in the second half of the eighteenth century, I am curious to know how it arose before 1750, what intellectual forces supported it, which compositions carried this designation, and what claims about liberty one could make in pre-Revolutionary France. Let's find that out.

---

28 "On n'en sent pas moins la force de la pantomime seule, et de la pantomime réunie au discours." Diderot, *Œuvres*, 4:1173.

29 Jacqueline Waeber, *En Musique dans le texte: Le mélodrame, de Rousseau à Schoenberg* (Paris: Van Dieren, 2005), ch. 1.

CHAPTER ONE

Bacchic Freedom

I N the prologue of his *pastorale-héroïque Isbé* (libretto by Henri-François, marquis de La Rivière; Opéra, 1742), composer Jean-Joseph de Mondonville did something thought-provoking: he presented the pantomime dance as a threat to *la belle danse*. Set at the Tuileries garden of Paris, the prologue begins with Lust (*Volupté*), who finds a bizarre nymph named Fashion (*La Mode*) threatening and turns to Amour, God of the Universe, for help. Instead of presenting Fashion as a charismatic character, Mondonville features her as an intrusive person, whose caprice, whose inconstancy, whose "weak pleasures" win over everyone. As Lust complains to Amour, "all the hearts in these places refuse to pay homage to you" (*tous les cœurs en ces lieux te refusent l'hommage*). To highlight Fashion as an intrusion, Mondonville introduced Italian characteristics that adulterated the French musical tradition. Take the French overture as an example. Instead of following tradition, by writing the second part as a fast section with imitative counterpoint, Mondonville wrote a section with Italianate stylistic features: a melodic sequence, chains of suspensions, unison writing, and a chromatic lament (Example 1.1). This unconventional, "Italianate" French overture set the stage for another unconventional element: a prelude featuring a chromatic ascending melody and invertible counterpoint that accompanies Fashion's entrance. After the prelude, Mondonville wrote yet another unconventional dance called "pantomime," followed by another dance in the same key marked "lively" (*gay*). Both were performed by five dancers called "Pantomimes," a group distinct from Amour's followers, Games (*jeux*) and Pleasures (*plaisirs*). Amour dislikes the "bizarre concerts" that accompany those pantomime dances, preferring instead the "sweet concerts" that are graceful and pleasurable. By the end of the prologue, the opposition is clear: Fashion brings forth "turbulent pleasures" so unsettling, the bizarre concerts so unjustified by Apollo, and a power over mortals so dominant that Amour leaves Paris for the fantastical land of Lignon. Granted, whether Apollo represents Louis XIV or not needs justification, Buford Norman cautions, but Voltaire did mention in *Anecdotes sur Louis XIV* (1748) that Louis XIV danced in some ballets as Apollo. In any case, the chorus rejoices in Amour's departure in the prologue of *Isbé*, singing: "Amour gives up victory to us" (*L'Amour nous cède la victoire*).[1]

---

1   For the lyrics of this prologue, see the livret *Isbé, pastorale-héroïque* (Paris: Ballard, 1742), 5–11. On this prologue, see David Charlton, *Opera in the Age of Rousseau: Music, Confrontation, Realism* (Cambridge: Cambridge University Press, 2015), 339. On *la belle danse* or *la danse noble*, see Nathalie Lecomte and Eugénia Roucher, *Dictionnaire de la musique en France aux XVIIe et XVIIIe siècles*, ed. Marcelle Benoit (Paris: Fayard, 1992), s.v. "Danse." On Apollo and Louis XIV, see Buford Norman, *Touched by the Graces: The Libretti of Philippe Quinault in the Context of French Classicism* (Birmingham, AL: Summa, 2001), 264, 294; Voltaire, *Œuvres complètes de Voltaire*, ed. Theodore Besterman and others (Oxford: Voltaire Foundation, 1968–), vol. 30C, 150. [*OCV*]

Example 1.1. Mondonville, *Isbé*, Overture, mm.43–64

Thus, Mondonville employed the long-standing tension between French and Italian music to represent the dispute between Fashion and Amour, a dispute that polarized the pantomime dance and *la belle danse* in this *pastorale-héroïque*.[2] It was necessary to motivate a plot with a problem, but it was uncommon to stage a conflict

2   On Italian music in France, see, for example, Georgia Cowart, "Carnival in Venice or Protest in Paris? Louis XIV and the Politics of Subversion at the Paris Opéra," *Journal of the American Musicological Society* 54, no.2 (2001), 265–302; Rebecca Harris-Warrick, "Staging Venice," *Cambridge Opera Journal* 15, no.3 (2003), 297–316; Graham Sadler and Shirley Thompson, "The Italian Roots of Marc-Antoine Charpentier's Chromatic Harmony," in Anne-Madeline Goulet and Gesa zur Nieden, eds, *Europäische Musiker in Venedig, Rom und Neapel, 1650–1750* (Kassel: Bärenreiter, 2015), 546–70.

Example 1.1. continued

about the cultural scene of contemporary Paris. *Isbé*'s prologue set at the Tuileries garden alluded to Jean Nicolas Servandoni's optical spectacles (*spectacles d'optiques*) performed at the Salle des machines of the Tuileries palace of 1738–42, starring, in *Les Aventures d'Ulisse* (March 1741), the English pantomime performer known as Mainbray, whose *pièce pantomime* called *Les Dupes, ou Rien n'est difficile en amour* had opened the 1740 season of the Saint-Germain fairground theater. The realistic staging in *Isbé* does not mean that Mondonville used this *pastorale-héroïque* as a *reportage* of Servandoni's spectacles; far from it, the presentation of pantomime as a threat in *Isbé* contradicted the popularity of pantomime dancers performed in various Parisian theaters. Writing in 1743, Claude and François Parfaict observed that pantomime was a "commonly used resource" at the fairground theaters in 1740. At the Saint-Germain fairground theater, Mainbray became producer and composer of *divertissements pantomimes* from 1740–43. At the Saint-Laurent fairground theater, the English troupe led by Henry Delamain staged no fewer than six new pantomimes in 1739. At the Théâtre Italien and the Opéra, Italian dancers who incorporated pantomime in their dances – the Arlequin Antonio Constantini in his mid-forties, his daughter Barbarina Campanini from Parma who was not even sixteen by July 1739, and her future husband Antonio Rinaldi from Naples – were extremely popular in 1739–40. If these pantomime performances were as warmly received as the Parfaict brothers reported, then Mondonville voiced in *Isbé* a concern that was not aired in published accounts of these performances.[3]

At stake here is not that Mondonville falsified the Parisian dance scene in *Isbé*, but that a cultural dynamic concerning dance emerged in response to the popularity of pantomime around 1740. Mondonville was not the only composer who treated pantomime as a different type of dance. The couple Campanini and Rinaldi (referred to as "M^r. Fosani and his wife" or "M^r. Ribaldini and Melle. Barbarini") performed with success pantomime dances that were added to three operas at the Opéra: Rameau's *Les Talents lyriques* (July 14, 1739), Pancrace Royer's *Zaïde, reine de Grenade* (September 5, 1739), and André Campra's *Les Fêtes vénitiennes* (July 19, 1740). Their success was reported in *Mercure de France* and, surprisingly, recognized by the music editor Madame Élisabeth Catherine Boivin (daughter of the royal music printer and bookseller Jean-Baptiste-Christophe Ballard and widow of music editor François Boivin, who had died in 1733), who promptly published in 1740 four music collections called *Airs italiens* and a "new pantomime" called *Le Sabottier* (clog maker), danced by "Fossan [sic]."[4] These collections were musical settings of pantomime dances that were added, ad hoc, to operatic performances. We do not know who wrote the music of the *Airs italiens*, and evidently the names of the composers were not as important as those of the dancers, but we do know that other composers around the same time became interested in writing music for pantomime dances. Around 1740 Madame Boivin also published the composer Nicolas Chédeville's collection of music called *Les Pantomimes italiennes dansées à l'Académie royale de musique*. A year before *Isbé* premiered, in 1741, Rameau composed the instrumental piece called "La Pantomime." The year after *Isbé* premiered, in 1743, composer Bernard de Bury (1720–85) wrote music for a pantomime dance, in the prologue of his *opéra-ballet Les Caractères de la folie* (lyrics by Charles Pint-Duclos; Opéra), which illustrates the conflict between Amour and Madness (*La Folie*), spotlighting Madness as Queen of the Universe, as opposed to Amour as God of the Universe in *Isbé*. These examples indicate that published music for pantomime performances became an artistic achievement in the early 1740s.

The culture of pantomime becomes more complex when one considers the discourse of pantomime in the *Querelle des anciens et des modernes* (Quarrel of the Ancients and Moderns), in the 1680s–1720s, an academic debate about the spirit of the modern time vis-à-vis that of antiquity. In this discourse, pantomime meant

3   On Servandoni, see Gösta M. Bergman, "La Grande mode des pantomimes à Paris vers 1740 et les spectacles d'optique de Servandoni," *Theatre Research/Recherches Théâtrales* 2, no.1 (1960), 71–81. On the pantomimes performed at the fairground theaters around 1740, see Claude and François Parfaict, *Mémoires pour servir à l'histoire des spectacles de la foire*, 2 vols. (Paris: Briasson, 1743), 2:141–44. On pantomimes in Paris, see Henri Lagrave, "La Pantomime à la Foire, au Théâtre italien et aux Boulevards (1700–1789). Première approche: historique du genre," *Romanistische Zeitschrift für Literaturgeschichte* 3–4 (1979): 408–30; Rizzoni; "Le Geste éloquent."

4   On their performances, see *Mercure de France* (July 1739), 2632; (September 1739, part 2), 2245; (July 1740), 1636; on Antonio Constanini, see Claude and François Parfaict, *Dictionnaire des théâtres de Paris*, 7 vols. (Paris: Lambert, 1756), 2:154–56. For the four collections of *Airs italiens*, see F-Po, CS-1404 (2, 3, 4, 7); for the "new Pantomime" *Le Sabottier*, see F-Po, CS-1404 (6).

a signature dramatic practice popular in antiquity. Among the publications on pantomime from the 1710s through 1730s, by Pierre-Jean Burette (1717), Dubos (1719,
rev. and expanded edn, 1733), and Bonnet (1723), Dubos's *Réflexions critiques sur la
poésie et sur la peinture* had the greatest impact on the intellectual movement known
as the Enlightenment. Expanding a section in the 1719 edition, Dubos discussed pantomime, declamation, and gesture in five of the eighteen chapters in volume three
of the 1733 edition, pointing out that ancient Roman pantomime actors made their
dances emotionally expressive and semantically suggestive. But if Dubos's *Réflexions
critiques* marked the beginning of the Enlightenment, then in what ways, if any, was
Dubos's argument related to Noverre's idea of ballet-pantomime as "a child of liberty" in *Lettres sur la danse* (1760)? What were the relationships between the cultural
history of pantomime and the history of liberty in the Enlightenment, and what roles
did music play in these histories?[5]

   In this first chapter I explain how composers recognized their moral liberty by
using pantomime in their compositions, by which I mean that composers were
acutely aware that they were adopting pantomime as an unconventional type of
dance whenever they used it in their musical compositions. I begin by explaining
Dubos's discussion of ancient Roman pantomime in the context of the Quarrel
of the Ancients and Moderns. I then discuss the compositions by Couperin and
Rameau which carry the designation of "pantomime." It is long known that Rameau
integrated his theatrical dances – air, or entrée, *ballet en action*, or what Cahusac
called *"ballet figuré"* – into his operas.[6] What is less often discussed, however, is that
he used pantomime to expand the expressive range of theatrical dance, showing his
moral liberty by thinking about music through pantomime.

DANCE OF THE ENLIGHTENMENT

To understand the Enlightenment as an intellectual movement in the eighteenth
century, it is necessary to trace the keywords that shaped this movement. One of
those was the "philosophical spirit" (*l'esprit philosophique*), defined by a contributor
to the *Encyclopédie*, Jaucourt, as "the gift of nature perfected by work, by art, and
by habit to judge everything sensibly."[7] The philosophical spirit should have broad

---

5   In his volume three Dubos discussed dance and pantomime in chapters 13, 14, and 16 and
     related topics of gesture and declamation in chapters 10 and 18. On Dubos's *Réflexions
     critiques*, see Edelstein, *The Enlightenment*, 37–43. On ballet-pantomime as a child of
     liberty, see Noverre, *Lettres*, 253.

6   A classic study on Rameau's dance music is Cuthbert Girdlestone, *Jean-Philippe Rameau:
     His Life and Work*, intro. Philip Gossett (1957; repr. Mineola, NY: Dover, 2014). On
     Rameau, pantomime, and *ballet figuré*, see Raphaëlle Legrand, "Louis de Cahusac et
     Jean-Philippe Rameau: Geste, danse et musique," *Les Cahiers du CIREM* 26–27 (1992–
     93), 31–40; Edith Lalonger and Jonathan Williams, "Music, Dance, and Narrative in
     Rameau's *Zaïs*: Bringing the Immortal Back to Life," *Dance Research* 33, no.2 (2015),
     212–26. On ballet figuré, see Thomas Soury, *Dictionnaire de l'Opéra de Paris*, vol. 1, s.v.
     "Ballet figuré."

7   "L'esprit *philosophique* est un don de la nature perfectionné par le travail, par l'art, & par
     l'habitude, pour juger sainement de toutes choses." Jaucourt, *Encyclopédie*, vol. 12, s.v.
     "Philosophique, esprit."

impact, radiating like a light outward from an origin. Jaucourt continued: "Residing with brilliance (*éclat*) in a small number of people, the philosophical spirit will spread (*répandra*), as it were, its influences on the entire body of the state, on all the works of the mind or the hands, and primarily on those of literature."[8] Dubos took this "philosophical spirit" as a key concept. He mentioned it seven times in his *Réflexions critiques* and, on one occasion, he linked the philosophical spirit directly to French opera: "As soon as we had produced operas, the philosophical spirit, which is excellent for highlighting the truth, provided that it comes after experience, has made us discover that the verses fullest of imagery (and generally speaking, the most beautiful) are not the most likely to succeed in music."[9]

Dubos offered two examples that supported his point. For a negative example, Dubos discussed Jean Racine's lyrics for Lully's *Idylle sur la paix* (1685), which consist of ample imagery: cannons, thunder, ramparts, ruins, Bellona, embattled legions, armor, snakes, skies, death. For a positive example, Dubos chose Lully's setting of Philippe Quinault's *Thésée* (1674), which depicts only one image – Amour throwing his darts away from Médée – an image that symbolizes unrequited love. To Dubos's mind, the philosophical spirit that characterized the Enlightenment manifested in the realm of aesthetics: music of the Enlightenment should be expressive rather than simply imitative. Composers inspired by the philosophical spirit should not just depict images with music; instead, they should use one passion that coheres the entire composition.[10]

As a historian, Dubos believed that history progressed cyclically: the aesthetic transition away from imitation toward expression had taken place many times, and could take place again. The Enlightenment in the eighteenth century, in his view, could well be another historical cycle. Inspired by Horace's *De Arte poetica*, Dubos observed that actors made theatrical declamation lively and expressive when they quickened their delivery. This observation might be obvious, but Dubos speculated that a new style might emerge when a dance changed from slow to fast, from simple to elaborate, from mechanical to expressive, and from a movement style shared by all characters to one customized for each character. His model of cyclic history explained stylistic progress in arts – whether this was simple and grave music replaced by exuberant music, as in Livius Andronicus's roman drama, the uniform recitation in Cicero's time replaced by emphatic pronunciation with foreign accents, or the slow and simple dance numbers of the 1650s replaced by Lully's quick and characterized airs. In Dubos's model, stylistic progress occurred in a cyclical rather than a linear manner, and a few examples were sufficient to kick-start a cycle.[11]

8 "L'esprit philosophique résidant avec éclat dans ce petit nombre de gens, il répandra pour ainsi dire, ses influences sur tout le corps de l'état, sur tous les ouvrages de l'esprit ou de la main, & principalement sur ceux de littérature." Jaucourt, *Encyclopédie*, vol. 12, s.v. "Philosophique, esprit."

9 "Dès que nous avons eu fait des Opéras, l'esprit Philosophique, qui est excellent pour mettre en évidence la vérité, pourvu qu'il chemine à la suite de l'expérience, nous a fait trouver que les vers les plus remplis d'images, & généralement parlant les plus beaux, ne sont pas les plus propres à réussir en musique." Dubos, *Réflexions*, 1:481–82.

10 On the philosophical spirit, see Dubos, *Réflexions*, 1:481–83.

11 Horace, *De arte poetica* 202–204, 211, 214–19; Dubos, *Réflexions*, 3:153–73.

Having established expression as a characteristic of the philosophical spirit, Dubos pointed out a distinction between ancient Roman pantomime (*saltatio*) and the French dance of his time (*notre danse ordinaire*). An ancient Roman pantomime expressed himself by gestures, whereas a dancer of Dubos's time performed dance steps: "*Saltatio* was not a dance in our manner, but a simple gesticulation."[12] Note that Dubos compared the ancients with the moderns in broad strokes, and he grouped Lully (who died in 1687) and Michel-Richard Delalande (who died in 1726) together, calling them "moderns," as opposed to the "ancients" Pylades and Bathyllus. But his comparison introduced a problem: he downplayed a generation of composers – Lully's son Louis, Campra, Philippe II, duc d'Orléans, and André Cardinal Destouches – who were active in the late reign of Louis XIV and the Regency (1715–23), creating the impression of a break in the history of music between Regency France and Enlightenment France.[13] To widen this imagined gap, Dubos considered French dance and ballet airs "placid" (*tranquilles*) and proposed modifying them in the manner of ancient Roman pantomime. His idea came from his critical reflection of theatrical dance during *his* present (primarily 1660s–1680s, and to some extent 1710s–1730s), not his *readers'* present (i.e., 1710s–1730s).[14]

Dubos's conception of "present" was common in the Quarrel of the Ancients and Moderns, but he developed an insight into movement and signification. He realized, in the 1719 edition, that the art of *saltatio* in antiquity consisted of "not only the art of our dance, but also the art of gesture, or this dance in which one did not dance, strictly speaking."[15] He never set out to write a history on "modern" (i.e., eighteenth-century) music and dance; rather, he identified a handful of Lully's expressive theatrical dances that signaled the Enlightenment: the funeral pomp in *Psyché* (1671) and *Alceste* (1674), the dancing old men in *Thésée* (1674), the dream scene in *Atys* (1676), the Hyperboreans who tremble in the cold in *Isis* (1677), and the *Entrée des cyclopes* in *Acis et Galathée* (1686). Granted, this is a small sample, but Dubos believed that this sample was sufficient to initiate a new aesthetic phase. Harris-Warrick has discovered that dance had *always* been a staple of French opera, and this discovery helps to contextualize Dubos's impact. Dubos earned a reputation soon after he published *Réflexions critiques*, in 1719. He was elected to Seat 39 of the Académie française in 1720, and was nominated as its perpetual secretary in 1722, the sixth person who held this position since its establishment in 1635. As a

---

12   "La *Saltatio* n'était point une danse à notre manière, mais une simple gesticulation." Dubos, *Réflexions*, 3:83. I use the pronoun "himself" because all ancient pantomime actors discussed by Dubos were male.

13   On the relationship between the Regency and the Enlightenment, see Edelstein, *The Enlightenment*, 25. On the aesthetic break from the Regency in the Enlightenment, see Elena Russo, *Styles of Enlightenment: Taste, Politics, and Authorship in Eighteenth-Century France* (Baltimore, MD: The Johns Hopkins University Press, 2007), 16–44.

14   On the Enlightenment and the critical reflection of the present, see Michel Foucault, "What is Enlightenment?" in Sylvère Lotringer and Lysa Hochroth, eds, *The Politics of Truth* (Los Angeles: Semiotext(e), 2007), 103. On ballet airs and "our ordinary dance," see Dubos, *Réflexions*, 3:318, 247.

15   "Il convient donc de se faire une idée de l'art appelé *Saltatio*, comme d'un art qui comprenait non-seulement l'art de notre danse, mais aussi l'art du geste, ou cette danse dans laquelle on ne dansait point, à proprement parler." Dubos, *Réflexions* (1719), 1:507.

historian, he believed that Lully purposefully employed François-Hilaire d'Olivet (*dit* Dolivet) to choreograph dances with gestural signs in *Thésée, Atys,* and *Isis,* while assigning Pierre Beauchamps or Antoine Desbrosses to stage ordinary dances.[16] He was especially impressed by the *Isis* example that depicted the Hyperboreans trembling in the cold without using "a single step [*pas*] of our ordinary dance." Evidently, he found a modern example of a "dance in which one did not dance," and he developed a key theoretical insight: although dance was related to drama in opera, a dance *step* was not a sign.[17]

Whereas Dubos proposed using "a dance in which one did not dance," the implementation at the theater had to be thought out, and Cahusac took the challenge. Cahusac was critical of Dubos's insufficient knowledge of eighteenth-century music and dance, but he nonetheless shared Dubos's general vision of creating a type of expressive, significative dance for the Enlightenment.[18] In his *La Danse ancienne et moderne* (1754), Cahusac, like Dubos, placed dance in the context of the Enlightenment. He warned against the abuses of non-imitative dance, proposing that what he called "action dance" (*danse en action*) would inspire the most "enlightened" spectator to analyze it and to feel the emotions in it during a performance. To further Dubos's claim, Cahusac situated his idea of *danse en action* alongside major Enlightenment writings: "In our theater, dance no longer needs anything other than guides, good principles, and a light (*lumière*) that, like the sacred fire, never goes out. Let us persuade ourselves that the epoch (*siècle*) that has produced, in letters, [Charles de Secondat Montesquieu's] *L'Esprit des lois,* [Voltaire's] *La Henriade,* [Georges-Louis Leclerc Buffon's] *Histoire naturelle,* and the *Encyclopédie* can go as far, in the arts, as the very century of Augustus."[19]

By the time Cahusac published his *La Danse ancienne et moderne,* in 1754, the time was ripe to update Dubos's *Réflexions critiques.* Many changes had taken place in French theatrical dance between 1733 and 1754. Rameau composed his first opera *Hippolyte et Aricie* in 1733, the same year that Dubos published the revised edition of *Réflexions critiques.* Between 1733 and 1754 Rameau established himself as the finest composer of French opera. The quarrel between supporters of Lully (called "Lullists") and Rameau (called "Ramists") in 1733–52 rendered Dubos's category of "modern" composers out-of-date.[20] But what made Cahusac particularly well-positioned to pen a revisionist study of Dubos's argument in 1754 is that he was not just another a historian like Dubos. He was primarily a practitioner in the French theatrical scene, working for years as a librettist who incorporated expressive dances

---

16   On the roles danced by François-Hilaire Dolivet, see Pascal Denécheau, *Dictionnaire de l'Opéra,* vol. 3, s.v. "Olivet (le père), François-Hilaire."

17   On Olivet's choreography, see Dubos, *Réflexions,* 3:247.

18   Cahusac, *La Danse,* 36.

19   "La danse, sur notre théâtre, n'a plus besoin que de guides, de bons principes, et d'une lumière qui, comme le feu sacré, ne s'éteigne jamais. Qu'on se persuade que le siècle qui a produit, dans les lettres, *l'Esprit des lois, la Henriade, l'Histoire naturelle,* et *l'Encyclopédie,* peut aller aussi loin, dans les arts, que le siècle même d'Auguste." Cahusac, *La Danse,* 230.

20   On the quarrel of Lullists and Ramists, see Paul-Marie Masson, "Lullistes et Ramistes, 1733–1752," *L'Année musicale* 1 (1911): 187–211; Mark Darlow, *Dissonance in the Republic of Letters: The Querelle des Gluckistes et des Piccinnistes* (Oxford: Legenda, 2013), 26–27.

into at least eight libretti he wrote for Rameau.[21] He moved to Paris in 1733, the year Dubos published his expanded *Réflexions critiques*, and finished *La Danse ancienne et moderne* when Diderot and d'Alembert were printing the early volumes of the *Encyclopédie*. He authored 130 articles for the *Encyclopédie*, including key articles "Ballet," "Dance," "Expression," and "Gesture," and co-wrote with Rousseau the articles "Chanson," "Chorus," and "Concert." Cahusac made a claim of *danse en action* as the dance of the Enlightenment because he had obtained extensive experience working with contemporary dancers and composers for the theaters in Paris, Fontainebleau, Choisy, and Bordeaux. In short, Cahusac was *the* person to bridge the gap between the discourse and practice of pantomime for the Enlightenment.

COMMEDIA DELL'ARTE AND PANTOMIME

What, exactly, did Dubos miss out on? Dubos knew little about the culture of pantomime in early eighteenth-century Paris. Many pantomime performers active in Paris around 1700 were performers of *commedia dell'arte*. Charles Allard, a director of the troupe of Allard at the fairground theaters in 1697, was called by the Parfaict brothers in 1743 "most skillful jumper [*sauteur*]," and "the greatest pantomime" of his time. These actors danced or mimed; sometimes, they could do both. Playing the stock character Scaramouch of the *commedia dell'arte* convention, Allard "performed dance superbly." Renaud, a "pantomime actor," played the role of Arlequin at the 1698 Saint-Germain fairground theater. Louis Nivelon, who performed at the Saint-Germain fairground in 1711, was crowned by the Parfaict brothers as "dancer of the first rank for the pantomime dance," and performed his original Swiss dance at the court many times in front of the king. The English Roger performed "ballets-pantomimes" in the Saint-Laurent fairground in 1729, and two years later, in 1731, he returned to the Saint-Laurent fairground with two other Englishmen, Renton and Haughton, and the three of them were called "excellent pantomime dancers newly arrived from London." The important point is not that these dancers were called "pantomimes," but that the Parfaict brothers had no qualms about describing their dance, *commedia dell'arte*, jumps, and pantomime as compatible elements. In this view, Dubos's theoretical distinction between dance steps and signs, penetrating as it is, seems reductionistic and inadequate as an analytical tool to *fully* explain the sophistication of pantomime performed in early eighteenth-century Parisian theaters.[22]

One might ask: since Dubos's insight was not shared by the Parfaict brothers and since Dubos's *Réflexions critiques* was crucial to the development of the Enlightenment, how should we take his lopsided bias in favor of the ancients? One approach is to place the history of Parisian pantomime in the context of *performance*

21   These libretti are *Les Fêtes de Polymnie* (1745), *Les Fêtes de l'Hymen et de l'Amour ou Les Dieux d'Égypte* (1747), *Zaïs* (1748), *Naïs* (1749), *Zoroastre* (1749), *La Naissance d'Osiris ou La Fête Pamilie* (1754), *Anacréon* (1754), and *Les Boréades* (1763). The livret *Nélée et Myrthis ou Les Beaux Jours de l'amour* (c.1754) was attributed to Cahusac.

22   On Allard, see Parfaict, *Mémoires*, 1:4; on Renaud, 1:12; on Nivelon, 1:117; on Roger, Renteon, and Haughton, 2:69–70; on the compatibility of dance and pantomime, see Harris-Warrick, *Dance and Drama*, ch. 4.

at various Parisian theaters, which took place around the time Dubos published his *Réflexions critiques*. Another approach is to examine the musical compositions in the 1730s and 1740s that carry the designation of pantomime. This is why we need to understand the contexts that motivated Rameau to publish his first musical composition on pantomime – a piece called "La Pantomime" – in 1741.

After Rameau moved to Paris permanently in late 1722, he had exposure to the *commedia dell'arte* convention, known generally as "base comedy" (*bas comique*).[23] The *commedia dell'arte* was the cornerstone of the Théâtre Italien, an Italian troupe that was expelled from Paris in 1697 and returned to Paris in 1716. Since its rise in the 1540s as marketplace entertainment in Italy, *commedia dell'arte* featured a type of comic routine called *lazzo*, which interrupts the plot by showcasing the performer's physical actions. In Paris, the emphasis on physical theater was important, for few French spectators understood Italian. Most Parisians attended these plays because they enjoyed the performances by the excellent Italian performers, who brought forth a degree of "agreeable variety" in their acting that overshadowed the "uniform regularity" of stylized acting at French theater. In *Arlequin muet par crainte* (1717), for example, the indiscreet Arlequin is threatened into keeping his master's secret. He promises to be mute and performs a *lazzo* in which he pretends to stitch together his lips, meaning he silences himself.[24]

The fairground theaters, especially at Saint-Laurent and the more substantial one at Saint-Germain, provided popular entertainment called *opéra-comique*; some of them consisted of pantomimes rich in social commentaries. Alexis Piron's *opéra-comique Le Mariage de Momus* (1722), for example, presents La Foire as the tenth muse, a fictional addition to the standard cohort of nine muses in Greek and Roman legends.[25] Personifying the fairground theaters, the twenty-year-old La Foire is a "brand-new muse." Cheerful, mute, but as lively as a fish (*vive comme un poisson*), La Foire can charm the audiences by her "pantomime."[26] With passion (*feu*) inherited from her father Bacchus and graces from her mother Venus, she expresses herself through physical action rather than speech. We do not know which gestures

---

23 On *bas comique*, see Cahusac, *La Danse*, 230. On *bas comique* and *haute comique*, see Martine de Rougement, *Le Vie théâtrale en France au XVIIIe siècle* (Paris: Champion, 2001), 122–26; Jacqueline Waeber, "'Le devin de la Foire?' Revaluating the Pantomime in Rousseau's *Devin du village*," in Waeber, ed., *Musique et geste*, 149–72. On the *grotteschi*, see Rebecca Harris-Warrick and Bruce Alan Brown, eds, *The Grotesque Dancer on the Eighteenth-Century Stage: Gennaro Magri and His World* (Madison, WI: The University of Wisconsin Press, 2005), chs. 1, 6, 7; Kathleen Kuzmick Hansell, "Theatrical Ballet and Italian Opera," in Lorenzo Bianconi and Giorgio Pestelli, eds, and Kate Singleton, trans., *Opera on Stage* (Chicago: The University of Chicago Press, 2002), 225–27.

24 *Le nouveau Mercure* (January 1718), 88–89, 91. On *lazzo*, see Mel Gordon, *Lazzi: The Comic Routines of the Commedia dell'arte* (New York: Performing Arts Journal Publications, 1983), 4.

25 On the history of *opéra-comique*, see Raphaëlle Legrand and Nicole Wild, *Regards sur l'opéra-comique: Trois siècles de vie théâtrale* (Paris: CNRS, 2002), chs. 1 and 2; on the Forain theaters, see Isabelle Martin, *Le Théâtre de la Foire: des tréteaux aux boulevards* (Oxford: Voltaire Foundation, 2002), 28–43.

26 Alexis Piron, *Œuvres complètes d'Alexis Piron*, pubd by Rigoley de Juvigny, 7 vols. (Paris: Lambert, 1776), 5:58.

La Foire makes in her pantomime, but we know that she performs a "dance" that demonstrates "pleasure," "glory," and "charms."[27] These descriptors suggest that La Foire's pantomime might include elements of *la belle danse* that confounded Dubos's tidy distinction between a dance step and a sign. While Dubos made this theoretical distinction, he did not consider the possibilities of nesting: a play called pantomime might include dance steps and, conversely, a dance might include signs abundant in pantomime. In *Le Mariage de Momus* the pantomime/dance scene imparted many layers of meanings: the long-standing tradition of dance, the art of pantomime developed in parallel to dance, inter-institutional rivalry in Paris, the social process of silencing engendered by such rivalry, narratives of victimhood and oppression, and creative representations of silences and mechanisms of silencing in the spectacles.[28]

That said, Dubos's distinction between a dance step and a sign was nonetheless important to the pantomime performances that had nothing to do with dance. For example, in Alain-René Lesage's novel *L'Histoire de Gil Blas de Santillane* (1732), which documents anecdotes about the fairground theaters, a pantomime actor pretends to keep a little pig inside his cloak. He imitates the sound of the pig so well that the spectators think he has hidden a real pig under his coat. A puzzled peasant complains about the spectators' enthusiasm over an illusion and calls for a competition with the pantomime actor. The next day the pantomime performs the same routine and earns an even bigger round of applause. This time the peasant makes a real pig screech under his cloak, and anticipates that spectators will appreciate the authenticity of the sound. But contrary to his expectation, spectators were not interested in an authentic screeching pig; rather, they were fascinated by the pantomime's superb *imitation* of its sound.[29]

Why did spectators prefer a human screeching like a pig to the genuine one? Lesage's episode illustrates a time-honored debate in the history of western aesthetics. It distinguishes between an ideal object, a real object, and the representation of an object, which Plato discussed in the allegory of the cave of his *Republic*. Whereas the peasant accepts nothing other than a real pig as the object of a spectacle, the Parisians prefer a *representation* to the real object. Lesage illustrated in this imaginary episode a classic philosophical debate about the value of imitation, using this episode to refer a pantomime to an imitator (*mime*) of everything (*panto-*).[30] In this epi-

27 La Foire's dance is remarked by Momus: "Ah! Grands dieux! Que j'entrevois / De plaisir & de gloire, / D'avoir tant d'appas à soi! / Ah, Jupiter! Donnez-moi / La Foire ..." Rigoley de Juvigny, *Œuvres complètes*, 5:60.

28 See my "Harpocrates at Work: How the God of Silence Protected Eighteenth-Century French Iconoclasts," in Patricia Hall, ed., *Oxford Handbook of Music and Censorship* (New York: Oxford University Press, 2017), 153–74.

29 Alain-René Lesage, *Histoire de Gil Blas de Santillane*, ed. Roger Laufer (Paris: Garnier-Flammarion, 1977), 171–74; Martin, *Le Théâtre de la Foire*, 87.

30 "Le nom de *pantomime* ... signifie *imitateur* de toutes choses." Jaucourt, *Encyclopédie*, vol. 11, s.v. "Pantomime." This definition was mentioned by John Weaver, *An Essay towards an History of Dancing* (London: J. Tonson, 1712), 158; Claude-François-Félix Boulenger de Rivery, *Recherches historiques et critiques sur quelques spectacles* (Paris: Jacque Merigot fils, 1751), 2. On the etymology of pantomime, see Dubos, *Réflexions*, 3:266. For this episode, see Lesage, *Histoire*, 155–56.

sode Lesage challenged Plato's skeptical attitude toward imitation, and supported Aristotle's argument for imitation in his *Poetics* (3.1): "Imitation comes naturally to human beings from childhood ...; so does the universal pleasure in imitations."[31]

Lesage's pantomime also raised the issue of gesture as a universal language, which was a defining feature of ancient Roman pantomime, as Dubos believed: "It was without speaking that pantomimes made themselves commonly understood."[32] In the eighteenth century, audiences' fascination with superb pantomime performances incentivized impresarios to present exceptional Italian and English actors/dancers in Paris. Shortly after the death of Louis XIV, in 1715, Luigi Riccoboni introduced to the Théâtre Italien the Harlequin Thomaso Antonio Vincentini (nicknamed Thomassin). Most French did not understand Italian, but Thomassin connected with his French audience all the same. His precise, expressive, and well-timed movements, without a word of Italian being spoken, impressed his French spectators. In a review of his performance in the French play *Arlequin sauvage* (1721), the *Mercure* complimented him on his "naïve graces" and "elegant bantering [*badinage*]," crowning him "the most excellent pantomime" and the "funniest actor" (*le plus joli comédien*) the Parisians had seen at the Théâtre Italien.[33]

What was impressive about Thomassin's performance was not about semantic *content*, but the communicating *skills* of gestural precision and degree of resemblance. In 1721 the *Mercure* complimented his keen observation: "Since he is unbiased, he judges the things he is made known of without error."[34] In the 1720s and 1730s, writers adopted the language of the Quarrel of Ancients and Moderns, summarized by Dubos, when discussing performances that employed bodily movements. In 1738, for example, an anonymous author published a pamphlet that related tightrope walking to ancient pantomime. To promote the English tightrope dancers (*les danseurs de corde*) of the troupe of La Meine at the Saint-Germain fairground in 1739, an anonymous author published a pamphlet on the tightrope dance. This author argued that their jumps, their balances, their surprising turns were never seen in Paris before, but these funambulists (*funambuli*), or tightrope walkers, were in fact mentioned in Terence's *Hecyra*, Horace's *Epistles*, and by writers Petronius, Juvenal, and Quintilian. These English dancers were originally more popular than the *opéra-comique* in the Saint-Laurent fair of 1738, but at the Saint-Germain fairground of the 1739 season, some six months later, they joined the *opéra-comique* and provided "new exercises, feats of strength, and surprising flexibility" in their performance, and they finished the spectacle with "some English ballets and a pantomime." Tellingly, to promote this assortment of entertainments, the author stressed in the pamphlet the intelligibility of their expression, and paraphrased a passage from Lucian of Samosata's *De Saltatione* about a pantomime who worked

---

31 On the cultural value of imitation, see Plato, *Republic* 514a–520c, 596b.

32 "C'était sans parler que les Pantomimes se faisaient entendre communément." Dubos, *Réflexions*, 3:265.

33 *Le Mercure* (June and July 1721, part 2), 22.

34 "Comme il est sans préjugé il juge sans erreur des choses qu'on lui fait connaître." *Le Mercure* (June and July 1721, part 2), 23.

as an interpreter for Nero, as he could communicate with Nero's "barbaric neighbor states" (*des voisins barbares*).[35]

One might find it absurd to consider tightrope walking a "universal language," however broadly defined, but the remarkable fact is that an author made this point in 1739. The Parfaict brothers also made a similar point, relating Thomassin to the ancient Roman tragic and comic actors Roscius and Esopus. Writing in 1733, Dubos did not seem to notice a pattern of dissemination that made pantomime an Enlightenment phenomenon. The art of pantomime had in fact been *spreading* – like a ray of light – across Europe, and this "ray" was spread by top *performers*. Thomassin was one of many exquisite itinerant actors who disseminated the craft of pantomime across national boundaries. His memorable acting was reported in the 1739 issue of *Les Amusements du cœur et de l'esprit*, a well-circulated journal in The Hague that published its fourth edition in 1742: "I focus on our charming Arlequin [i.e., Thomassin]: you know what the charms of this pantomime are. What pleasant clumsiness; what a variety of tones; what an abundance of *lazzis*."[36] His reputation reached Frankfurt, and in a poem "In Praise of Arlequin" (*Éloge d'Arlequin*) published in the journal *Le Perroquet* of 1741 (reissued in a collection in 1742), the poet praised Thomassin's skill in making his hands and fingers speak and his capacity to play different roles: "When, in the same performance, he brings together different roles with artistry, he seems indeed to be a child, a statue, and a parrot all at once."[37]

Thomassin's transnational success raised a question about who qualified as modern equals of ancient Roman pantomimes in Enlightenment France. Should Thomassin be considered a modern version of such ancient Roman pantomimes as Roscius, Esopus, Pylades, or Bathyllus? Dubos offered no answers to this question, but he made some observations instead: Roger – the English ballet master and Pierrot who performed at the Saint-Laurent fairground theater in 1729 and 1731 – made himself understood without opening his mouth; some Chinese actors performed without speaking, like the ancient Roman pantomimes; Persian dances were in effect scenes of pantomime. Dubos was interested above all in Anne, Duchess of Maine, at Sceaux, an enlightened princess who, Dubos thought, had enough natural spirit (*esprit naturel*) and knowledge (*lumières*) to revive the idea of ancient pantomime at the 1714–15 Grandes Nuits at the chateau of Sceaux, southwest of Paris, by having the dancers Baton and Françoise Prévost mime the scene in act four of

---

35   On the troupe of La Meine, see Parfaict, *Mémoires*, 2:133–34. On Nero's pantomime, see Lucien, *Éloge*, 32; *Lettre écrite à un ami sur les danseurs de corde, et sur les pantomimes qui ont paru autrefois chez les Grecs & chez les Romains, & à Paris en 1738* (Paris: Valleyre, 1739), 7.

36   "C'est à notre charmant Arlequin, que je m'arrête: vous savez quelles sont les grâces de ce Pantomime. Quelle aimable balourdise; quelle variété de tons, quelle abondance de lazzis." *Les Amusements du cœur et de l'esprit* 4 (January 1739; 4th edn, 1742), 222–23. On Roscius and Esopus, see Dubos, *Réflexions*, 3:136–37. On Thomassin and Roscius and Esopus, see Claude and François Parfaict, *Dictionnaire des théâtres de Paris*, 7 vols. (Paris: Rozet, 1767), 6:173.

37   "Quand dans la même Pièce avec art il rassemble, / Des Rôles différents & semble être en effet / Tout à la fois Enfant, Statue, & Perroquet." *Le Perroquet, Mélange de diverses pièces intéressantes pour l'esprit et pour le cœur*, 2 vols. (Frankfurt: François Varrentrapp, 1742), 2:638.

Pierre Corneille's tragedy *Horace* (1640), where Horace kills Camille. The dancers themselves were moved to tears during the performance, complete with music, bodily gestures, and walks (*démarches*), but without any dance steps (*pas de danse*). Note that Dubos made none of these observations in the 1719 edition of *Réflexions critiques*; he added them to the 1733 edition. This fact indicates that Dubos began to be aware that there were indeed some modern versions of ancient pantomimes after 1719, but he had some reservations: he questioned Roger's knowledge of Pylades and Bathyllus, which made him appear supercilious; he disregarded the popular culture in Paris, which made his idea of Enlightenment elitist. In any case, his global and trans-historical vision nonetheless promoted a universalist worldview that set the tone of the Enlightenment.[38]

Writers accepted Dubos's claim in different degrees. Cahusac found *bas comique* far more imitative than *la belle danse*, but he insisted that even the finest imitations without expression were inadequate for the Enlightenment if they failed to express emotions: "Every dance must *express*, paint, redraw in the eyes some affection of the soul. Without this condition, it loses the character of its original function. It is no more than an abuse of art."[39] [emphasis mine] Jaucourt, by contrast, upheld Dubos's elitist attitude in 1765: "Their [the pantomimes'] mute play (*jeu muet*) conveyed the [meanings of the] poems in their entirety, unlike the mimes that were only some inconsequential buffoons."[40] Their positions support the basic point that the Enlightenment was what Edelstein calls a "narratological" phenomenon, but to study pantomime as a *cultural* phenomenon one must move beyond the narratological level. If anything, the case study of Thomassin reminds us to set aside the abstract divide between the elite and the popular and to study the agents and material culture responsible for shaping the culture of pantomime.[41]

RETHINKING FRENCH DANCE

Dubos's general disregard of eighteenth-century pantomimes notwithstanding, attempts to revive ancient Roman pantomime in England and France offered examples of a serious type of pantomime distinct from the *bas comique* tradition. Roger collaborated in London with John Weaver in *Perseus and Andromeda* in 1728. Weaver had published in 1706 an English translation of Raoul Anger Feuillet's *Chorégraphie ou L'Art de décrier la danse* (1700), and he called *la belle danse* "serious

38 Dubos, *Réflexions*, 3:289–90. On the Enlightenment and elitism, see Edelstein, *The Enlightenment*, 88.

39 "Toute danse doit exprimer, peindre, retrace aux yeux quelque affection de l'âme, sans cette condition, elle perd le caractère de son institution primitive. Elle n'est plus qu'un abus de l'art." Cahusac, *La Danse*, 221. On expressive dancing, see Rebecca Harris-Warrick, "'Toute danse doit exprimer, peindre …': Finding the Drama in the Operatic Divertissement," *Basler Jahrbuch für historische Musikpraxis* 23 (1999), 187–210.

40 "Leur jeu muet rendait des poèmes en entier, à la différence des mimes qui n'étaient que des bouffons inconséquents." Jaucourt, *Encyclopédie*, vol. 11, s.v. "Pantomime."

41 On a critique of the elitist Enlightenment, see Robert Darnton, "The High Enlightenment and the Low-life of Literature in Pre-Revolutionary France," *Past and Present* 51, no.1 (1971), 81–115. On the Enlightenment as a narratological phenomenon, see Edelstein, *The Enlightenment*, 3.

dancing" in *An Essay towards an History of Dancing* (1712). Like Dubos, Weaver admired ancient Roman pantomime; both authors might have consulted accounts of Pylades and Bathyllus from François Hédelin Aubignac's *La Pratique du théâtre* (1657) or Lucian's *De Saltatione*. While Weaver staged many comic pantomimes in London, as Richard Semmens has shown, his serious English pantomimes provided an alternative to *commedia dell'arte*.[42]

The cultural significance of the English pantomime was recognized not just at the theater or in writings about dance, but in the musical genre of character pieces. In his last keyboard collection, *Pièces de clavecin* (1730), composer François Couperin differentiated the Italian *commedia dell'arte* from the ancient Roman pantomime. He composed a character piece called "L'Arlequine" (in the twenty-third *ordre* of this collection) to be played in a "grotesque" way, as opposed to "La Pantomime" (in the twenty-sixth *ordre*) to be played "happily and marked, and with great precision" (*Gaiement et marqué, et d'une grande précision*).[43] There is no evidence that "La Pantomime" imparts any sentiment or any narrative, but these two character pieces suggest a distinction between an actress ("L'Arlequine") and a pantomime performer ("La Pantomime").[44]

These examples showed that pantomime in Enlightenment France was grounded in *culture*. What makes pantomime a telling topic for cultural history is that it appealed to the illiterate, a demographic that amounted to some 70 per cent of the French population in 1700, and some illiterate French workers acted out pantomime in their ateliers as entertainments.[45] In addition to the issue of literacy, pantomime also raised the issue of class. The Parfaict brothers remarked in 1743 that the public went to the fairground theaters during the day, whereas people of quality went there in the evenings. The orphaned Jean Monnet, who became director of the Opéra-Comique in 1743 and hired Noverre as ballet master, started out in Paris with limited literacy by charming Marie Louise Élisabeth d'Orléans, Duchesse of Berry, with his

42 John Weaver, *A History of Mimes and Pantomimes* (London: J. Roberts, 1728), 3, 25, 43–49; on the earliest mention of Pylades and Bathyllus in the seventeenth century, see François Hédelin Aubignac, *La Pratique du théâtre* (Paris: Antoine de Sommaville, 1657), 200; on Weaver's comic pantomimes on the London stage, see Richard Semmens, *Studies in the English Pantomime, 1712–1733* (Hillsdale, NY: Pendragon, 2016), 14.

43 Four choreographies carrying the word "Arlequin" in the titles came from sources dated 1695–1728, and they are documented in Lancelot, *La Belle Dance*, 251, 289, 312, 338. On the grotesque dance style, see Kathleen Kuzmick Hansell, "Eighteenth-Century Italian Theatrical Ballet: The Triumph of the Grotteschi," in Harris-Warrick and Brown, eds, *The Grotesque Dancer*, 15–32.

44 Couperin claimed that he finished the set three years before the publication date of 1730, in 1727. Thus, there is no reason to link Roger's performances in 1729 to Couperin's *Pièces de clavecin*. See François Couperin, *Quatrième livre de pièces de clavecin* (Paris: s.n., 1730) [unpaginated preface], and "La Pantomime," 64–65.

45 On the literacy rate in France, see Daniel Roche, *France in the Enlightenment*, trans. Arthur Goldhammer (Cambridge, MA: Harvard University Press, 1998), 428; Robert Darnton, "Workers Revolt: The Great Cat Massacre of the Rue Saint-Séverin," in *The Great Cat Massacre and other Episodes in French Cultural History* (New York: Basic Books, 1984), 100–101.

impersonations.[46] These pieces of evidence point up a historical reality that Dubos did not consider. Although Dubos imagined that Lully's expressive dances *spread* to other dances as if they were driven by a philosophical spirit, in reality many factors contributed to the culture of pantomime in eighteenth-century France.

One of the common genres of music in the culture of pantomime was the vaude-ville (i.e., a familiar tune known as a "timbre" sung to new lyrics), commonly used in the *opéra-comique*. Charles-François Pannard experimented with what the Parfaict brothers called a "very new and very amusing" idea, based on the vaudeville tradi-tion. In his *L'Acte pantomime ou Le Pot pourri* (Saint-Germain fairground theater, 1732), he asked the actors to experiment on performing the vaudevilles in "mute scenes." That is, "the symphony played the airs of them [the vaudevilles], and the actors imparted the sense and the words of them through their gestures."[47] This experiment failed, for most audiences did not possess enough knowledge of vaude-villes to follow these mute vaudevilles, but this failure provided the foundation for a "strongly applauded" *opéra-comique* called *La Muse pantomime* (Saint-Laurent fair-ground theater, 1737).[48]

In addition to vaudevilles, some composers also supplied music for the per-formances at the Théâtre Italien, the fairground theaters, the Comédie-Française, and Servandoni's spectacles at the Tuileries. These composers included Charles-Guillaume Alexandre, Adolphe-Benoît Blaise, Pierre-Just Davesne, Robert Des Brosses, Egidio Duni, Foulquier, Francesco Saverio Germiniani, Jean-Claude Gilliers, Barthélemy Giraud, Louis-Gabriel Guillemain, and Charles Sodi.[49] Most of their music is not extant, but there were attempts to preserve it in text. For the pantomime *Les Vendanges de Tempé* (Saint-Laurent fairground theater, 1745), which enjoyed a "prodigious success," the Parfaict brothers presented the play in their *Dictionnaire des théâtres de Paris* (1756) using an uncommon two-column layout: on the left side of the page one reads actor's movements, including dances; on the right side one reads the vaudevilles played by the orchestra; each corresponds exactly to a dramatic event printed on the left side of the page. This layout shows an attempt to translate dramatic events into musical segments with some precision, but a musi-cal score would serve as a better tool for correlating music and gesture with a much higher degree of precision.[50]

46 On the spectators at the fairground theaters, see Joachim Christoph Nemeitz, *Séjour de Paris* (Leiden, Amsterdam: Jean van Aboude, 1727), 174–75; Parfaict, *Mémoires*, 1:xxiv–xxv. On Jean Monnet, see *Supplément au Roman comique, ou Mémoires pour servir à la vie de Jean Monnet*, 2 vols. (London: s.n., 1772), 1:2.

47 "Cette Pièce, dont l'idée était très-neuve, & fort plaisant, fut exécutée en scènes muettes, & sur des paroles de différents Vaudevilles connus. La symphonie en jouait les airs, & les Acteurs faisaient entendre par leurs gestes le sens et les paroles des Vaudevilles." Parfaict, *Mémoires*, 2:76–77. For the text of this *opéra-comique*, see Waeber, ed., *Musique et geste*, 265–77.

48 On *La Muse pantomime*, see Rizzoni, "Le Geste éloquent," 129.

49 On composers who wrote music for the pantomimes, see Rizzoni, "Le Geste éloquent," 132–36.

50 See Parfaict, *Dictionnaire* (1756), 6:73–82. On the table format and the issue of translation, see Ellen Lockhart, *Animation, Plasticity, and Music in Italy, 1770–1830* (Berkeley, CA:

Two other uses of music contributed to the culture of pantomime. The first one referred to a genre of pantomime made up of dances. The "two new panto-mimes" added to the prologue of a re-run of Campra's *Les Fêtes venitiennes* on July 31, 1740, danced by Rinaldi and Barbarini, comprised of a number of short dances. As shown in the collection *Airs italiens*, published afterwards, they included the standard dance types of *la belle danse* of loure, forlana, menuet, and allemande. The "pantomime" added to the entrée of the Ball of the same performance, comprised also of short dances, including rigaudon and gigue.[51] This use of pantomime, in per-formance and publication, demonstrates that pantomime was employed by danc-ers and publishers as a genre that *included* – and was not in opposition to – *la belle danse*. This use directly challenged Dubos's duality of dance step and sign, reducing its significance to the theoretical rather than the practical level. The second one referred to the music of a pantomime dance adapted as a popular tune set to new lyrics. The music of a pantomime dance, like a vaudeville, was repurposed (or "par-odied") for a new group of audiences. For example, the pantomime dance added to Jean-Baptiste Niel's ballet *L'École des amans* in 1745 was set to a song called "Good Education or a Well-Educated Girl" (*La Bonne Éducation ou La Fille bien instruite*), published also by Madame Boivin sometime between 1747 and 1753 in two collec-tions of songs called *Le Tribut de la toilette*. This source demonstrates how the art of pantomime "spread" from the theater to residences, from evening performances of pantomime dances to the formal daily morning ritual called the *toilette*, practiced primarily by privileged females and recorded notably by François Boucher's paint-ing *La Toilette* (1742).[52]

These various uses of pantomimes were among the spectacles that Rameau encountered after he settled in Paris in 1722. Sylvie Bouissou claims that Rameau developed a genuine fascination with the hybrid genres of farces and burlesques performed at the fairground theaters, suggesting that he was not nearly as elitist as Dubos was. Certainly, the fairground theaters offered opportunities for budding artists. Noverre danced the role of Borée in a parody of *Les Indes galantes* called *L'Ambigu de la Folie, ou Le Ballet des dindons* (Opéra Comique, 1743), and his first major work, the divertissement *Les Fêtes chinoises* (Marseilles of Strasburg, before 1750), earned critical acclaim at the 1754 Saint-Laurent fairground theater. Rameau's earliest theatrical experience was to compose music for Alexis Piron's mono-logue *Arlequin-Deucalion* in 1722. They collaborated again on the *opéras-comiques* *L'Endriague* (1723), *L'Enrôlement d'Arlequin* (1726), *La Robe de dissension* (1726), the unperformed *Le P.[ucelage], ou La Rose*, and the *pastorale Les Courses de Tempé* (Comédie-Française, August 30, 1734). Rameau might have gotten the idea of the mute character of Hébé of his *tragédie lyrique Castor et Pollux* (1737) from La Foire of Piron's *Le Mariage de Momus*.[53]

    University of California Press, 2017), 47–52.

51   *Airs italiens de la IV. et V. Pantomime* (Paris: Le Clerc; Madame Boivin, 1740), 1–9. F-Po CS 1404 (5).

52   *Le Tribut de la toilette*, 2 vols. (Paris: Madame Boivin, [between 1747 and 1753]), 2:586–88.

53   On Rameau and the fairground theaters, see Sylvie Bouissou, *Jean-Philippe Rameau: Musicien des Lumières* (Paris: Fayard, 2014), ch. 7. On the fairground theaters and

Of these *opéras-comiques, L'Endriague* includes an episode that mocks dance. The plot is about a place called Coqsigrüopolis, whose residents sacrifice a virgin to the monster Endriague every six months. This plot offers opportunities to dramatize the political risk of indiscretion. The first scene presents a doctor who, afraid of Caudaguliventer (the great priest of the god Popocambéchatabalipa), asks his wife to remain quiet. Endriague, a crocodile-like monster with elephant-sized legs, gobbles down the virgin, and terrifies the whole village into silence. A genie comes onstage to frighten the villagers. The plot uses the familiar themes related to oppression – threat, fear, silence, and resistance – and mocks the theaters that had privileges (i.e., the Théâtre Italien, the Comédie-Française, and the Opéra). Terpsichore, the muse of dance, performs ironically a *tambourin* and boasts about her dancing: "My foot is not touching the ground. / My body is slim and light. / Ah, ah, do I not have good bearing?"[54] It was common to have characters such as Terpsichore or Master of Dance satirize dance at the Théâtre Italien and the fairground theaters, but in *L'Endriague* Terpsichore takes a step further: she relates the silenced villagers in the play to the Parisian spectators, implying that they were metaphorically petrified by the lifeless plays performed at the Parisian theaters that had royal privileges.[55]

Rameau reused the idea of Terpsichore as a parodic technique later, in his instrumental piece "La Pantomime," published in his *Pièces de clavecin en concerts* (1741).[56] Rameau probably knew of Couperin's "La Pantomime," but instead of differentiating two kinds of performers, as Couperin did, Rameau composed a piece called "La Pantomime" that differentiated a pantomime *dance* from *la belle danse* (e.g., the menuets and tambourins in the same collection). The tempo marking "lively" (*vive*) in "La Pantomime" recalls the *loure un peu gaie* of Rameau's *Castor et Pollux* (1737), but this meter of 6/8 time and fast tempo defy the standard slow *loure* in 6/4 time (e.g., the three *loures* choreographed by Guillaume-Louis Pécour and Antoni of Sceaux (or Anthony, Antony) (1704, 1713, and 1725) and the *loure grave* he had composed for "La Danse" of *Les Fêtes d'Hébé ou Les Talents lyriques* (1739)). By setting a slow *loure* to music in a fast tempo, Rameau used music to capture the effect of a pantomime performing the supposedly serious *loure*.[57]

---

the Enlightenment, see Russo, *Styles*, 221–51. On Hébé, see Harris-Warrick, "Ballet, Pantomime, and the Sung Word," 47–48.

54 "Mon pied ne touche pas terre! / Ma taille est fine et légère; / ah, ah, n'ai-je pas bon air?" Alexis Piron, "L'Endriague," in Piron, *Œuvres complètes*, 3:131–91, at 185. On this *opéra-comique*, see Graham Sadler, "Rameau, Piron, and the Parisian Fair Theatres," *Soundings: A Music Journal* (1974): 13–29, at 14–16; Bouissou, *Jean-Philippe Rameau*, 238–43.

55 Piron, "L'Endriague," 188; on the dances in *L'Endriague*, see Bouissou, *Jean-Philippe Rameau*, 242–44; on using Terpsichore as an element of irony, see Nathalie Rizzoni, "Un Représentant pittoresque de Terpsichore: Le maître à danser dans le théâtre français de la première moitié du XVIIIᵉ siècle," in Alain Montandon, ed., *Sociopoétique de la danse* (Paris: Anthropos, 2012), 207–22.

56 On the categories of pieces in this set, see Bouissou, *Jean-Philippe Rameau*, 541–49.

57 Paul-Marie Masson, *L'Opéra de Rameau* (Paris: Henri Laurens, 1930), 396. For a definition of the *loure*, see *Encyclopédie*, vol. 9, s.v. "Loure." The three choreographies of *loure* are documented in Lancelot, *La Belle Dance*, 74, 158, 228.

It was common in the *opéra-comique* to mock a dance. In Pannard's *opéra-comique L'Impromptu* (1733), for example, the dance masters at the Opéra charge six louis for a *loure*, twice the price for a menuet. In the one-act *opéra-comique Les Noms en blanc* (1736 or possibly 1739), Nicholas Fromaget included a character called M. de La Loure.[58] Rameau's "La Pantomime" suggests a parody of a *loure* performed by a pantomime actor. What did a parody mean? In his *Discours sur l'origine et sur le caractère de la parodie* (1738–40), the abbé Claude Sallier claimed that the Greek word "parody" comprises the prefix "para-" (which means both "beside" and "contrary to") and the word "ode" (which means "song"). The word "parody" means, paradoxically, "an idea of resemblance *and* an idea of opposition."[59] [emphasis mine] A slight change of a word in a verse is sufficient to parody the whole work. Sallier's definition helps to explain what it meant for a pantomime to perform a perverse type of *loure*. A *loure* ought to be slow because it consists of two step units per measure. A quick tempo would require the dancer to rush through the dance, creating a comic effect by bringing to the surface the *possibility* of missteps. Any dancer who had embodied knowledge of the *loure* would have understood the risks when performing a slow dance to fast music. Years later, in 1765, Calzabigi would use the term "high dance" (*la haute danse*), which refers to an elevated class of dancing, but already in 1741 Rameau revealed in "La Pantomime" that *la belle danse* belonged to an elite type of dance. His "La Pantomime," therefore, was an outcome marking a different type of dance through modifying a common, unmarked dance type.[60]

LINKING DANCE TO DRAMA

After using pantomime to parody the *loure* in an instrumental piece, Rameau adapted pantomime as a type of dance at the theater. The first pantomime he wrote for the lyric stage appeared in the prologue of the *ballet bouffon Platée* (1745). Rameau had used dances to show narrative and emotion in his operas before, notably in the *Oracle figuré* of *Les Fêtes d'Hébé* and the Rose scene of *Les Indes galantes*. He also wrote music, now lost, for a pantomime performed by Marie Anne Cupis de Camargo and the Italian Pierre Sodi, an actor credited by the Parfaict brothers for being "born with a unique talent for the performance and choreography of

58　Rizzoni, "Un représentant," 211, 218.

59　"La préposition [du mot de Parodie] παρά jointe à ce substantif ὠδή, y attache tout-à-fois une idée de ressemblance, & une idée d'opposition." Claude Sallé, *Histoire de l'Académie Royale des Inscriptions et Belles Lettres*, 19 vols. (Paris: L'Imprimerie royale, 1718–81), 7:398.

60　On Rameau's *loures*, see Bernadette Lespinard, "De l'adaptation des airs de danse aux situations dramatiques dans les opéras de Rameau," *Jean-Philippe Rameau: Colloque internationale* (Paris: Champion, 1987), 480–82. On the embodied knowledge of Baroque dance, see Harris-Warrick, *Dance and Drama*, 84. On *la haute danse* as the synonym of *la belle danse*, see Calzabigi, *Scritti teatrali e letterari*, ed. Anna Laura Bellina, 2 vols. (Rome: Salerno, 1994), 1:172. Note that Calzabigi's *la haute danse* does not mean the vigorous style of *danse par haut* (or *danse haute*) that consists of high jumps. See Lecomte and Roucher, "Danse."

pantomime dances."[61] But in *Platée*, Rameau called a dance performed onstage an *air pantomime*. Rameau's use of the designation "pantomime" followed a growing interest in pantomime around 1740, but to understand why Rameau made a claim of originality in this *air pantomime* in *Platée*, we need to first understand the *comédie-ballet La Princesse de Navarre*. Both operas were performed to celebrate the wedding, on February 23, 1745, of the Dauphin of France, Louis (son of Louis XV), and María Teresa Antonia Rafaela (daughter of Philip V of Spain), during the War of Austrian Succession (1740–48).

La Princesse de Navarre was purposefully created as an original *genre* for nationalistic purposes. In early 1744 Louis XV wanted to use a new spectacle to exert French cultural power, a spectacle that served as his wedding gift for the Dauphine. He did not want one of those "spectacles for the eyes" that other nations could produce; rather, he wanted an original genre of spectacle that should amuse the court, promote beautiful arts, and glorify his reign: "So we wanted the one in charge of composing the celebration to create one of these dramatic works, in which divertissements in music are part of the subject, where joking is mixed with the heroic, and in which we see a mixture of opera, of comedy, and of tragedy."[62] The idea of mixing genres stressed out the librettist Voltaire, who shared Dubos's elitist attitude against *bas comique*: "I am almost frozen by my work [*La Princesse de Navarre*] for the court ... How to amuse them, how to make them laugh? Me, working for the court! I dread making only foolish things (*des sottises*)."[63]

Whereas Voltaire tried to avoid elements of *bas comique* in *La Princesse de Navarre*, the preparation for the royal wedding in Paris sparked a Dubosian discussion about pantomime and dramatic realism. A month before the wedding festivities, in January 1745, an untitled comic pantomime similar to Molière's *Sganarelle* and *Mascarille* provided entertainment for members of the Court who were busy preparing for the wedding festivities.[64] The content of this untitled pantomime was insignificant, but its reception was noteworthy. It prompted an anonymous author to relate it to ancient Roman pantomime, which was discussed by Dubos. In an essay published in *Mercure de France*, an author claimed that ancient Roman pantomimes presented such dramatic realism as dignity in heroic ballets, gallantry in pastorals, or fury in demonic dance, and criticized theatrical dances in French opera: sailors should not

61 "Sodi, (Pierre) Romain, né avec un talent singulier pour la composition & l'exécution des danses Pantomimes." On Sodi, see Parfaict, *Dictionnaire* (1767), 5:179. Sodi and Mlle Camargo danced three pantomimes in *La Princesse de Navarre* and none of them is indicated in the libretto or the score. On Rameau and these pantomimes, see Bouissou, *Jean-Philippe Rameau*, 584–88.

62 This goal is stated in the preface: "On a donc voulu que celui qui a été chargé de composer la fête, fit un de ces ouvrages dramatiques, où les divertissements en musique forment une partie du sujet, où la plaisanterie se mêle à l'héroïque, et dans lesquels on voit un mélange de l'opéra, de la comédie, et de la tragédie." *OCV*, 28A:173–74.

63 "Je suis d'ailleurs presque glacé par mon ouvrage pour la cour ... Comme les amuser, comme les faire rire? Moi travailler pour la cour! J'ai peur de ne faire que des sottises." Voltaire, letter to Pierre Robert Le Cornier de Cideville dated May 8, 1744 (D2968). [EE]

64 "Cette Pantomime a été choisie pour divertir la Cour aux Noces de Monseigneur le Dauphin." *Mercure de France* (January 1745, part 1), 163.

carry their oars; peasants should not put on wigs as if they were ladies at the court, and magicians should not wear rustic bonnets. This author was not the first one who criticized the quality of theatrical dance in French opera. He echoed Gabriel Bonnot de Mably, who had pointed out in 1741 that it was absurd for the demons in Rameau's *Dardanus* (1739) to perform a jolly dance. Inspired by this comic panto-mime, so insignificant that it did not even have a title, the critic of *Mercure de France* declared, "every good dancer must be [a] pantomime at the theater."[65]

Voltaire meanwhile found a way to incorporate comic elements in his *La Princesse de Navarre* without resorting to base comedy. Inspired by historical events of 1369, during the Hundred Years' War, Voltaire designed a plot about Constance, the princess of Navarre, who had fled from her enemies Don Pedro and the Duke of Foix, and had taken refuge in the country home of the baron Don Morillo, a comic character who shows but a provincial and thus inauthentic version of gal-lantry. Don Morillo falls in love with Constance, but she has no romantic interest in him; instead, she becomes enamored of a soldier called Alamir, who, despite his lower-class status, has a gallant bearing. As it turns out, this "soldier" is the Duke of Foix in disguise.[66] Voltaire designed comic situations around Don Morillo's daugh-ter, known as Sanchette, who dreams of becoming a genuine noblewoman, although she is a "simple child, naïve, [and has] as much coquetry as ignorance."[67] The plot dramatizes tensions between high and low, gallantry and naiveté, pretense and truth. Sanchette serves as a comic imposter by overreaching herself, mimicking the behav-iors of a real noblewoman when she fantasizes about gallantry. Voltaire probably thought that this plot about fake and real nobles would amuse the genuine nobles who attended the royal wedding.

Although Voltaire came up with a script that consists of comic ideas, Rameau reversed one of Voltaire's ideas that was particularly unsuitable for wedding festivi-ties. In the duet sung by a fortune-teller couple in Act 1 Scene 6, Voltaire portrayed happy marriage as "rare," but Rameau reversed Voltaire's meaning, turning the word "rare" to "sweet." Whereas Voltaire highlighted marriage as a prolonged period of slavery, Rameau asserted that a happy relationship prevents a sense of entrapment. Whereas Voltaire stressed that marriage inevitably introduces dangerous knots, Rameau countered that equal partnership makes a happy relationship.[68] Rameau further mitigated Voltaire's skepticism by musical means. Beginning in E major, the duet modulates to the dominant, B major, emphasizing the words "slavery" (*esclavage*) in mm.4–5 and "dangerous" (*dangereux*) in mm.8–9, before returning to the home key of E major. Rameau underscored his own interpretation of Voltaire's

---

65 "Tout bon danseur doit être Pantomime sur le Théâtre." *Mercure de France* (January 1745, part 1), 166. For Mably's remarks, see Gabriel Bonnet de Mably, *Lettres à Mme la marquise de P*** sur l'opéra* (New York: AMS Press, 1978), 114.

66 *OCV*, 28A:129.

67 "Je la [Sanchette] fais une enfant simple, naïve, et ayant autant de coquetterie que d'ignorance." Voltaire, letter to comte d'Argental, dated June 5, 1744 (D2985). [EE] On *bienséances*, see Downing A. Thomas, "Rameau's *Platée* Returns: A Case of Double Identity in the *Querelle des bouffons*," *Cambridge Opera Journal* 18, no.1 (2006), 6–8. On the coquette, see Russo, *Styles*, 118–23.

68 On Rameau's revision of Voltaire's text, see *OCV*, 28A:202, n.20.

text by musical means, repeating the melodic motive E–C-sharp–D-sharp–E on the words "marriage" and "equality" in mm.11–14, and reiterating the verse by the end of the duet. He also had the strings play polyphonically until the section on marriage and equality, when they play in thirds, creating a textual clearing that emphasizes the words "marriage" and "equality."[69]

By revising the meaning of Voltaire's text, Rameau obviously exercised his creative agency in different stages of his compositional process, making the opera more congruous with the theme of the wedding celebrations. Rameau thus exhibited, according to John Locke's definition of liberty in *An Essay Concerning Human Understanding* (1690), the "power to begin or forbear."[70] This idea of liberty was elaborated in the article "Moral Liberty" of the *Encyclopédie* (1765), attributed to Jacques-André Naigeon and the abbé Claude Yvon, who summarized ideas on liberty written by philosophers including Baruch Spinoza, Thomas Hobbes, Locke, Bernard Le Bovier de Fontenelle, Gottfried Wilhelm Leibniz, and Voltaire. In it, moral liberty was not an abstract idea; it should instead be realized through action: "The power of making up one's mind is not more dependent on mental abilities than on the power to paint, to engrave, and to write."[71]

Whereas Rameau disagreed with Voltaire, both worked together in other instances by emphasizing the social meaning of dance. Following the Lullian convention, the duet discussed above would lead directly to dances, but Rameau and Voltaire interrupted this sequence of singing and dancing with a brief spoken dialogue, where Sanchette asks the Duc of Foix if the singing and dancing festivities (*fêtes*) represent his love for her.[72] The Duc of Foix offers an evasive reply, claiming that these festivities are nothing other than his craze (*folie*), a word defined later by Cahusac as "an absence of or a distraction from reason."[73] Their exchange leads to a *menuet*, in which the Duc of Foix refuses to dance with Sanchette, while Sanchette's

---

69 According to Lionel Sawkins, Rameau's revised libretto was employed at the wedding festivities in 1745. See his "Voltaire, Rameau, Rousseau: A Fresh Look at *La Princesse de Navarre* at its Revival in Bordeaux in 1763," *Studies on Voltaire and the Eighteenth Century* 265 (1989), 1334–40. Russell Goulbourne argues against taking Rameau's variant as the definitive version. On a comparison of these two versions, see *OCV*, 28A:212–13, n.20 and Sawkins, ibid., 1336–37. For the score, see Jean-Philippe Rameau, *Œuvres complètes*, published under the direction of Camille Saint-Saëns, vol. 11, *La Princesse de Navarre, Les Fêtes de Ramire, Nélée et Myrthis, Zéphyre* (Paris: Durand; New York: Broude Brothers Limited, 1968), 31–32.

70 John Locke, *An Essay Concerning Human Understanding*, ed. Pauline Phemister (Oxford: Oxford University Press, 2008), 141.

71 "Le pourvoir de se déterminer n'est pas plus dépendant des dispositions du cerveau, que le pouvoir de peindre, de graver & d'écrire." Naigeon and Yvon [attributed], *Encyclopédie*, vol. 9, s.v. "Liberté [Morale]." On the sources that informed this entry, see Dan Edelstein, Robert Morrissey, and Glenn Roe, "To Quote or not to Quote: Citing Strategies in the *Encyclopédie*," *Journal of the History of Ideas* 74, no.2 (April 2013), 200 n.20.

72 Harris-Warrick, *Dance and Drama*, 50.

73 "La folie est une absence ou un égarement de la raison." Cahusac, *Encyclopédie*, vol. 5, s.v. "Enthousiasme [Philosophie/Belles Lettres]."

father, Don Morillo, asks Constance to dance with him.[74] Dances at the balls, Harris-Warrick observes, were not about self-enjoyment or self-expression, but about displaying their skills in front of spectators. Since one couple at a time danced and others watched them dance, this *pre*-dance scene demonstrates the mixed responses of acceptance and refusal. Two dances – *menuets* and a *tambourin en rondeau* – offer a real princess (Constance) access to aristocratic sociality and prevent a comic imposter (Sanchette) from dancing. Talking about liberty, the Duc of Foix exercises what Leibniz called a "liberty of indifference." He has the choice to dance or not dance with Sanchette, and he opts out.[75] The linkage of dance and class indicates that Rameau thought about the dramatic meanings of dance, as he wrote in a letter dated May 29, 1744: "In fact, it is necessary to be involved in the show, having studied its nature for a long time, to paint it as accurately as possible, have all the characters present, be sensitive to dance, to its movements, not to mention all the accessories, know the voices, the actors, etc."[76] The expression "sensitive to dance" resonated with the definition of the "philosophical spirit" by Jaucourt, and was explained by Cahusac: "We usually watch dance only as an isolated decoration [*agrément*] at the lyric theater. It must, however, always be intimately related to the principal action."[77] Rameau carried forward this thinking to *Platée*, the other spectacle he composed for the same wedding festivities. As with *La Princesse de Navarre*, *Platée* was a new spectacle. In it, Rameau employed pantomime as an original type of dance.

BACCHUS, THE GOD OF LIBERTY

We have seen the trend to publish pantomime music around 1740, but it is in *Platée* that Rameau related Bacchus explicitly to the themes of originality and liberty. The librettist of this opera, Jacques Autreau, originally wrote it as a comic opera for the Opéra. The title *Platée* refers to the Battle of Plataea, the last land battle of the Greek-Persian war, in 479 BC, which took place in the city of Plataea – a battle that led to the Peloponnesian War. After being threatened twice to desert their land, the Plataens collaborated with the Athenians in the critical battle of Plataea

---

74 The stage direction reads: "Les acteurs de la comédie sont rangés sur les côtés; Sanchette veut danser avec le Duc de Foix qui s'en défend. Morillo prend la Princesse de Navarre et danse avec elle." Jean-Philippe Rameau, *Œuvres complètes*, vol. 9, ed. Paul Dukas (Paris: A. Durand, 1906), 33. On various functions of these stage directions (also called *didascalies*), see Harris-Warrick, *Dance and Drama*, 28–31.

75 Françoise Dartois-Lapeyre, "Les divertissements dansés dans les opéras de Rameau," in *Jean-Philippe Rameau: Colloque*, 513–14. On the balls at the French court and spectatorship, see Harris-Warrick, *Dance and Drama*, 267. On the liberties of contingency and indifference, see Gottfried Wilhelm Leibniz, *Essais de Théodicée* (1710; Paris: Aubier, 1962), 135. [AFTFL]

76 "Il faut être en fait du spectacle, avoir longtemps étudié la nature, pour la peindre le plus au vrai qu'il est possible; avoir tous les caractères présents, être sensible à la danse, à ses mouvements, sans parler de tous les accessoires; connaitre les voix, les acteurs, etc." *Mercure de France* (June 1765), 54–55.

77 "On est dans l'habitude de ne regarder la danse au théâtre lyrique, que comme un agrément isolé. Il est cependant indispensable, qu'elle y soit toujours intimement liée à l'action principale." Cahusac, *La Danse*, 237.

and defeated the Persians. According to Jaucourt, Plataea symbolized war victory and originated the Games of Liberty in antiquity. This liberty is different from the moral liberty we have discussed above because it indicates what Hobbes called, in *Leviathan* (1651), "free commonwealths": "The Athenians, and Romans were free; that is, free commonwealths: not that any particular men had the liberty to resist their own representative; but that their representative had the liberty to resist, or invade other people."[78] This military history left its traces in the history of comedy. Playwright Aristophanes included an episode of Plataea in his comedy *Frogs*. By adopting *Platée* as a subject matter of an opera, Autreau alluded to both ancient Greek military history and ancient Greek theater. The allusions to the war victory in antiquity helped create an image of a strong France in the middle of the ongoing War of Austrian Succession.[79]

In keeping with the allusion to liberty in the title of *Platée*, the libretto employs the deity of Bacchus as an icon of liberty. Bacchus, the Roman version of the powerful Greek god Dionysus, can use alcohol to transcend realities. As the god of wine noted in Ovid's *Metamorphoses* and Euripides's *Bacchae*, Bacchus represents ecstasy and intemperance, but he also makes their followers unfree by making them morally indecent, by altering their minds, by giving them superhuman strength and animalistic brutality, and, in the case of Agave and Pentheus, by causing Agave to commit prolicide. According to Menestrier's *Des Ballets anciens et modernes selon les règles du théâtre* (1682), "the satyrs danced in honor of Bacchus, and their dance was not very decent because they hardly danced until they were warmed with wine."[80] Charles Rollin pointed out in 1740 that the Dionysian festivities were morally suspect, for in ancient times they included aspects of violence, consumption of raw meat suggesting cannibalism, obscenity, and even murder. The operas *Orphée* (1690), *Enée et Lavinie* (1690), and, as Don Fader points out, *Penthée* (1705) even painted Bacchus as a destructive power.[81] Yet, the cultural meaning of Bacchus took a turn in the eighteenth century by signaling liberty – what Hobbes called an "absence of opposition."[82] Numerous *airs à boire*, published between 1691 and 1737 in collections called *Recueils d'airs sérieux et à boire*, celebrate Bacchus as a harmless god of revelry. Cahusac noted Bacchic dances as sensual expressions of "liberty and joy" (*la liberté et la joie*). Diderot likewise emphasized the relaxing and voluble effects that

---

78 Thomas Hobbes, *Leviathan*, ed. John Charles Addison Gaskin (Oxford: Oxford University Press, 1996), 143.

79 Aristophanes, *Frogs*, 694; Jacques Autreau, *Œuvres de Monsieur Autreau*, 4 vols. (Paris: Briasson, 1749), 4:50. This image was crafted by the second volume of the February 1745 issue of *Mercure de France*; almost the entire volume was on the royal wedding.

80 "Les Satyres dansaient à l'honneur de Bacchus, & leur Dance était peu honnête, parce qu'ils ne dansaient guère qu'ils ne fussent échauffez de Vin." Claude-François Menestrier, *Des ballets anciens et modernes selon les règles du théâtre* (Paris: René Guignard, 1682), 12.

81 On Bacchus as a destructive power, see Don Fader, "*Le Régent en Bacchus*? French Noble Self-Construction, Operatic Allegory, and Philippe d'Orléans's *Penthée* (1703)" (paper, American Musicological Society/Society of Music Theory Annual Meeting, Milwaukee, WI, November 6, 2014).

82 Hobbes, *Leviathan*, 139.

Bacchus's wine brings forth: "We sacrificed male goat and magpie to him [Bacchus]. The goat eats shoots; wine causes the magpie to speak."[83]

Platée was not the first opera that presented itself as a new spectacle. Lully had presented *Atys* (1676) and *Achille et Polixène* (1687) as new spectacles as well, but *Platée* differs from them by having the prologue serve as a *framing* device that presents the ensuing three-act comedy proper as a "new" spectacle. This frame shows the agency of the librettists Adrien-Joseph Valois d'Orville and Sylvain Ballot de Sauvot, who added to Autreau's script a divertissement that begins with an *air pantomime*.[84] The prologue, known as the birth of comedy (*la naissance de la comédie*), depicts a process through which a comedy is born. Set in a Greek vineyard protected by the god of wine, Bacchus, the prologue begins with Thespis, the inventor of comedy, lying asleep on the ground. A Satyr wakes him up and asks him to sing the praises of Bacchus, the "god of liberty" and "father of sincerity." Thespis finds himself empowered by the Bacchic orgy to speak the truth. He calls the young and beautiful Maenads out for their infidelity, threatening to disclose their secrets. Thespis is encouraged by Thalia, the muse of comedy, who plans to stage a play with the god of raillery, Momus, to teach the mortals a lesson. The three of them decide to mock everyone and laugh about everything. Momus suggests staging the story of Jupiter, king of the Roman gods, who once came up with a scheme that cured his wife Juno of jealousy and pride. This trio is joined by Eros, the god of love, and the formation of this team brings us to the end of the prologue, where the chorus sings, "Let us make a new spectacle" ("*Formons un spectacle nouveau*"), and ascribes the power of Bacchus to Hippocrene, the sacred fountain on Mountain Helicon in Boeotia that gushes out extraordinary streams of water which empower those who drink it with poetic inspiration. Thus, the prologue refers reflexively to the opera as a new spectacle, produced with the protection of the boundlessly creative Bacchus.

The climax of the prologue culminates at the beginning of the divertissement, which is marked by an *air pantomime* that consists of a high *density* of dissimilar thematic materials. Lully had employed mimed action and dancing in *Les Fêtes de l'Amour et de Bacchus*, and Louis de Lacoste's *tragédie Philomèle* (1705) includes an *air de furies* danced by the Bacchantes.[85] Yet Rameau presents in this *air pantomime* neither a narrative nor any emotion, offering instead thematic abundance. At the beginning of this *air*, a broken-chord melodic figure establishes D major as the home key, which leads to an ascending scalar sextuplet motive (m. 496, Example 1.2).

83 Charles Rollin, *Histoire ancienne des Égyptiens, des Carthaginois, des Assyriens, des Babyloniens, des Mèdes, et des Perses, des Macédoniens, des Grecs*, 5 vols. (Paris: Estienne, 1740), 5:667; Cahusac, *La Danse*, 76. On Bacchus, see Diderot, *Encyclopédie*, vol. 2, s.v. "Bacchus."

84 On *Achille et Polixène*, see Laura Naudeix, *Dramaturgie de la tragédie en musique (1673–1764)* (Paris: Honoré Champion, 2004), 207; on the prologue as a preface, see Rebecca Harris-Warrick, "Le Prologue de Lully à Rameau," in Michel Noiray and Solveig Serre, eds, *Le Répertoire de l'opéra de Paris (1671–2009): Analyse et interprétation* (Paris: École des Chartes, 2010), 200–204; Naudeix, *Dramaturgie*, 219.

85 On mimed action and dancing in Lully's *Les Fêtes de l'Amour et de Bacchus*, see Harris-Warrick, *Dance and Drama*, 157–61. On Bacchus, see Robert A. Green, "Aristophanes, Rameau and *Platée*," *Cambridge Opera Journal* 23, nos.1–2 (2012), 8. I thank Olivia Bloechl for asking me to consult Lacoste's *Philomèle*.

Example 1.2. Rameau, *Platée*, Prologue Scene 3, "Air pantomime," mm.494–516
Reproduced with the kind permission of the Société Jean-Philippe Rameau

On danse.

A more lyrical motive follows (mm. 503–506), and the section concludes with a descending scalar motive in sextuplets (mm. 514–15). As a pantomime does not belong to *la belle danse*, it does not consist of any "dance rhythm," but Rameau developed a distinct approach to this dance.[86] In this section of just twenty-two measures, Rameau used no fewer than four thematic ideas, emphasizing the *density* of dissimilar thematic materials (i.e., the number of discernible themes *per* section), rather than the sheer number of dissimilar thematic materials. A typical piece of *la belle danse*, such as a menuet, has a low thematic density, for the entire dance is unified by one "dance rhythm." By contrast, with four thematic ideas in a section of just twenty-two measures, Rameau's *air pantomime* has a much higher thematic density. Rameau was probably inspired by Mondonville, who wrote the "pantomime"

86 None of the 539 dances listed in Francine Lancelot's catalogue bears the designation of "pantomime" and two choreographies represent Bacchus or the Bacchante. See her *La Belle Dance*, 96, 162.

Example 1.2. continued

in his 1742 *Isbé* (prologue/iv) as a dance in binary form. He presented five thematic ideas in the first section of twenty-one measures, and he developed these ideas in the second section. In the "pantomime" added to the prologue of the 1740 re-run of Campra's *Les Fêtes vénitiennes*, the anonymous composer used four thematical

Example 1.2. continued

ideas in a section of eleven measures.[87] Rameau must have enjoyed experimenting with thematic density in his dances. He used low thematic density in the *rigaudons* and *contredanse en rondeau* of the same divertissement in *Platée*, and high thematic density in the unperformed acte de ballet *Zéphire ou Les Nymphes de Diane* (*c.*1750). In *Platée*, therefore, the exceptionally theme-rich *air pantomime* generates a dance-and-chorus sequence.[88]

The high thematic density of the *air pantomime* resembles the mimetic versatility of a pantomime, which is an indicator of a pantomime performer's creativity. An ancient Roman pantomime described by Lucian and Dubos performed as many as five different roles in succession. Boulenger de Rivery also reported, in *Recherches sur les mimes et pantomimes* of 1751, that an ancient Roman pantomime was admired by having "more than one soul in one body."[89] Pantomimes in the *commedia dell'arte*

87 For the score of these pantomime dance, see Mondonville, *Isbé* (Paris: Madame Boivin), 15–16; *Airs italiens de la IV. et V. Pantomime, dansées par Mr. Fossani et son épouse. Au Prologue et dans l'Acte du Bal des Festes Venitiennes* (Paris: Madame Boivin, [s.d.]), 1. F-Po, CS 1404 (5).

88 On *Zéphire*, see Harris-Warrick, "Ballet, Pantomime, and the Sung Word," 46.

89 "Dans un seul corps tu as plus d'une âme." Boulenger de Rivery, *Recherches*, 81; Dubos, *Réflexions*, 3:279.

tradition also showed instantaneous transformations. For example, in Mainbray's *pièce pantomime* called *Les Dupes, ou Rien n'est difficile en amour* (1740), Arlequin strikes the head of a black dwarf and transforms him into a buffet; later, he transforms himself into a black man, and, by the end of the play, he strikes the bottom of a painting and turns it into a prison.⁹⁰ In this *air pantomime*, Rameau used Bacchus as a god of liberty to validate an uncommonly generous amount of distinct musical ideas for a dance. Rameau's pantomime as a symbol of creativity was consistent with Dubos's idea of creativity. Evoking Hobbes's idea of the absence of opposition as the condition for poetic creation, Dubos wrote that "the less the imagination is restricted, the more freedom a poet has for invention."⁹¹

In the context of the entire opera, the *air pantomime* marks a brief structural pivot, which joins together the prologue and the opera proper. Brevity was a characteristic of ancient Roman pantomime. As Boulenger de Rivery noted, "They [the pantomime performances] did not need any denouement. They [the pantomime actors] escaped from the theater often at the moment when we least expected it, and the play was over."⁹² Noverre also mentioned in his *Lettres sur la danse* (1760) that the tableaux of a ballet-pantomime must be "varied," and that each tableau must "last only an instant."⁹³ By placing this thematically rich *air pantomime* at the beginning of a divertissement, Rameau made the *air pantomime* a structural elision, at once the goal of the prologue and the threshold of comedy. He also made it present miscellaneous musical ideas. Just as the magpie starts to "speak" when it gets drunk, as Piron and Diderot imagined, Rameau captured in his *air pantomime* a brief but pronounced state of intoxication at the inception of a creative act, a "liminal" state – as it were – for pre-creating a comedy in which originality met with liberty.

What, then, is the relationship between the liberty as portrayed in the *air pantomime* of *Platée* and liberty as understood in the Enlightenment? The attributed authors of the article "Moral Liberty" in the *Encyclopédie* offered a conceptual framework. Citing Gottfried Wilhelm Leibniz's *Essais de théodicée sur la bonté de dieu, la liberté de l'homme et l'origine du mal* (1710), they claimed that the essence of liberty "consists in the *intelligence* that envelops a clear knowledge of the object of deliberation, in the *spontaneity* with which we make decisions, and in the *contingency*, that is, the exclusion of logical or metaphysical *necessity*."⁹⁴ [emphasis mine] Since his actions did not follow any logical, metaphysical, or physical necessity, Bacchus

---

90 Mainbray, *Les Dupes ou Rien n'est difficile en amour* (Paris: [De Lormel], 1740), 7, 18, 22.

91 "Moins elle [l'imagination] est resserrée, plus il lui [au poète] reste de liberté pour inventer." Dubos, *Réflexions*, 1:319.

92 "Ils n'avoient besoin d'aucun dénouement; ils s'échappaient du Théâtre souvent à l'instant où l'on s'y attendait le moins, & la pièce était finie." Boulenger de Rivery, *Recherches*, 25.

93 "Ses Tableaux [de la danse] doivent être variés, & ne durer qu'un instant." Noverre, *Lettres*, 3.

94 "Son essence [L'essence de la liberté] consiste dans l'intelligence qui enveloppe une connaissance distincte de l'objet de la délibération. Dans la spontanéité avec laquelle nous nous déterminons, & dans la contingence, c'est-à-dire dans l'exclusion de la nécessité logique ou métaphysique." Naigeon and Yvon [attributed], *Encyclopédie*, s.v. "Liberté [Morale]."

was an excellent representation of spontaneity and contingency. In addition to the Bacchic revelry, singing, and dancing that are ordinarily blessed by him, Bacchus was portrayed by Ovid and Euripides as an extraordinary god: he was born twice, first prematurely by his mother, Semele, and the second time by his father, Zeus, who carried him in his thigh; he was a god who looked like a little girl; he looked like a foreigner. This extraordinary god was portrayed as doing extraordinary things: he bewitched his aunts and turned them into Bacchantes; he made a ship stand still in the sea; he transformed sailors into fish; he released his priest from a prison by making the doors fly open on their own and making chains fall from the priest's shoulders; he turned the mother of Pentheus, king of Thebes, into a Bacchante who mistook her son/king for a beast and slaughtered it/him. Above all, Bacchus had an extraordinary presence. Ovid underscored in the *Metamorphoses* that Bacchus could reveal himself unannounced, and described him as "a god more truly present than all others." He could make his power felt without being physically present. He is present when one gets drunk. Under the auspices of Bacchus, water rushed out of a rock when a bacchant struck her thyrsus against it; wine spurted up when another bacchante thrust her fennel rod into the ground; milk spilled out of the ground when the Bacchae scratched the ground; streams of honey spilled out of their thyrsi.[95] Although Bacchus never appears onstage in *Platée*, spectators who had read Ovid and Euripides would not *assume* that he was absent; instead, spectators would expect that Bacchus would alter the reality with his extraordinary power. Jacques Cazotte, indeed, claimed that he felt the omnipresence of Bacchus in the opera: "I feel the drunk joy of the grape pickers in the ballet of *Platée*."[96] Granted, Rameau was one of many composers who wrote a dance about Bacchus or the Bacchantes (e.g., Lully's pastorale *Les Fêtes de l'Amour et Bacchus* (1672)), but Rameau ingeniously deployed the pantomime in *Platée* as an unconventional type of dance that illustrates the supramundane, invisible presence of Bacchus. Its high motivic density illustrates an inchoate state, suggesting not a premeditated, but a spontaneous act of creation. Hence, Rameau illustrated in this *air pantomime* elements of liberty as understood in the Enlightenment.

So far, we have discussed how Rameau acted as a creative agent by exercising his free will within the confines expected of a composer in his compositional process. His creative agency left tangible evidence in his musical settings of pantomimes. But he did not stay on the level of fixing the text; rather, he tried to make sure that his artistic ideas were realized in the performance, making performance a necessary extension of his creative process. There is evidence that the texts – his scores of pantomimes – conditioned performers' interpretations of the texts, which ultimately led spectators, such as Jacques Cazotte, to notice an overall sense of liberty transmitted through the performance.

Soon after Rameau made the air pantomime represent contingency and spontaneity in the 1745 version, he reinforced these effects in the 1749 re-run at the

---

95 Ovid, *Metamorphoses* 3.837–935; Euripides, *Bacchae* 678–765.

96 "Je sens la joie ivre des vendangeurs du Ballet de Platée." *La Querelle des bouffons: texte des pamphlets*, ed. Denise Launay, 3 vols. (1973; Geneva, 1992), 1:340. On Bacchus as a revelatory god, Ovid, *Metamorphoses* 3.859–63.

Académie Royale de Musique in Paris. Rameau strengthened the effect of liberty in the celebratory chorus "Let's Sing of Bacchus" (*Chantons Bacchus*) that follows the *air pantomime*. In it Thespis sings in alternation with the chorus.[97] Compared with the 1745 version, the score published in 1749 includes an additional stage direction, "they dance if they want to" (*On danse si l'on veut*), whenever Thespis sings the line "May each of these gods in turn satisfy our souls in this place" ("*Que tour à tour / Dans ce séjour, / Ces dieux remplissent nos âmes*"). This variant indicates a special effect. It modifies the conventional alternation of singing and dancing in the performance practice of dance-song (a vocal piece with dance elements) and *chœur dansé* (a chorus number including singing and dancing) by allowing dancers the *option* to dance whenever Thespis sings. Bacchus not only creates the entire spectacle – he also lets them exercise their volition during the performance. Rameau highlighted Bacchus's invisible presence in the 1749 version by allowing dancers to move with spontaneity and contingency. Rather than having dancers act as the chorus's surrogates or "body doubles," Rameau allowed dancers to choose the *kind* of doubles they wanted to be by exercising a freedom of motion (to be discussed in Chapter Four), which was theorized by David Hume in his *A Treatise of Human Nature* (1739–40): "By the will, I mean nothing but the internal impression we feel and are conscious of, when we knowingly give rise to any new *motion* of our body, or new perception of our mind."[98]

Dancing during Thespis's solo singing may distract spectators from paying full attention to Thespis, of course, but loosening the strict alternation between solo singing and dancing in *Platée* may also represent freedom. Charles Batteux argued in *Les Beaux-arts réduits à un même principe* (1746) that a perfect imitation of *belle nature* must have the qualities of both exactitude and freedom. Whereas exactitude *regulates* imitation, freedom *animates* it. Hence, artists should capture the freedom in nature even though such a freedom may manifest as imperfections: "Nature always appears naïve and ingenuous. Because it is free, it proceeds without study and without reflection … In an effort to achieve this freedom, great painters sometimes let their brushes play on the canvas. Sometimes symmetry is broken. Sometimes a disorder is affected in some small part. Here, it is a careless ornament; there, it is even a flaw, left on purpose. The law of imitation demands it."[99] Batteux's idea of a perfect

---

97   Usually singing alternates with dancing in French opera. See Harris-Warrick, *Dance and Drama*, 55.

98   See Jean-Philippe Rameau, *Opera Omnia*, series 4, vol. 10, ed. M. Elizabeth C. Bartlet, 45, and 393 [critical notes]. [*OOR*] On dancers as surrogates, see Mary Cyr, "The Dramatic Role of the Chorus," in Thomas Bauman and Marita Petzholdt McClymonds, eds, *Opera and the Enlightenment* (New York: Cambridge University Press, 1995), 113; Lois Rosow, "Performing a Choral Dialogue by Lully," *Early Music* 15, no.3 (1987), 330; on the alternation of singing and dancing, see Harris-Warrick, *Dance and Drama*, 40–55. On dancing and stage movement, see Thomas Betzwieser, "Musical Setting and Scenic Movement: Chorus and *Chœur dansé* in Eighteenth-Century Parisian Opéra," *Cambridge Opera Journal* 12, no.1 (2000), 13–14, 19. On free will and freedom of motion, see David Hume, *A Treatise of Human Nature*, ed. David Fate Norton and May J. Norton, 2 vols. (Oxford: Clarendon Press, 2007), 1:257.

99   Charles Batteux, *The Fine Arts Reduced to a Single Principle*, trans. James O. Young (Oxford: Oxford University Press, 2015), 46.

imitation, therefore, formed the aesthetic foundation for Noverre's idea of "beautiful chaos" (*un beau désordre*) in ballet-pantomime.[100]

PANTOMIME AS THE OTHER DANCE

After composing *Platée*, Rameau again looked to pantomime for a creative outlet in his acte du ballet *Pygmalion* (1748). By the time he composed music for this ballet, Rameau had already thought about representing Bacchic's power in *Platée*. For the ballet *Pygmalion*, based on a well-known story of the animation of a Statue, Rameau brought the musical and kinetic representation of the supernatural to a new level. To understand how he did it, we need to look at the music sources that show the different stages of Rameau's creative process. On the score published in 1748 he wrote two staging directions – "a moment of silence" (*silence d'un moment*) and "the statue comes alive" (*La Statue anime*) – that appear on the same vertical axis on the page. Their locations on the page suggest that a musical pause generates a moment of heightened anticipation for the animation of the Statue. Yet, a manuscript copy of Rameau's score (H.720), sent to Louis XV for the 1754 revival at Fontainebleau, includes a copyist's handwritten annotations, which separated these two stage directions: the instruction of a moment of silence stays in the same location, while the second instruction was moved to the beginning of the next system.[101] The annotations suggest that Rameau – assuming that he authorized them – kept thinking about the most effective way to stage this crucial dramatic moment even after he published the score. For the re-run at Fontainebleau, he decided to separate a moment of silence into two portions: first, a pause – then the Statue comes alive. Rameau used the moment of silence as Dubos's concept of an "instituted sign," which emphasizes a suspenseful soundless moment as a primordial state that marks the marvelous transformation of Statue into a human being.[102]

Immediately after the transformation, the process of acculturation begins. Rameau integrated dance into the plot, using it to civilize the Statue/woman. Rameau used nine dances – gavotte, menuet, another gavotte, chaconne, loure, passepied, rigaudon, sarabande, and tambourine – that form a dance sequence. Rameau grouped all these dances together, to be performed continuously without a pause. His decision made sense because they all belong to the category of *la belle danse*, what Dubos called "ordinary dances," or what Cahusac and Noverre called *la danse simple* or the "alphabet" of theatrical dance, as opposed to what Cahusac called "composite dance" (*la danse composée*), which forms "a sustained action" (*une action suivie*). Cahusac criticized La Motte for failing to use simple dance to advance

---

100 Noverre, *Lettres*, 10. On naturalness and gesture in ballet-pantomime, see Sibylle Dahms, *Der konservative Revolutionär: Jean Georges Noverre und die Ballettreform des 18. Jahrhunderts* (Munich: Epodium, 2010), 86–97.

101 Rameau, *Pygmalion, acte de ballet* (Paris: Boivin, 1748), 13. F-Pn H.720.

102 On H.720, see Olivier Opdebeeck, "*Pigmalion* de Rameau: étude des sources et propositions pour une édition," in *Jean-Philippe Rameau: Colloque*, 248. I borrow the term "staging annotation" from Antonia L. Banducci: see her "Staging and Its Dramatic Effect in French Baroque Opera: Evidence from Prompt Notes," *Eighteenth-Century Music* 1 (2004), 3. On the natural and instituted signs, see Dubos, *Réflexions*, 3:223–24.

dramatic action: "La Motte only knew simple dance. He varied it in his operas, giving it some national characters, but it was introduced without any prescribed action."[103]

Like Lully, Rameau saw merits in both types of dance. Moreover, his use of both types in this scene in effect realized Dubos's idea of significative dance. He dismantled the binary opposition of simple dance and composite dance by having the animated Statue dance with the Graces during the last three measures of the *loure* (Example 1.3). This characteristic instantly reframed the entire dance series from a *performance* for the spectators (including the animated Statue) into a dance *lesson* in which the Graces civilize the animated Statue through teaching her a variety of dances. With a simple staging technique, Rameau turned an otherwise lengthy series of decorative dances, which have little bearing on the drama, into a special dramatic event. Rameau also used keys to highlight this civilizing process. He used C major for the passepied and rigaudon, both danced by the Graces, and he turned this key into the dominant of F minor of the sarabande, which was called, deliberately, "Sarabande for the Statue." The tonal sequence of C major to F minor has at its core the harmonic progression of dominant to tonic. In dramatic terms, the Graces' dances, decorative as they should be, move the drama forward by getting the Statue ready to dance. With four flats, F minor marks the darkest, the most monstrous tonal point of the entire opera, a key that serves as the exact inverse of E major, with four sharps, that presents the animation of the Statue as the brightest, the most wondrous point of the opera. Using the key of F minor as another instituted sign, Rameau spotlights this sarabande as an especially surreal dance in this stagy dance series.[104]

One of the most remarkable moments of *Pygmalion* is Rameau's treatment of *la belle danse* and pantomime not as independent but as mutually influencing types of dances.[105] Rameau used the F minor of the sarabande to modulate to F major of the following tambourin, a key that functions as what Cynthia Verba calls a "tonal anchor."[106] Responding to Pygmalion's call for celebrating Amour, people come onstage and perform two pantomimes, a *pantomime niaise un peu lent* (a rather

103 "La Motte n'a connu que la danse simple. Il l'a variée dans ses opéras, en lui donnant quelques caractères nationaux; mais elle y est amenée, sans aucune action nécessaire." Cahusac, *La Danse*, 236. On *la danse simple* and *la danse composée*, see Cahusac, *La Danse*, 222; Noverre, *Lettres*, 181. On the centrality of the dance series in *Pygmalion*, see Lois Rosow, "Opera in Paris from Campra to Rameau," in Simon P. Keefe, ed., *Cambridge History of Eighteenth-Century Music* (Cambridge: Cambridge University Press, 2009), 281.

104 On the dance sequence framed as a performance, see Harris-Warrick, "Ballet, Pantomime, and the Sung Word," 37. On the dancing master scene, see ibid., *Dance and Drama*, 262–66. On Rameau's animation scene, see Thomas Christensen, *Rameau and Musical Thought in the Enlightenment* (New York: Cambridge University Press, 1993), 218–31. On another key with four flats – A-flat major – as a sign of monstrosity, see Charles Dill, "Rameau's Imaginary Monsters: Knowledge, Theory and Chromaticism in *Hippolyte et Aricie*," *Journal of the American Musicological Society* 55, no.3 (2002), 456–58.

105 The published reduced score reads: "Peuple et les précédents. L'amour sort." But H.720 offers a more precise direction : "air gay: pour l'entrée du Peuple qui viens admirer la statue." Rameau, *Pygmalion*, H.720, 28.

106 On Rameau's tonal anchoring strategy, see Cynthia Verba, *Dramatic Expression in Rameau's Tragédie en musique: Between Tradition and Enlightenment* (New York: Cambridge University Press, 2013), ch. 2.

Example 1.3. Rameau, *Pygmalion*, Scene 4, "Menuet, Gavotte, Chaconne vive, Loure," mm.8–57

Entrée

Example 1.3. continued

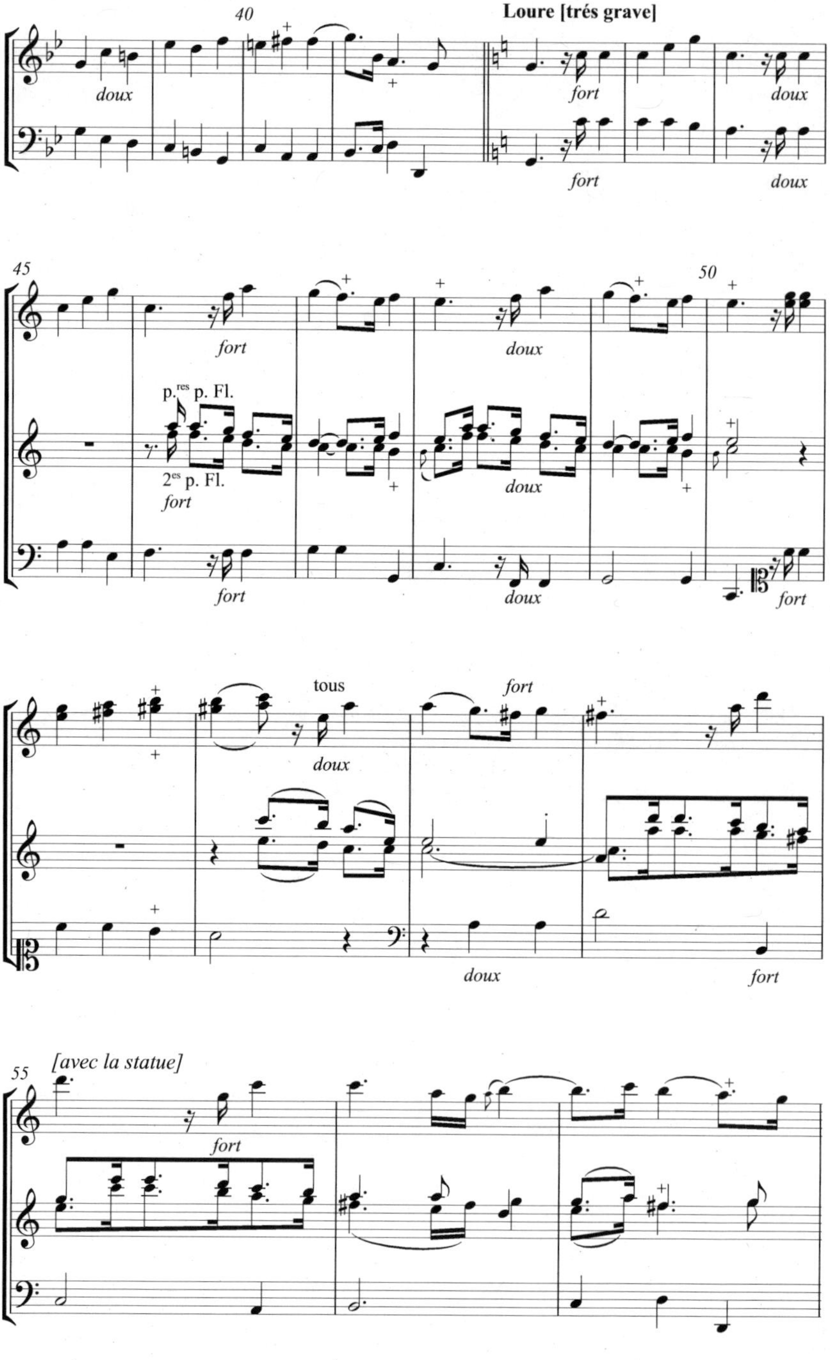

slow pantomime for the simpletons), followed by a "very brisk (*vive*)" pantomime, which demonstrate their admiration for the animated – and *civilized* – Statue. Like the elided dances, these two pantomimes, both in F major, form a connected pair. Revealingly, a melodic ornament adds an expressive element to this pantomime. A repeated E, reaching upwards to the melodic highpoint of G, is decorated melodically by an ascending double appoggiatura; and in H.720 the copyist inserted the word "admiration" above this ornament in m.15, turning this commonplace ornament into yet another instituted sign (Example 1.4).

Example 1.4. Rameau, *Pygmalion*, Scene 5, "Pantomime niaise et un peu Lente," mm.1–32 and "2e Pantomime très vive," mm.1–33

48

Example 1.4. continued

*Très vite on continue de danser
comme si l'air continuait toujours,
et sur le commencement du suivant
il y a surprise etc.*

2ᵉ Pantomime très vive

A dance of "admiration" was not new. One example was performed in Italy around 1480 for Gian Galeazzo Sforza, duke of Milan, and his wife Isabella of Aragon, where the characters Jason and the Argonauts "took the Golden fleece, with which they covered the table [in a magnificent hall], having danced a noble entrée that expressed their admiration at the sight of so beautiful a princess and of a prince so worthy of possessing her."[107] What is new, however, in Rameau's *Pygmalion*, is that the simpletons' expressive gesture of reaching for the Statue illustrates the singularity of their passion. The expression of one sentiment exemplifies the philosophical spirit that Dubos had identified in Lully's *Thésée*. For Cahusac, who championed Dubos's argument, Rameau's pantomime would provide an up-to-date example of Dubos's dance of the Enlightenment.

Rameau thought through his music for the pantomime dance carefully: he used the moment of admiration to begin a short, tonally unstable section. Three descending melodic statements form a sequence. The first statement (mm.18–19, Example 1.4) suggests but never settles firmly in D minor. The second one (mm.20–21), with its B-natural in the bass, moves away from D minor towards C major. The last one (mm.22–23) arrives in D minor, only to modulate again to C major in m.29, the dominant of the tonal anchor, F major. The temporary tonal instability, in contrast to the tonally related dance sequence, peaks at the end of the pantomime for the simpletons, when Rameau suspended the harmonic resolution of a dominant seventh chord in F major. The violin plays a descending stepwise melody from G to B-flat, supported by E in the bass, forming the first inversion of the dominant seventh on C in F major. In m.32, the leading note E in the bass signals a tendency to resolve to the tonic of F, and the B-flat in the melody reinforces this tendency. These two pitches, forming a diminished fifth interval, produce a strong tendency to resolve to F and A. At this harmonically tense moment, Rameau suspends this diminished fifth interval for one measure (i.e., between the last measure of the first pantomime and the first measure of the second one), before resolving it to the F-major chord, and rearticulates the tonal anchor. Recalling a moment of absolute silence right before the animation of the Statue, these suspended dissonances highlight this one-measure pause as another sign.

Neither the libretto nor the printed score offers any explanation for this one-measure rest, but the handwritten staging annotations in H.720 provide noteworthy details. Above the one-measure silence the copyist wrote: "Very quickly they continue to dance as if the air were to keep going, and at the beginning of the following [air] there is surprise, etc."[108] This staging direction asks the simpletons to be temporarily spellbound by the eerily moving Statue and deliberately misaligns music and gesture. This deliberate misalignment (*hors de cadence*), as Calzabigi called it, belonged to strolls (*baladins*) in base comedy performed by Italian grotesque

---

107 "Ils portaient la fameuse Toison d'or, dont ils couvrirent la table, après avoir dansé une entrée noble qui exprimait leur admiration à la vue d'une princesse si belle, et d'un prince si digne de la posséder." Cahusac, *La Danse*, 137.

108 "Très vite on continue de danser comme si l'air continuait toujours, et sur le commencement du suivant il y a surprise etc." Rameau, *Pygmalion*, H.720, 36.

dancers.[109] Unaware of the suspended ending of the first pantomime, the simpletons tune out and continue to dance as if they were still dancing to music, and they snap out of this mindless state only when they hear the beginning of the quick pantomime that follows, and resume dancing. Contrary to the animated Statue, who demonstrates her freedom of motion by walking and dancing, these simpletons behave, according to the authors of the article "Moral Liberty" of the *Encyclopédie*, as if they were children, fools, or sleepers who enter an "unfree" state because they do not demonstrate enough intelligence to master their free will: "With sleep having relaxed the machine of the body, and weakened all movements, the spirits cannot flow freely."[110]

The simpletons' temporary loss of sensitivity to music shows the reverse of the animated Statue who has demonstrated musical and dance competencies, which prove her physical coordination and muscular flexibility. As a result, *la belle danse* and pantomime correspond very tidily to two classes, the Graces and the people, which represent respectively royalty and the common people. The smooth transition from one dance to another dance in the dance series contrasts sharply with the interrupted pantomime pair. Contrary to the Graces, who have taught the Statue (danced by Mademoiselle Puvigné) how to dance and pay attention to the smooth transitions between consecutive dances, the simpletons marvel at the Statue so much that they momentarily cease to pay attention to the music.

Not all early eighteenth-century pantomimes illustrated claims of the Enlightenment as clearly as Rameau's *Pygmalion*. Pantomime performed in private entertainments for the nobles at Versailles for Louis XV showed how base comedy and elitism overlapped. For three winter seasons, from December 1747 through April 1750, a variety of amusements – including *tragédie en musique*, divertissement, fragment, comedy, *pastorale-héroïque*, ballet-pantomime, and comic excerpts – were performed at the Théâtre des Petits Appartements. Louis XV must have been amused to see the French nobles, including counts and countesses, marquises, chevaliers, dukes and duchesses, act in comedies in front of him. In addition to performing as the stock characters such as Pleasures and Graces, they also act as members of the lower class: valets, peasants, slaves, and pastoral characters such as fauns, nymphs, shepherds, and hunters. One could imagine Louis XV watching French courtiers masquerade as foreigners – Americans, Germans, or Chinese. He might be amused by a colonial fantasy when they travestied as slaves who dressed like their master. For example, Jeanne-Antoinette Poisson, Marquise de Pompadour performed as Princess Europe in the divertissement *Jupiter et Europe* and performed in the *Extraite de la Foire Saint Germain* in February 1750. Instead of distancing themselves from the *commedia dell'arte*, as Dubos did, the court appropriated these theatrical works

---

109 Calzabigi, *Scritti*, 1:170. On *baladin* and *bas comique*, see Cahusac, *Encyclopédie*, vol. 2, s.v. "Baladin."

110 "Le sommeil ayant détendu la machine du corps, & en ayant amorti tous les mouvements, les esprits ne peuvent couler librement." Naigeon and Yvon [attributed], *Encyclopédie*, vol. 9, s.v. "Liberté [Morale]."

for private royal entertainment. They formed what Adolphe Jullien jokingly called "Théâtre de société *royale*."[111] [emphasis mine]

If it is true that these entertainments relativized the cultural authority of *la belle danse*, the reverse is also true, for pantomime was used in these works precisely to reassert its cultural superiority. The ballet-pantomime *L'Opérateur chinois* (December 12, 1748), for example, depicts the commotion of a village. Mlle Puvigné, the same dancer who had performed the animated Statue in Rameau's *Pygmalion* four months earlier in Paris, appeared onstage in Versailles in front of Louis XV as a simpleton (*une niaise*). Dances, including the concluding contredanse, offered a graceful summary to the "varied actions" (*des actions variées*) that resembled the rowdy fairground (*le tumulte d'une Foire*).[112] *Le Pédant*, another pantomime, presented a story about students and peasants eager to dance as soon as the pedant leaves.[113] Contrary to Mondonville's *Isbé*, this pantomime re-legitimated *la belle danse* as the pinnacle of French dance.

Rameau continued to employ pantomime as a dance for his operas in the 1750s. About a decade after the performance of Mondonville's *Isbé*, Boulenger de Rivery foresaw in pantomime a "new type of pleasure," stressing the originality in pantomime as a source of pleasure rather than a threat.[114] His observation coincided with the Italian dancer Cosimo Maranesi's serious ballet-pantomime at the theater of the Saint Laurent fair in 1751. Rameau composed a *pantomime noble* for *La Guirlande* (1751), pointedly differentiating this serious pantomime from base comedy. He composed a pantomime for the *pastorale-héroïque Acante et Céphise, ou La Sympathie* (1751), and another for the *comédie-ballet Les Paladins* (1760). In the *pastorale-héroïque Daphnis et Églé* (1753), two young shepherdesses dance a pantomime marked "air gracieux sans lanteur," showing the expressions of surprise and joy. Rameau modified *La Pantomime* from *Pièces de clavecin en concert* for the 1757 revival of *Les Surprises de l'Amour*, eliminating the transgressive reference of *loure vive* and the programmatic title. He used an "action pantomime" in the 1758 version of the entrée *L'Enlèvement d'Adonis* of *Les Surprises de l'amour* that illustrated a mixture of action and dancing, exemplifying Cahusac's *danse en action* as the dance for the Enlightenment.

Rameau used pantomime as a *danse en action* in addition to employing *la belle danse* as the icon of nobility in *Anacréon* (livret written by Cahusac in 1754), an

---

111 *Recueil des comédies et ballets représentés sur le théâtre des petits Appartements*, F-Po C.2768 (1–4). On these works, see Adolphe Jullien, *La comédie à la cour* (Paris: Firmin-Didot, 1885), 139–247.

112 "Généralement tous les Acteurs qui sont sur la Scène, par des actions variées, peignent le tumulte d'une Foire." "L'Opérateur chinois," *Recueil des comédies et ballets représentés sur le théâtre des petits Appartements pendant l'Hiver de 1748 à 1749*, 6. F-Po C.2768 (2).

113 For a summary of *Les Fêtes chinoises* performed in Paris on July 1, 1754, see Jean Desboulmiers, *Histoire de l'opéra comique*, 2 vols. (Paris: Deladoué, 1770), 2:323–24; see Jennifer Thorp, "From *Les Fêtes chinoises* to *Agamemnon revenged*: Ange Goudar as Commentator on the Ballets of Jean-Georges Noverre," in Michael Burden and Jennifer Thorp, eds, *The Works of Monsieur Noverre Translated from the French* (Hillsdale, NY: Pendragon Press, 2014), 4–5.

114 Boulenger de Rivery, *Recherches*, iv–v.

entrée he added to the 1757 revival of *Les Surprises de l'amour*. As with *Platée*, this pantomime shows the unrestrained bodily movements that characterize Bacchus's followers.[115] Followers of Amour and the Maenads enter the stage in an entrée. They perform an action-filled pantomime, in turn featuring rounds of rushing, showing their surprise, stopping, and paying homage. The followers of Bacchus and Amour scurry onto the scene, mimetically accompanied by sixteenth-note streams, and are surprised to see Amour. They stop and bow to her. They rush again, and soon stop and look at the Graces. At last, the followers of Bacchus and Amour make Anacréon's mistress Lycoris dance with them. The rounds of rushing and stopping and bowing make this action-packed pantomime qualitatively different from the previous dance entrée and the pair of menuets that follow. Rameau introduced action to dance in a pantomime, while keeping *la belle danse* in the conventional sense.[116]

Rameau's treatment of pantomime as the other dance, without renouncing *la belle danse*, was in line with the principle of compatibility in Hume's discussion of liberty and necessity. In *A Treatise of Human Nature* Hume claimed that the actions of matter obey physical law and thus follow the principle of necessity; he also observed that human behaviors can be inconstant and irregular. Yet the irregularity of these behaviors did not contradict the logic of cause and effect; rather, these irregular behaviors reveal the existence of hidden causes. Hence, liberty and necessity were compatible. In *An Enquiry Concerning Human Understanding* (1748, translated into French in 1758), Hume furthered this argument by justifying irregularity: "The irregular events, which outwardly discover themselves, can be no proof, that the laws of nature are not observed with the greatest regularity in its internal operations and government."[117] In his compositions Rameau made pantomime a dance that suited a range of dramatic situations – from the abundance of ideas to unrestrained rushing-about to absent-mindedness, and even to formlessness – a dance that was compatible with *la belle danse* after all.

RAMEAU THE PANTOMIME

The examples discussed in this chapter demonstrate that Rameau used the art of pantomime as a kind of dance while maintaining *la belle danse* as a cultural icon of French high art. His operatic pantomimes demonstrate Dubos's idea of philosophical spirit. In his review of the 1749 re-staging of *Platée* at the Académie Royale de Musique, Charles Collé found the idea of the prologue excellent, although its music was "dishonorable for our nation if we let such awful things be played in public."[118]

---

115 An early example of unrestrained bodily movement comes from the mascarade *Le Mariage de la grosse Cathos* (1688). See Rebecca Harris-Warrick and Carol G. Marsh, *Musical Theatre at the Court of Louis XIV: Le Mariage de la grosse Cathos* (Cambridge: Cambridge University Press, 1994), 52, 132–33.

116 Rameau eliminated this pantomime and the two menuets from the 1758 re-run. See *OOR*, series 4, vol. 27, part 2, XXXVI.

117 Hume, *A Treatise of Human Nature*, 1:257–62; Hume, *An Enquiry Concerning Human Understanding*, ed. Peter Millican (Oxford: Oxford University Press, 2007), 63.

118 "[L]a musique en est bien jolie, mais il est déshonorant pour notre nation qu'on laisse jouer en public des choses aussi détestables." Charles Collé, *Journal et mémoires de*

His comment indicates that the court and the city, Versailles and Paris, held two distinct sets of cultural expectations. Even though it was acceptable to stage *Platée* at Versailles in 1745, critics did not find it appropriate for Paris in 1749. Collé's opinion indicates that the meanings of a stage work were at once co-created by the creators and the spectators, subject to institution- and city-specific expectations. This level of localized meaning challenged *la belle danse* as a national icon in mid-eighteenth-century France. Despite Louis XV's nationalistic mandate, in the middle of a war, of performing a genre of spectacle unique to France instead of some "spectacles for the eyes" that other nations could produce, French spectators felt invested in declaring what was and was not "French" to them shortly after the end of that war.[119]

Audiences noticed in Rameau's pantomimes signs of artistic novelty and related Rameau himself to a pantomime. In the "Lettre sur Omphale" (1752) Grimm commended the F-minor sarabande danced by the animated Statue in *Pygmalion*. He noted the originality in the *pantomime niaise* of *Pygmalion* and admired the novelty in Rameau's other pantomimic dances, including the Rose in *Les Indes galantes* and the fourth act of *Zoroastre*. Grimm did not just regard Rameau's pantomimes as innovative – he also drew a parallel between Rameau the composer and the shape-shifting sea god Proteus, who, according to Menestrier and Cahusac, resembles a skillful pantomime, thereby associating the creative Rameau with a pantomime actor: "What a Proteus, always novel, always original, always grasping the true and the sublime of each character."[120]

Rameau, the metaphoric pantomime, was recognized by his other contemporaries. Compared with dances in Lully's time, Noverre noticed in 1760 more variety in dance. Dance steps and positions are manifold; different body movements follow one another in quick succession; tempos are mixed; links are numerous. But, unlike Dubos, who envisioned some of Lully's theatrical dances as model pantomimes for the Enlightenment, Noverre paid special tribute to Rameau: "Dance owes all its progress to the traits and the spiritual conversations that are in his [Rameau's dance] airs."[121] Nicolas Bricaire de la Dixmerie wrote similarly, in *Les Deux Âges du goût et du génie français* (1769), that Rameau helped push dancing beyond the simple graces

Charles Collé, 3 vols. (Paris: Didot, 1868), 1:49.

119 On the parterre as the representation of the nation, see Jeffrey Ravel, *The Contested Parterre: Public Theater and French Political Culture 1680–1791* (Ithaca, NY: Cornell University Press, 1999), 193–202.

120 "Quel Protée toujours nouveau, toujours original, toujours saisissant le vrai et le sublime de chaque caractère." Friedrich Melchior Grimm, *Correspondance littéraire, philosophique et critique*, 16 vols. (Paris: Garnier frères, 1877–82), 16:307. On Proteus who changes shape, see Homer, *Odyssey* 4.468–73; Ovid, *Metamorphoses* 2.11. On the connection between Proteus and a skillful pantomime actor/dancer, see Menestrier, *Des ballets*, 124 and Cahusac, *La Danse*, 95.

121 "C'est aux traits & aux conversations spirituelles qui règnent dans ses airs, que la Danse doit tous ses progrès." Noverre, *Lettres*, 144. On Rameau and *danse en action*, see Bouissou, *Jean-Philippe Rameau*, 368–70, 587.

characteristic of most of Lully's dances, bringing about "in dance the same revolution as in our music."[122]

After studying all musical compositions that Rameau named "pantomime," I realize that Rameau exercised his moral liberty over and over by adapting pantomime as a type of dance that imparts various narrative or expressive content. He belonged to a generation of composers who wrote music for pantomimes, but unlike his peers, he composed music that consists of signs. This is *not* to say, however, that Rameau had less liberty when he composed examples of *la belle danse* for the theater, but further research needs to be undertaken to shed light on this topic. If anything, we know for a fact that Rameau attempted to capture dancers' movements in ways that were more specific and more consistent than those of his peers.

Rameau's pantomimes paved the path for the next generation of composers, including philosopher and composer Rousseau, some twenty-nine years younger than Rameau. Rousseau also developed his views on dance and pantomime in late 1745, in the aftermath of the same royal wedding, for he was asked by the Duke of Richelieu to revise Rameau's *La Princesse de Navarre* as *Les Fêtes de Ramire* for a performance at Versailles. Like Rameau, who thought musically through pantomime, Rousseau found in pantomime a way in which spectators could develop moral liberty for themselves. An investigation of the pantomimes in his *intermède Le Devin du village* (1752–53) leads us to the core ideas of cognition and spectatorship in the Enlightenment. This is the subject of the next chapter.

---

122 "Il [Rameau] a causé dans la danse la même révolution que dans notre Musique." Nicolas Bricaire de la Dixmerie, *Les Deux Âges du goût et du génie français* (La Haye and Paris: Lacombe, 1769), 522.

CHAPTER TWO

Freedom from an Evil Spell

I N the last chapter I discussed how the composers Mondonville, Couperin, Rameau, and others used pantomime in their musical compositions. In this chapter I turn to another composer Jean-Jacques Rousseau, who was also a music theorist and a philosopher. Rameau and Rousseau often appear side-by-side in studies of eighteenth-century French music, not only because Rousseau composed *Les Fêtes de Ramire*, but also because they debated on many important musical topics – most famously the theoretical relationships between harmony and melody. Yet, despite copious studies on Rameau's dances and Rousseau's pantomimes, Rousseau's thoughts on dance are not fully understood.[1] Like Rameau, Rousseau was interested in pantomime as a type of dance that could expand the expressive range of dance. Like Rameau, Rousseau thought about *la belle danse* in the civilizing process. Yet, unlike Rameau, who used pantomime to explore the idea of artists' freedom that could be illustrated in performance, Rousseau used pantomime to explore spectators' moral liberty when they responded to a stimulating performance. In other words, while Rameau focused on *text* and its effect on *performance*, Rousseau, fully aware of the significance of his text, emphasized the issue of *reception* of an effective performance at the theater. In his *intermède* called *Le Devin du village* of 1753, which was a great operatic phenomenon in late eighteenth-century France, Rousseau found a way for spectators to recognize their moral liberty through watching, interpreting, and sharing the content of pantomime among themselves. This chapter is about how he made this discovery.

Le Devin du village consists of three characters: a village couple called Colin and Colette, and a fortune teller called the Soothsayer (*Le Devin*). We will begin our discussion with fortune telling, known in the eighteenth century as "soothsaying."[2]

What did soothsaying mean in the Enlightenment? It might be unsurprising that soothsaying was rationalized in the Enlightenment as a useful skill (similar to what we now call "counselling," "informed prediction," or "educated guess") rather than a mystical practice but, surprisingly, Rousseau retained some mystique surrounding this term. In the *Encyclopédie* Louis de Jaucourt identified two types of fortune

---

1   On Rameau and Rousseau's musical thinking, see, for example, Cynthia Verba, *Music and the French Enlightenment: Rameau and the Philosophes in Dialogue*, 2nd edn (New York: Oxford University Press, 2016), chs. 2 and 3. On Rousseau and pantomime, see Jacqueline Waeber, "'Le devin de la foire?' Revaluating the Pantomime in Rousseau's *Devin du village*," in Waeber, ed., *Musique et geste*, 149–72.

2   *Le Devin du village* was staged 324 times from 1753 to 1789. These numbers are obtained in http://chronopera.free.fr/ on July 5, 2018. On the reception of *Le Devin du village* in France in the 1770s, see Michael O'Dea, "Rousseau's Ghost: *Le Devin du village* at the Paris Opera, 1770–1779," in Maria Gullstam and Michael O'Dea, eds, *Rousseau on Stage: Playwright, Musician, Spectator* (Oxford: Voltaire Foundation, 2017), 209–25.

tellers – prophets and soothsayers – and defined them as folks good at making pre-
dictions about the future. Although both types could predict events that were yet to
take place, Jaucourt explained that none of them in fact possessed any *real* supernatural power. Like psychologists nowadays, soothsayers excelled at knowing a person
well enough to anticipate their behavior. Like logicians or social scientists, prophets
speculated on the likelihood of future happenings by using techniques that we now
call data collection and deduction.[3] But it is surprising that Rousseau created in his
Le Devin du village the character "Soothsayer" (*Le Devin*) who retains a sense of mysticism. The Soothsayer claims that his "art" reveals to Colin that his lover, Colette,
has fallen in love with a gentleman from the city. After Colin recognizes his tendency
towards constancy and his materialism as character flaws, the Soothsayer has Colin
believe that a mystical "art" has destroyed "some malicious spirit" (*quelque esprit
malin*) that has corrupted him. To reinforce an aura of mystique, the Soothsayer
declares that "I have freed you both from a cruel evil spell" (*Je vous ai délivrés d'un
cruel maléfice*). By using the expression "free from" (*délivrer de*), Rousseau suggests
that the Soothsayer can help Colin and Colette become less encumbered by the
constraints of materialism. His vision was echoed in the *Encyclopédie* article on
Pythagoreanism: "You who want to be a *philosophe* propose to free your soul from
all the bonds that constrain it."[4]

One might find it odd that the Soothsayer thinks of fortune telling as a useful skill,
but his thinking was consistent with the Enlightenment's emphasis on the usefulness
of knowledge. In his *Discours préliminaire* of the *Encyclopédie*, d'Alembert mentioned
that the *Système figuré des connaissances humaines* (commonly known as the "tree of
knowledge") illustrates links between pleasing and useful categories of knowledge.
In *Émile*, Rousseau made a case for astronomy as a useful subject when the boy Émile
finds his way out of the countryside by following the stars. In *La Danse ancienne et
moderne*, Cahusac began by arguing that theory of arts was useful. Abstract theory,
in other words, could become applied knowledge. In this Enlightenment context,
even soothsaying that carried a vestige of mystique could become a useful skill.[5]

---

3   Jaucourt, *Encyclopédie*, vol. 13, s.v. "Prophète, Devin." On mysticism and the French
    Enlightenment, see Dan Edelstein, "Introduction to the Super-Enlightenment," in Dan
    Edelstein, ed., *The Super-Enlightenment: Daring to Know Too Much* (Oxford: Voltaire
    Foundation, 2010), 1–33.

4   "Toi qui veux être philosophe, tu te proposeras de délivrer ton âme de tous les liens qui
    la contraignent." Diderot [attributed], *Encyclopédie*, vol. 13, s.v. "Pythagorisme." The
    Soothsayer's verse is quoted in Jean-Jacques Rousseau, *Œuvres complètes*, ed. Bernard
    Gagnebin and Marcel Raymond, 5 vols. (Paris: Gallimard, 1959–1995) 2:1109. [*OC*] On
    Rousseau's ideas of liberty, see Robert Wokler, *Rousseau, the Age of Enlightenment, and
    Their Legacies*, ed. Bryan Garsten (Princeton, NJ: Princeton University Press, 2012),
    155–84.

5   On the utility of knowledge, see d'Alembert, *Preliminary Discourse*, 15–16. On utility
    and theory of arts, see Cahusac, *La Danse*, 45–46. On astronomy and utility, see *CWR*,
    13:112. On the mystique of the Soothsayer, see Jacqueline Waeber, "'Le Devin de la foire'?
    Pantomime et jeu muet dans *Le Devin du village*," in Jacques Berchtold, Christophe
    Martin, and Yannick Seite, eds, *Rousseau et le spectacle* (Paris: Armand Colin, 2014),
    105–30.

What, then, makes the art of pantomime "useful"? I argue in this chapter that Rousseau used the art of pantomime to impart a moralizing message in *Le Devin du village*: to free Colin and Colette from an evil spell. However, the intriguing aspect is not the message itself, but the *development* of his thinking that led to this message. The best approach to explain how he arrived at this message is to examine his pantomime dance – a major component in the 1753 version of his *intermède* – in the context of Rousseau's moral writings and plays. To this end, I begin this chapter with Rousseau's *Discours sur les sciences et les arts* (generally known as the *First Discourse*, published in January 1751), in which he mentioned "pantomime" for the first time. I then explain his concept of useful art in the preface to his play *Narcisse*, a text that Rousseau completed around the same time that he composed the pantomime of *Le Devin du village*. I follow this analysis with a discussion on how Rousseau used pantomime as a cognitively demanding section for the onstage spectators – Colin, Colette, and the Soothsayer – which leads to the two points I want to make in this chapter: my first point is that Rousseau had these three characters watch spectacles critically rather than passively, employing their advanced cognitive faculties to reflect upon signs and develop their moral positions. In short, Rousseau designed a *useful* pantomime in *Le Devin du village* by making it a vehicle for spectators to recognize and cultivate their own moral liberty.[6] My second point is that Rousseau fit this pantomime into his long-term thinking about moral liberty. Less than a decade after he premiered *Le Devin du village*, he theorized self-governance when he discussed "moral liberty" in his *Du Contrat social* of 1762: moral liberty makes us our own masters because it is "the obedience to the law we prescribed to ourselves."[7]

ROUSSEAU ON ITALIAN PANTOMIME

Eighteenth-century composers considered pantomime first and foremost a type of dance, but they experimented with its content and function for expressive or dramatic purposes. For many scholars, Rousseau's thoughts about dance are best represented by Letter No.23 in Part Two of his novel *Julie, ou La Nouvelle Héloïse* (1761): "If the Prince is joyous, they take part in his joy, and dance; if he is sad, they want to cheer him up, and they dance."[8] As this quote indicates, Rousseau

---

6 On signs, see Dubos, *Réflexions*, 1:305–307. On Rousseau's theory of spectatorship, see Jean-Paul Sermain, "Le Spectacle de La Nouvelle Héloïse," in Berchtold, Martin, and Seite, eds, *Rousseau et le spectacle*, 227–36; Joseph Harris, *Inventing the Spectator: Subjectivity and the Theatrical Experience in Early Modern France* (Oxford: Oxford University Press, 2014), 198–222.

7 *OC*, 3:365. On Rousseau and practicality, see William Weber, "Learned and General Musical Taste in Eighteenth-Century France," *Past & Present* 89 (1980), 79. On moral liberty, see Paul Hoffmann, *Dictionnaire de Jean-Jacques Rousseau*, ed. Raymond Trousson and Frédéric S. Eigeldinger (Paris: Honoré Champion, 2006), s.v. "Liberté (morale)"; Wokler, *Rousseau, the Age of Enlightenment*, 174–75.

8 "Si le prince est joyeux, on prend part à sa joie, et l'on danse: s'il est triste, on veut l'égayer, et l'on danse." *OC*, 2:287. Scholarly works that cite this sentence include Marian Hannah Winter, *The Pre-Romantic Ballet* (Brooklyn: Dance Horizons, 1974), 111; Susan Leigh Foster, *Choreography & Narrative: Ballet's Staging of Story and Desire* (Bloomington, IN: Indiana University Press, 1998), 17; Harris-Warrick, "Toute danse," 187.

criticized the uniform function of joyful dancing in French opera regardless of the opera's subject matter. This kind of festive dancing suspends the dramatic action; it invites spectators to shift their focus from the forward momentum of the drama to the decorative dances; it represents nothing other than dancing. This type of festive dancing is, Agamben might say, "inoperative" and has "zero symbolic value."[9] But this criticism in *Julie* does not best represent Rousseau's thinking about dance. To present a fuller picture, I trace Rousseau's uses of dance and pantomime in his tragedy *La Découverte du nouveau monde* (1740 or 1741) and the *ballet-héroïque Les Muses galantes* (1743–45), and I discuss them in relation to his *First Discourse*.

Given his criticism of *la belle danse* in *Julie*, one might be surprised to learn that Rousseau himself used this type of dance in his theatrical works. In his tragedy on the life of Christopher Columbus, *La Découverte du nouveau monde* (written in Lyon and Charmettes in 1740 or 1741), Rousseau showcased in dances the French gallantry and levity that the personification "Europe" approves, using these dances to astonish the gazes of the savage people.[10] *La belle danse*, in this tragedy, is employed as an icon of western civilization. Elsewhere, in his *ballet-héroïque Les Muses galantes* (1743–45), Rousseau used examples of *la belle danse* – a musette and a forlane – to condone sensuous pleasure. The fact that Rousseau used these dances in this ballet does not mean that he fully endorsed *la belle danse* and its role in the civilizing process; quite the contrary, he was critical of it. In the preface to the unpublished libretto, Rousseau called this ballet "mediocre," admitting that he wrote it to question French "habit and prejudices."[11]

Contrary to Rameau, who sometimes used pantomime in opposition to *la belle danse*, Rousseau imagined no correlation between the two in his early works. In the *First Discourse*, Rousseau argued that advances in arts and sciences introduce moral decline. Whereas he argued that government and laws formed the foundation of society, he also considered science, letters, and the arts less "despotic" and perhaps even more "powerful." The civilized subjects – the "happy slaves" as Rousseau called them – cultivated refined taste and softness of character. With education and sociable exchanges, the French developed "natural yet engaging manners, equally remote from Teutonic simplicity and Italian pantomime."[12]

9   On the idea of "inoperativity," see Giorgio Agamben, *Nudities*, trans. David Kishik and Stefan Pedatella (Stanford, CA: Stanford University Press, 2011), 112; Bloechl, *Opera*, ch. 1.

10 "Que nos jeux enchanteurs brillent de toutes parts. / De ce people sauvage étonnons les regards." *OC*, 2:829.

11 "Cet ouvrage est si médiocre en son genre, et le genre en est si mauvais, que pour comprendre comment il m'a pu plaire, il faut sentir toute la force de l'habitude et des préjugés." *OC*, 2:1051. On *Les Muses galantes*, see Samuel Baud-Bovy, "De l'*Armide* de Lully à l'*Armide* de Gluck: Un siècle de récitatif à la française," in Jean-Jacques Eigeldinger, ed., *Jean-Jacques Rousseau et la musique* (Neuchâtel: La Baconnière, 1988), 37–40. On the genesis of *Les Muses galantes*, see Jacqueline Waeber, "Rousseau on Music: A Case of Nature vs. Nurture," in Eve Grace and Christopher Kelly, eds, *The Rousseauian Mind* (London: Routledge, 2019), 297–307.

12 *CWR*, 2:5.

FROM ITALIAN PANTOMIME TO COMMUNICATION

To Rousseau's mind, "Italian pantomime" was, alongside "Teutonic simplicity," the opposite of the "natural and engaging" manners that the French elites aspired to. What he meant by "Italian pantomime" probably included various kinds of spectacles performed in Paris that incorporated elements of the Italian *commedia dell'arte* tradition. At the Salle des Machines of the Tuileries palace, as mentioned in Chapter One, the Italian Servandoni staged visual spectacles in 1738–42 and again in 1754–58, and showcased pantomimes in *La Descente d'Énée aux enfers* (1740), *Les Travaux d'Ulysse* (1741), and *Le Triomphe de l'amour conjugal* (1755). At the Théâtre Italien Jean-Baptiste François Dehesse choreographed at least fifty-eight pantomime ballets between 1747 and 1757. The Comédie-Française began to hire ballet masters – Dourdet, Pierre Sodi, and Jean-Pierre Bigot de La Rivière – in 1753, although all three of them danced there and worked across theatrical institutions, and it staged the first pantomime ballet, *La Fête villageoise*, in 1754. Rousseau's observation of the vogue of Italian pantomime in Paris was confirmed by Boulenger de Rivery, who mentioned in 1751 that the genre of ballet-pantomime had been successful at the Théâtre Italien and the fairground theaters since the suppression of the *opéra-comique* in 1745.[13]

These performances of pantomimes stimulated discussion not about the politics of comportment, but about the communicative capacity of gesture, a discussion that applied Dubos's duality of signs and dance steps to the theater. In addition to those pantomimes discussed in the last chapter, two pantomimes added into French operas in the 1740s stimulated discussion about gesture as a means of communication, a theme crucial to Rousseau when he composed *Le Devin du village*.

The first one is called "Pantomime of a Venetian gardener" (*Pantomime du jardinier vénitien*), which was performed at the end of the entrée called *Les Sujets indociles*, an entrée that was newly composed for the 1745 re-run of Niel's 1744 *ballet mis en musique* called *L'École des amans* (Opéra, April 27, 1745).[14] The pantomime *Les Sujets indociles* is about the rivalry between Amour and Bacchus, a topic that recalled the Bacchic theme in Rameau's *Platée*, which had premiered at Versailles about a month earlier, on March 31, 1745. Niel discovered Rameau's pantomime as a new resource for the re-run of his ballet: he even quoted the opening motif of Rameau's pantomime to indicate the presence of Bacchus (see mm.119–23 of Example 2.1). This instance of borrowing indicates instant and warm reception of Rameau's pantomime among his peers and provides another piece of evidence of the vogue of pantomime in the 1740s.

---

13 Boulenger de Rivery, *Recherches historiques*, i. On these pantomimes, see Harris-Warrick and Carol G. Marsh, "The French Connection," in *The Grotesque Dancer*, 175–88; Michèle Sajous-d'Oria, "*Alceste* selon Servandoni ou *Le Triomphe de l'amour conjugal*: spectacle orné de machines et animé d'acteurs pantomimes," in Daniel Brandenburg and Martina Hochreiter, eds, *Gluck auf dem Theater: Kongressbericht Nürnberg 7.–10. März 2008*, Gluck-Studien 6 (Kassel: Bärenreiter, 2011), 61–70.

14 "On y [*L'École des amans*] a fait les changements qui ont paru être souhaités par le public, & on y a ajouté un acte nouveau pour lui donner l'étendue convenable à la saison." *Mercure de France* (April 1745), 133.

Example 2.1. Jean-Baptiste Niel, "Les sujets indociles" (1745), quatrième entrée added to *L'École des amans* (1744), Scene 4, mm.117–131

Fashionable as pantomime dance was in the 1740s, connection between pantomime and drama varied. In the case of *Pantomime du jardinier vénitien*, no evidence indicates its semantic content: in keeping with other published pantomime dances around 1740, Niel did not write any annotation on the score. Commentators did not write about its semantic or affective content, much less how it was related to the drama. In this case, critics simply reported that the new pantomime was fairly well-received. The reviewer of *Mercure de France* provided more details, commending the "genius" of the choreographer and the "lively lightness" of the dancers.[15]

---

15   "Cet acte est terminé par un Ballet-Pantomime où brille le génie du Compositeur & la vive légèreté des exécutants." *Mercure de France* (April 1745), 135.

Hence, this pantomime was treated as a welcomed ad hoc addition to a performance, not as a component integral to the compositional thinking or dramatic logic of the ballet. Niel's interest in pantomime was not shared by all, however. In an essay called *Suite des réflexions sur les ballets*, published in the same *Mercure de France* issue in which this performance was reviewed, the reviewer voiced his reservations about the category of pantomime dance, claiming, in the anti-Dubosian manner, that gestures alone "can never explain intelligibly what one means."[16] As the mixed opinions show, the 1745 revival of *L'École des amans* stimulated discussion not about *la belle danse* or the politics of comportment, but about the intelligibility of physical gesture in a pantomime dance, an issue that was at the heart of Dubos's insight on signs as he had theorized in *Réflexions critiques*. The question of how any choreographer or any dancer could ever "explain" anything "intelligibly" through the art of pantomime would remain open for decades to come, but in 1745, this question of how physical gestures could impart any semantic meanings reframed the debate on pantomime from a type of dance to a means of communication. By reframing this debate, critics in fact followed Dubos's thinking about dance steps and signs, treading away from the realm of imagination towards that of reason in the Enlightenment.

The second pantomime was a dance for three dancers called a *pas de trois*, which was performed at the end of a divertissement called *Zélie* (1749–50) at the Théâtre des Petits Appartements of Versailles. This pantomime dance was acclaimed, according to Adolphe Jullien, as the "most entertaining pantomime" ever performed at that theater. It shows a nymph avoiding a faun's amorous advances, but Amour forces her to yield to him. The music is suggestive in a general way. The pantomime ends with the violin playing a descending scale three times, which creates a decrease in dynamics from strong (*fort*) to less strong (*moins fort*) to sweet and slow (*doux et lent*), suggesting that the nymph gives in gradually. These examples show that despite published criticisms, composers and choreographers continued to explore the communicative potential of pantomime around 1750.[17]

LANGUAGE AS ACTION

Immediately following the 1740s, a decade in which a culture of pantomime was firmly established in Paris and Dubos's discourse on it spread from Paris to other European cities, Rousseau became interested in the art of pantomime. Within about two years, between his *First Discourse* (January 1751) and the second version of *Le Devin du village* (March 1753), Rousseau imagined uses of pantomime in practical and conceptual terms, separating the genealogy of dumb shows (e.g., dumb shows in antiquity, Lully's character dances, *lazzi* in *commedia dell'arte*, Weaver's

16 "Les gestes du Pantomime ... ne peuvent jamais seuls expliquer intelligiblement ce qu'ils veulent dire." *Mercure de France* (April 1745), 137.

17 "Cette comédie ... fut suivie de la plus divertissante pantomime qui ait jamais paru sur le théâtre des petits cabinets." Adolphe Jullien, *Histoire du théâtre de Madame de Pompadour dit Théâtre des petits cabinets* (Paris: Baur, 1874), 38. For a manuscript copy of the score of the "pas de trois," see *Zélie, divertissement nouveau représenté devant le Roy sur le Théâtres des Petits Appartements à Versailles, Le 13, Février 1749*, F-Po CS-1175, 103–105. On the connection between *Zélie* and *Le Devin du village*, see Charlton, *Opera*, 154–57.

English pantomime) from an archaeology of communication (e.g., language, gesture, music, sign).

To understand Rousseau's pantomimes, one must understand the genesis of *Le Devin du village*. As Jacqueline Waeber has shown, Rousseau worked on *Le Devin du village* in three stages. The first stage took place in March 1752. Rousseau composed at least two airs and a duet and had them rehearsed in June 1752. He reworked these materials for the performance at the court at Fontainebleau on October 18, 1752, which was the first version and included only the first seven scenes. He finished it for the premiere on March 1, 1753, at the Opéra, by adding an overture and the eighth and final scene, and he published the score shortly after the 1753 performance.[18]

Here is a summary of the *intermède*, an expansion of the brief synopsis I mentioned earlier. The *intermède* begins with Colette, a distraught village girl, who suspects that her lover Colin is unfaithful to her. She approaches the Soothsayer for help, hoping that he can return Colin to her. The Soothsayer tells her that Colin has some connection with another woman but assures her that he still loves her. The Soothsayer then comes up with a scheme. He tells Colin that Colette is planning to leave him for a certain *Monsieur* from the city, leaving Colin to realize that he prefers Colette. Colin then meets with Colette and apologizes to her, but she, following the Soothsayer's advice, tells Colin that she does not love him anymore. Colin panics and tells Colette that he is no longer the disloyal lover he was. Colette forgives him and they make up. The Soothsayer comes onstage and declares that he has freed Colin and Colette from an evil spell and asks young villagers to imitate them. At the end, the chorus celebrates their reunion; Colin and Colette sing a romance, and the three of them watch a pantomime about their own story. They sing a final strophic song (*chanson*), taking turns to share what they have learned.[19]

The plot seems straightforward, but the ending is baffling. Why did Rousseau place the pantomime after the romance and before the chanson? In the pages that follow, I offer my explanation for its dramatic and musical functions based on Rousseau's thinking on communication, cognition, and the utility of theater. One way to begin this inquiry is to examine Rousseau's uses of speech as action in the *intermède*.[20]

Rousseau uses speech *as* action in Scene 2, when the Soothsayer promises Colette that he will cure Colin of his vanity: "I declare I shall bring the fickle one back to your feet."[21] The Soothsayer takes action by making a declaration, as opposed to the gallants who charm listeners with their speeches (*discours*). Colette, for one, notices the lure of the gallants' speeches: "If of the gallants of the town / I had listened to

18 On these two versions, see Jacqueline Waeber, "'Cette horrible innovation': The First Version of the Recitative Parts of Rousseau's 'Le Devin du village,'" *Music & Letters* 82, no.2 (2001), 177–213.

19 The term "vaudeville" is employed in the livret instead of "chanson", see *OC*, 2:1111.

20 On speech as action, or "speech acts," see John Langsaw Austin, *How to Do Things with Words* (Cambridge, MA: Harvard University Press, 1962), 1–11, 22.

21 "Je prétends à vos pieds ramener le volage." *OC*, 2:1101. Translation adapted from *CWR*, 10:217.

the speeches, / Ah! How easy it would be for me / to form other ties of love!"[22] The ever-practical Soothsayer also teaches Colette how to use her speech as an act. He tells her to pretend to be slightly coquettish in front of Colin so that, paradoxically, the illusion of her inconstancy will cure Colin's fickleness. Note that the Soothsayer does not ask Colette to take concrete action, such as dating another man; instead, he only asks Colette to *pretend* to have such a lover.[23]

Uses of language as action have a long history, but the idea that language could function as action stimulated fresh ideas when Enlightenment philosophers redefined the field of rhetoric from narrowly conceived rhetorical rules to a broadly defined art of communication. In the "System of knowledge" of the *Cyclopedia* (1728), Chambers identified the rhetorical figure as the main area in the study of rhetoric, but this emphasis gradually lost its appeal in the Enlightenment. This loss could be traced back to Nicolas Boileau's translation of Cassius Longinus's *Peri hypsous* as *Traité du sublime* (1674), which treated the sublime as a *concept* of transcendence rather than a literary *style*.[24] Inspired by this reading of the sublime, Bernard Lamy's *De l'art de parler* (1675) and César Chesneau Du Marsais's *Des Tropes* (1730) questioned why generations of teachers had emphasized the rhetorical figure as the primary topic of rhetoric. Their work was followed by Claude Buffier, who realized in his *Traité de l'éloquence* (1728) that it was a mistake to focus on rhetorical rules and figures rather than eloquence, which should be inspired by nature. In response to Buffier's point, Diderot rethought the study of rhetoric as the art of communication rather than a set of rules. In his *Système figuré des connaissances humains* (1750), he redesigned Chambers's system of knowledge. He divided the art of communication into two categories: the science of the qualities of discourse (including rhetoric and the mechanics of poetry), and the science of the instrument of discourse, meaning pedagogy and grammar (including signs, prosody, and syntax). He subdivided the category of signs into gesture (which includes pantomime and declamation) and character (which includes hieroglyphs). In this newly conceived system of knowledge, Diderot separated the *qualities* of discourse from the *instrument* of discourse, placing rhetoric within a more inclusive domain of communication.[25]

Like Diderot, Rousseau wrote about the effectiveness of teaching and learning of rhetoric at school. He pointed out in his *First Discourse* that children did not learn to speak their native languages at school, but to speak languages they did not use. They wrote verses they did not understand, and they wrote arguments without learning how to differentiate truth from error. They might know the definitions of big words such as magnanimity, equity, moderation, humanity, and courage, but they knew little of what these words really meant. The problem with this kind of pedagogy, Rousseau argued, was the disconnect between language and action: "One no longer

22 CWR, 10:217.

23 "Pour vous faire aimer davantage, / Feignés d'aimer un peu moins." *OC*, 2:1102.

24 Robert Doran, *The Theory of the Sublime from Longinus to Kant* (New York: Cambridge University Press, 2015), 111.

25 On rhetoric in eighteenth-century France, see Marc Fumaroli, *Histoire de la rhétorique dans l'Europe modern (1450–1950)* (Paris: Presses universitaires de France, 1999).

asks if a man is upright, but rather if he is talented, nor of a Book if it is useful, but if it is well written."[26]

These examples illustrate the dualistic thinking that undergirds much of *First Discourse*. Rousseau assumed a mutual exclusivity – the either/or thinking – that left little room for inclusivity – the both/and thinking. Can a man be both upright *and* talented? Can a book be both useful *and* well written? Rousseau did not answer these questions, and he made an exaggeration that reinforced the polarity between language and action: "There are a thousand prizes for fine discourses, none for fine actions."[27] In his *Fragment sur la liberté* (1750?), Rousseau rearticulated this polarity, pointing out that some politicians' actions contradicted their words: "Listen to our Politicians argue: they have nothing but the defense and the advantage of people in view. Watch them act: they work only to oppress them."[28]

Rousseau concluded his *First Discourse* by rearticulating a duality of language and action. Whereas Athenians knew how to *speak* well, Spartans knew how to *act* well.[29] Though lacking in nuance, this duality provides a conceptual axis for Rousseau's *Le Devin du village*. Framed by this axis, Rousseau employed pantomimic episodes and an extensive section of pantomime that display physical movements as action while suppressing speech. This duality also explains why the Soothsayer believes he can cure Colin's inconstancy with his speech, which functions as an action.

REDEMPTIVE ARTS

Rousseau used speech as action for curative ends in *Le Devin du village* ("I have freed you both from an evil spell") and, for Rousseau, the idea of curative speech was consistent with that of a "curative" portrait. The fact that *Le Devin du village* is an opera may make it challenging to study on a par with Rousseau's other writings, but this opera afforded him the very theatrical experiment through which he sub-stantiated his ideas in music and gesture – communicative mediums other than just language. To illustrate how this opera complemented his writings, then, we should read the second version of *Le Devin du village* alongside the preface to *Narcisse*, where Rousseau clarified the arguments he had made in the *First Discourse*.

After Rousseau had written the *First Discourse*, which denounced arts and sciences as corrupting, he defended this thesis for three years, from 1750 through 1752: and in December 1752 he wrote a preface to his comedy *Narcisse ou L'Amant de lui-même*. This preface was written after the Fontainebleau performance of *Le Devin du village* and was published shortly before the performance at the Opéra. It helps connect the reception of the *First Discourse* with the play *Narcisse* and the two versions of *Le Devin du village*.[30]

26   *CWR*, 2:18–19.

27   Jean-Jacques Rousseau, *The Major Political Writings of Jean-Jacques Rousseau: The Two Discourses and the Social Contract*, trans. and ed. John T. Scott (Chicago: The University of Chicago Press, 2012), 31.

28   *CWR*, 4:12.

29   Rousseau, *The Major Political Writings*, 36.

30   *CWR*, 5:326. The publication of *Narcisse* was announced in the March 1753 issue of *Mercure de France*, 156–77.

The preface to *Narcisse* deserves attention because Rousseau imagined it as a stand-alone text that is related – but not subsidiary – to the play. Rousseau wrote it years after he finished the play itself, and it marks two phases – one before, another after the *First Discourse* – of Rousseau's writings. Rousseau began working on the comedy *Narcisse* (his only spoken play performed in public) when he was eighteen. He first wrote it in Chambéry from 1732 to 1740, brought it with him to Paris in 1742, and had it accepted by the Théâtre Italien around 1746. As the Théâtre Italien postponed the performance, Rousseau showed it to the actor and playwright Joseph-Baptiste Sauvé, nicknamed La Noue, of the Comédie-Française, who staged it on December 18 and December 20, 1752. According to his *Confessions*, Rousseau criticized the play as a "bad piece" (*une mauvaise Pièce*) but commended the preface as "one of his good writings" (*un de mes bons écrits*). His remarks suggest that the preface is not a typical introduction to a play but is a text in its own right.[31]

Why did Rousseau publish the preface to *Narcisse* and revise *Le Devin du village* when he was denouncing arts and sciences in the *First Discourse*? Those who read Rousseau's *First Discourse* as a self-sufficient argument, such as his contemporary, Charles Bordes, might use Rousseau's *Narcisse* and *Le Devin du village* as evidence of his self-contradiction. Yet this impression of self-contradiction disappears if one reads the *First Discourse* as one of many stages in an evolving line of thinking rather than as a definitive argument. Rousseau emphasized in the preface to *Narcisse* that there were exceptions to the arts and sciences that he had dismissed categorically in the *First Discourse*. Some institutions – including academies, libraries, and theaters and other amusements – were exceptions, not because they could "bring people to do good," but because they could "give some diversion to the wickedness of men."[32] As mentioned above, Rousseau suspected, in the *First Discourse*, that sciences, letters, and arts were more "powerful" than government and law, but he added in the preface to *Narcisse* that even if most arts and sciences were sources of vice, some exceptions might do public good by limiting the negative impact of vice. He found it unrealistic to eradicate vices, but he believed that the pleasing appearance afforded by these exceptions could still offer the public traces of virtue. Of all the types of arts, Rousseau found the temporal arts of music and theater particularly useful for providing some cure for society. In the preface to *Narcisse*, he claimed, "Whereas these things have done a great deal of evil to society, it is very essential to *use* them today as a medicine for the evil they have caused."[33]

To understand how Rousseau considered *Narcisse* a kind of theatrical medicine for society, we should understand how his version deviates from the myth of Narcissus in the third book of Ovid's *Metamorphoses*. For Ovid, Narcissus is a handsome man who offends his male and female admirers, one of whom curses him for loving no one except himself. Narcissus subsequently falls in love with his reflection in the water, a shadow that he mistakes for substance. He seeks love and is the object

---

31 *OC*, 1:388; see Jacques Scherer's critical commentaries in *OC*, 1:1860–61.

32 *CWR*, 2:196. Charles Bordes presented his *Discours sur les avantages des Sciences & des Arts* at the Académie des Sciences & Belles-Lettres de Lyon on June 22, 1751 and published it in the first part of the December 1751 issue of *Mercure de France*, 25–64.

33 *CWR*, 2:197–98.

he is seeking, and he finally comes to the realization that he is the boy whose reflection in the water he admires: "Touch may be forbidden, / but looking isn't: then let me look at you / and feed my wretched frenzy on your image."[34] Rousseau revised Ovid's story by mixing the theme of narcissism with cross-dressing. He designed the protagonist Valère as a man who adores a portrait of himself cross-dressed as a woman, without recognizing that he is in fact the sitter of that portrait. Instead of falling in love with a reflection in the water, Valère is infatuated with his image *en travestie*. The portrait indisputably misrepresents his gender, but this misrepresentation also reveals a facet of femininity hidden under Valère's typical masculine appearance. Rather than distort the truth of Valère's gender, this portrait *unveils* truth precisely by means of misrepresentation. As his sister says of him, "With his delicacy and with the affectation of his adornment, Valère is a sort of woman hidden under the clothes of a man, and this portrait seems less to disguise him than to return him to his natural state."[35]

Rousseau probably got the idea of a portrait from literary and theatrical works on sex change. Gabriel-François Coyer's fantastical satire, *L'Année merveilleuse, ou Les Hommes-femmes* (1748), tells the story of the uncommon conjunction of five planets causing sex change, transforming men into women and vice versa.[36] This fantastical topic was popular in contemporary comic theater. Pierre Rousseau's *L'Année merveilleuse*, performed fourteen times at the Théâtre Italien beginning on July 18, 1748, has La Folie transform a male officer into a female fop (*une petite maîtresse*), a female dancer into a male dancer, and a schoolgirl into an effeminate young man.[37] Rousseau's *L'Année merveilleuse* trounced another comedy on the theme of metamorphosis, *La Grande métamorphose* (Verneuil, 1751), by an anonymous author, who tried in vain to get his work staged at the Théâtre Italien. Another play, *Les Métamorphoses extravagantes*, which was staged in The Hague in 1748, also employed the subject matter of sex change.[38]

In *Narcisse*, Rousseau used the portrait of a cross-dresser as a tool of redemption. Like Ovid's Narcissus, Rousseau's Valère is obsessed with his appearance. He asks his servant Frontin, "How do you find me this morning? I don't have any fire at all in my eyes; I have a poor color; it seems to me that I am not at all up to the usual standard."[39] Once he sees the portrait, Valère thinks he sees the prettiest face

---

34 Ovid, *Metamorphoses*, 3.517–658, 620–22.

35 *CWR*, 10:125. On unveiling a hidden truth, see Jean Starobinski, *Jean-Jacques Rousseau: Transparency and Obstruction*, trans. Arthur Goldhammer, with intro. Robert Morrissey (Chicago: The University of Chicago Press, 1988), 73–75. On art concealing art, see David Marshall, "Rousseau's Pygmalion and the Theatre of Autobiography," in Gullstam and O'Dea, eds, *Rousseau on Stage*, 161. On a subject desiring his/her body in *Narcisse*, see René Démoris, "*Narcisse*: ou comment l'auteur se donne en spectacle," in Berchtold, Martin, and Seite, eds, *Rousseau et le spectacle*, 100.

36 Gabriel-François Coyer, *Découverte de la pierre philosophale. L'année merveilleuse avec un supplément* (Pegu: s.n., 1748), 12.

37 Pierre Rousseau, *L'Année merveilleuse* (Paris: Cailleau, 1748), 11.

38 See Walter E. Rex, "Sexual Metamorphoses on the Stage in Mid-Eighteenth-Century Paris: The Theatrical Background of Rousseau's *Narcisse*," *SVEC* 278 (1990), 269–73.

39 *CWR*, 10:130.

in the world, and he finds his real fiancée Angélique less attractive by comparison. Infatuated by this anonymous beauty, he decides not to marry Angélique until he knows the availability of this mysterious "woman." His doubt amuses Frontin, who, once punished for his indiscretion and still wary of saying anything inappropriate in front of his master, refrains from disclosing the real identity of the woman in the portrait.[40] Meanwhile, Valère's infatuation with merely an *image* of an anonymous female offends Angélique, who takes his infatuation as evidence of Valère's inconstancy and demands him to pick his bride. Torn between these two "women," Valère experiences what Walter Rex calls a "homeopathic shock" and recognizes his own character flaw. The portrait thus serves as a tool of redemption. Valère sets aside the portrait and falls at Angélique's feet, asking her to forgive him: "It is done; you have won, beautiful Angélique, and I feel how inferior the feelings born out of caprice are to those that you inspire in me."[41]

What makes the portrait a curative tool is that Rousseau's portrait of a cross-dresser brings forth the power of dramatic realism. The painting in *Narcisse* functions as a tool of healing, not because it offers a realistic image of the man who needs to be cured of his narcissism, but because it offers an inaccurate imitation that *illuminates* his inner flaw. Rousseau discussed this value of portrait in his second preface to *Julie*: "A portrait always has some value provided it is a good likeness, however strange the original."[42] With the idea of a portrait of cross-dresser, Rousseau made his *Narcisse* different from Ovid's *Narcissus* in major ways: whereas Ovid's Narcissus falls in love with his reflection in the water, Rousseau's Valère falls in love with his cross-dressed image in a painting; whereas Ovid's Narcissus's downfall stems from one vengeful ex-admirer, Rousseau's Valère, tricked by his sister, recognizes his fault. Unlike Ovid, who advances a moral lesson about the destructive outcome of self-absorption, Rousseau takes Valère's awakening as a lesson for spectators: "The pretext is to correct Valère: but the true motive is to laugh at his expense."[43]

Not everybody notices the redemptive element in *Narcisse*, for it can only be recognized by spectators who exercise the cognitive operation of reflection. The portrait helps Valère recognize his infidelity, which is interpreted by Angélique as a sign of effeminacy and character imperfection; she praises his remorse as a marker of his masculinity: "Yes, Valère; he was a woman up to now: but I hope that he will be a man from now on, and greater than these little weaknesses that degrade his sex and his character."[44] Valère agrees with Angélique and recognizes that Angélique's scheme has cured his vanity. "Come, fair Angélique, you have cured me of a ridiculousness that was the shame of my youth, and from now on I am going to prove

---

40 Indiscretion is a theme in Quinault's *L'Amant indiscret* (1654) and Molière's comedies *L'École des femmes* (1662) and *L'Étourdi* (1653/55). See Russell Goulbourne, *Voltaire Comic Dramatist* (Oxford: Voltaire Foundation, 2006), 22.

41 *CWR*, 10:156–57; see Rex, "Sexual Metamorphoses," 267.

42 *CWR*, 6:7. On illumination, see Starobinski, *Jean-Jacques Rousseau*, 77.

43 *CWR*, 10:128.

44 "Oui, Valère; c'était une femme jusqu'ici: mais j'espère que ce sera désormais un homme, supérieur à ces petites faiblesses qui dégradaient son sexe et son caractère." *OC*, 2:1015.

with you that when one loves well, one no longer considers oneself."[45] Rousseau considered this curative function in theater important not to all spectators, but only to those who would and could reflect upon the performance. In *Émile* (1762), Rousseau stressed a theatrical work's educational value specifically for thoughtful spectators: "I take him [Emile] to the theater to study not morals but taste, for it is here that taste reveals itself to those who know how to reflect."[46]

The idea that reflection may promote self-governance is grounded in Enlightenment empiricism. Building upon Locke's ideas of sensation and reflection, but rejecting his neglect of signs, Condillac argued in his *Essai sur l'origine des connaissances humaines* that signs provide the necessary condition for knowledge acquisition. He believed that any individual who knows how to pay attention can reflect. He believed that the cognitive operation of reflection leads to the mental activities of distinguishing, composing and decomposing, comparing, and analyzing. He believed that these operations form the foundation of the still higher levels of cognitive processes of judgment, reasoning, and conception – processes that lead ultimately to human understanding. Unlike sentimentalist thinkers such as David Hume and Adam Smith, Condillac believed that reflection was a matter of cognition rather than feelings.[47] By having the protagonists Angélique and Valère talk at the end of *Narcisse* about the lessons they have learned, Rousseau demonstrated how spectators can develop their own cognitive faculty of reflection. Rousseau, in other words, applied Condillac's theory of human knowledge to the theater. In this sense, Rousseau's *Narcisse* is useful to society, not just because its plot shows how a narcissist can be redeemed, but also because it underscores the cognitive component of reflection in the process of self-awakening.[48]

ARTIFICE, MIMESIS, AND SELF-GOVERNANCE

While an artifice such as a portrait helps Valère develop self-governance, it remains unclear how Valère's transformation has any relevance to spectators' ethics. What made Rousseau so sure that spectators would learn from Valère? Rousseau did not consider the issue of identification in *Narcisse*, but he did so in *Le Devin du village*, where he illustrates the role of mimesis – that is, imitation of someone's behavior – in his theory of spectatorship.

Like *Narcisse*, *Le Devin du village* illustrates how artifice, such as a lie, may cure character flaws. Following the Soothsayer's plan, Colin confronts Colette in a type of accompanied recitative called *récitatif obligé* (Scene 6), in which they are choked

45   *CWR*, 10:160.

46   *CWR*, 13:516.

47   On sensation and reflection, Locke, *An Essay*, 54–63. Condillac, *Essai sur l'origine des connaissances humaines*, ed. Aliènor Bertrand (Paris: Vrin, 2002), 47; Downing A. Thomas, *Music and the Origins of Language: Theories from the French Enlightenment* (Cambridge: Cambridge University Press, 1995), 62; on language as the condition of knowledge, see Condillac, *Essai*, 71–72.

48   On reflection, see Michael L. Frazer, *The Enlightenment of Sympathy: Justice and the Moral Sentiments in the Eighteenth Century and Today* (New York: Oxford University Press, 2010), 4.

with intense emotions, represented by orchestral interludes that fill in the gaps when they fall silent. They hesitate to speak to each other at first, and in the end reveal their fear of losing each other.[49] Colin admits his inconstancy but takes no responsibility for his moral failure, instead blaming his inconstancy on some "malicious spirit" (*l'esprit malin*). He wants Colette, but she, all dressed up, lies about not wanting him anymore. Her lie prompts Colin to withdraw from her, an action that makes Colette disclose the truth: "I am afraid of a fickle lover!" (*Je crains un amant volage!*) Her revelation marks a critical dramatic turning point. Her lie helps Colin recognize the harmful effect caused by his inconstancy.

Using a lie as an artifice, Rousseau demonstrates in *Le Devin du village* how Colin recognizes his character flaw. The Soothsayer enters onstage and takes credit for their reunion, singing: "I have freed you from a cruel evil spell" (*Je vous ai délivrés d'un cruel maléfice*). The *Encyclopédie* (1765) defines the word "*maléfice*" as magic or sorcery. An "evil spell" (*un cruel maléfice*) indicates the Soothsayer's self-proclaimed access to a supernatural source.[50] Yet Rousseau portrayed the Soothsayer as a rational person adept at interpreting signs. The "spell" he casts before Colin is not mystical; it offers only a *performance* intended to deceive and enchant, but his spell as false magic is instrumental in helping Colin develop moral imperatives for himself. One could say that the Soothsayer's fake spell frees Colin from the *real* spell of material temptation. Yet, the important point here is not about the opposition of reason and magic, but the *continuity* between the Soothsayer's performance and Colin's self-governance. The Soothsayer's spell belongs to one of those exceptional arts that may not turn Colin into a virtuous man but may *prevent* him from turning his vices into crimes. In the by-and-large anti-theatrical *Lettre à d'Alembert sur les spectacles* (1758), Rousseau rephrased this point, stressing that a theater may redeem the spectators who live in a place filled with corrupted people because it may prevent "bad morals from degenerating into brigandage."[51]

Unlike in *Narcisse*, in which Valère's self-governance has unclear social impact, Rousseau made clear in *Le Devin du village* that Colin's self-awakening has a positive impact on the spectators onstage. The Soothsayer declares Colin and Colette's influence on spectators, and asks the chorus to celebrate the union of Colin and Colette and to "imitate them," implying that the chorus should take the couple as moral exemplars: "Come, young boys; come lovable girls: / Gather together, come, imitate them."[52] Following the Soothsayer's request, the chorus celebrates the return of Colin to Colette and the Soothsayer's "dazzling power" (*le pouvoir éclatant*), an expression that mystifies the Soothsayer's fictitious "evil spell." But this time, spectators would understand that the Soothsayer's "spell" can have this power *precisely*

---

49 On the portrayal of passions in a *récitatif obligé*, see Waeber, "Rousseau's 'Pygmalion' and the Limits of (Operatic) Expression," in Gullstam and O'Dea, eds, *Rousseau on Stage*, 108.

50 "Maléfice, s.m. (Divinat.) sorte de magie ou sorcellerie." *Encyclopédie*, vol. 9, s.v. "Maléfice."

51 *CWR*, 10:298. On Rousseau's anti-theatrical position, see Patrick Primavesi, "The Dramaturgy of Rousseau's *Lettre à d'Alembert* and Its Importance for Modern Theatre," in Gullstam and O'Dea, eds, *Rousseau on Stage*, 58.

52 *CWR*, 10:224.

because it is artful. The spell – be it a craft, a lie, a trick, or a performance – aims precisely at deceiving and instructing them. Hence, Rousseau's Soothsayer advances a rationalized type of soothsaying in the guise of magic. His "art" is a combination of his sign-reading skills, his ability to apply a principle of cause-and-effect to foresee future happenings, his insightful use of speech as acts, and his aptitude for performing whatever "magic" he can muster to enchant. Downing Thomas might say that the Soothsayer's common-sense approach to problem solving presents a "natural, domesticated form of magic"; indeed, it is this rationalized soothsaying – one no less "dazzling" than the occult type – that makes it useful to the village by promoting social good.[53]

How did Rousseau justify the promotion of social good in the theater, where dramatic characters customarily scheme against one another? In *Le Devin du village* Rousseau dramatized the dynamics of performers and spectators in the plot and established a connection by identifying with characters' behavior. By asking the chorus to "imitate the couple," the Soothsayer teaches them to change their behavior in light of the lesson that the couple has learnt. Once again, Rousseau re-articulated his bias for action over language. His call for action – to "imitate" the village couple – applies the aesthetic concept of mimesis to a practice. By asking the spectators to follow the village couple, Rousseau extended imitation from a compositional device (e.g., tremolos that represent an earthquake) to spectators' behavior. This is not to say that all actions in theater deserve to be imitated, of course. Evoking book three of Plato's *Republic*, Rousseau stated in *Lettre à d'Alembert* that authors should provide spectators only *useful* lessons (*des leçons utiles*), "for it is not good that we be shown all sorts of imitations, but only those of things that are decent (*honnêtes*) and befitting free men (*des hommes libres*)."[54] In the case of *Le Devin du village*, the Soothsayer specifically urges onlookers – the spectators onstage such as the chorus, and, by extension, the spectators in the theater – to imitate the village couple. By linking the act of spectating to the act of imitating a decent behavior, Rousseau showed how mimesis can be *made* useful by promoting self-governance.[55]

PANTOMIME AND IMAGINATION

Now that we have discussed the general moralizing purpose of *Le Devin du village*, we can examine how Rousseau employed the pantomime to that effect. To do so, we need to compare the 1752 version performed in Fontainebleau with the 1753 version performed at the Opéra in Paris. The metaphor of medicine explains how Rousseau used the pantomime that he added to the 1753 version as a "useful" component for spectators to cultivate morality for themselves.

Rousseau considered using pantomime during a period when composers Rameau, Niel, Dauvergne, and others were experimenting with pantomime as a kind of dance

---

53   On magic, see Downing A. Thomas, *Aesthetics of Opera in the Ancien Régime, 1647–1785* (New York: Cambridge University Press, 2002), 249; Waeber, "'Le Devin de la foire?,'" 118–27.

54   *CWR*, 10:339.

55   Harris, *Inventing the Spectator*, 5. On the removal of the boundary separating actor and spectator, see ibid., 222.

(and, to a limited extent, as acting) in their operas. By the time *Le Devin du village* appeared onstage in Fontainebleau on October 18, 1752, Rousseau had finished the first seven scenes. He approved some changes introduced to the 1752 version, but he did not publish these changes in the 1753 score. As Jacqueline Waeber has shown, a manuscript copy currently kept at the Bibliothèque de l'Assemblée Nationale – MS PB – includes what *Mercure de France* called a "very brilliant" divertissement comprising a pastiche of twelve numbers, prepared by the composer François Francoeur. Half of these numbers came from Rameau's operas.[56] This pastiche includes a fragment of the pantomimes taken from Rameau's *Pygmalion* that highlights the jarring pause between them discussed in Chapter One.[57] This fragment was crossed out, and Rousseau never discussed the pantomimes of Rameau's *Pygmalion* in his writings, but MS PB suggests that he might have considered using them in his *Le Devin du village*. Rousseau replaced this fragment with another pantomime created by Rameau's composition student Dauvergne.[58] Taking these two pantomimes into account in the creative process of *Le Devin du village*, the pantomime that Rousseau added to *Le Devin du village* for the 1753 version was in fact his third attempt to incorporate a pantomime into it.

These three pantomimes reveal Rousseau's process of revising *Le Devin du village*. Rameau's pantomime pair in the *Pygmalion* shows little narrative content. Dauvergne's pantomime is tonally closed, consisting of alternations of sharply contrasting thematic segments that make this pantomime syntactically distinct from the thematically uniform dances in binary or rondeau form.[59] Compared to these two, Rousseau's pantomime demonstrates a high degree of thematic individuation and semantic suggestiveness. The verbal instructions printed on the published score demarcate musical units and correlate each unit to one stage direction. This precise degree of musical-textual correlation can effectively regulate dancers' gestures by aligning each unit in relation to each musical segment, resulting in a fresh effect, commended explicitly by *Mercure de France*: "In the divertissement, we have savored especially the pantomime, whose music appeared full of character and whose dance fit the music perfectly."[60]

---

56 *Mercure de France* (December 1752, part 1), 173. On the final divertissement, see Waeber, "Cette horrible innovation," 212–13. On pantomime as acting, see Waeber, "'Le Devin de la foire?,'" 112–18.

57 This fragment is no.7 of the final divertissement. See Waeber, "Cette horrible innovation," 213.

58 The choice of Dauvergne was fitting, for he had composed two pantomimes, one for the second entrée "L'Amour timide" and another, a pantomime of Bacchus's company Silenus, for the fourth entrée "L'Amour enjoué" of the *ballet-héroïque Les Amours de Tempé*, which was premiered at the Opéra on November 7, 1752. See *Mercure de France* (December 1752, part 1), 170.

59 These are No.2 entrée, No.3 the air gracieux, No.4 the two rigaudons, No.6 the two passepieds, No.9 the gigue, and No.10 the two airs vifs, and No.12, the contredanse in rondeau form that concludes the divertissement. See Waeber, "Cette horrible innovation," 212–13.

60 "Dans le divertissement on a surtout goûté la Pantomime, dont la musique a paru pleine de caractère, & dont la danse parfaitement bien adaptée à la musique." *Mercure de France*

Rousseau designed a self-contained pantomime as a key component in the divertissement of the last scene. By "self-contained" I mean that his pantomime forms a "play-within-a-play," or what André Gide called a *mise en abyme*, in *Le Devin du village*. Waeber has discussed the details of this pantomime, but it is unclear how it correlates structurally and dramatically to the entire *intermède*.[61] This is an important inquiry because the pantomime forms a substantial portion of the last scene of Rousseau's 1753 version. It was initially rejected by the Opéra, which might be related to its inventive conception of presenting an action through music, dance, and gesture – one that formed a kind of *danse en action* that Cahusac would theorize a year later in his *La Danse ancienne et moderne*. In fact, Rousseau conceived a continuous dramatic action as a guiding principle for this divertissement, which included the pantomime, as he claimed in his *Confessions*: "This divertissement ought to be *in action* [*en action*] from beginning to end, and on a coherent subject, which in my view, provided some very pleasant tableaux."[62]

To grasp the structural significance of Rousseau's pantomime, we should take a closer look at the structure of Scene 8, the last scene added to the 1753 version. It begins with a chorus celebrating the reunion of Colin and Colette. Colin sings a romance as a response to the chorus, accepting himself as a peasant and looking forward to leading a simple life with Colette. This romance suspends the forward momentum of the dramatic action. Here comes Rousseau's pantomime, which offers an abstracted summary of the first seven scenes, enacting a process of corruption that the Soothsayer has thwarted. The pantomime is performed by three dancers and is watched by Colin, Colette, and the Soothsayer. Remarkably, Rousseau wants these three protagonists to *watch* this dumb show about their story, as the Soothsayer claims after the pantomime: "It is necessary that all is presented to us again" (*Il faut tous à l'envi / nous signaler ici*).[63] This remark is strange. Why does the Soothsayer say that they must watch it again? Wouldn't it be redundant for them to watch a dumb show illustrating their own story?

Here is what Colin, Colette, and the Soothsayer see in the pantomime: a village girl dances, and a courtier from the city watches her dance. This courtier tries to seduce her: He first offers her a purse; she refuses it with disdain. He then offers her a necklace. This time, she accepts it, tries it on, and enjoys her new look. A villager, evidently her lover, comes onstage and is disheartened to see her accepting the jewelry. In response to the villager's distress, the girl returns the necklace to the courtier. The girl's rejection hurts the courtier, who threatens the villager. This threat alarms the girl, who tries to calm the courtier down, while signaling the villager to leave. The villager refuses to leave, and the courtier escalates his threat by motioning to

---

    (April 1753), 174. On two types of stage directions (i.e., the melodic and pantomimic types), see Waeber, "'Le Devin de la foire?,'" 109.

61   This term was coined by André Gide in the early 1890s and was discussed in Lucien Dällenbach, *The Mirror of the Text*, trans. Jeremy Whiteley with Emma Hughes (Chicago: The University of Chicago Press, 1989), 8. On this pantomime, see Jacqueline Waeber, "Décor et pantomime du *Devin du village*: Une étude didascalique," *Annales de la Société Jean-Jacques Rousseau* 45 (2003), 131–65.

62   *CWR*, 5:320.

63   *OC*, 2:1111.

kill him. This time, the village couple throw themselves at the feet of the courtier – a gesture that begs the courtier to spare the villager's life. Touched by this gesture, the courtier gives in and unites the couple. Other villagers come to celebrate the union of the village couple and applaud the compassionate courtier.

On the face of it, the pantomime offers a playback of the story about Colin and Colette, but a closer look reveals that it offers a modified version of this story. The village couple obviously represent Colin and Colette, but the courtier has no corresponding character in the first seven scenes of the *intermède*. On one level, this courtier represents a fictive "fine gentleman of the town" whom the Soothsayer wants Colin to believe is his love rival: "It is no Shepherd [*Berger*] that she prefers to you, / It is a fine Gentleman of the Town [*un beau Monsieur de la Ville*]."[64] On a more abstract level, this courtier represents Colin's vanity. As the Soothsayer observes in Scene 2, Colin likes to dress like a courtier: "Colin wants to be brave; he loves to show off: / His vanity has given you [Colette] an insult, / For which his love must atone."[65] In comparison to the narrative presented in the first seven scenes, the pantomime departs in three major ways. First, no courtier offers anything to Colette in the first seven scenes, whereas in the pantomime a courtier repeatedly attempts to seduce Colette with jewelry and money. Second, Colette is not the only person subject to temptation. As she points out in Scene 6, it is *Colin* who has received a costly ribbon from a certain Lady, indicating that Colin – and not Collette – is morally corrupt.[66] Third, no one threatens the villager in the first seven scenes, but the courtier threatens the villager repeatedly in the pantomime.

Accordingly, Rousseau's pantomime provides not an accurate summary of Colin's relationship with Colette, but a *fictional* account of an amorous relationship based on their deteriorating relationship. Although the pantomime comes after the end of the dramatic action, it does not move the narrative forward; rather, it loops *backward* by revisiting important events of the plot. The pantomime disrupts the forward momentum of dramatic linearity by recalling the dramatic happenings thus far. It displays an abstracted moral story about the perils of corruption and presents a corrective to corruption. Positioned at the end of the *intermède*, the pantomime dance offers an extension of the plot, not by introducing another scene, but by *deepening* the scenario. It creates a warped sense of time, asking spectators to experience the progress of time by retracing its path, going both forward and backward in time. It is the experience of this bi-directional temporality that generates a sense of deepening, making the pantomime present a narrative abyss (*mise en abyme*) in *Le Devin du village*.

At the theater, a narrative abyss has profound implication for spectatorship. Watching a play forms the basis of interpretation and discussion with fellow members of the audience. This basis can be adapted for dramatic purposes, as watching other people *watch* a play can be a dramatic event. Diderot, for example, dramatized himself – Moi – watching the performance of the domestic tragedy *Le Fils naturel*

64 *CWR*, 10:219.

65 *CWR*, 10:217.

66 During his compositional process, Rousseau played down his criticisms of nobility for fear of coming across as offensive. See Waeber, "'Le Devin de la foire?,'" 114 n.1.

(1757) and his discussion with Dorval, a protagonist of *Le Fils naturel*, in three conversations called *Entretiens sur le fils naturel* (1757). Their discussions in turn introduce the sequel of *Le Fils naturel* called *Le Père de famille* (Comédie-Française, 1761). Crucially, topics of pantomime and declamation figure prominently in *Le Fils naturel* and the *Entretiens*. In the second conversation, Diderot mentioned the moment the cynic philosopher Demetrius became convinced by a pantomime performer's communicative ability, linking his idea of pantomime with Lucian's *De Saltatione* and applying Dubos's idea of pantomime to the spoken theater: "The pantomime performs, and the philosopher [Demetrius], transported, exclaims, 'I do not only see you; I hear you. You speak to me from your hands.'"[67]

If, according to Diderot, watching a play formed a foundation for the sociable activity of discussion, then what does it mean to watch a play embedded within a play? In *Le Devin du village* Rousseau presented two superimposed narratives, an account of the reality that *embeds* its fictionalized re-enactment. This structure has implications for spectatorship. Spectators are to make a conscious effort not just to understand the pantomime (i.e., the fictionalized re-enactment of the reality), but also to *imagine* its relevance to the first seven scenes of the *intermède* (i.e., to understand how and why the reality is fictionalized in the pantomime). To do so, they need to forgo the passive mode of spectatorship, to stop viewing themselves as what Locke called "white paper" – which passively receives sensory perceptions – and adopt an active and thus advanced mode of spectating, engaging their cognitive operation of imagination to convert weak sensory perceptions of the gestural and musical signs in the pantomime into enduring ideas. In *Le Neveu de Rameau* Diderot used the play-within-a-play structure to display two parallel narratives – what Rameau's nephew would like to be and what he is, the real and the imaginary. In both cases, the use of imagination was essential. In his *Lettre à d'Alembert*, Rousseau stressed the significance of imagination in spectatorship, which is a cognitive operation that enables spectators to perceive an object in front of them as more appealing than it is: "The immediate power of the senses is weak and limited; it is through the intermediary of the imagination that they make their greatest ravages."[68] By placing the pantomime in the last scene of the *intermède*, Rousseau made the 1753 version more cognitively demanding than the 1752 version.

ACTOR'S GESTURES AND ORCHESTRAL MUSIC

What makes the condensed plot presented in the pantomime different from the opera is that it is made of musical-gestural units, unlike most of the *intermède*, which employs sung text. It is cognitively challenging for spectators to recognize and to decipher these units as nonverbal signs. Rousseau's pantomime also places demands on spectators on an affective level: Cahusac emphasized in *La Danse ancienne et moderne* that "gesture is more precise than speech."[69] Rousseau agreed, emphasizing

---

67 "Le pantomime joue, et le philosophe, transporté, s'écrie: 'Je ne te vois pas seulement; je t'entends. Tu me parles des mains.'" Diderot, *Œuvres*, 4:1144; this episode is also included in Lucian, *Éloge de la danse*, 32.

68 *CWR*, 10:350. On "white paper," see Locke, *An Essay*, 54.

69 "Le geste est plus précis que le discours." Cahusac, *La Danse*, 3:150.

in his *Essai sur l'origine des langues* that gestures, compared to spoken language, are "more expressive and say more in less time."[70] But he also considered visual signs not as effective as aural ones when it came to moving spectators. One can understand visual signs in a single glance, but it takes time to experience aural signs and to *feel* the emotions conveyed by them. One might not be too affected by the sight of person in a painful situation, for example, but one would likely be moved to tears if one were to take the time to listen to that person's account of his pain. As Rousseau continued in his *Essai sur l'origine des langues*, "pantomime alone, without discourse, will leave you almost unperturbed; discourse without gesture will wrest tears from you."[71] At issue for Rousseau was not the distinction between pantomime and discourse, but the element of *time* that distinguishes showing/seeing from telling/listening. The content of the discourse concerned him less than the tonal inflections – or "accents" – of the delivery. These "accents" underscore the affective dimension of speech by penetrating to "the bottom of the heart," and helping us to "feel what we hear."[72]

Since it takes time for one to experience feelings, the technique of aligning music with gesture shapes spectators' experience of musical-gestural units as signs. As with Rameau, who used written stage directions to correlate music and gesture in *Pygmalion*, Rousseau also employed this technique in Scene 2 (when Colette approaches the Soothsayer for help), and he redeployed this technique on a larger and most consistent scale in the pantomime. Fifteen stage directions printed above the musical staff, which fall into three categories, suggest that each marks the beginning of a musical-gestural unit. Rousseau used the term "entrée" to indicate *la belle danse*. For example, three dancers enter the scene separately, dancing in three entrées: "entrée of the village girl," "entrée of the courtier," and "entrée of the villager." A second category describes action: for example, "the courtier notices her"; "she dances while he is looking"; "he offers her a purse"; "she refuses it." The third indicates expressions: the village girl refuses the courtier's gift "with disdain"; she tries the necklace on and, feeling adorned, looks at her reflection "with complaisance."[73]

These stage directions meticulously tie actors' gestures to segments of orchestral music. The notational technique heightens the semantic suggestiveness of instrumental music. In the article "Sonata," in the *Dictionnaire de musique*, in response to Fontenelle's question "sonata, what do you want from me?" (*sonate, que me veux-tu?*), Rousseau claimed: "To know the meaning of all the jumble in sonatas

70   *CWR*, 7:290.

71   *CWR*, 7:292.

72   *CWR*, 10:291–92.

73   For a table for these stage directions, see my "'Tout, dans ses charmes, est dangereux': Music, Gesture, and the Dangers of French Pantomime, 1748–1775," *Cambridge Opera Journal* 20, no.3 (2010): 241–68, at 252. For a classification of gestures on eighteenth-century stage, see Dene Barnett, *The Art of Gesture: The Practices and Principles of 18th-Century Acting* (Heidelberg: Carl Winter, 1987), 26–87. On the indexicality of dance, see Stephen Rumph, *Mozart and Enlightenment Semiotics* (Berkeley, CA: University of California Press, 2012), 83–84; on aligning music with gesture, see Lockhart, *Animation*, 35–36.

with which one is overwhelmed, one would have to act like that bad painter who was obliged to write underneath his figures – 'this is a tree; this is a man; this is a horse.'"[74] As each segment of this pantomime imparts one unit of semantic meaning, a sequence of these segments would form a musical-gestural narrative that makes the pantomime a dance in action, accompanied by what Ellen Lockhart calls "through-composed" music that unfolds in real time.[75] This technique does not necessarily mean that gesture and music are of equal importance. In his *Lettre sur la musique française* (1753), Rousseau considered music a guiding force for gesture: "This accompaniment goes so well with the song and is so exactly proportioned to the words that it often seems to determine the action and to dictate to the Actor the gesture he should make."[76] Later, Rousseau revised this point and understood these two mediums as mutually reinforcing. According to the entry "Actor" in the *Dictionnaire de musique*, a performer at the Opéra should not just be a good singer, but also an excellent pantomime, for a performer should match his acting to the instrumental accompaniment: "His steps, his looks, his gesture, everything must go well with the music incessantly."[77]

To make sense of the pantomime, therefore, is to make sense of each dance unit (including entrées) in relation to the orchestral music composed unambiguously to accompany it, and to feel the emotions conveyed by the dancers. Consequently, Rousseau's pantomime represents the pantomime of the Enlightenment because it meets the criteria of emotional expressivity and semantic suggestiveness that Dubos had envisioned for the dance of the Enlightenment.

CONDILLAC'S FIRST IDEAS AND COMPLEX IDEAS

What is fascinating is that Rousseau's technique of aligning music with gesture in the pantomime was compatible with theory of cognition, for it allows spectators to develop what Condillac called "complex ideas" on the basis of "first ideas" – terms borrowed from Locke's "simple ideas" and "complex ideas."[78] The pantomime of *Le Devin du village* showcases a self-contained moralistic play that prompts the onstage onlookers – Colin, Colette, and the Soothsayer – to offer their reflections of it in the chanson sung after the pantomime. The sequence of a pantomime followed by a chanson can be explained by Condillac's *Essai*. Arguing against René Descartes, who thought that one must begin to obtain knowledge through abstract principles or definitions, Condillac proposed that one must start with some "first ideas," obtained through the process of sensing or reflecting. These first ideas enable one to acquire knowledge by connecting ideas – combining the simplest ideas into more complex ones. While Colin, Colette, and the Soothsayer develop first ideas by

---

74 "Pour savoir ce que veulent dire tous ces fatras de Sonates dont on est accablé, il faudrait faire comme ce Peintre grossier qui était obligé d'écrire au-dessous de ses figures; *c'est un arbre, c'est un homme, c'est un cheval.*" *OC*, 5:1060.

75 Lockhart, *Animation*, 36, 72.

76 *CWR*, 10:155.

77 "Ses pas, ses regards, son geste, tout doit s'accorder sans cesse avec la Musique." Rousseau, *Dictionnaire de musique*, s.v. "Acteur," *OC*, 5:637.

78 On simple and complex ideas, see Locke, *An Essay*, 64–98.

watching the pantomime, in the final chanson they exercise a higher cognitive level, sharing complex ideas contingent upon their experience, gender, and social status.[79]

Rousseau knew Condillac in 1742, a decade before he staged *Le Devin du village* at Fontainebleau and played a part in the publication of Condillac's first major work, *Essai sur l'origine des connaissances humaines*. According to book seven of *Les Confessions*, the two of them sometimes dined together in Paris in 1745, when Condillac had just finished the manuscript. Rousseau recognized the significance of this work but knew that *Essai*'s topic of metaphysics was unfashionable at the time. He thus introduced Condillac to Diderot, who shared Rousseau's interest in it and had the Parisian printer Durand publish it in 1746, even though it was published anonymously under the fictitious imprint of Pierre Mortier of Amsterdam.[80]

In his *Essai* Condillac bypassed the *genealogy* of pantomime in the framework of the Quarrel of Ancients and Moderns, offering instead an *archaeology* of communication based on his theory of the origin of language, a topic Locke did not discuss in his *Essay*. Condillac conceived of language as a type of verbal sign. He discussed in his *Essai* signs used by humans before the invention of language as the primary means of communication. Compared to verbal language, the "language of action" (*langage d'action*) – a term Condillac borrowed from William Warburton's *The Divine Legation of Moses* (1741, French translation 1744) – acts with greater force on human imagination and thus makes a more lasting impression. A common means of communication in the Jewish tradition, the language of action was reserved for serious occasions concerning religion or government. The ancients called this language of action "dance," as in 2 Samuel 6, where David danced in front of the ark.[81]

Condillac drew a connection between ancient dance and dances in the modern age, offering a conceptual link that connected the genealogy of pantomime with the archaeology of communication. Condillac adopted Dubos's ancient-vs-modern framework, arguing that dance had evolved into two main types – one of gestures and another of steps – since antiquity. The former indicated a means of communication, whereas the latter expressed emotions. Turning his attention from the ancients to moderns, Condillac subdivided dances of steps into Italian and French. The dance of steps in Italy evolved into the *commedia dell'arte* style of pantomime, and the dance of steps in France became *la belle danse*, which was graver and simpler than the Italian, with a comparably more limited expression. Contrary to d'Alembert, who would give credit in 1759 to both French and Italian styles in *De la liberté de la*

---

79 Condillac, *Essai*, 181–83. On the relationship between this essay and music, see Thomas, *Music and the Origins of Language*, ch. 3.

80 *OC*, 1:347, see also 1:1424 n.3.

81 "And David danced before the Lord with all his might; and David was girded with a linen ephod. So David and all the house of Israel brought up the ark of the Lord with shouting, and with the sound of the trumpet." 2 Sam. 6:14–15 (King James Bible). On the term "langage d'action," see *Essai sur les hiéroglyphes des égyptiens*, 2 vols. (Paris: Hippolyte-Louis Guerin, 1744), 1:58; see also Hans Aarsleff, "Philosophy of Language," in Knud Haakonssen, ed., *Cambridge History of Eighteenth-Century Philosophy*, 2 vols. (Cambridge: Cambridge University Press, 2006), 466; on the origin of language, see Condillac, *Essai*, 99–106; Thomas, *Music and the Origins of Language*, 12–56.

musique, Condillac favored none of these national dances in 1746.[82] He acknowledged that all of them had their strengths, but preferred the kind of dance that
imparted semantic meaning: "A dance that expresses grace and dignity is good; a
dance that creates a sort of conversation or dialogue seems to me better." The type
he least favored was the Italian type of acrobatic dance that displayed nothing other
than physical virtuosity, which "merely requires strength, dexterity, and agility." He
found *la belle danse* flawed, as well. He claimed: "The flaw of the French is to limit
the arts by wanting to make them simple."[83]

Using the vocabularies theorized in Condillac's *Essai,* Rousseau used dance as
dance, and dance as *langage d'action* in his *Le Devin du village.* This pairing is consistent with the Dubosian duality of dance step versus sign, and Noverre described, in
his *Lettres sur la danse et sur les ballets,* their uses in practice: "The symmetrical figures from the right to the left are only tolerable, in my opinion, in the *corps d'entrée,*
which are not of an expressive nature, and which, imparting nothing, are performed
only to give the principal dancers time to catch their breath again."[84] Dancers should
perform less as dancing masters whose meticulously practiced steps would appear
mechanical, and more like fiery "actors" (*comédiens*) who, taking the ancient Roman
pantomime actors Pylades and Bathyllus as models, can communicate or speak with
their gestures.[85] In *Le Devin du village* the village girl, the courtier, and the villager
come onstage in three entrées and present in each one a dance that expresses what
Condillac would call "grace and dignity," without attempting to convey any semantic content. These entrées thus serve as decorative dances. The rest of the pantomime shows sections of *langage d'action.* Whereas Condillac's concept of *langage
d'action* connects Dubos's idea of pantomime with his theory of human knowledge,
Rousseau established in the pantomime of *Le Devin du village* the opposing relation
of the dance entrée and *langage d'action.*

To highlight *langage d'action,* Rousseau conveyed in the pantomime the dangers of corruption, through gestural and musical ruptures as signs. Whereas all the
cadences performed in the entrées fall on downbeats, the first segment of *langage
d'action* begins with a diminished seventh chord that replaces the final cadence of
the courtier's entrée, in m.72. The half cadence in mm.67–68 sets up the expectation of a full cadence in m.72. The tonic chord, however, defies the proper sense
of arrival expected of a cadence by entering an eighth note earlier, in m.71. This
precipitous arrival places the cadence unexpectedly on a weak beat, generating a

---

82   On d'Alembert's position, see Robert Isherwood, "The Conciliatory Partisan of Musical
     Liberty: Jean Le Rond d'Alembert, 1717–1783," in Georgia Cowart, ed., *French Musical
     Thought, 1600–1800* (Ann Arbor, MI: UMI Research Press, 1989), 96–119. On this
     collaboration, see David Charlton, "New Light on the *Bouffons* in Paris (1752–1754),"
     Eighteenth-Century Music 11, no.1 (2014), 31–54.

83   "Le défaut des Français, c'est de borner les arts à force de vouloir les rendre simples."
     Condillac, *Essai,* 104. Translation adapted from Condillac, *Essay,* 119.

84   "Les figures symétriques de la droite à la gauche, ne sont supportables, selon moi, que
     dans les corps d'entrée, qui n'ont aucun caractère d'expression, & qui ne disant rien,
     sont faits uniquement pour donner le temps aux premiers danseurs de reprendre leur
     respiration." Noverre, *Lettres,* 8.

85   Noverre, *Lettres,* 17–18.

sense of cadential let-down. The sense of premature arrival is reinforced by another surprise: a diminished seventh chord on F-sharp in m.72, emphasized by a fermata as an agogic accent, displaces the cadence on the strong beat. Thoughtfully incorrect voice-leadings also underpin this cadential displacement. In the second beat of m.71, the bass line falls a diminished octave from F to F-sharp (in m.72) via B-flat, and the melody played by the first violin shoots up a major seventh interval from B-flat (m.71) to A (m.72). The bass line displaces the B-flat tonic chord by a diminished seventh chord on the strong beat in m.72, which signals a tonal and metric rupture, moving the anticipated B-flat major abruptly at the cadential point toward G minor. Rousseau amplifies this unprepared tonal swerve further by setting it in G major, the parallel major of G minor (m.73 of Example 2.2).

What does this jarring cadential displacement mean? The tonal swerve – what Jean Starobinski calls a "negative sign," indicative of hostility – calls for justification, and indeed Rousseau offered an explanation for it by inserting a stage direction in the score: "He [the courtier] discovers the village girl" (*Il aperçoit la villageoise*) (mm.72–73 of Example 2.2).[86]

By eighteenth-century acting standards, the courtier's look does not seem to carry enough dramatic weight to warrant such a musical rupture, but it marks the beginning of corruption that has significance, according to Rousseau's *First Discourse*. A look is unusually significant precisely because it seems so banal, and the verb *apercevoir* – to "begin to see" or "discover" – does not serve any special indicative, imitative, or expressive function according to acting manuals of the time.[87] This verb does not indicate the use of the hands or arms. The performer playing the courtier may turn his head and cast a look at the village girl, which would qualify as what Gilbert Austin called, in *Chironomia* (1806), a gesture of commencement or emphasis of little import. But when one places this seemingly insignificant moment in the context of Rousseau's *First Discourse*, the courtier's look at the village girl – his *first* look at her – takes on significance by marking the *origin* of corruption. This look initiates two rounds of temptation. The cyclical structure demonstrates a direct correlation between stages of corruption and resistance to temptation: the bigger the temptation, the more difficult to resist.

The cyclical structure requires spectators to use their cognitive ability to make comparisons to grasp the process of intensification. Condillac proposed in his *Essai* that analysis stemming from connecting ideas necessitates the process of discovery. The challenge is to design a process that *optimizes* connections between ideas and facilitates the operation of comparison. Condillac's concept of comparison explains why this apparently inconsequential look bears structural significance. These two rounds of temptation offer materials for spectators to *compare*, on the cognitive level, the intensity of corruption. After the courtier discovers her, the village girl resumes dancing, but this time – though the music and probably her dance remain the same – her dancing is watched by the courtier (*Elle danse tandis qu'il la regarde*). She becomes what Laura Mulvey calls an object of the male gaze and thus prey

---

86 Starobinski, *Jean-Jacques Rousseau*, 157.

87 "APERCEVOIR … Commencer à voir, découvrir." *Dictionnaire de l'Académie française* (1762), s.v. "Apercevoir."

Example 2.2. Rousseau, *Le Devin du village*, Scene 8, "Pantomime," mm.65–80

for a sexual predator.[88] To highlight the moral significance of this cycle through music, Rousseau composed a symmetrical eight-measure period starting in m.80, which sets up a normative phrase structure. The subsequent phrase accompanies the courtier's first seductive move: he offers her a purse, a gesture that confirms that he is a source of corruption. Rousseau's disruptive music signals her resentment. The C minor in m.92 is interrupted by unprepared octave jumps on C in the melody. The melodic leaps, played very loudly, accompany the village girl's rejection of the courtier's money (*Elle la refuse avec dédain*), posing sharp melodic and dynamic contrasts to the courtier's refined, alluring, sweet (*doux*) stepwise melody of mm.89–92 (Example 2.3). The octave, as Rousseau defined in his *Dictionnaire de musique*, is "the most perfect of consonances; it is, after the unison, that of all the chords whose ratio is the simplest."[89] Rousseau liked this utter simplicity, as he wrote in *Julie*, "for my part, I am convinced that of all harmonies, there is none so agreeable as singing in unison, and that if we need chords, it is because our taste has been depraved."[90] Thus, an ethic underlies Rousseau's compositional choices: the octave jumps represent the village girl's aversion to corruption, expressed in a natural, prompt, transparent manner.

The potentially corrupting look, followed by two cycles of seduction, can be explained by Condillac's theory of human understanding. He argued that learning should serve a social purpose, and that a meticulously thought-out sequence of events enables understanding: "A thing said once in its proper place is clearer than when it is repeated several times in different places."[91] Prolixity is tiresome; divisions and subdivisions may cause confusion; digressions are distracting, and redundancy exhausts the mind. Coming from a rhetorical tradition that stresses an orator's speech as much as a reader's response, Condillac emphasized the significance of personal experience in the pursuit of truth. The goal, he emphasized, is not to convince the reader by argumentation or by logic, but to illustrate the *process* through which one discovers the truth. To demonstrate the effectiveness of learning, one who thinks he has obtained the truth should be able to explain to others how he has gotten to know it, since knowledge acquisition serves personal as much as social purposes. If the point of obtaining knowledge is to share it with others, then Rousseau's cyclical design would make the peril of incremental corruption understandable for a broad audience.[92]

Using a cyclic design, Rousseau encouraged spectators to compare two rounds of temptation. Just in case his spectators missed the dramatic meaning of the octave leaps, Rousseau provided another explanatory stage direction, spelling out exactly

88 Laura Mulvey, *Visual and Other Pleasures*, 2nd edn (New York: Palgrave Macmillan, 2009), 19.

89 "L'Octave est la plus parfait des Consonances; elle est, après l'Unisson, celui de tous les Accords dont le rapport est le plus simple." *OC*, 5:944. On transparency, see Starobinski, *Jean-Jacques Rousseau*, 315–16. On the unison, see Jacqueline Waeber, "Jean-Jacques Rousseau's 'Unité de mélodie,'" *Journal of the American Musicological Society* 62, no.1 (2009), 79–143, at 120–25.

90 *CWR*, 6:499.

91 Condillac, *Essay*, 218.

92 Condillac, *Essay*, 188–89.

Example 2.3. Rousseau, *Le Devin du village*, Scene 8, "Pantomime," mm.87–93

what it means: "She refuses it [the purse] with disdain." After establishing the dramatic meaning of the octave leaps, the second round of temptation begins. The
courtier tries harder, giving her a necklace. These two rounds of temptation illustrate what Condillac called the cognitive operation of comparison that leads to
the operation of reflection: "Once the ideas have been determined, they must be
compared."[93] Rousseau repeated the same point in his *Essai sur l'origine des langues*:
"Reflection is born of compared ideas, and it is the multiplicity of ideas that leads to
their comparison."[94]

The climax of the pantomime illustrates how the cognitive operations of imagination and reflection create sympathy, which means, according to David Hume's *A
Treatise of Human Nature* (1739–40), "to receive by communication their [others']
inclinations and sentiments, however different from, or even contrary to our own."[95]

93 Condillac, *Essay*, 212.

94 *CWR*, 7:306.

95 Hume, *A Treatise of Human Nature*, 1:206.

Sympathy occurs the moment after the courtier threatens to kill the villager, when the village couple give in and kneel before the courtier, begging him to spare the villager's life. The stage direction again offers helpful explanation, asking that the courtier "allows himself to be touched and unites them" (*Il se laisse toucher et les unit*). In *Essai sur l'origine des langues* Rousseau emphasized the meaning of the reflexive verb "to allow oneself to be touched" (*se laisser toucher*): "How do we allow ourselves to be moved to pity?" (*Comment nous laissons-nous émouvoir à la pitié?*)[96] Pity, though natural to man, remains inactive until imagination activates it. It allows one to sympathize, that is, to be *transported* outside oneself and to identify with the person who suffers. Pity, therefore, is the result of sympathy that comes from imagination. Rousseau continued, "He who imagines nothing feels only himself; he is alone in the midst of mankind."[97] The crucial point in this climax is not that Colin and Colette beg the courtier for mercy, but that the courtier *allows himself* to be moved by their action. In this process, the courtier employs his cognitive operations of reflection and imagination to realize that he and his rival – despite their differences in class and educational background – are both vulnerable to rejection.[98]

Remarkably, Rousseau used noticeable musical ruptures in the pantomime to individuate segments of *langage d'action*. The octaves of mm.92–93 form a distinct musical-gestural unit, which anticipates another unit of mm.175–78, when the village couple beg for their lives. An unprepared modulation from D major to G minor is reinforced by the triple time that unexpectedly replaces quadruple time; a slow tempo replaces a quick one, and a slow quarter-note rhythm replaces a fast eighth-note stream. A stepwise melodic descent of a third in mm.175–77, evoking the *topos* of lament, imitates what Rousseau might call "vocal inflexions" of cries and complaints, or what Condillac called a *fusion* of natural and arbitrary signs.[99] This four-measure unit ends on a D-major chord, which is at once the half cadence of the G minor and the dominant chord of the following joyful G-major denouement (m.178 of Example 2.4). The homo-rhythmic texture, the melodic descent, and the ambiguous C-minor mode modulating towards G minor mark a moment of solemnity. This segment has a simple, direct, and transparent effect; its semantic meaning apparently does not depend on any explanatory sung text or stage direction. The sight of the couple begging in front of the courtier, accompanied by the music that resembles human cries, offers an affective context in which even the pitiless courtier develops sympathy.[100]

96   *CWR*, 7:306.

97   *CWR*, 7:306. For the definition of sympathy, see Jaucourt, *Encyclopédie*, vol. 15, s.v. "Sympathie [Physiologie]." See also Thomas, *Aesthetics of Opera*, ch. 7; Ruth HaCohen, "The Music of Sympathy in the Arts of the Baroque; or, the Use of Difference to Overcome Indifference," *Poetics Today* 22, no.3 (2001), 618.

98   On music and social bonding, see Olivia Bloechl, "On Not Being Alone: Rousseauean Thoughts on a Relational Ethics of Music," *Journal of American Musicological Society* 66, no.1 (2013), 262.

99   *CWR*, 10:322. On the fusion of natural and arbitrary signs, see Condillac, *Lettres inédites à Gabriel Cramer*, ed. Georges Le Roy (Paris: Presses universitaires de France, 1953), 85–86.

100 On music and moral effects, see *CWR*, 10:327.

84

Example 2.4. Rousseau, *Le Devin du village*, "Pantomime," mm.168–181

The pantomime positioned near the end of the *intermède* therefore creates a narrative abyss by allowing spectators to see and hear for themselves the perils of corruption. It epitomizes how to reject material temptation and demonstrates how this rejection may foster sociality through shared vulnerability. The pantomime illustrates Condillac's theory of knowledge acquisition by distinguishing the cognitive phase of sensory perception from that of the formation of ideas. Like Condillac, Rousseau cautioned in his *Essai sur l'origine des langues* that sensory stimulants such as colors or sounds do not have power over the people who perceive them. To move someone, these "simple objects of the senses" need to offer the recipient not just something aesthetically pleasing, but something deeper that can touch the soul: "Even songs that are only pleasant and say nothing are still tiresome; for it is not so much the ear that carries pleasure to the heart as the heart that carries it to the ear."[101] Rousseau might not agree with Condillac, but he sided with Condillac in arguing against Locke, who never thought about the problem of the origin of language, and who assumed that sensation and reflection could take place without language. Like Condillac, Rousseau emphasized spectators' *agency*, exercised through higher-level cognitive processes.[102]

Specifically, spectators act as agents by formulating "complex ideas" for themselves, based on the first ideas presented in the pantomime. Once the pantomime comes to an end, the *mise en abyme* ends and the forward dramatic momentum resumes. The Soothsayer sings a brief recitative, admitting that he cannot leap like the dancers and proposing instead to sing a new song (*une chanson nouvelle*), in which the three protagonists – the Soothsayer, Colin, and Colette – share their points of view of this pantomime. Its strophic form offers a suitable structure that accommodates disconnected reflections. Thus, this chanson becomes yet another tool at the Soothsayer's disposal, transforming the pantomime into a participatory theater, turning Colin, Colette, and the Soothsayer from protagonists into spectators and back to protagonists who reflect upon what they have watched.[103] The Soothsayer begins by emphasizing the utility of art, as if he were to revise Rousseau's rejection of arts and sciences in the *First Discourse*: "Art is favorable to Amour, / and Amour knows how to charm artlessly" (*L'Art à l'Amour est favorable, / Et sans art l'Amour sait charmer*). Collette sings the second stanza, making a point unrelated to the one the Soothsayer has expressed. She evokes the idea of good savage (*le bon sauvage*, a natural man who lives in the society): "here" (i.e., a place where one is distanced from temptation), Amour "follows the innocence of simple nature"; but in "other places" (i.e., places corrupted by arts and sciences), he seeks "a borrowed

101 *CWR*, 10:324. See Deirdre Loughridge, "Who Measured the Wind and Made the Fingers Move," *Journal of the American Musicological Society* 66, no.1 (2013), 273.

102 David Kasunic, "Rousseau's Cat," *Journal of the American Musicological Society* 66, no.1 (2013), 268.

103 Thomas, *Music and the Origins of Language*, 45. On participatory theater, see Jérôme Brillaud, "If You Please! Theater, Verisimilitude, and Freedom in the Letter to d'Alembert," in Christie McDonald and Stanley Hoffmann, eds, *Rousseau and Freedom* (Cambridge: Cambridge University Press, 2010), 89.

shine from adornment."[104] Colin sings the next stanza and offers another set of reflections. He learns a lesson about constancy (what Rousseau called in *Lettre à d'Alembert* "the maxim of exciting the passions by obstacles"), noting that a flighty heart is retained, paradoxically, by coquetry, and that a faithful shepherd is less loved than a fickle one.[105] Colette concludes the chanson by singing the last stanza, declaring that she now knows how to love. This declaration naturally leads to joyful singing and dancing typical of a French opera. The reflections expressed by Colette, Colin, and the Soothsayer are uncoordinated, independent, divergent, illustrating the point of alienated spectatorship that Rousseau would make in *Lettre à d'Alembert*: "People think they come together in the theater, and it is there that they are isolated."[106]

The socially alienated nature of spectatorship at the theater demonstrates the cognitive process through which inequality is cultivated. The significant point is that the chanson does not advance a single moral shared by all three of them. Nor does anyone of them mention the courtier as a moral exemplar. The courtier's actions – deciding not to kill his love rival and reuniting the village couple – are left unacknowledged. The chanson demonstrates the incongruous lessons that each socially alienated spectator formulates after they watch the pantomime. The musical-gestural units in the pantomime are the same for everyone, but everyone interprets them differently. The dissimilarity of their interpretations demonstrates how the complex idea of inequality is born. As Condillac wrote, "The materials are the same in all human beings, but their agility in the use of signs varies, which causes the inequality we find among them."[107]

The divergent responses by the three protagonists mirror that of Rousseau's contemporary viewers, who likewise offered disparate responses to Rousseau's *Le Devin du village*. In *Les Trois Chapitres* (early March 1753), Diderot imagined a character called the Petit Prophète de Boehmischbroda, who, crying like a spoiled child, complained that there was no fête at the end of *Le Devin du village* and was chided by a Voice: "You will not see the fête … because joy is not there. You must not be upset any longer and you must not always play bad minuets (*mauvais menuets*), out of spite for a natural type of expression, and you do not like to play bad minuets."[108] Charles Palissot de Montenoy observed in 1757 how this pantomime, abundant with musical and gestural signs, enabled him to recognize a common perceptual ground and an intersubjective bond he shared with Rousseau and the Renaissance Italian painter Antonio Allegri, or Correggio: "This ballet [i.e., the pantomime] so new, for which pains were taken to draw up a plan, is precisely what we see at our theaters every day, to the point that on reading it, I found myself the composer, and that

---

104 "Ici de la simple Nature / L'Amour suit la naïveté; / En d'autres lieux, de la parure / Il cherche l'éclat emprunté." *OC*, 5:1111. On the good savage, see Trousson and Eigeldinger, eds, *Dictionnaire*, s.v. "Sauvage (Bon.)"

105 *CWR*, 10:315.

106 *CWR*, 10:262. On Rousseau's point of social alienation, see Harris, *Inventing the Spectator*, 200–201 n.5.

107 Condillac, *Essay*, 82–83.

108 "Tu ne verras point la fête … car la joie n'y est pas; il ne faut pas que tu te fâches davantage et que tu fasses toujours de mauvais menuets, car tu es colère de ton naturel, et tu n'aimes pas à faire de mauvais menuets." Diderot, *Œuvres*, 4:146.

I could have spoken like Correggio ... Many ideas that he has woken in me are common."[109] In the entry "Intermède" of the *Encyclopédie* (vol. 8, 1765), the author (possibly Diderot) observed that *Le Devin du village* caused polarized reactions at the theater: "It had to make spectators of a common taste weep, and the spectators of a more unguarded (*délié*) taste laugh."[110]

PERSUASION WITHOUT CONVINCING

If musical-gestural units are presented in *Le Devin du village* as serviceable means of communication at the lyric theater (serviceable because Rousseau still finds it necessary to prescribe their meanings with verbal annotations in the score), then how is this tool different from language?

In theory, the pantomime in *Le Devin du village* creates a space in which indicative and expressive gestures are presented simply and directly, a space in which "mute eloquence" reigns.[111] Phrases of irregular lengths resemble the irregularities and anomalies of language at their origins. The pantomime, with its jarring syntax and musical ruptures, resembles the unknown language similar to the inscriptions on the ruins of Tchelminar discussed by Jean-Baptiste Siméon Chardin in 1735.[112] In *Essai sur l'origine des langues* Rousseau related pantomime to a form of nonverbal communication that was lost when Europeans began to gesticulate while speaking. His pantomime, then, offers a representation of the kind of communication at the pre-linguistic stage of civilization, in which signs such as hieroglyphs were communicated with directness and immediacy: "What the ancients said most vividly they expressed not by words, but by signs; they did not say it, they showed it." Rousseau noticed a remnant of this mode of communication in his time, observing that the Italians and inhabitants of Provence gestured before speaking: "The object, presented before speaking, stirs the imagination, arouses curiosity, [and] holds the mind in suspense and anticipation of what is going to be said."[113]

In practice, however, Rousseau knew that the meanings of musical-gestural units were perplexing to many spectators. What does a look mean? What does it mean to double a tone at an octave? To counter his mistrust in the intelligibility of these units, Rousseau designed a pantomime in *Le Devin du village* as part of a double exposure to corruption, presenting a first-hand experience of vice, followed by an abstracted

---

109 "Ce ballet si neuf, dont on prend la peine de dessiner un plan, est précisément ce que nous voyons tous les jours à nos théâtres, au point qu'en le lisant, je me suis trouvé compositeur moi-même, et que j'aurais pu dire comme le Corrège: (...) tant les idées qu'il a réveillées chez moi sont communes." Charles Palissot de Montenoy, in "Petites Lettres," *Œuvres complètes*, 6 vols. (Paris: Collin, 1809), 1:307–308. On intersubjectivity and common sense, see Sophia Rosenfeld, *Common Sense: A Political History* (Cambridge, MA: Harvard University Press, 2011), 23.

110 "Il a dû faire pleurer les spectateurs d'un goût commun, & rire les spectateurs d'un goût plus délié." *Encyclopédie*, vol. 8, s.v. "Intermède [Belles-Lettres/Musique]."

111 *CWR*, 7:291. On the notion of persuasion, see Bryan Garsten, *Saving Persuasion: A Defense of Rhetoric and Judgment* (Cambridge, MA: Harvard University Press, 2006), ch. 2.

112 *CWR*, 7:297–98.

113 *CWR*, 7:290.

and enriched re-enactment of it. This double exposure illustrates the importance of advanced cognitive operations for interpreting nonverbal signs. Bacon argued for this type of *re*-experience in his *Novem organon scientiarum* (1620), claiming that ideas are poorly formed unless they are formed again. Condillac restated Bacon's point in his *Essai*, and Rousseau provided an illustration of the same point in *Le Devin du village* by having the protagonists reflect upon the content of the pantomime in a chanson positioned after it. The musical-gestural units in the pantomime stimulate the cognitive operations of reflection and analysis precisely because their semantic meanings are ambiguous. This is the reason Condillac argued in *La Logique* (1780) that the *langage d'action* demands analysis: "He who listens with his eyes will not hear, if he does not break down this action in order to observe in it the movements one after another."[114]

Rousseau was ambivalent about the intelligibility of nonverbal signs; he found musical-gestural signs "persuasive," and language "convincing." This distinction is made in many Enlightenment writings. Batteux, in *Les Beaux-arts réduits à un même principe* (1746), ranked speech above voice and gesture in its capacity to express ideas: "Speech can instruct us and convince us; it is the vehicle of reason. But tone of voice and gesture are the vehicles of the heart. They move us, win us over, and persuade us."[115] Diderot expanded on Batteux's point in his *Lettre sur les sourds et muets* (1751): "French is designed to instruct, to enlighten, and to convince; Greek, Latin, Italian, and English to persuade, to move, and to deceive."[116] Rousseau also claimed to use the preface to *Narcisse* to convince, and not to persuade: "As long as I convince my adversaries, I care very little about persuading them."[117] He later speculated in his *Essai sur l'origine des langues* that the earliest form of language (what he calls the "first language") persuaded rather than convinced audiences: "Instead of arguments it would have aphorisms; it would persuade without convincing, and depict without reasoning."[118] Rousseau revisited this point in *Du Contract social* (1762), defending nonverbal signs not as undeveloped and uncivilized, but as reliable and canonical: "Since the Legislator is ... unable to use either force or reasoning, he must necessarily have recourse to another order of authority, which can win over without violence and persuade without convincing."[119]

---

114 "Celui qui écoute des yeux n'entendra pas, s'il ne décompose pas cette action, pour en observer l'un après l'autre les mouvements." Condillac, *La Logique, ou Les Premiers Développements de l'art de penser* (Paris: L'Esprit, 1780), 91.

115 Batteux, *The Fine Arts*, 129. On the differences between these two words, see Tracy B. Strong, "Music, the Passions, and Political Freedom in Rousseau," in McDonald and Hoffmann, eds, *Rousseau and Freedom*, 94–102.

116 "Le français est fait pour instruire, éclairer et convaincre; le grec, le latin, l'italien, l'anglais pour persuader, émouvoir et tromper." Diderot, *Œuvres*, 4:32.

117 *CWR*, 2:186.

118 *CWR*, 10:296.

119 *CWR*, 4:156.

UNITY OF LANGUAGE

In addition to making pantomime a persuasive medium by the Enlightenment standard, Rousseau theorized pantomime as an operatic component. This leads to my last point about the concept of "unity of language" in Rousseau's discussion of French opera.

Since Rousseau included both a dance entrée and *langage d'action* in his pantomime, his idea of pantomime includes an imitative type of dancing resembling communication at the origins of language. He made this point in the entry "pantomime" of his *Dictionnaire de musique*, which was reprinted word-for-word in the *Supplément à l'Encyclopédie* (1776–77). Unlike the entry "Opéra [1]," which includes materials published in printed sources such as Sébastien de Brossard's *Dictionnaire de musique* (1705) or Dubos's *Réflexions critiques*, Rousseau wrote this entry anew. Evidently, he had one example in mind: the pantomime in his *Le Devin du village*:

> Pantomime, s.f. A dance number in which two or more Dancers perform an Action while Dancing that also bears the name of Pantomime. The Airs of the Pantomimes typically consist of a main couplet that often returns during the course of the Piece, and which must be simple, for the reason discussed in the entry *Contre-danse*, but this couplet is interweaved with more salient ones, which speak – as it were – and make an image, in situations where the Dancer must make a definite expression.[120]

Rousseau implied in this entry the opposition of non-imitative and imitative types of dance, reframing Dubos's opposition of dance (non-imitative) and signs (imitative). In doing so, Rousseau indicated a shift in emphasis not simply from a genealogy of pantomime to an archaeology of communication, but also to the *hierarchy* of imitative arts in French operatic poetics. Although music, according to d'Alembert, is a borderline imitative art, dance is even less imitative. Writing in response to a proposed 1759 revival of *Le Devin du village* at the Opéra, Rousseau explained dance in *Julie* in terms of what he called the "unities of language" in opera, referring to the integration of such diverse theatrical mediums as sung or spoken text, acting, song, dance, costumes, and stage settings in a way analogous to a monolingual opera: "It would not be less out of place if it [dance, or the fourth of the fine arts] did imitate something; because of all the unities, none is more indispensable than that of language; and an Opera in which the action took place half in song and half in dance, would be even more ridiculous than one spoken half in French, half in Italian."[121] Rousseau did not address how one could add imitative elements

---

120 "Pantomime, *s.f.*: Air sur lequel deux ou plusieurs Danseurs exécutant en Danse une Action qui porte aussi le nom de Pantomime. Les Airs des Pantomimes ont pour l'ordinaire un couplet principal qui revient souvent dans le cours de la Pièce, et qui doit être simple, par la raison dite au mot *Contre-Danse*: mais ce couplet est entremêlé d'autres plus saillants, qui parlent, pour ainsi dire, et font image, dans les situations où le Danseur doit mettre une expression déterminée." *OC*, 5:968.

121 *CWR*, 6:235. On the dating of this letter, see *OC*, 2:1504–05. On this letter as a satirical account of French opera, see Jean-Jacques Eideldinger, "Pour une esthétique de l'art lyrique," in *OC*, 5:1711. On the aesthetic of imitation in French opera, see his article "Imitation [1]," *OC*, 5:860–61.

to non-imitative *la belle danse*, as Rameau did in *Pygmalion*; rather, he made a less subtle claim that *la belle danse* is fundamentally non-imitative, and that framing it in a dramatic context cannot alter this basic property.

Rousseau's framing of *la belle danse* and pantomime as imitative/non-imitative dances makes pantomime a *dance* of the Enlightenment by reconciling an archaeology of communication with a genealogy of pantomime. As indicated by the *Système figuré des connaissances humaines* of the *Encyclopédie*, pantomime can be *both* an operatic component and a means of communication, both philosophy and poetry, both reason and imagination. This cross-domain property alone does not cause problems when one treats them separately, but it causes problems when one uses the *criteria* of one domain to question the other, dismissing *la belle danse* as decorative according to the criterion of semantic clarity or, conversely, criticizing pantomime as an anti-dance using the criterion of *la belle danse*. Dubos did not realize that he conflated these two orders of inquiry; even Rousseau conflated them occasionally, calling the *opéra-ballet* "bizarre" in the entry "Ballet" of his *Dictionnaire de musique*: even the best dancers "do not know how to *tell* you anything else except that they dance well."[122] [emphasis mine] In this view, the decorative dance *became* a problem in the discourse on pantomime of the Enlightenment.

Diderot shared Rousseau's criticism of *la belle danse* as non-imitative in the *troisième entretien* of *Entretiens sur le fils naturel* (1757), asserting that *la belle danse* was still waiting for a genius, and that it was bad everywhere (*mauvaise partout*) because it was not a genre of imitation (*un genre d'imitation*):"I would very much like to be told the meaning of all these dances that follow an established path – such as the minuet, the passepied, the rigaudon, the allemande, the sarabande."[123] Coming from the communicative rather the operatic angle, Rousseau questioned the dramatic function of *la belle danse* in his *Julie*: "What are minuets, rigaudons, chaconnes in a tragedy?"[124]

How should one use dance in an opera? Rousseau addressed the problem of unity in the entry "Opéra [1]" of his *Dictionnaire de musique*. Music, poetry, and decoration form a unified whole (*un tout*). Anything that would suspend the dramatic action or distract the audience would reduce dramatic effect. *La belle danse*, charming as it can be, could become a "counter charm" in French opera when it undermines operatic unity. Rousseau argued against using the divertissements strictly as diversion, for it would leave audiences less moved at the end of the act than at the beginning of it. The Italians, he noted, stopped inserting comical *intermèdes* into *opera seria*, because the presence of these two genres would cause mutual harm. For the same reason, one should not suspend or interrupt a tragic action by dance steps such as *entrechats*, but one could perform a ballet after the opera, when festivity extends the opera without suspending any dramatic action while providing the spectators a brief moment

---

122　"Les meilleurs Danseurs ne savent vous dire autre chose sinon qu'ils dansent bien." *OC*, 5:649.

123　"Je voudrais bien qu'on me dît ce que signifient toutes ces danses, telles que le menuet, le passe-pied, le rigaudon, l'allemande, la sarabande, où l'on suit un chemin trace." Diderot, *Œuvres*, 4:1183.

124　*CWR*, 6:235.

of rest. This moment is one of inoperativity, which exemplifies what Agamben calls a "cerebral Sabbath."[125] Inasmuch as Rousseau made a case for pantomime in French opera, he came to the same conclusion that Rameau did in recognizing the aesthetic value of decorative dance.

Whereas Rousseau, like Rameau, recognized value in both non-imitative dance and imitative pantomime, he insisted on separating language and nonverbal signs in French opera. He asked, "How to allow at the same time two languages that are mutually exclusive, and connect the art of pantomime to speech that makes it super-fluous?"[126] Gesture, the primary means of communication for deaf-mutes, is sup-plemental for those who can speak. Since one does not usually reply to a spoken message by means of gestures, and vice versa, Rousseau thought that one should not use speech if one opts for pantomime. He clarified when and how to use language for pantomime in an opera: "So suppress speech if you want to use dance: as soon as you introduce pantomime into the opera, you must banish poetry from it."[127] On this note, we can revisit Rousseau's remarks about dancing in Letter No.23 of Part Two of *Julie*, as quoted above: "If the Prince is joyous, we share in his joy, and dance; if he is sad, we wish to cheer him up, and dance." It is now clear that this much-cited remark does not fully represent Rousseau's views on dance. As a matter of fact, Rousseau thought that ballet placed after the opera, like a little spectacle performed after tragedy, would offer an enjoyable closure. But his argument for this positioning of ballet also made him reject the genre of ballet-pantomime: "To begin with some *ballets en action*, without having previously established the convention of gestures, is to speak a language to people who do not have a dictionary, and who, consequently, will not understand it."[128] In the case of *Le Devin du village*, the placement of the pantomime *after* the main action of the *intermède*, and *before* the chanson, provides an *optimal* condition, Condillac might say, for spectators to analyze musical and gestural signs in the pantomime. This location entails a dramatic context (i.e., the "dictionary" in Rousseau's formulation) that allows spectators to gather simple ideas before generating complex ones.

I explain in this chapter how Rousseau's pantomime in *Le Devin du village* differs in kind from Rameau's pantomimes, but both justify the co-existence of *la belle danse* and pantomime in French opera. Unlike Rameau, who made little attempt to have musical-gestural units resemble a verbal narrative, Rousseau organized musical-gestural units into signs so that spectators could follow the resulting pantomime

125 *OC*, 5:959–62. On the cerebral Sabbath, see Giorgio Agamben, *Homo Sacer: Sovereign Power and Bare Life*, trans. Daniel Heller-Roazen (Stanford, CA: Stanford University Press, 1998), 62.

126 "Comment admettre à la fois deux langages qui s'excluent mutuellement, et joindre l'Art Pantomime à la parole qui le rend superflu?" *OC*, 5:960–61.

127 "Supprimez donc la parole si vous voulez employer la Danse: sitôt que vous introduisez la Pantomime dans l'Opéra, vous en devez bannir la Poésie." *OC*, 5:961.

128 "Commencer par donner des Ballets en action, sans avoir préalablement établi la convention des gestes, c'est parler une Langue à gens qui n'en ont pas le Dictionnaire, et qui, par conséquent, ne l'entendront point." *OC*, 5:961–62.

as continuously as if it were a narrative. His pantomime provides a narrative abyss that enables the protagonists to become alienated from their viewing experience, seeing a dilemma anew in a nonverbal theatrical medium in order to reflect upon the perils of corruption. Through the subsequent cognitive processes of reflection, imagination, and sharing of their reflections, spectators may develop morality for themselves, like the self-awakening experienced by Valère and Colin. Rousseau's pantomime, therefore, exemplifies a useful type of art analogous to soothsaying and the painting of a cross-dresser in his play *Narcisse*.

How does Rousseau's pantomime relate to the topic of liberty? Surprisingly, Rousseau kept these two topics separate in his writings. Nowhere did he make a direct connection between them: He asked spectators to develop liberty on their own by reflecting on a supposedly moralizing pantomime. He relinquished any control of the spectators' responses, but he offered a *possibility* of moral improvement through the process of identification with his onstage characters. On this note, we can revisit the claim of Rousseau's anti-theatrical stance. Was he really as anti-theatrical as *Lettre à d'Alembert* suggests? Two quotes that follow help to answer this question: In the final scene of *Le Devin du village*, the chorus sings its praises to the Soothsayer, who has made the theater useful: "Let's sing the dazzling power / Of the Soothsayer of our Village / He brings back a fickle lover / And makes him happy and constant."[129] If these verses are evidence of Rousseau's pro-theatrical stance, then he drastically revised this position in *Lettre à d'Alembert*, where he criticized the theater – in this second quote – as useless: "The moral effect of the theater can never be good or salutary *in itself*, since, in reckoning only its advantages, we find no kind of real utility without drawbacks which outweigh it."[130] How to reconcile these two positions? My answer is that they do not contradict each other because the first quote praises a carefully thought-out way of using the theater, and the second objects to a blanket proposition about the utility of theater. The seeming contradiction highlights the point of a *possibility* of moral improvement at the theater. Rousseau added, "Now, as a consequence of its very lack of utility, the theater, which can do nothing to improve morals, can do much toward changing them."[131] Whether or not the theater was useless depended upon what the *spectators* took as signs. For this reason, seeing something we can identify with onstage, without being told what to look for, turning audio-visual signals into signs, using our imagination to connect them, shaping them into a story, comparing and contrasting similar ideas, turning simple ideas into complex ones, sharing reflections about them with fellow spectators, and accepting divergent interpretations as the inevitable and desirable outcome of alienated spectatorship *may* allow us to free ourselves from whatever evil spells that enslave us.

129 *CWR*, 10:225.
130 *CWR*, 10:292.
131 *CWR*, 10:292.

CHAPTER THREE

Things that Move

I N a 1999 production of Christoph Willibald Gluck's French version of *Alceste* (1776), conductor Sir John Eliot Gardiner and theater director Robert Wilson offered an intriguing interpretation of Act 1 Scene 3: Although Gluck explicitly asked the priests and priestesses to perform a "pantomime" in this scene, nobody appeared onstage in Wilson's production; instead, Wilson sent a gigantic cube slowly spinning down onto the empty stage.[1] Though solemn, refined, and breathtakingly beautiful, this scene prompts me to raise a question: What does it mean when the body is removed, or displaced by an object, in a pantomime?[2]

Wilson's interpretation is disconcerting because it eliminates the body that is *supposed* to be onstage; it is not simply an issue of performance practice, for the body played an essential role in the relationship between acting and liberty in the Enlightenment. In the article "Pantomime," in the *Supplément à l'Encyclopédie* (1776–77), Marmontel distinguished two types of actors: he criticized one as the "copyist of the poet," while praising the pantomime actor: "Between the action of the actor and that of the pantomime there must be the difference between slavery and liberty."[3] By correlating an actor with enslavement and a pantomime with liberty, Marmontel made clear that a live performer was an important means through which audience members grasped the idea of liberty.

What makes Marmontel's thesis particularly relevant to the Enlightenment is not just that he published it in the supplement of the *Encyclopédie*, the greatest intellectual achievement of the Enlightenment, but also that he was a frequent participant in social gatherings hosted by Paul-Henri-Dietrich Thiry, baron d'Holbach, whose salon provided an intellectual hub of Enlightenment in Paris from around 1750 to 1780.[4] Writers who frequented that space published a range of thoughts about liberty. D'Holbach's protégé, Naigeon, attributed as the co-author of the article

---

1   Christoph Willibald Gluck, *Alceste* (Halle: Arthaus Musik, 2000), DVD. The stage direction in the score reads: "Temple d'Apollon avec la Statue de ce Dieu, grand Prêtres et Prêtresses, Peuple qui entre successivement." The word "pantomime" is printed in the first measure in the score. Gluck, *Alceste* (Paris: Au Bureau abonnement musical, 1776), 43.

2   On staging and opera, see David Levin, *Unsettling Opera: Staging Mozart, Verdi, Wagner, and Zemlinsky* (Chicago: The University of Chicago Press, 2007), 1–36; on bodily eloquence, see Angelica Goodden, *Actio and Persuasion: Dramatic Performance in Eighteenth-Century France* (Oxford: Clarendon, 1986).

3   "Il doit donc y avoir entre l'action du comédien & celle du pantomime la différence de l'esclavage à la liberté." Marmontel, *Supplément à l'Encyclopédie*, vol. 4, s.v. "Pantomime."

4   On Marmontel's participation in d'Holbach's salon, see Alan Charles Kors, *D'Holbach's Coterie: An Enlightenment in Paris* (Princeton, NJ: Princeton University Press, 1976), 19–21.

"Liberty (Moral)" of the *Encyclopédie* (1765), proclaimed that "We are the masters of our homes, not as God is in the world, but as a wise prince is in his states, or a good father of the family is in his household."[5] By sharp contrast, d'Holbach himself denied, in *Système de la nature* (1770), that human beings are free: "Man is *not* free at any instant of his life. He is not master of his build that he takes from nature. He is not master of his ideas or changes of his brain due to causes that, despite himself and without his knowledge, are acting continuously upon him."[6] [emphasis mine]

In this chapter I use these conflicting views as a framework to understand facets of liberty in the pantomimes that Gluck used in his French operas.[7] Not all of these pantomimes in his French operas were dances – some were sections of a natural-istic style of acting. The first half of this chapter discusses pantomime as a type of dance in *Orphée et Euridice* (1774), *Alceste* (1776), and *Iphigénie en Tauride* (1779). The discussion leads into the second half of the chapter, on pantomime as a style of acting, and I will illustrate it with an example in *Armide* (1777). Placing these pan-tomimes in the context of the Enlightenment, I make two points. The first point is about aesthetics and signification. The eighteenth century was a transitional period in the history of aesthetics, moving away from the mimetic paradigm (art in rela-tion to external nature) towards the romantic paradigm of expression (art in rela-tion to the artist), and this transition illustrated Dubos's idea of the Enlightenment (see Chapter One).[8] What Dubos did not anticipate, however, is that *music* – and not just lyrics – played an important role in this aesthetic change. Instead of using music to copy things in exterior nature (e.g., birdsong) or to arouse in the audience the same passion one would experience in nature (e.g., a horrifying storm), Gluck imparted "accessory ideas" in his music by using multiple referents for one sign, be it a word or an object or an idea. This brings me to my second point, about signifi-cation and liberty. By using pantomimes in his French operas, Gluck wrote musical "signs" that had multiple meanings. To understand these meanings, according to the Enlightenment writings on liberty, was to ask audiences to exercise their "liberty to think" (*la liberté de penser*).[9]

5   "Nous sommes les maîtres chez nous, non pas comme Dieu l'est dans le monde, mais comme un prince sage l'est dans ses états, ou un bon père de famille l'est dans son domestique." Naigeon and Yvon [attributed], *Encyclopédie*, vol. 9, s.v. "Liberté [Morale)."

6   "L'homme n'est point libre dans aucun des instants de sa durée. Il n'est pas maître de sa conformation qu'il tient de la nature; il n'est pas maître de ses idées ou des modifications de son cerveau qui sont dues à des causes qui malgré lui et à son insu agissent continuellement sur lui." D'Holbach, *Système de la nature*, 2 vols. (Paris: Fayard, 1990), 1:243.

7   On Gluck in Paris, see Daniel Heartz, *Music in European Capitals: The Galant Style, 1720–1780* (New York: Norton, 2003), 801–881; Gerhard Croll and Renate Croll, *Gluck: Sein Leben. Seine Musik* (Kassel: Bärenreiter, 2014), 171–245.

8   On imitation and expression in French music, see Marian Hobson, *The Object of Art: The Theory of Illusion in Eighteenth-Century France* (New York: Cambridge University Press, 1982), part V; Béatrice Didier, *La Musique des lumières* (Paris: Presses Universitaires de France, 1985), 19–40; Thomas, *Music*, 143–72; Verba, *Music the French Enlightenment*, 34–55.

9   On Gluck's music and the aesthetic of imitation, see Thomas, *Aesthetics of Opera*, ch. 9; David Charlton, "Storms, Sacrifices: The 'Melodrama Model' in Opera," in David

THE INDISPENSABLE PANTOMIME

By the time Rousseau published his *Dictionnaire de musique*, which consists of his entry on "Pantomime," many ballet-pantomimes had been performed in Paris, and many had failed. Marmontel observed in his *Poétique française* (1763) that "we have a thousand examples of fêtes [that are] ingeniously staged at the theater, but we also have a thousand of them that are ill placed."[10] In this context, Gluck came to France in 1774 after having produced in Vienna, among other works, three Italian reform operas – *Orfeo ed Euridice* (1762), *Alceste* (1767), and *Paride ed Elena* (1770) – and the ballet-pantomimes *Le Festin de pierre, ou Don Juan* (1761), *Citera assediata* (1762), *Les Amours d'Alexandre et de Roxane* (1764), *Sémiramis* (1765), and *Achille in Sciro* (1765). Gluck did not use pantomime in his first French opera, *Iphigénie en Aulide* (premiered on April 19, 1774), but he used one in his second opera for Paris, *Orphée et Euridice* (premiered on August 2, 1774), which was a revision of the Italian *Orfeo ed Euridice*. As Bruce Alan Brown demonstrates, the Italian version was already influenced by works performed at the French theater in Vienna, and it already realized what Daniel Heartz calls the "total" theater. In the French version of *Orfeo ed Euridice*, Gluck streamlined the Italian opera further by logically connecting the pantomimes to the plot.[11]

One of the major features in *Orphée et Euridice* is its rich economy of sensuous stimuli, for Gluck emphasized the body by correlating the sense of sight with that of hearing. For *Orphée et Euridice*, Gluck and his librettist, Pierre-Louis Moline, pledged to stay close to the Italian *Orfeo ed Euridice* (1762) but made revealing modifications nonetheless.[12] In the Italian version, the opening scene focuses on audiences' aural experience. The opening chorus asks Euridice's spirit to "listen" to her unhappy husband (*ed ascolta il tuo sposo infelice*), who "calls" her and "grumbles" while weeping (*che piangendo ti chiama, e si lagna*). Later in the same scene, Orfeo sings in a recitative that "Euridice resounds in every valley" (*In ogni valle Euridice risuona*) and states that it is the stream that "answers" his cries by "whispering" (*Pietoso al pianto mi ova mormorando il rio, e mi risponde*). By stressing the sense of hearing in the opening scenes, Gluck and the librettist Calzabigi reserved the sense of sight for Orfeo's fateful look at Euridice in the Underworld, even though Calzabigi had warned in 1767 against the abuse of visual stimuli (e.g., using real horses in painted forests) and of

---

Charlton, ed., *French Opera, 1730–1830: Meaning and Media* (Ashgate, Aldershot: 2000), X:1–61. On principle and accessory ideas, see Aarsleff, "Philosophy of Language," 455–56.

10 "Nous avons sur le théâtre mille exemples de fêtes ingénieusement amenées; mais nous en avons mille aussi de fêtes placées mal-à-propos." Marmontel, *Poétique française* (Paris: Lesclapart, 1763), 355. [ARTFL]

11 On Italian reform opera, see Daniel Heartz, *Haydn, Mozart, and the Viennese School* (New York: Norton, 1995), 143–234. On the ballet-pantomime in Vienna, see Bruce Alan Brown, *Gluck and the French Theatre in Vienna* (Oxford: Clarendon, 1991), 143–93, 282–357, 358–81. On the ballet-pantomime in Europe, see Arianna Beatrice Fabbricatore, *La Querelle des Pantomimes: Danse, culture et société dans l'Europe des Lumières* (Rennes: Presses universitaires de Rennes, 2017).

12 "On a suivi aussi littéralement qu'il était possible l'original dans la traduction." *Orphée et Euridice* (Paris: Delormel, 1774), 4.

hearing (e.g., performing concertos with the voice).[13] Gluck drew specific attention in *Orphée et Euridice* to these two senses. The opening chorus asks Euridice's ghost if she "hears" their lamentation at all (*Euridice! Si ton ombre nous entend*), and asks her to "see" their suffering and "see" their tears (*vois nos pleines, vois les larmes*). By explicitly addressing the sense of sight, Gluck enriched the economy of sensuous stimuli in *Orphée et Euridice* by making it more visually stimulating than *Orfeo ed Euridice*.[14]

To stimulate these two senses, Gluck narrated the pantomime (what he called "*ballo*" in the Italian version) with music and gesture. The dance scenario of this *ballo* reads:

> This ballet represents the funeral rites that the ancients celebrated around the tombs of the dead. These consisted of sacrifices, censing, strewing flowers and wreathing the tomb with them, in pouring midland wine on it and dancing around it with acts of grief, and in singing the praises of the departed one. In the most solemn of [these rites] youths dressed as genii were introduced, and given attributes and actions suited to the character and station of the person entombed: Thus in this ballet around the tomb of Euridice there weep genii representing cupids, one of whom, in the guise of Hymen, extinguishes his torch as a symbol of the conjugal union being broken by death.[15]

This extensive description indicates a variety of bodily movements – strewing flowers, pouring wine, singing, dancing, weeping, a cupid extinguishing his torch, and so on – but Gluck did not organize them into discernible semantic units or align them with musical segments as Rousseau did in *Le Devin du village*.

What he did do, in addition to retitling the *ballo* a "pantomime," was to streamline the opening scene on a structural level. He divided the recitative of the Italian version into two parts. In the first recitative, Orphée asks the dancers to cover Euridice's tomb with flowers, which leads to a pantomime where dancers act out his command. In the second recitative, Orphée asks the dancers to leave him alone, which leads to a shortened repetition (*ritournelle*) of the same pantomime, during which dancers exit the stage. Whereas the Italian *ballo* presents a medley of prosaic activities, each of the two French pantomimes displays gestures that are clearly mentioned in the preceding recitative. In other words, Gluck used a recitative to introduce a pantomime, projecting semantic meanings mentioned in the recitative onto the pantomime. Using two recitative-pantomime pairs instead of one *ballo*, Gluck integrated the pantomimes into the plot more tightly than he did in the Italian version. This

---

13   Patricia Howard, *Gluck: An Eighteenth-Century Portrait in Letters and Documents* (Oxford: Clarendon, 1995), 79.

14   On ocularcentrism, see Martin Jay, *Downcast Eyes: The Denigration of Vision in Twentieth-Century French Thought* (Berkeley, CA: University of California Press, 1993), 83–108. On synesthesia in music discourse, see Mark Darlow, "*Nihil per saltum*: Chiaroscuro in Eighteenth-Century Lyric Theatre," in Sarah Hibberd and Richard Wrigley, eds, *Art, Theatre, and Opera in Paris, 1750–1850: Exchanges and Tensions* (Farnham: Ashgate, 2014), 37–52. Note that Condillac did not discuss the combination of seeing and hearing in his *Traité des sensations* (1754).

15   Translation taken from Brown, *Gluck*, 367.

technique of recitative-pantomime pairing builds a stronger dramatic trajectory, enabling spectators to follow the content of pantomime more easily during the performance, without needing to refer to the libretto.[16]

On the motivic level, Gluck used a motif of sighing to correlate the vocal numbers and the pantomimes. This motif first appears as an appoggiatura, C–B-natural, in m. 2 of the introduction to the C-minor opening chorus, and the appoggiatura develops into a neighbor-note motif, G–A-flat–G, in mm.3–4. This motif creates dramatic meanings when the chorus laments Euridice's unexpected death. A vocal ensemble links the neighbor-note version of the sigh motif to the sighing, moaning, and lamenting Orphée (*Il soupire, il gémit, il plaint sa destinée*) (m.42, Example 3.1). The motif operates on three concurrent layers. In the first layer, the soprano solo in m.42 hovers chromatically around G, oscillating between its upper neighbor, A-flat, and its lower neighbor, F-sharp. In the second layer, the altos and tenors sing in parallel thirds in note value double that of the soprano solo, moving chromatically upwards from D and B-natural to E-flat and C, before returning to D and B-natural. In the third layer, Orphée utters nothing but Euridice's name, singing an appoggiatura E-flat to D in mm.44–45 and the neighbor-note motif G–A-flat–G in m.45. These three layers correlate a musical sigh with the sighing Orphée, and with Euridice's name; they relate, through music, Orphée's sorrow at Euridice's death. Importantly, Gluck constructed a dense motivic web based on this sigh motif in the pantomime, making the opening measures of the opera the motivic source, like a musical gene, that coheres the entire opening scene. With this economical design, he came up with a new compositional solution, distinct from Rousseau's, that could project semantic and affective meanings onto the pantomimes without *needing* to align every gesture performed by dancers with a corresponding musical segment.

A motivic web built upon a gesture (a sigh), a word (the name of Euridice), and a musical topos (lament) illustrate how Gluck's music *embodies* grief. Since the sung numbers condition spectators' perception of the pantomimes, Gluck provided a context for his spectators to feel the sorrow. Friedrich Melchior Grimm responded to Gluck's deliberate effort; he found himself affected by "the dolorous and piercing cries with which Orphée interrupts, in a manner so true and with such pathos, the sensitive and sweet song of the nymphs who are crying over Euridice's tomb."[17] A correspondent for the *Journal des beaux-arts* made a similar observation: "Gluck has tied ballets to the [dramatic] action of this opera very well. They are an essential part of the opera, as in [Rameau's] *Castor*, and much better than [those] in *Iphigénie* [*en Aulide*]."[18] It is not remarkable that Gluck made ballets and pantomime dances part of the dramatic fabric of French operas; what is remarkable is that Gluck

16 On Gluck's revision of *Orfeo ed Euridice*, see Alessandra Martina, *Orfeo/Orphée: Storia della trasmissione e della recezione* (Turin: De Sono, 1995); on the functions of these synopses, see Fabbricatore, *La Querelle des Pantomimes*, 145–214.

17 "Les cris douloureux et pénétrants par lesquels Orphée interrompt d'une manière si vraie et si pathétique le chant sensible et doux des nymphes qui pleurent sur le tombe d'Eurydice." Grimm, *Correspondance littéraire*, 10:472.

18 "M. Gluck a très bien lié dans cet Opéra les Ballets à l'action, ils en font une partie essentielle comme dans *Castor*, & beaucoup mieux que dans *Iphigénie*." *Journal des beaux-arts et des sciences* (September 1774), 546. On the uses of dance in French opera,

Example 3.1. *Gluck, Orphée et Euridice*, Act 1 Scene 1, "Ah! dans ce bois," mm.39–45

tightened their connection within the *vocal* context of the opera – not just on the structural level as in Lully's operas, but on the motivic level – by employing music, text, and gesture to confer affective and semantic meanings to the pantomime dances. In doing so, Gluck not only provided another example of expressive theatrical dance of the Enlightenment – he also illustrated how music can embody sorrow in a clearly defined and perceptible manner.[19]

---

see Catherine Kintzler, "La Danse, modèle d'intelligibilité dans l'opéra français de l'âge classique," *Ateliers* 11 (1997), 72–73.

19   On using theatrical dances in the vocal context of French opera, see Harris-Warrick, *Dance and Drama*, ch. 2.

Example 3.1. continued

What made Gluck's pantomime dances in *Orphée et Euridice* "essential" to the opera is that Gluck integrated them seamlessly into the plot. The musical-gestural-textual correlations created a logic of cause and effect, making the pantomimes follow the principle of causality and seem logical. This compositional logic was qualified as "natural" in writings of the Enlightenment. As d'Holbach argued in *Système de la nature*, "In nature where everything is related, no effect exists without cause, and in the physical world as well as the moral world, everything that has happened is a necessary series of visible or hidden causes that are forced to behave according to their own essence."[20]

A COMPOSER'S VISIONS

As a composer, Gluck was known in his time for his unusual care for visual effects in his operas. According to Noverre, who choreographed dances for several of Gluck's operas in Vienna and Paris, Gluck complained about the chorus during a rehearsal of the Italian *Alceste*. He sang; he made gestures; he threw his wig onto the floor, but the chorus acted like they were inanimate statues: "The statues have ears and do not hear at all; [they have] eyes and see nothing."[21] Gluck also paid attention to the dramatic effects of theatrical dances. In 1779 Étienne-Nicolas Méhul saw Gluck at work, composing, probably a dance for *Echo et Narcisse* (1779), in which a nymph figures prominently. Instead of turning over his dances to the choreographer Noverre, Gluck himself made *révérence*, trying out dance steps like *glissades*, *tricotets*, and *entrechats*, and mimed the delicate looks of a female nymph. Evidently, Gluck did not write off dance steps as devoid of dramatic meaning, as Dubos had suggested, but tried to put theatrical dances to dramatic uses.[22] Similarly, the editor of the *Journal de musique* Olivier de Corancez recalled in 1788 that Gluck always pictured himself in the middle of the parterre, imagining audio-visual effects of an opera: "Once his opera was assembled in this way, and its individual numbers characterized, he considered his work completed, even though he had not yet composed anything."[23]

It is important to understand how Gluck's acute visual sensibility informed his compositional choices, as this audio-visual thinking helps explain why he added the stage props of the lyre and the helmet to the opening scene of *Orphée et Euridice*. These props are hung on the tree at the beginning of the opera.[24] Few spectators

---

20 "Dans une nature où tout est lié il n'existe point d'effet sans cause; et dans le monde physique ainsi que dans le monde moral, tout ce qui est arrivé est une suite nécessaire de causes visibles ou cachées, qui sont forcées d'agir d'après leurs propres essences." D'Holbach, *Système de la nature*, 1:246.

21 "Les statues ont des oreilles et n'entendent point; des yeux et ne voient rien." Noverre, *Lettres sur la danse, sur les ballets et les arts*, 4 vols. (St Petersburg: Jean Charles Schnoor, 1803), 2:160. On staging the chorus, see Daniela Philippi, "'Gluck les distribua derrière les coulisses:' Zum Einsatz der Chöre in Glucks *Alceste*," in Ursula Kramer and Wolfgang Birtel, eds, *Chöre und chorisches Singen* (Mainz: Are, 2009), 139–53. On Gluck's visual emphasis and its implications on staging, see Thomas Betzwieser, "*Le chœur et son double*. Glucks Konzept der szenischen Chor-Bewegung und seine Umsetzung auf der aktuellen Opernbühne," in Nicola Gess, ed., *Barocktheater Heute* (Bielefeld: Transcript Verlag, 2008), 49–61.

22 Gustave Denoiresterres, *Gluck et Piccinni: 1774-1800*, 2nd edn (Paris: Didier, 1875), 261.

23 "[S]a Pièce ainsi combinée & ses morceaux caractérisés, il regardait son Ouvrage comme fini, quoiqu'il n'eût encore rien écrit." *Journal de musique* 237 (August 24, 1788), 1022–23; translation adapted from Howard, *Gluck*, 249.

24 The stage direction reads: "Orphée est assis sur un coté du théâtre, contre un arbre, où il a suspendu son casque & sa lyre; entièrement livré à sa douleur, il ne fait que répéter à

would notice them until Amour draws attention to the lyre in Act 1 Scene 3, reminding Orphée that he is a singer, after all: "If the sweet harmonies of your lyre, / if your melodious accents / sooth the fury of the tyrants of these places, / you will bring her back from the dark empire."[25] Gluck revised the following episode substantially. Whereas Orfeo sings a recitative in which he complains about being forbidden to look at Euridice in the Underworld, Orphée thanks the gods for a chance to rescue Euridice. He picks up his lyre and the helmet and then sings the virtuosic Italianate ariette "L'espoir renaît dans mon âme," which Gluck had used in his serenata *Il Parnasso confuso* (Vienna, 1765) and his *Atto d'Aristeo* (Parma, 1759). Symbolizing Orpheus's musical and martial capacities, these two stage props empower Orphée to embark on his rescue.

The ariette "L'espoir renaît dans mon âme" consists of vocally demanding passages, but the problem is that Gluck was not expected to flaunt vocal virtuosity by the time he composed *Orphée et Euridice*. The addition of this ariette to *Orphée et Euridice* reversed the aesthetic principle of simple, direct, and natural music of Italian opera reform that Gluck had mastered. As mentioned above, Calzabigi had voiced his opposition to the abuse of superfluous ornaments, and he restated this objection in a 1767 letter to the imperial chancellor, Prince Wenzel Anton Kaunitz: "It is ridiculous to hear [a singer] prolong the word '*amore*,' for instance, with a hundred notes when nature has limited it to three, given that, in my opinion, one note must never be worth more than one syllable."[26] His view was known in France, for his preface to the Italian version of *Alceste* (1769) was translated by François-Louis Gand Le Bland Du Roullet, librettist of the French *Alceste*, and was published in *Gazette de littérature* in 1774. Calzabigi's anti-virtuosic stance was shared by his contemporaries, including Francesco Algarotti, but Gluck saw no point in carrying forth this reform principle from Italian opera to French opera.[27] By contrast, Gluck reintroduced vocal virtuosity to *Orphée et Euridice*, but he did so not just to show off a singer's vocal prowess for its own sake, as in the case of Italian opera, but for dramatic reasons. At this instance, vocal virtuosity is necessary because the grief-stricken Orphée, who could not utter anything other than Euridice's name, needs to rediscover his lyrical voice – and to reconstruct his identity as a singer – before he can embark on a rescue mission in the Underworld. After all, according to Ovid's *Metamorphoses*, it was Orpheus's singing that summoned Hymen to Thrace in the first place. Through singing with gusto in this ariette, Orphée develops self-affection, and experiences a

---

tout moment le nom d'Euridice." *Orphée et Euridice*, 9.

25　According to the livret, "Si les doux accords de ta lyre; / Si tes accents mélodieux / apaisent la fureur des tirants de ces lieux: / Tu la ramèneras du ténébreux empire." *Orphée et Euridice*, 14.

26　"Il est ridicule d'entendre prolonger le mot '*amore*' (par exemple) sur cent notes alors que la nature l'a limité à trois, vu que selon moi une note ne doit jamais valoir avantage qu'une syllabe." Calzabigi, "Lettre au chancelier Kaunitz, Vienne, le 6 mars 1767," ed. Michel Noiray, *L'Avant-Scène Opéra* 256 (2010), 76.

27　Francesco Algarotti, *Essai sur l'Opéra, traduit de l'italien du comte Algarotti* (Paris: Ruault, 1773), 36–37.

re-becoming of the legendary Orpheus, the singer. To Gluck's mind, Orphée finds himself again *through* singing vocally demanding passages.²⁸

Gluck designed the process of re-becoming by employing what Bill Brown calls the "misuse value" of the lyre. The lyre, which symbolizes musicality, is a useless object when no one plays it, obviously, but when Orphée holds it during the ariette, he *misuses* it. In this instance, however, misusing justifies in turn the coloratura passages sung by Orphée that highlight the words *flamme* (passion) and *revoir* (see again). In this ariette, the grieving Orphée is *re*-embodied, as J. Q. Davies might say, by his own virtuosic singing.²⁹ As the only virtuosic aria in this opera, this ariette empowers Orphée as much as the spectators. Martha Feldman analyzes the da capo aria in terms of a rhetorical exchange between the singer and the audiences, and this type of exchange was understood by Cahusac as a circulation of enthusiasm between the performers and the audiences: "It is enthusiasm that makes one feel: it augments by degree. It passes from the soul of the actors to that of the spectators, and note that as the spectators are aroused, the performance of the actors becomes more animated. Their mutual fire is like a tennis ball that the lively and rapid skill of the performers sends back and forth."³⁰ Indeed, the critic of *Mercure de France* wrote that the ariette "cannot be more brilliant, better arranged, more contrasted, and more appropriate for bringing out the talent of the singer and a superb voice such as Le Gros's."³¹ By the end of the aria, Orphée the singer has re-emerged from his stupefied state, re-empowered by his voice, and is ready to rescue Euridice in the Underworld. By misusing the lyre and using vocal virtuosity as a means of empowerment, Gluck revised the anti-virtuosic aesthetic: Display of instrumental or vocal virtuosity might be minimized, but there was no reason to eliminate virtuosity altogether; rather, virtuosity should be deployed at dramatic moments that demand a forceful voice.

28   Ovid, *Metamorphoses* 10.4. On self-affection, see Jacques Derrida, *Voice and Phenomenon: Introduction to the Problem of the Sign in Husserl's Phenomenology*, trans. Leonard Lawlor (Evanston, IL: Northwestern University Press, 2011), 68.

29   On the misuse of things, see Bill Brown, *Other Things* (Chicago: The University of Chicago Press, 2015), 21–22, 51. On re-embodiment, see James Q. Davies, *Romantic Anatomies of Performance* (Berkeley, CA: University of California Press, 2014), 8.

30   "C'est l'*enthousiasme* qui se fait sentir, il augmente par degrés, il passe de l'âme des acteurs dans celle des spectateurs; & remarquez qu'à mesure que ceux-ci s'échauffent, le jeu des premiers devient plus animé; leur feu mutuel est comme une balle de paume que l'adresse vive & rapide des joueurs se renvoie." Cahusac, *Encyclopédie*, vol. 5, s.v. "Enthousiasme [Philosophie/Belles-Lettres]." On aria and exchange, see Martha Feldman, *Opera and Sovereignty: Transforming Myths in Eighteenth-Century Italy* (Chicago: The University of Chicago Press, 2007), 42–96.

31   "L'air de la fin du premier acte, *l'espoir renaît dans mon âme*, ne peut être plus brillant, mieux ordonné, mieux contrasté & plus propre à faire ressortir le talent d'un habile chanteur & d'une voix superbe, tel que M. le Gros." *Mercure de France* (September 1774), 195.

DENATURING PLEASURES

After *Orphée et Euridice*, Gluck's French *Alceste* (1776), a revision of the Italian *Alceste* (1767), demonstrates another attempt to make pantomime necessary to a French opera, but this time the pantomime dance was considered a threat to operatic pleasures.

When he reworked the Italian *Alceste* for the French version, Gluck once again paid attention to dances and pantomimes. In the Italian version of *Alceste*, Noverre had choreographed three pantomimes, one in each act, in addition to four regular ballets. In the French version, Gluck retained the pantomimes – *les danses sacrées*, what he called in score "pantomime" and a "pantomime for the sacrifice" (*pantomime pour le sacrifice*) – for Act 1 and eliminated the first two scenes from Act 2. Gluck added a joyous divertissement (consisting of a *passacaile*, an andante, an allegro, and a slow dance marked *lent*) that celebrates the improved health of King Admète. For the concluding divertissement of Act 3, he wrote three of the six dances (a march, an andante, and a chaconne), and used the other three by François-Joseph Gosse, or Gossec (another andante, a menuet, and a gavotte).[32] Although he included the final divertissement, he considered it peripheral to the opera. Echoing Rousseau, Gluck claimed that the dances made *Alceste* "neither better nor worse, because it [the divertissement] comes at the end of it."[33]

Despite Gluck's deliberate effort to incorporate pantomimes and dances into the French *Alceste*, the Parisian critics found the dances unsatisfactory. On the day after the premiere on April 23, 1776 Louis Petit de Bachaumont wrote that the opera was brilliant, but the ballets were "miserable," for there were no "airs de violin" and "nothing cheerful." Another critic, François Arnaud, said that Gluck's *Alceste* would mortify spectators' tastes and pleasures.[34] He made a Dubosian remark that dance steps on their own did not express passions or impart semantic ideas:

> Would you not want the priests [and] priestesses to come adore and pray while beating out *entrechats*? Do not all these movements, perfectly in accordance with those of the orchestra, depict what they must depict? Do they not express what they must express? Now, Monsieur, be so kind as to say to me which passions or ideas the *cabrioles*, the *entrechats*, the *gargouillades* and the *moulinets* awaken in you.[35]

---

32 On Act 3 of *Alceste*, see Gluck's letter to Du Roullet dated July 1, 1775, in Howard, *Gluck*, 65–66. On the final chaconne in *Alceste*, see Gerhard Croll, "'Apollo non in macchina.' Zur Scena ultima der Wiener *Alceste*," in Brandenburg and Hochreiter, eds, *Gluck auf dem Theater*, 60.

33 Letter to Kruthoffer dated June 30, 1776, in Howard, *Gluck*, 158.

34 Louis Petit de Bachaumont, *Mémoires secrets pour servir à l'histoire de la république des lettres en France*, 36 vols. (London: Adamsohn, 1777–89), 9:97; Arnaud, "Le souper des enthousiastes," repr. in François Lesure, *Querelle des gluckistes et piccinnistes*, 2 vols. (Geneva: Minkoff, 1984), 1:63. On this quarrel, see Darlow, *Dissonance*, 52–61.

35 "Ne voudriez-vous pas que des Prêtres, des Prêtresses vinssent adorer & prier en battant des entrechats? Tous ces mouvements, parfaitement d'accord avec ceux de l'Orchestre, ne peignent-ils pas ce qu'ils doivent peindre, n'expriment-ils pas ce qu'ils doivent exprimer? Or, Monsieur, auriez-vous la bonté de me dire, quelles sont les passions

In Gluck's defense, Du Roullet made a distinction between dance and panto-mime in *Lettre sur les drames-opéra* (1776). Taking the first act of Lully's *Atys* as an example, Du Roullet reasoned that it would be absurd to have the people perform a dance for the goddess Cybelle. He proposed having them admire her in a fête pan-tomime. Du Roullet criticized the inflexibility of Quinault's convention of inserting dance into every act of a *tragédie en musique* and regretted that French librettists "have almost totally neglected pantomime." This remark was unfair to Lully. As Harris-Warrick shows, Lully had repeatedly incorporated a pantomimic element in his theatrical dances. A handful of his pantomimic dances (though the designation of "pantomime" was not employed), Dubos argued, provided early examples for the pantomime dances in the Enlightenment. Still, eliciting "the laws of reason and of good sense," Du Roullet criticized the French for overusing the dramatically unnec-essary though conventional dances, and for ignoring Gluck's dramatically necessary though unconventional pantomimes.[36]

In response to Du Roullet's criticisms, Secretary of the Opéra Nicolas Le Bourguignon de La Salle countered by explaining the practical challenges of employing the art of pantomime at the Opéra. He acknowledged Du Roullet's dis-tinction between dance and pantomime, but disagreed with Du Roullet's aesthetics: "These days, these furies that Tartary spews out and who, holding torches, stand in the way of Pollux who wants to visit his brother in the Underworld, are they not utterly ridiculous?"[37] La Salle found the aesthetic gap between dancing and pan-tomime insurmountable. His opinion recalled the observation that Ange Goudar had made in 1759: "There is an infinite distance between dance (*la danse*) and pan-tomime (*la composition*). For dance, strength and agility are usually enough, but for pantomime, one must use imagination, mind, and insight."[38] The problem was acute at the Opéra, which was expected to offer a plurality of pleasures. As Voltaire wrote in his epicurean poem *Le Mondain* (1736): "We must go to this magical palace [the Opéra] / Where fine poetry, dance, music, / The art of deceiving the eyes by colors, / The art made more successful as it appeals to our hearts, / From a hundred pleas-ures make a single pleasure" (lines 94–97).[39] If the leading dancers Jean Bercher

---

ou les idées que réveillent en vous les cabrioles, les entrechats, les gargouillades & les moulinets." Lesure, *Querelle*, 1:46–47.

36 Du Roullet, "Lettre sur les drames-opéra," 38–44; repr. in Lesure, *Querelle*, 2:144–50. On the pantomimic element in Lully's theatrical dances, see Harris-Warrick, *Dance and Drama*, 119–30.

37 "De nos jours, ces furies que vomit le Tartare, & qui, la torche à la main, s'opposent au passage de Pollux, qui veut aller faire une visite à M. son frère dans les Enfers, ne sont-ils pas du dernier ridicule?" Lesure, *Querelle*, 2:180–81.

38 "Il y a cependant une distance infinie de la Danse à la Composition. Pour l'une il suffit ordinairement de la force & de l'agilité, mais pour l'autre il faut de l'imagination, de l'esprit & de la pénétration." Ange Goudar, *Observations sur les trois derniers ballets pantomimes qui ont paru aux Italiens & aux François* ([Paris: Nicolas-Bonaventure Duchesne], 1759), 42.

39 "Il faut se rendre à ce palais magique, / Où les beaux Vers, la Danse, la Musique, / L'Art de tromper les yeux par les couleurs, / L'Art plus heureux de séduire les cœurs / De cent plaisirs font un plaisir unique." André Morize, *L'Apologie du luxe au XVIIIe siècle et "Le Mondain" de Voltaire: étude critique sur "Le Mondain" et ses sources* (Paris: s.n., 1909;

(alias Dauberval), Allard, Maximilien-Léopold-Philippe-Joseph Gardel, and Marie-Madeleine Guimard were to perform pantomime, they would have to dance in a style they did not master, and forgo the type of dance they were trained to perform. Consequently, the principle of dramatic necessity would overpower institutionalized dance. The quality of their performance would decline, and the pantomimes would only complicate the subject matter and spoil (*dénaturer*) the very operatic pleasures that defined French opera.[40]

If pleasures were understood as institutionalized products, then one might come up with an argument in defense of *all* types of dances performed at theatrical institutions (e.g., the Opéra), especially theatrical dances based on *la belle danse*. To make this claim, one must acknowledge that *la belle danse* and pantomime were fundamentally distinct, although this distinction was not sharp in the years around 1740. Rousseau made this point in his *Dictionnaire de musique*, and Marmontel made a similar point in his *Poétique française* (1763): "In general, we must distinguish the [type of] dance that is only dance and the one that depicts an action."[41] But in the *Supplément de l'Encyclopédie* Marmontel made a strong case for *all* types of dance, including *la danse simple* that Cahusac had snubbed as "an easy resource that replaces a lack of imagination" when used in solemn situations.[42] No matter which style dancers performed, Marmontel argued, the activity of dancing was *already* a natural act of self-expression: "We do not dance to express our sentiment or our thought. We dance to dance, to follow the natural activity to which youth, health, rest, [and] joy move us."[43]

By making a basic observation that humans *naturally* enjoy dancing for the sake of dancing, Marmontel shifted the debate about pantomime from institution history to the Enlightenment. He constructed his argument by navigating the conceptual diagram of the *Système figuré* away from pantomime and back to dance, from communication back to opera, from human science back to *poésie*, and from reason back to imagination. His point recalled an episode that Rousseau discussed in his *Lettre à d'Alembert* (1758), about group dancing by amateurs in public. Instead of dancing at a theater, this group, the Regiment of Saint-Gervais, danced impromptu around the fountain in the city square in Geneva:

> The harmony of five or six hundred men in uniform, holding one another by the hand and forming a long ribbon which wound around, serpent-like; in cadence and without confusion, with countless turns and returns, countless sort of figured evolutions, the excellence of the tunes which animated them, the sound of the

---

Geneva: Slatkine, 1970), 137. On the pleasures in French opera, see Catherine Kintzler, *Poétique de l'opéra français de Corneille à Rousseau*, 2nd edn (Paris: Minerve, 2006), 33–35.

40 La Salle, *Réponse*, 18–19; repr. in Lesure, *Querelle*, 2:181–82.

41 "Il faut distinguer en général la danse qui n'est que danse, et celle qui peint une action." Marmontel, *Poétique française*, 355.

42 "Dans les occasions solennelles, il [la danse simple] est d'une ressource aisée, qui supplée au défaut d'imagination." Cahusac, *La Danse*, 167.

43 "On ne danse pas pour exprimer son sentiment ou sa pensée. On danse pour danser, pour obéir à l'activité naturelle où nous met la jeunesse, la santé, le repos, la joie." Marmontel, *Supplément à l'Encyclopédie*, vol. 4, s.v. "Pantomime."

Drums, the glare of the torches, a certain military pomp in the midst of pleasure, all this created a very lively sensation that could not be experienced coldly.[44]

Their dance, which already demonstrated camaraderie within a regiment, had broader social impact. Although it was late at night, the women who were already in bed got up and watched through their windows as their husbands danced. Noting that their wives were watching them, the men changed the purpose of their dancing. Rather than dancing to express themselves, they danced *as if* they were performing for their audiences. Soon their wives came to join them; their servants brought wine, and the children got up and joined their parents. A group dance then turned into a public communal celebration. It ended with embraces and laughs, and the square was filled with universal gaiety, leading Rousseau to conclude that "the only pure joy is public joy."[45]

The claim that dancing in any style at all – *la belle danse*, pantomime, and others – was already "natural" was supported by Enlightenment materialism. In his *La Morale universelle* (1776), d'Holbach explained why dancing is natural and universal: "Indicated by the nature of our body fluids, the movements of which are periodic, dance, we find, is practiced by all the peoples on earth, both savages and the civilized."[46] The gist of the materialist argument is that dancing is caused by nature, and human beings have no choice but to follow their impulse to dance. In this view, even non-imitative dance was *not* unnatural, although it is usually devoid of the natural signs found in imitative types of dance such as pantomime.

BARBAROUS JOY

While Rousseau and Marmontel considered joyous dancing natural, not artificial, they did not discuss how "natural" it would be to express a darker, menacing type of joy through dancing, or how this type of menacing dance would change the idea of "natural" expression. To begin with, this dark joy illustrated the concept of "animal liberty" (*la liberté animale*) in the Enlightenment. According to the article "Evidence" in the *Encyclopédie*, animal liberty is always found in a confused human being (*un homme en désordre*). Animal liberty meant "a conflict of affective sensations which limit the soul's attention to illicit passions ... [and] must be distinguished from moral liberty or liberty of intelligence."[47] The idea of animal liberty explains what Gluck called "ballet-pantomime" in his *Iphigénie en Tauride* (libretto by Nicolas-François Guillard, 1779).

In collaboration with the choreographer Noverre, Gluck used one ballet-pantomime in *Iphigénie en Tauride*, and this ballet-pantomime illustrates dark, barbarous,

---

44 *CWR*, 10:351n.

45 "Il n'y a de pure joie que la joie publique." *OC*, 5:124.

46 "Indiquée par la nature des fluides de notre corps, dont les mouvements sont périodiques, nous la trouvons établie chez tous les peuples de la terre, tant sauvages que policés." D'Holbach, *La Morale universelle* (Amsterdam: M. M. Rey, 1776), 237. [ARTFL]

47 "Cette liberté animale ou ce conflit de sensations affectives qui bornent l'attention de l'âme à des passions illicites ... doit être distinguée de la liberté morale ou d'intelligence." François Quesnay [attributed], *Encyclopédie*, vol. 6, s.v. "Évidence."

masochist joy. The livret lists four divertissements, two in the first act, one in the second act, and one in the fourth and final act. Only one – the divertissement in Act 2 Scene 4, in which the furies torment and terrorize Oreste – is labeled in the livret as a "ballet-pantomime."[48] The second divertissement, in Act 1 Scene 4, showcases Scythians who express "barbarous joy" – a perverted, sadistic rejoicing in others' suffering – on the cusp of sacrificing Oreste and Pilade as offerings.[49] *Journal de Paris* acknowledged the terrifying effect of this divertissement: "The dance number is relevant to the situation, and conveys perfectly the barbarous joy of these savages, who are already enjoying the torture of the two unfortunate persons."[50] But, to Bachaumont's mind, there was neither overture nor ariette in the opera, and there was only *one* dance, implying that *Iphigénie en Tauride* could barely meet the expectation for multiple sensory pleasures. After the premiere Noverre added another ballet-pantomime to the end of the opera about Oreste liberating the enchained Scythians, followed by a *real*, conventional joyous dance that celebrates the liberation of the Scythians. The music of this second ballet-pantomime was supplied by Gossec, and not Gluck, which indicates that Gluck considered it non-essential but accepted it nonetheless as a functional operatic component.[51]

What is ingenious in *Iphigénie en Tauride* is that Gluck interlinked terror and barbarous joy through his music. He used terraced dynamics in the ballet in Act 1 Scene 4 (Example 3.2) – bouncing back and forth between extremes of *forte* and *piano* in a short, eight-measure ballet that makes use of no conventional dance rhythm. This ballet suggests animal liberty (i.e., a conflict of affective sensations) and represents the Scythians' barbarous joy. Gluck also used similar terraced dynamics in the terrifying ballet-pantomime in Act 2 Scene 4, when Oreste is tormented by furies while he is half awake. In this half-awake state, where dream and reality overlap, he mistakes his sister Iphigénie for the ghost of his deceased mother Clytemnestra, whom he had murdered after learning that she had killed his father.[52] Gluck connected

---

48 "Les Euménides sortent du font du Théâtre, & entourent Oreste. Les unes exécutant autour de lui un Ballet-Pantomime du terreur; les autres lui parlent."*Iphigénie en Tauride* (Paris: Delormel, 1779), 16.

49 *Iphigénie en Tauride*, 9. On Noverre's role in *Iphigénie en Tauride*, see Croll and Croll, *Gluck*, 235–36.

50 "L'air de danse est relatif à la situation, & rend parfaitement la joie barbare de ces Sauvages, qui jouissent d'avance du supplice de ces deux malheureux." Review first published in *Journal de Paris* on May 19, 1779 and compiled by Du Roullet in *Mémoires pour server à l'histoire de la Révolution opérée dans la Musique par M. le Chevalier Gluck* (Naples and Paris: s.n., 1781), 428–29.

51 Bachaumont, *Mémoires*, 14:58. On the addition of the second ballet-pantomime, see Armand Gastoué, "Gossec et Gluck à Opéra de Paris: Le ballet final d'*Iphigénie en Tauride*," *Revue de musicologie* 16, no.54 (May 1935), 87–99.

52 The content of this ballet-pantomime reads: "Accablé par l'excès même de sa douleur, il tombe dans un sommeil profond, pendant lequel les furies viennent le tourmenter, lui reprocher ses crimes, lui montrer l'ombre de sa mère égorgée par lui, & dégoutante du sang qui coule encore de sa blessure." *Mercure de France* (June 1779), 53. On the economical design of this opera, see Julian Rushton, "'Iphigénie en Tauride': The Operas of Gluck and Piccinni," *Music & Letters* 53, no.4 (1972), 411–30. On the convention of the dream scene in French theater, see Adrian La Salvia, "Zwischen Klassik und Romantik:

Example 3.2. Gluck, *Iphigénie en Tauride*, Act 1 Scene 4, "Ballet," mm.81–88

Traum-Szenen im französischen Musiktheater," in *Von Gluck zu Berlioz: Die französische Oper zwischen Antikenrezeption und Monumentalität*, ed. Thomas Betzwieser (Würzburg: Königshausen & Neumann, 2015), 87–109.

these scenes of barbarous joy and tormenting terror through the musical feature of terraced dynamics, laying bare the undercurrent shared by the brutish Taurians, in reality, and the horrifying furies, in the dream.

In addition to terraced dynamics, Gluck used the diminished seventh chord to interlink an illusion and a memory. In the ballet of Act 1 Scene 4 (Example 3.2), the diminished seventh chord creates a dissonant, nervous beginning in m.81. It resolves as a secondary dominant chord to A-major chord, in m.81 and m.83, which is the dominant of D minor. Gluck used the diminished seventh chord again in Act 2 Scene 5, and he explained this usage in a letter to Guillard dated June 17, 1778: in this scene, Oreste sees in a dream the ghost of his mother when he exclaims "my mother, heaven," but in reality it is Iphigénie in front of him.[53] Oreste's scream climaxes in the word "mother" (*mère*), accompanied by a diminished seventh chord on F. This chord, the "pathetic harmony," as Rousseau called it in *Lettre à M. Burney* (1777), in effect brings back Iphigénie's memory of her mother, who appears as a ghost after having slain her husband. Remarkably, this memory is also marked by a diminished seventh chord in m.288 in Act 1 Scene 1, precisely on the word *mère*: "This frightening ghost was my mother."[54]

The correlation between an illusion and a memory indicates a kinship that is unknown to Iphigénie and Oreste. Because the diminished seventh chord highlights Iphigénie's recollection of her mother in Act 1 Scene 1, the repetitions of the word "mother" and the diminished seventh chord in Act 2 Scene 5 become what Condillac called "accidental signs" that create a *déjà vu* effect.[55] For Iphigénie and Oreste, these accidental signs disclose an intersubjective bond unbeknown to either of them until they recognize one another as siblings in the last act. At the moment of recognition, in Act 4 Scene 2, Iphigénie and Oreste sing "brother" and "sister" simultaneously on the first beat of m.158. Iphigénie then cries "Oreste," which is accompanied by yet another diminished chord on A (i.e., A-C-D-sharp) in m.158. The point is not just that the recognition of their consanguineal relation takes the siblings Iphigénie and Oreste by surprise, but also that Gluck had *already* disclosed their intersubjective bond, though not their kinship, through meticulous placements of the diminished chord throughout the opera.

Apart from using diminished chords, Gluck employed modified repetition of lyrics as accidental signs. At the beginning of the opera, the storm subsides and calm returns to nature. In Act 1 Scene 1 Iphigénie sings, "calm reappears, but, alas, the storm still stays deep in my heart" (*Le calme reparait; mais au fonds de mon cœur, Hélas! L'orage dure encore*). In Act 2 Scene 3 Oreste tries to manage his anger and

---

53 "Les Euménides paraissant à Oreste seulement en songe, et en sa fantaisie, cela détruit l'idée qu'il croit voir sa mère en voyant Iphigénie, il doit encore être occupé de son songe, en disant ces paroles: *ma mère! Ciel!* Autrement ils seraient sans aucun effet." Christoph Willibald Gluck, *Sämtliche Werke*, founded by Rudolf Gerber, continued by Gerhard Croll, series I, vol. 9, *Iphigénie en Tauride* (Paris version of 1779), ed. Gerhard Croll (Kassel and New York: Bärenreiter, 1973), vii.

54 "Ce spectre affreux, c'était ma mère!" *Iphigénie en Tauride*, 4. On the diminished seventh chord, see *CWR*, 7:494.

55 On kinship, see Marshall Sahlins, *What Kinship Is—And Is Not* (Chicago: The University of Chicago Press, 2013), 19–31. On accidental signs, see Condillac, *Essay*, 36.

sings a verse, "calm returns to my heart" (*le calme rentre dans mon cœur*), which reminds spectators of Iphigénie's verse. The return of calm after an emotional furor recalls Iphigénie's experience of the subsiding storm. Although words are arbitrary signs, by definition, they double in this instance as accidental signs.

Gluck used accidental signs elsewhere in this opera. Syncopated rhythm, quick alternations of staggered dynamics, streams of repeated sixteenth notes, and fast scalar ascents represent the storm and the *Sturm und Drang* topos at the beginning of the opera, forming what Heartz calls a part of the "dramatic argument."[56] This storm represents Iphigénie's apprehension, linking a physical phenomenon with a psychological state. The *Sturm und Drang* topos also represents the barbarous joy of human sacrifice in the Scythian dance that is meant to quell King Thoas's fear of his mortality. By connecting these scenes through a common *Sturm und Drang* musical topos, Gluck used accidental signs that single out fear as an intersubjective emotion shared by Iphigénie, Oreste, and King Thoas.

Thus, in *Iphigénie en Tauride*, the *Sturm und Drang* topos depicts a storm *and* represents a subconscious condition. By the time Oreste proclaims that calm returns to his heart, the syncopated rhythm and *sforzando* jabs played by the viola serve as accidental signs that betray his inner disquiet (Example 3.3). Gary Tomlinson reads this instance as an indicator of "the advent of a new subjectivity [in the history of opera], one whose soul can be divided at fundamental levels."[57] There is no question that Gluck's music marks a metaphysical dimension, but an emphasis on metaphysics (i.e., the soul) should not overlook the physical dimension (i.e., the storm and the body) in the context of Enlightenment materialism. In fact, Gluck's music conveys as much *metaphysical* force as *physical* force. It is the unity of the soul and the body – what Michel Foucault called, aptly, "the soul with the brain" – that makes this scene gripping. Gluck reportedly explained Oreste's subconscious fear: "Oreste lies" because "he mistakes the collapse of his organs for calm, but the fury is always there."[58] His point is that Oreste is conscious only of parts of his body and his soul, and that orchestral accompaniment discloses his fear, which he is unaware of. The critic of *Mercure de France* also explained covert meanings in Gluck's evocative orchestral music that reveal the truth: "But listen to the instrumental parts, they will tell you that there is despondency, and not rest. They will tell you that Oreste has lost not the feeling of his pains, but only the strength to express them."[59]

The disclosure of hidden emotions in Gluck's orchestral music illustrates how little control human beings have over their subconsciousness and therefore how *unfree* human actions are. It is at this level of analysis that Gluck operated as a

---

56 Heartz, *Haydn*, 145.

57 Gary Tomlinson, *Metaphysical Song: An Essay on Opera* (Princeton, NJ: Princeton University Press, 1999), 59.

58 "Il [Oreste] ment, s'écria Gluck, il prend pour calme l'affaissement de ses organes, mais la furie est toujours là." Olivier de Corancez, "Suite de la Lettre sur le Chevalier Gluck," *Journal de Paris* 234 (21 August 1784), 1011. On embodiment, see Foucault, *Madness and Civilization: A History of Insanity in the Age of Reason*, trans. Richard Howard (New York: Vintage, 1988), 92.

59 "Mais écoutez les instruments, ils vous diront que c'est là de l'accablement, & non du repos: ils vous diront qu'Oreste a perdu, non le sentiment de ses peines, mais seulement la force de les faire éclater." *Mercure de France* (June 15, 1779), 176–77.

Example 3.3. Gluck, *Iphigénie en Tauride*, Act 2 Scene 3, "Le calme rentre dans mon coeur,"
mm.22–41

thinking composer in the spirit of the Enlightenment. His music exemplifies d'Hol-bach's idea of liberty in *Système de la nature*: "The actions of men are *never* free. They are always necessary results of their temperament, of their received ideas, of the true or false notions they have of happiness."[60] [emphasis mine]

THE IMPERFECTION OF LANGUAGE

It is well known that Gluck composed richly evocative orchestral music. It is less well-known, however, that his orchestral accompaniment approximates the nat-uralistic style of acting known as "pantomime." As Marmontel remarked in his "Essai sur les révolutions de la musique" (1777), "even those [operas] by Philippe Quinault, where a sweeter feeling reigns, more graduated in its nuances, and where violent passions burst out only at intervals, do not have these hurried, tumultuous, rapid movements of Gluck's operas, reduced almost to pantomime."[61] Marmontel's remarks show that the discourse of pantomime bifurcated in the 1750s to the 1770s. In addition to discussing pantomime as an alternative type of dance, writers referred it to an emerging naturalistic style of acting. To explain the relationship between

60 "Les actions des hommes ne sont jamais libres; elles sont toujours des suites nécessaires de leur tempérament, de leurs idées reçues, des notions vraies ou fausses qu'ils se font du bonheur." D'Holbach, *Système de la nature*, 1:228.

61 "Ceux même de Quinault, où règne un sentiment plus doux, plus gradué dans ses nuances, & où les passions violentes n'éclatent que par intervalles, n'ont pas ces mouvements pressés, tumultueux, rapides des Opéras de M. Gluck, réduits presque à la Pantomime." Lesure, *Querelle*, 1:173.

Example 3.3. continued

pantomime as acting, and Gluck's music, we need to first examine differences between language and gesture. Then, as Heartz points out, we need to discuss the naturalistic style of acting performed by the English actor Garrick, one of the best actors in the eighteenth century, who performed at d'Holbach's place when he traveled to France.[62]

62   See Daniel Heartz, "From Garrick to Gluck: The Reform of Theater and Opera in the Mid-Eighteenth Century," in Rice, ed., *From Garrick to Gluck*, 257–70. On Garrick and d'Holbach, see Kors, *D'Holbach's Coterie*, 112.

Example 3.3. continued

In the eighteenth century, language was considered imperfect because it posed challenges for words to represent complex ideas. As John Locke discussed in *An Essay Concerning Human Understanding* (1690), words such as "murder" and "sacrilege" are complex ideas because neither has necessary connections with any visible action. The action of pulling the trigger of a gun, for example, might be the only visible gesture made by a shooter, but this gesture has no predetermined relationship with supplementary ideas such as death, homicide, or punishment that are required to define the word "murder." For this word to become a legal term, therefore, the connections among supplementary ideas associated with the word "murder" had to be spelled out precisely – which is why French lawyer Antoine-Gaspard Boucher d'Argis revised the definition of "murder" published in the *Dictionnaire de droit et de pratique* (2nd edn, 1749) for the article on murder in the *Encyclopédie*: A "homicide" should happen by accident or in a fight, whereas a "murder" should be premeditated, take place in an ambush, and a convicted "murderer" should receive the death penalty.[63] Without this level of definitional precision, language would become an imperfect means of communication, since a word would fail to "excite in the Hearer the same idea it stands for in the mind of the speaker."[64]

Contrary to unreliable language (i.e., a word does not have a meaning shared by all users), gesture bypassed the problem of mutual intelligibility. In the chapter on dance in *Observations sur la musique et principalement sur la métaphysique de l'art* (1779), Chabanon recalled Dubos's argument that dance in antiquity did not refer narrowly to dance steps, but more broadly to the art of gesture and of pantomime. There was nothing new in his summary. What was new, however, was that

---

63 Antoine-Gaspard Boucher d'Argis, *Encyclopédie*, vol. 10, s.v. "Meurtre."

64 Locke, *An Essay*, 259. On the imperfection of words, see Sophia Rosenfeld, *A Revolution in Language: The Problem of Signs in Late Eighteenth-Century France* (Stanford, CA: Stanford University Press, 2011), 25–26.

Chabanon used Dubos's argument to make a point about language and gesture, claiming that the "ocular language" of gesture was less clear but more *expressive* than verbal language: "The gesture of fury says infinitely more than the word fury."[65]

Chabanon's recognition of the differences between language and gesture, as two distinct means of communication, had implications in reality and at the theater. Following Locke, Chabanon used the example of "murder" to illustrate the difference between language and gesture:

> The gesture applied to a metaphysical word becomes the physical demonstration and the detailed definition of it. Love embraces; hatred kills; pride disparages. The truth of such a language has something frightening about it: it says what words do not say: Every day we pronounce and hear the phrase "I hate" without being intimidated. Who would not be intimidated if the gesture of murder replaced the word?[66]

Such a substitution could cause grave problems in real life, no doubt, but it might provide a source of pleasure at the theater. Aristotle argued in his *Poetics* (3.1) that there is "universal pleasure in imitations" of any situation; this very point was applicable to Garrick not because he actually murdered someone, but because he amazed his Parisian spectators by *pretending* to murder someone, notably in the murder scene of Shakespeare's *Macbeth*.

What made Garrick's acting style remarkable? One of Garrick's most captivating performances was the dagger scene in Act 2 Scene 1 of Shakespeare's *Macbeth*. This scene shows Macbeth's reactions to an opportunity to kill King Duncan. When this opportunity arrives, he becomes delirious, hallucinating a dagger floating in mid-air that directs him to the king's chamber. Shakespeare wrote: "Is this a dagger, which I see before me, / The handle toward my hand?" (lines 33–34) Driven by an object of his imagination, Macbeth finds himself propelled by his desire to assassinate the king. How could an actor perform this scene convincingly? Shakespeare's script offers little help, for he did not provide any stage directions at this instance, and thus Garrick proposed in *An Essay on Acting* (1744) that actors should think beyond the literal meaning of Shakespeare's verses. At issue here is not the dagger flying in the air, Garrick emphasized, but Macbeth, who is unable to control his murderous *desire*. This approach steers theatrical illusion away from what Marian Hobson calls the "correspondence" theory of truth – which asks the actor to imagine what is *not* there – to a "revelatory" one, which discloses something hidden.[67] In the "revelatory" mode, Garrick would generate a *deep* interpretation of Shakespeare's verses, rendering the action of chasing a flying dagger as just one option among many. Similar to Gluck's Oreste, who mistakes Clytemnestra for his deceased mother in his

---

65 "Le geste de la fureur dit infiniment plus que le mot fureur." Chabanon, *Observations sur la musique et principalement sur la métaphysique de l'art* (Paris: Pissot, 1779), 87.

66 "Le geste appliqué à un mot métaphysique, en devient la démonstration physique, & la définition détaillée. L'amour embrasse, la haine tue, l'orgueil met au-dessus de soi. La vérité d'un tel langage a quelque chose d'effrayant: elle dit ce que les mots ni disent pas: tous les jours on prononce & l'on entend ce mot, je hais, sans être ému; qui ne le serait pas, si le geste du meurtre remplaçait la parole?" Chabanon, *Observations*, 89.

67 Hobson, *The Object of Art*, 15–16.

half-awake state, Garrick's Macbeth appears delusional, preoccupied by an obsessive thought, making a high density of uninterrupted gestures that "show an unsettled motion in his eye, like one not quite awaked from some disordering dream; his hands and fingers should not be immovable, but restless, and endeavoring to disperse the cloud that overshadows his optic ray, and bedims his intellects."[68]

Crucially, Garrick's revelatory style of acting was referred to by his Parisian spectators as "pantomime," a designation that recalls the expressive type of declamation and acting in ancient Roman theaters that Dubos had considered fitting for the Enlightenment. On July 12, 1751 Garrick performed this scene for an intellectual circle at a dinner during his first trip to Paris. After watching Garrick's acting, Collé declared that his style of acting indicative of intense sensibility exemplified "tragic pantomime":

> He filled us with terror; it is impossible to paint a situation better, to convey it with more fervor, and at the same time to exercise better self-control. His face expresses all the passions one after another, without making any grimace, although this scene is full of dreadful and tumultuous movements. What he performed for us was a kind of tragic *pantomime*, and by this single performance I would not be afraid to assert that this actor is excellent in his art.[69] [emphasis mine]

Note that Collé observed simultaneously Garrick's Macbeth and his *detachment* from the Macbeth he created – an observation that pointed to a phenomenology of acting that Diderot later called the paradox of an actor.[70]

What made Garrick's acting so memorable was that he demonstrated through his acting a piercing understanding of character. In July 1765 Grimm wrote about Garrick's performance of the dagger scene, which he had seen in a room without costumes and staging. To his mind, Garrick was able to create what Diderot calls, in *De la poésie dramatique* (1758), an ideal model (*modèle idéal*) of the character that was informed by a deep reading of the text: "All the changes that take place in his features come from the way he is affected *inwardly*. He never exaggerates the truth, and he knows this other inconceivable secret of embellishing himself without the help of anything but passion."[71] [emphasis mine]

---

68 David Garrick, *An Essay on Acting* (London: Bickerton, 1744), 17; on non-interruption, see Hobson, *The Object of Art*, 176.

69 "Il nous inspira la terreur; il n'est pas possible de mieux peindre une situation, de la rendre avec plus de chaleur, et de se posséder en même temps avantage. Son visage exprime toutes les passions successivement, sans faire aucune grimace, quoique cette scène soit pleine de mouvements terribles et tumultueux. Ce qu'il nous joua était une espèce de pantomime tragique, et par ce seul morceau je ne craindrais point d'assurer que ce comédien est excellent dans son art." Collé, *Journal et mémoires*, 1:332. On bodily expression of intense sensibility, see Thomas, *Music*, 152–53.

70 *Paradoxe sur le comédien* was first alluded to in 1769 and was reworked several times afterwards. It was first published posthumously in 1830.

71 "Tous les changements qui l'opèrent dans ses traits proviennent de la manière dont il s'affecte intérieurement; il n'outre jamais la vérité, et il sait cet autre secret inconcevable de s'embellir sans autre secours que celui de la passion." Grimm, *Correspondance*, 6:319. On the ideal model, see Diderot, *Œuvres*, 4:1329–50; Joseph R. Roach, *The Player's*

Garrick was not the only actor of his generation who adopted a penetrating style of pantomimic acting that stimulated spectators' imagination. Rousseau had emphasized spectators' cognitive operation of imagination in *Lettre à d'Alembert* (1758): "The hand emerging from the wall and writing unknown words at the feast of Balthazar ... makes one shudder ... Even on the stage, not everything should be said to the eyes, but the imagination must also be excited."[72] Rousseau's point about the significance of imagination in spectatorship was shared by commentators. In a letter to Voltaire dated November 28, 1760, Diderot demonstrated what Lorraine Daston calls the technique of "attentive observation" in his description of the French actress Clairon's performance of Act 3 of Voltaire's *Tancrède*, using "pantomime" as a catchword for a style of acting abundant with natural signs:

> Oh, my dear master, if you saw Clairon moving across the stage, half knocked over on the executioners who surround her, her knees failing under her, her eyes closed, her arms falling, as if she were dead. If you heard the cry she let out on seeing Tancrède, you would remain more convinced than ever that silence and pantomime sometimes have a pathos that all the resources in oratorical art do not attain. I have in my mind a dramatic moment when everything is mute, and when the spectator remains suspended in the most terrifying alarm.[73]

As with Diderot, Goudar also used the word "pantomime" in his *Remarques sur la musique et la danse* (1773) to describe Clarion's naturalistic acting style, seeing in her the modern, female incarnation of the all-male ancient Roman pantomimes and, in addition to Garrick, as yet another example of Dubos's conception of the pantomime for the Enlightenment: "If Mademoiselle Clairon had been born in the age of the Romans," he wrote, "one would not have failed to put her in the rank of the top pantomimes."[74]

Bear in mind that these commentators dissociated the word "pantomime" from the *bas comique* shunned by Dubos, but it took time for this dissociation to gain acceptance. In 1762 Voltaire welcomed Garrick's penetrating acting style for Shakespearean tragedies, but he was reluctant to use the term "pantomime" to describe it: "I beg my dear brother to tell brother Plato [Diderot] that what he calls

---

Passion: Studies in the Science of Acting (Ann Arbor, MI: University of Michigan Press, 1985), 125, 133.

72   *CWR*, 10:340n.

73   "Ah! Mon cher maître, si vous voyiez la Clairon traversant la scène, à demi renversée sur ses bourreaux qui l'environnent, ses genoux se dérobant sous elle, les yeux fermés, les bras tombants, comme morte; si vous entendiez le cri qu'elle pousse en apercevant Tancrède, vous resteriez plus convaincu que jamais que le silence et la pantomime ont quelquefois un pathétique que toutes les ressources de l'art oratoire n'atteignent pas. J'ai dans la tête un moment de théâtre où tout est muet, et où le spectateur reste suspendu dans les plus terribles alarmes." Diderot, *Œuvres*, 5:331. On the technique of attentive observation, see Lorraine Daston, "Attention and the Values of Nature in the Enlightenment," in Lorraine Daston and Fernando Vidal, eds, *The Moral Authority of Nature* (Chicago: The University of Chicago Press, 2004), 100–126.

74   "Si Mademoiselle Clairon était née du temps des Romains, on n'eût pas manqué de la mettre au rang des premières pantomimes." Ange Goudar, *De Venise: Remarques sur la musique et la danse* (Venice: Palese, 1773), 71.

pantomime I have always called 'action.' I do not like the term 'pantomime' for trag-edy."[75] But Voltaire later changed his view. In 1766 he used the term "pantomime" without apprehension: "We want dramatic acting. We are putting pantomime in place of eloquence. What can succeed in the study becomes cold onstage."[76]

That it took a few years for Voltaire to accept the term "pantomime" indicates that pantomime gained acceptance in the mid-1760s, which marked a new phase in the history of pantomime in eighteenth-century Paris. Garrick stayed in Paris for six months in 1764–65, and Jaucourt's article "pantomime" in the *Encyclopédie* appeared in December 1765. Jaucourt noticed in ancient Roman pantomimes a disinclination to interpret words of a script literally, preferring instead multiple interpretations of a word. He suspected that ancient pantomimes favored a deep kind of interpretation of a script. He recognized that a work should be what Umberto Eco called "open": a script of a work provided but a suggestive blueprint, not a prescription, for perfor-mance. In his view, a play as a text was incomplete, and it could only be *made* com-plete by superb actors who supplied supplementary details during the performance. Like Garrick, ancient Roman pantomimes "managed to give meaning to gesture, not only the words taken in the proper sense, but even the words taken in the figurative sense. Their silent performance rendered poems in their entirety, unlike mimes who were only inconsequential buffoons."[77]

THE TALL MAN VERSUS THE GREAT MAN

How could an actor provide a deep interpretation of a play? A much-discussed example of deep reading came from a competition between two Roman pantomime actors during the reign of Augustus: Hylas and his teacher Pylades. This competi-tion was discussed in Georges de Scudéry's *L'Apologie du théâtre* (1639) and pro-voked debates in the eighteenth century. In his interpretation of a monologue about Agamemnon, king of Argos, Hylas took the epithet "*Agamemnon le Grand*" to mean a tall man. Hylas's teacher, Pylades, who introduced the serious style of pantomime to ancient Rome, faulted Hylas for depicting a "tall" man (*un homme grand*) rather than a "great" man (*un grand homme*). A great man, it goes without saying, does not have to be tall, and a tall man is not necessarily a great man. To offer a less literal, deep interpretation of a great man, Pylades forwent delineating his height and build, portraying instead a man in profound meditation. His interpretation indicates that

---

75 "Je prie mon cher frère, de dire au frère Platon [Diderot], que ce qu'il appelle pantomime, je l'ai toujours appelé action. Je n'aime point le terme de pantomime pour la tragédie." Letter from Voltaire to Étienne Noël Damilaville dated c.March 30, 1762 (D10397). [EE]

76 "On veut du jeu de théâtre; on met la pantomime à la place de l'éloquence. Ce qui peut réussir dans le cabinet devient froid sur la scène." Letter from Voltaire to Jacques Lacombe dated September 19, 1766 (D13574). [EE]

77 "Les pantomimes virent à bout de donner à entendre par le geste, non seulement les mots pris dans le sens propre, mais même les mots pris dans les sens figuré; leur jeu muet rendait des poèmes en entier, à la différence des mimes qui n'étaient que des bouffons inconséquents." Jaucourt, *Encyclopédie*, vol. 11, s.v. "Pantomime." On Jaucourt's article, see Franck Salaün, "L'imagination au défi: la grande pantomime du *Neveu de Rameau*," in Franck Salaün and Patrick Taïeb, eds, *Musique et Pantomime dans le Neveu de Rameau* (Paris: Hermann, 2016), 246.

a king's psychological depth, not his physique, should be significant to the body politic. Whereas Scudéry criticized Pylades's rendition as a "misinterpretation" (*un contresens*), Dubos found it perceptive: "A man greater than the others was a man who thought more deeply than they did."[78]

The competition between Pylades and Hylas illustrates the distinction between imitation and *emulation*. In the third book of the *Republic*, Plato discussed imitation in the sense of emulating good models for self-improvement (396c–d). For Plato, Dionysius of Halicarnassus developed a concept of emulation based on imitation, seeking to *recreate* rather than *reproduce* events in writings. This concept of emulation as re-creation played a significant role in the eighteenth-century discourse of pantomime. Dubos claimed, in *Réflexions critiques*, that Pylades did not imitate Hylas, but *emulated* him by surpassing his student's interpretative skills. The meaning of outdoing a model was rearticulated in the *Dictionnaire de l'Académie française* (4th edn, 1762): Emulation "is a kind of jealousy that leads to match or surpass someone in something praiseworthy."[79]

Eighteenth-century writers used the contest between Pylades and Hylas to ponder the capacity of emulation afforded by pantomime. Both Noverre and Gasparo Angiolini (in collaboration with Calzabigi) mentioned them as ancient authorities of mime, but Cahusac fictionalized his account of this contest as if it were a play, complete with dialogue and dances for Pylades to perform. In Cahusac's colorful account, Agamemnon was not just one king among many, but a *super* king who commanded twenty lesser sovereigns:

> Pylades [as Agamemnon] then appears with a noble and proud countenance. His dance serious, his arms crossed, his steps slow, his movements sometimes animated, often suspended, his gaze sometimes fixed on the ground, sometimes turned toward the sky, [he] portrayed a man occupied with the greatest matters that he saw, weighed up, and compared, as a king.[80]

Cahusac then elaborated Dubos's point about emulation. Hylas, who merely had some talent for acting, could only perform what Pylades had taught him, whereas

78 "Un homme plus grand homme [*sic*] que les autres, c'était un homme qui pensait plus profondément qu'eux." Dubos, *Réflexions*, 3:271–72. On this episode, see Georges de Scudéry, *L'Apologie du théâtre* (Paris: Courbé, 1639), 86–87. On the body politic, see Ernst H. Kantorowicz, *The King's Two Bodies: A Study in Mediaeval Political Theology* (Princeton, NJ: Princeton University Press, 1957), 3–23.

79 "Émulation. s.f. Espèce de jalousie qui excite à égaler ou à surpasser quelqu'un en quelque chose de louable." *Dictionnaire de l'Académie française*, 4th edn (1762). On emulation, see Gunter Gebauer and Christoph Wuff, *Mimesis: Culture-Art-Society*, trans. Don Reneau (Berkeley, CA: University of California Press, 1992), 36; Stephan Halliwell, *The Aesthetics of Mimesis: Ancient Texts and Modern Problems* (Princeton, NJ: Princeton University Press, 2002), 293–94.

80 "Pylade paraît alors avec une contenance noble et fière. Sa danse grave, ses bras croisés, ses pas lents, ses mouvements quelquefois animés, souvent suspendus, ses regards tantôt fixes sur la terre, tantôt tournés vers le ciel, peignaient un homme occupé des plus grandes choses qu'il voyait, qu'il pesait, qu'il comparait en roi." Cahusac, *La Danse*, 118.

Pylades, in emulating Hylas, surpassed his student – and thereby his former self – and advanced the craft of pantomime.[81]

After Cahusac used the Pylades-versus-Hylas competition to make a case for artistic progress, two new interpretations of competition, around 1780, steered the discussion away from artistic progress to signification and aesthetics. On the one hand, Chabanon, in *Observations sur la musique* (1779), applauded Pylades's criticism of Hylas's performance but found Dubos's reading of it unconvincing. The fact that a man is lost in profound thought, he reasoned, does not *in itself* have any predetermined meaning. Such a situation could refer to a hero or a villain, to the great Agamemnon or to his father, the cowardly and ferocious Atreus. What Chabanon meant is that the meaning of any gesture is necessarily undefined. Although theorized as a natural sign at the origin of language, the meaning of any gesture is *inevitably* as arbitrary as that of a word, for even the meaning of a natural sign as readily intelligible as a cry of passion would necessarily depend on the whims of an interpreter.[82] On the other hand, Engel, in his *Ideen zur einer Mimik* (1785), used the difference between "a tall man" and "a great man" to differentiate painting (*malen*) from expression (*ausdrucken*). Informed by Quintilian's *Institutio oratoria*, Engel remarked that most comic actors considered their craft to be sheer mimicry, but the finest actors, such as Pylades, aspired to "*express* the sense [rather] than the words." [emphasis mine] Instead of merely imitating exterior properties of characters, a great actor should aim to act out the mental states that bring about observable behaviors.[83]

Drawing knowledge from the substantive distinction between Agamemnon the "tall" man and Agamemnon the "great" man, between painting and expression, and between literal and deep interpretations, Garrick's performance of the dagger scene illustrated the expressive acting style that stimulated spectators' imagination. In France Garrick realized that not many French understood English, so he resorted to gesturing whenever he failed to make himself understood verbally. When he was traveling in the provinces, he gained first-hand experience of the potential of gesture as a universal type of language capable of transcending cultural and linguistic barriers. One day he saw a father holding his child by an open window. The toddler suddenly sprang from his father's arms, fell from the window, and died. The father's heartbreaking reaction to this tragedy was to Garrick's mind a "language of nature" so immediately intelligible that it required no translation. He re-enacted this tragic accident in Paris in 1765 for a group of English and French guests, performing that father's "silent, but expressive language of unutterable sorrow." Few in the room

---

81 On Pylade's art of emulation, see Dubos, *Réflexions*, 3:272. On Pylade and Hylas, see Burden and Thorp, eds, *The Works of Monsieur Noverre*, 276; Calzabigi, *Scritti*, 1:147; Cahusac, *La Danse*, 116–18.

82 Chabanon, *Observations*, 88. On the relationship between a sign and its interpreter, see Condillac, *Essay*, xxiv–xxv, 36.

83 André Morellet considered the terms "painting" and "expression" as synonyms in music. See André Morellet, "De l'expression en musique," *Mercure de France* (November 1771), 114; Johann Jakob Engel, *Ideen zur einer Mimik* (Berlin: s.n., 1785), 371, translated as *Practical Illustrations of Rhetorical Gesture and Action*, trans. Henry Siddons (London: Richards Phillips, 1822), 209.

could tell whether Garrick "imitated" or "emulated" the grieving father, of course, but the *accuracy* of his imitation of the grieving father was less relevant than the *expressiveness* of his performance. Apparently, his performance was convincing; it caused the "greatest astonishment" followed by "abundant tears" in the audience.[84]

Note that Garrick's expressive acting approximated the type of expressive pantomime performed by the ancient Roman pantomimes. According to Dubos, Roscius performed in a pantomime (*un jeu muet*) the meaning of a phrase that Cicero had just written, and he could express the same idea in various ways.[85] Significantly, Diderot compared Garrick to Roscius in a commentary he wrote about a bust created by his sculptor friend, Jean-Baptiste Le Moyen II, which was on display in the salon of 1765: "The bust of Garrick is good. It is not the child Garrick who strolls about in the street, who performs, jumps, pirouettes, and wanders in the room. It is Roscius commanding his eyes, his brow, his cheeks, his mouth, all the muscles of his face, or rather his soul."[86] Diderot's point emphasizes Garrick's supreme degree of bodily control. It was in *Garrick's* acting that French writers recognized the pantomime of the Enlightenment that Dubos had envisaged. Jaucourt even crowned Garrick an omni-competent successor to the ancient Roman pantomimes: "Does not the theater of London now have a pantomime who could be put against Pylades and Bathyllus? The famous Garrick is an actor all the more marvelous, as he equally performs all sorts of tragic and comic characters."[87]

DAGGER SCENES

In what ways was Garrick's pantomimic style of acting relevant to music? Ellen Harris argues that Garrick's craft – showcasing a character's subtle and abundant psychological changes in unspoken moments – might have been inspired by the pauses in Handel's music.[88] I propose that his influence also went in the other direction. A musical moment analogous to Garrick's interpretation of the dagger scene in *Macbeth* comes from another dagger scene in Gluck's *Armide* (1777).

Dagger scenes offer telling musical and textual details for analysis not only because they represent extreme emotions, but because different treatments of these emotions indicate national styles. During the *Querelle des bouffons*, Diderot compared Lully's dagger scene with one in *Sesostri re d'Egitto* (Rome, 1751), by the

---

84   Thomas Davies, *Memoirs of the Life of David Garrick*, 2 vols. (London: printed for the author, 1780), 2:80–83.

85   Dubos, *Réflexions*, 3:232.

86   "Le buste de Garrick est bien. Ce n'est pas l'enfant Garrick qui baguenaude dans la rue, qui joue, saute, pirouette et gambade dans la chambre; c'est Roscius commandant à ses yeux, à son front, à ses joues, à sa bouche, à tous les muscles de son visage, ou plutôt à son âme." Diderot, *Œuvres*, 4:445.

87   "Le théâtre de Londres ne possède-t-il pas à présent un pantomime qu'on pourrait opposer à Pylade & à Bathylle? Le fameux Garrick est un acteur d'autant plus merveilleux, qu'il exécute également toutes sortes de sujets tragiques & comiques." Jaucourt, *Encyclopédie*, vol. 11, s.v. "Pantomime."

88   Ellen T. Harris, "Silence as Sounds: Handel's Sublime Pauses," *Journal of Musicology* 22 (2005), 552–56.

Spanish-born Italian composer Domingo Miguel Bernabe Terradellas. Recalling the Italian-vs-French music framework, Diderot denounced Lully's setting, calling it "a listless psalmody, a melody without fire, without soul, without strength, and without genius."[89]

What "melody" meant was elaborated by Rousseau, who considered Italian music superior to French music in his *Lettre sur la musique française* (November 1753) because the Italian language allows a composer to write music according to the concept of "unity of melody," which, as Waeber explains in detail, means that the music should follow the lyrics by conveying a single melody to the ear and a single idea to the mind. Italian melody that modulates abruptly from one key to another without transitions can depict every imaginable emotion, image, and idea. Compared to language, music is a more dependable medium for an actor: "Someone who would not play the role from the words alone will play it quite correctly from the Music, because it performs its function of interpreter so well."[90]

Rousseau's concept of "unity of melody" is important because it legitimated the concept of an "accessory idea." These two concepts were discussed in Antoine Arnauld and Pierre Nicole's *La logique, ou L'Art de penser* (1662), and Diderot related these concepts to music in his *Lettre sur les sourds et muets* (1751). Diderot said, "When the musician knows his art, the accompaniment parts will contribute to either strengthening the expression of the vocal part, or adding *new ideas* that the subject asked for, and that the vocal part could not have conveyed."[91] [emphasis mine] Rousseau developed this point by establishing a hierarchy of musical ideas. As these "new" ideas draw meaning from the dominant vocal part, they should play the accessorial role. Orchestral accompaniment may function like eclipses by allowing accessory ideas to come to the surface at the intervals when singers temporarily stop singing. The interplay between the vocal and the orchestral parts creates a dialogic effect: "If the meaning of the words includes an accessory idea which the song is not able to render, the Musician will insert it into the rests or into the held notes in such a way that he may present it to the Listener without distracting him from the meaning of the song."[92]

Rousseau illustrated his concept of the "unity of melody" in his *Lettre sur la musique française* with his analysis of Armide's monologue "Enfin, il est en ma

89 "Les scènes d'*Armide* ne sont en comparaison de celles de *Nitocris* [*Sésostris*] qu'une psalmodie languissante, qu'une mélodie sans feu, sans âme, sans force et sans génie." Diderot, *Œuvres*, 4:137. Laurent Versini questioned what Diderot knew about Terradellas's opera, which was neither performed nor published in France; see ibid., 4:132. On Lully's operas in eighteenth-century France, see Benoît Dratwicki, "Lully d'un siècle à l'autre, du modèle au mythe (1754–1774)," in Agnès Terrier and Alexandre Dratwicki, eds, *L'invention des genres lyriques français et leur redécouverte au XIXe siècle* (Lyon: Symétrie, 2010), 310, 318.

90 *CWR*, 7:156. On the unity of melody, see Waeber, "Jean-Jacques Rousseau's 'unité de mélodie,'" 79–143.

91 "Quand le musicien saura son art, les parties d'accompagnement concourront ou à fortifier l'expression de la partie chantante, ou à ajouter de nouvelles idées que le sujet demandait, et que la partie chantante n'aura pu rendre." Diderot, *Œuvres*, 4:46.

92 *CWR*, 7:156. On the eclipses, see Charlton, *Opera*, 50. On the dialogue between the vocal line and the orchestral accompaniment, see Waeber, *En musique*, ch. 1.

puissance" in Act 2 Scene 5 of Lully's *Armide* (1686; re-run at the Opéra in 1746) – one he called "the most perfect model of true French recitative."[93] During the course of this recitative, Armide decides not to kill Renaud but to make him fall in love with her so that she has the option to hate him as revenge. A dagger in hand, Armide announces that she is going to pierce Renaud's unconquerable heart (*Je vais percer son invincible cœur*), but she instantly flounders. Rousseau rebuffed Lully's use of a cadence landing on an E-minor chord in m.28 (Example 3.4). This moment, right after Armide sings the word "heart" (*cœur*), should mark the first *movements* that signal her pity or her love for Renaud, and these movements justify a gap (*jour*) for the orchestral accompaniment. By the time Armide sings "What turmoil seizes me? What makes me hesitate?" (*Quel trouble me saisit? Qui me fait hésiter?*), in mm.32–34, the resolution of the $V^{4/2}$ chord to I^6 chord in G major in m.32 arrives too late and offers too little musical contrast to represent the "prodigious change" (*le change-ment prodigieux*) that Armide should have just experienced: "But Heavens! Is it indeed a question of tonic and dominant at a time when all harmonic connection should be interrupted, when everything should portray disorder and agitation!"[94] To Rousseau's mind, Lully missed a great opportunity at this instance to fill in the blanks – that is, to introduce accessory ideas in the orchestral accompaniment that support one unified melody.

Rousseau's words "movement" and "disorder" make one think of materialism. As defined in the article "Passions (Eloquence)" in the *Encyclopédie*, every movement of the will (*volonté*) brings about a change in the mind (*esprit*), and these movements influence even the body.[95] The psycho-physiological state of "disorder" indicates the presence of thoughts that are yet to be fully formed. As Diderot wrote in *Essai sur le mérite et la vertu* (1745): "Wherever the excess or weakness of affections, the indolence or impetuosity of inclinations, the absence of natural feelings or the presence of some foreign passions characterize two kinds [of feelings] that are assembled and mixed together in the same individual, there must be imperfection and disorder."[96] By imagining the unity of melody that exposes rapid transitions from one psychological movement to another, Rousseau anticipated a point that d'Holbach made in *Système de la nature* about disorder in nature: "The disorder in a being is … only its passage to a new order. The faster this passage is, the greater the disorder is for the being that experiences it."[97]

By laying bare the depiction of "movement" and "disorder" in the music, Rousseau conceptualized the "unity of melody" as a solution that a composer can

---

93 *CWR*, 7:168.

94 *CWR*, 7:170. On this monologue, see Baud-Bovy, "De l'*Armide* de Lully à l'*Armide* de Gluck," 71–75; Thomas, *Aesthetics*, ch. 3.

95 *OC*, 5:324; *Encyclopédie*, vol. 12, s.v. "Passions [Éloquence]."

96 "Partout où l'excès ou la faiblesse des affections, l'indolence ou l'impétuosité des penchants, l'absence des sentiments naturels ou la présence de quelques passions étrangères, caractériseront deux espèces rassemblées et confondues dans le même individu, il doit y avoir imperfection et désordre." Diderot, *Œuvres complètes de Diderot*, ed. J. Assézat, 20 vols. (Paris: Garnier frères, 1875–77), 1:98. [ARTFL]

97 "Le désordre dans un être n'est … que son passage à un ordre nouveau. Plus ce passage est rapide, et plus le désordre est grand pour l'être qui l'éprouve." D'Holbach, *Système de la nature*, 1:94.

Example 3.4. Lully, *Armide*, Act 2 Scene 5, "Enfin il est en ma puissance," mm.21–41

'Armide tenant un dard à la main'

Example 3.4. continued

use to alleviate the problem of wooden acting in contemporary French opera, using musical means to compensate for a visual shortcoming. He explained, "Our most beautiful airs are always in the monologues and never in the scenes, because, since our Actors possess *no skill* in pantomime [*jeu muet*] and since the Music indicates no gesture and depicts no situation, the one who remains silent does not know what to do with himself while the other sings."[98] [emphasis mine] This remark is critical to this book because Rousseau wrote the first version of *Lettre sur la musique française* between August and December of 1752, a period in which, as discussed in Chapter Two, he included gesture, dance, and pantomime in his *Le Devin du village* for performances at Fontainebleau and the Opéra. His theorization and practical application of pantomime gave birth to the idea of unity of melody, which initiated another phase of discourse on pantomime.

Rameau, however, took issue with Rousseau's point. In a response to Rousseau's *Lettre sur la musique française* entitled *Observations sur notre instinct pour la musique* (1754), Rameau disagreed with Rousseau's emphases on contrasts of register, dynamics, and tempos, all of which were to his mind mere superficial modifications of the melody that failed to match his idea of modulation, which meant musical phrasing informed by harmonic, tonal, and poetic syntaxes. Rameau argued that expression of feelings characteristic of French music should come from harmony. He was unconvinced by Rousseau's suggestion of accessory ideas that disclose Armide's unspoken thoughts and whatever invisible "movements" might take place *between* her verses. Regarding any significative potential of the pause in m.28 of Armide's monologue, Rameau queried: "To demand orchestral accompaniments when one can do without them, is this not an uncalled-for quibble? Does the actor need his inner feelings to be combed, and does the singer need anything other than a rest in this case?"[99]

98   *CWR*, 7:164.

99   "Exiger des accompagnements d'Orchestre lorsqu'on peut s'en passer, n'est-ce pas là une chicane déplacée? Le Comédien a-t'il besoin qu'on peigne ses sentiments intérieurs,

Rousseau did not answer these questions but, years later, Gluck addressed them when he reworked Quinault's libretto of *Armide* for the Opéra (September 23, 1777). He likely disagreed that orchestral accompaniment at this instance is some "inappropriate chicane," and might doubtless have claimed that Armide *does* need the music to depict emergent movements, thoughts, and feelings. Gluck, in fact, studied Rousseau's musical writings, including his *Lettre sur la musique française*, and was familiar with the debate about Lully's monologue. In the letter dated February 1773, published in *Mercure de France*, he declared that he admired Rousseau's analysis of Lully's monologue.[100] In light of these pieces of tangible evidence, I propose that Gluck's setting of the same monologue in *Armide* illustrates Rousseau's concept of "unity of melody" by making orchestral accompaniment resemble pantomime. Although Gluck told Du Roullet, in a letter dated October 14, 1775, that he "did not intend to remove a line from Quinault's libretto," he did make some telling changes: he set it to music without the prologue; he added four lines to Act 3; and he replaced the word "*vais*" with "*veux*" in the verse "I am going to pierce his invincible heart" (*Je vais percer son invincible cœur*).[101] The substitution of this one word gives nuances to the meaning of this verse. Rather than draw attention to Armide's immediate *action*, expressed in the *futur proche* "I am going to" (*je vais*), Gluck emphasized her intense *desire* to kill, expressed in the modal verb, "I really want to" (*je veux*). The word "want" (*veux*) emphasizes not the visible action of stabbing Renaud but her invisible desire to kill him.

By emphasizing Armide's desire rather than her action, Gluck rejected Lully's conception of this scene. Unlike most eighteenth-century re-runs of Lully's *Armide* (1746, 1761, 1762, 1764, 1765, 1766) which condensed Act 4, Gluck's setting of the monologue illustrates Rousseau's idea of the "unity of melody." Lully's setting remains in E minor throughout, but Gluck's recitative begins in A minor and ends in E minor.[102] Like the pantomime in *Orphée et Euridice*, Gluck did not provide any

---

et le Chanteur a-t'il besoin d'autre chose que d'un silence en ce cas?" Rameau, *The Complete Theoretical Writings of Jean-Philippe Rameau*, ed. Erwin R. Jacobi, 6 vols. (Rome: American Institute of Musicology, 1967–72), 3:308. On Rameau's remarks on this recitative, see Charles Dill, "Rameau Reading Lully: Meaning and System in Rameau's Recitative Tradition," *Cambridge Opera Journal* 6, no.1 (1994), 1–17.

100 "L'étude que j'ai faite des ouvrages de ce grand homme sur la Musique, la Lettre entr'autres dans laquelle il fait l'analyse du monologue de l'*Armide* de Lully, prouvent la sublimité de ses connaissances & la sûreté de son goût, & m'ont pénétré d'admiration." Lesure, *Querelle*, 1:10.

101 Howard, *Gluck*, 149. Gluck also changed the word "dagger" to "dart" and "vengeance" to "fury" in the monologue. See Gabriele Buschmeier, "Glucks *Armide*-monologue, Lully und die 'Philosophes,'" in Axel Beer and Laurenz Lütteken, eds, *Festschrift Klaus Hortschansky zum 60. Geburtstag* (Tutzing: H. Schneider, 1995), 169, n.10, n.11. The libretto follows Quinault's original and uses the word "vais." Klaus Hortschansky draws attention to this modification in Gluck, *Sämtliche Werke*, series I, vol. 8a/b, *Armide*, 2 vols., ed. Klaus Hortschansky (Kassel and New York: Bärenreiter, 1987, 1991), 183. On the four lines added to Act 3, see Carl Van Vechten, "Notes on Gluck's *Armide*," *The Musical Quarterly* 3, no.4 (1917), 545.

102 One example of streamlining Lully's *Armide* is the 1746 version by François Rebel and François Francoeur. On reworking Lully's opera in the eighteenth century, see Dratwicki, "Lully d'un siècle à l'autre," 345; Lois Rosow, "How Eighteenth-Century Parisians Heard

stage directions, but he imparted accessory ideas in the almost three-measure-long orchestral accompaniment after Armide sings the verse "*Je veux percer son invincible cœur*" (Example 3.5). This verse clearly projects onto the pause a *desire* to kill. Like his pairing of recitative and pantomime, through this verse Gluck informed his audiences of the content of the long pause, turning these few measures into a microcosm of his recitative/pantomime pairs. The orchestra plays two contrasting sets of thematic materials in this extended pause. In the last two quarter beats of m.17, the orchestra plays a rushing scalar ascent in B minor, a topos of anger that suggests Armide's murderous intent. But during the next two measures, in mm.18–19, Gluck replaced this topos of anger with one of hesitation. A melodic motif of B–D–B in m.18, supported by a B-minor tonic chord, leads to the same melodic motif transposed a major second above, C-sharp–E–C-sharp, supported by a $V^{6/5}$ in B minor. This progression indicates a harmonic motion away from the tonic of B minor, creating a harmonic distancing effect that suggests hesitation. In m.20 this moment of hesitation is interrupted abruptly by the same B-minor scalar ascent, suggesting a resurgence of Armide's murderous desire. The juxtaposition of these two opposing musical passages discloses her competing thoughts, while she remains speechless.

Like Garrick's pantomimic acting, Gluck's orchestral accompaniment depicts the yet-to-be-sorted-out thoughts that rush through Armide's mind. Gluck showed that his music could paradoxically reveal the *presence* of unspoken thoughts in the *absence* of speech, and that the state of speechlessness does not preclude any movements and disorder in one's mind. Rousseau wrote about this paradox in the article "Opéra [1]" of his *Dictionnaire de musique*: "It is one of the great advantages of the Musician to be able to depict *things* that cannot be heard, while it is impossible for the Painter to depict those that cannot be seen."[103] Rousseau here made a case for the representational capacity of music. The "things" that can be represented by music include those that may not be perceptible in the phenomenal world. The effect is similar to LUI's pantomimes in Diderot's *Le Neveu de Rameau*, which, as Béatrice Didier claims, "exceeded and upset all objective materiality of imitation."[104] Grounded in the theory of imitation, Rousseau considered unexpressed emotions or unarticulated thoughts that should be taking shape in Armide's mind to be some of the "things" that come up naturally. What Rousseau's concept of "unity of melody" offers is a replacement of the schematic division between the vocal part and its instrumental accompaniment with a more dynamic, more reciprocal, and more dialogic mode of interaction between them. As Gluck's orchestral accompaniment and Garrick's pantomimic acting make clear, the existence of inarticulate thoughts that are out of Armide's conscious control illustrate d'Holbach's materialist thesis that human actions are unfree.

Lully's Operas: The Case of Armide's Fourth Act," in John Hajdu Heyer, ed., *Jean-Baptiste Lully and the Music of the French Baroque: Essays in Honor of James R. Anthony* (Cambridge: Cambridge University Press, 1989), 219–21.

103 *CWR*, 7:456.

104 Didier, *La Musique des lumières*, 38.

Example 3.5. Gluck, *Armide*, Act 2 Scene 5, "Enfin, il est en ma puissance," mm.12–22

PANTOMIME, IMITATION, AND LIBERTY

In view of Gluck's uses of unity of melody, typifying d'Holbach's claim that human actions are unfree, what does it mean that Marmontel, one of the regular members of d'Holbach's coterie, related pantomime to liberty?

When Marmontel noticed in the actor and the pantomime an analogy between slavery and liberty, he perceived liberty as what Hobbes called the absence of opposition. Heartz also noticed this meaning of liberty. He observed in Jean-François de Saint-Lambert's article "Genius" of the *Encyclopédie* (1757) that a genius, as understood in the eighteenth century, could exercise liberty by escaping from the constraints of rules: "The rules and laws of taste would give obstacles to the genius; he

Example 3.5. continued

breaks them to fly to the sublime, the pathetic, the great."[105] The meaning of escape, of breaking away, of overcoming obstacles provides a Hobbesian foundation for Marmontel's distinction between an actor and a pantomime. Contrary to an actor, who was subjugated to a literal interpretation of the text, a pantomime performer exercised interpretive liberty by breaking free of the confines of literal meanings.

105 "Les règles & les lois du goût donneraient des entraves au génie; il les brise pour voler au sublime, au pathétique, au grand." Jean-François de Saint-Lambert, *Encyclopédie*, vol. 7, s.v. "Génie"; On taste and genius, see Heartz, "From Garrick to Gluck," 260–61.

Example 3.5. continued

*) Im Libretto heißt es: "Je vais percer".

Based on a Hobbesian view, Marmontel defended the idea of liberty by revisiting Dubos's idea of emulation. In 1759 he made an essentialist association of Italian music with liberty: "The taste of the nation [Italy] leaves them complete liberty."[106] But in 1777 Marmontel turned against this essentialist conception of Italian style, decoupling liberty from the Italian style and connecting the idea of liberty to a pan-European model of pantomime. He concluded his "Essai sur les révolutions de la musique" by claiming that musical progress relies on the concept of emulation: "Liberty, mother of emulation, will reign over the lyric theater."[107]

How does imitation ensure stylistic continuity while facilitating creativity? In 1754 Cahusac had censured unimaginative imitation as regressive, as aping, as failing to be a human. In *Poétique française* (1763) Marmontel made a similar criticism against pantomime in Spanish comedy: "This people [the Spanish] … make gestures as if performing pantomime; [they] have created this mute play [*jeu muet*] which, sometimes by a lively and pleasant expression and often by grimaces bringing a man closer to the monkey, sustains only an intrigue deprived of art, of sense, of mind, and of taste."[108] But in the 1770s and 1780s Marmontel reconceptualized imitation, giving this age-old technique a new emphasis in any creative process. In his *Essai* he observed that a genius learned by studying good models, and he elaborated this point in the article "Imitation" of his *Éléments de littérature* (1787): "To imitate a

---

106 "Le goût de la Nation [l'Italie] leur laisse toute liberté." Marmontel, "Examen des réflexions de M. D'Alembert sur la liberté de la musique," *Mercure de France* (July 1759, part 2), 92.

107 "La liberté, mère de l'émulation, régnera sur la Scène Lyrique." Lesure, *Querelle*, 1:190.

108 "Ce peuple d'ailleurs pantomime, a donné lieu à ce jeu muet, qui quelquefois par une expression vive et plaisante, et souvent par des grimaces qui rapprochent l'homme du singe, soutient seul une intrigue dépourvue d'art, de sens, d'esprit et de goût." Marmontel, *Poétique française*, 391–92. On imitation and aping, see Cahusac, *La Danse*, 220.

writer, an orator, or a poet is not to translate [a piece], to copy it slavishly. It is, in the strictest sense, to penetrate his thought and to convey it with liberty."[109]

By considering imitation as an act through which one recreates rather than reproduces a work, Marmontel rejected Cahusac's point and saw in the act of imitation a path toward liberty. To imitate *with liberty* means first to know good models well, after which the artist can exercise advanced cognitive skills as outlined in Condillac's *Essai sur l'origine des connaissances humaines*. Struck by imagination, with a mind enriched by memory and a soul fulfilled by the beauties of the model, one would proceed to imitate by producing a new work of the same genre. In doing so, one would participate in a tradition, studying how masters such as Molière and Jean de La Fontaine emulated masterworks, and how they in turn produced their best works. Whereas the slavish imitators copied masterworks as an end, the ambitious imitators *emulated* them. Certainly, not all writers differentiated emulation from imitation, but by the same token, even writers who practiced the art of imitation recognized in imitation a source of creation. La Fontaine wrote in the poem "À Monseigneur l'Évêque de Soissons" (1671) that "my imitation is not a [condition of] slavery: / I only take the idea, and the turns, and the laws / that our masters themselves once followed."[110] Thus imitation is not the opposite of originality; instead, it provides a tried-and-true path *towards* originality through which one ought to exercise moral liberty. Citing La Fontaine, Jaucourt declared in the article "Imitation (Poetry, Rhetoric)" of the *Encylopédie* that "imitation must be done in a noble, generous manner, and full of liberty. Good imitation is a continual invention."[111]

How, then, did the semantic ambiguity of gesture and music affect the process of imitation as creation? Marmontel noticed that the ideas presented in pantomime are as "vague as dreams" (*vagues comme les songes*). His point recalls Chabanon's comment about the indefinite meaning of instrumental music.[112] Just as music does not have precise and distinct meanings, gestures, too, lack definite referents. But, if music and dance can only convey something vague, can pantomime really turn dance into an imitative art? It depends, Chabanon might say. Whether music and dance could be considered imitative at all depends not on a plot they serve, nor on skilled performers, but rather on an *interpreter* willing to triangulate the dyadic sign/object relationship. Chabanon added that neither music nor dance is inherently imitative, but both may be *perceived* as such when an interpreter makes a deliberate

---

109 "Le génie s'enrichit par l'étude des bons modèles." Lesure, *Querelle*, 1:171; "IMITATION. Imiter un écrivain, un orateur, un poète, ce n'est pas le traduire, le copier servilement; c'est dans le sens le plus étroit, se pénétrer de sa pensée, & la rendre avec liberté." Marmontel, *Éléments de littérature*, 6 vols. (Paris: Chez Née de la Rochelle), vol. 4, s.v. "Imitation."

110 "Mon imitation n'est point un esclavage: / Je ne prends que l'idée, et les tours, et les lois / que nos maitres suivaient eux-mêmes autrefois." La Fontaine, *Œuvres diverses* (Paris: Gallimard, 1942), 646. [ARTFL]

111 "L'imitation doit être faite d'une manière noble, généreuse, & pleine de liberté. La bonne imitation est une continuelle invention." Jaucourt, *Encyclopédie*, vol. 9, s.v. "Imitation [Poésie/Rhétorique]." On imitation and originality, see Philippe Vendrix, "La Notion de révolution dans les écrits théoriques concernant la musique avant 1789," *International Review of the Aesthetics and Sociology of Music* 21, no.1 (1990), 74.

112 On Chabanon and the semantic indeterminacy of music, see Thomas, *Music*, 32.

effort to link the semantically vague music and dance to the semantically more distinct verbal language. He argued, "A *work* of the mind is necessary for attaching a
situation and analogous words to this sensation; and it is this last operation that
makes music and dance two imitative arts."[113] [emphasis mine]

One can develop Marmontel's argument by claiming that the semantic ambiguity
of music and gesture offered *precisely* the condition for spectators to exercise their
moral liberty to an interpretive end. Marmontel noted in the article "Pantomime"
of the *Supplément à l'Encyclopédie* an inverse relation between gesture and speech.
The more difficulty we have expressing ourselves through speech, whether due to
distance, an impaired organ, or limited linguistic proficiency, the more reason we
have to communicate with one another via gesture: "It is therefore especially for the
most passionate movements of the soul that pantomime is necessary."[114] For all their
semantic imprecision, gesture and music function as effective means of communication that compensate for the imperfection of language. Sophia Rosenfeld argues that
a range of literary and theatrical devices – including silent tableaux, melodramatic
gestures in domestic dramas, and action dance – helped to solve the epistemological
problem of the imperfection of words in the eighteenth century by presenting them
as prototypes of a universal language.[115] I add that instrumental music was understood to solve the same problem. On this point, Marmontel agreed with Chabanon
by highlighting the role of an interpreter who would seek out distinct meanings in
instrumental music. The semantically vague property shared by music and pantomime *rewarded* rather than frustrated audiences because it turned the interpretation of nonverbal signs into an exercise through which audiences generated what
Thomas calls self-knowledge: "The only voice that can be given to the pantomime
actor is that of the symphony, because it is vague and indistinct, because it does
not interfere with the action, because while helping us to guess the sentiment and
thought, it still allows us to enjoy *our* insight, or rather the talent that knows how to
express everything without the aid of the word."[116] [emphasis mine]

The act of reading meaning *into* the semantically ambiguous music and dance
takes on importance in the discourse on the imperfection of words. In truth,
it is precarious to assume that words convey meanings as clearly as they should.
Montesquieu, for example, pointed out, in a chapter called "Diverse significations
given to the word 'liberty'" in his *De l'esprit des loix* (1748), that the word "liberty"

---

113 "Il faut un travail de l'esprit pour attacher à cette sensation une situation & des mots
analogues; & c'est cette dernière opération qui fait de la Danse & de la Musique
deux Arts imitatifs." Chabanon, *Observations*, 97. On the interpreter in the process of
identification, see Michel Noiray, *Vocabulaire de la musique de l'époque classique* (Paris:
Minerve, 2005), 107.

114 "C'est donc surtout aux mouvements de l'âme les plus passionnés que la pantomime est
nécessaire." Marmontel, *Supplément à l'Encyclopédie*, s.v. "Pantomime."

115 Rosenfeld, *A Revolutionary in Language*, 57–85.

116 "La seule voix qu'on peut donner à l'acteur *pantomime*, est celle de la symphonie, parce
qu'elle est vague & confuse, qu'elle ne gêne point l'action, qu'en nous aidant à deviner
le sentiment & la pensée, elle nous laisse encore jouir de notre pénétration, ou plutôt
du talent qui sait tout exprimer sans le secours de la parole." Marmontel, *Supplément
à l'Encyclopédie*, s.v. "Pantomime." On the generation of self-knowledge, see Thomas,
Music, 162–64.

has pliable meanings. Whereas the Muscovites took the word "liberty" to mean the liberty to grow a long beard, other cultures used this word to refer to the privilege of possessing weapons or the power of using violence. Because the meaning of "liberty" was culturally specific, Montesquieu defined it in *Mes Pensées*, a collection of fragments, in relative rather than in absolute terms. As a political concept, liberty did not indicate a type of government, but a *privilege* granted by a ruling body. In a state ruled by the people, the rich and the powerful serve the poor, and the weak enjoy their liberty; but, in a monarchy, the opposite is true: the powerful people are those who have liberty.[117]

Since the meaning of liberty comes from a *relation*, as Montesquieu argued, it is Marmontel's *comparison* between an actor and a pantomime that makes possible the connection between pantomime and liberty. Marmontel's point is not that pantomime embodies liberty; rather, his point is that a pantomime exercises moral liberty through providing a deep interpretation of a play, as opposed to an actor who adheres narrowly to its literal meaning. Marmontel's point is consistent with what Thomas calls a broader "shift away from an aesthetic of singular referentiality and towards a rhetorical concern with affective response and interpretation."[118] What Marmontel contributed to this discourse, however, was that pantomime constructed the idea of liberty in two interconnected processes: first, by coming up with multiple interpretations of a sign, a pantomime actor or actress exercised moral liberty; and second, by interpreting the gestures performed by a pantomime as signs, spectators exercised their moral liberty. Both processes assumed that human beings had the ability to think, and *this* is a critical point. Although human beings have no control over our actions, as d'Holbach argued, we have the liberty to think (*la liberté de penser*).

Three years after he wrote *Système de la nature*, d'Holbach himself made a case for the liberty to think, in his *Système social* (1773). In a chapter pointedly entitled "Of the liberty to think" (*De la liberté de penser*), d'Holbach argued that the liberty to think provides the foundation for the liberty of communication: "Free communication of ideas, instruction, and the publication of useful discoveries are interesting things for all of society. Every good citizen owes his talents and his knowledge [*lumières*] to his associates. Therefore, in a well-governed country, man has the right to think, speak, and write."[119] Strikingly, this very passage provided a basis for Article 11 of the *La Déclaration des droits de l'homme et du citoyen* (1789) on liberty of expression as a right, as quoted in the Introduction: "The free expression [*communication*] of thought and opinions is one of the most precious rights of man: thus every citizen may freely speak, write, and print, subject to accountability for abuse of this

117 Montesquieu, *De l'Esprit des loix*, ed. J. Brethe de la Gressaye, 4 vols. (Pairs: Les Belles lettres, 1950–61), 2:59–60 [ARTFL]; Monstesquieu, *My Thoughts (Mes pensées)*, trans. and ed. Henry C. Clark (Indianapolis, IN: Liberty Fund, 2012), 254, entry 884.

118 Thomas, *Music*, 171.

119 "La libre communication des idées, l'instruction, la publication des découvertes utiles sont des choses intéressantes pour toute Société. Tout bon citoyen doit ses talents et ses lumières à ses associés. Ainsi, dans un pays bien gouverné, l'homme est en droit de penser, de parler et d'écrire." D'Holbach, *Système social ou principes naturels de la morale et de la politique* (Paris: Fayard, 1994), 333.

liberty in the cases determined by law."[120] Hence, in the Enlightenment context culti-vated by d'Holbach's coterie, pantomime was understood to develop the liberty of performers and spectators, helping them to think and to express themselves more readily than did actors. Small wonder that members of d'Holbach's coterie enjoyed watching Garrick act, for in doing so they became acutely aware of their *own* moral liberty to think.

In this chapter I discuss two kinds of pantomime in Gluck's French operas – panto-mime as a dance and pantomime as acting – and the intellectual stakes of thinking about pantomime in the Enlightenment. Let's return to the question I asked at the beginning of this chapter: why does the body matter? We need the body onstage not necessarily out of obedience to Gluck's authorial intent, nor should we put the body back onto the stage only to counteract some non-representational staging at the turn of the twenty-first century. Rather, I argue that we need the body onstage to remind us that humans were believed, in writings of the Enlightenment, to have the liberty to think. The body is indispensable because Gluck presented it in his Paris operas as a legible text that reveals interpersonal communication and psychoso-matic complexities in ways that are irreducible to – and irreplaceable by – orchestral accompaniment or stage props. I explained in Chapter Two that Rousseau fused music, gesture, and text into one semantic unit by way of a notational technique of precise alignment – and I continued that theme in this chapter by explaining how Gluck, in operatic pantomime, used a number of techniques to interrelate music, dance, and text: dense motivic layering, sequential pairing of recitative and panto-mime, stylistic and textual repetitions, and accessory ideas in orchestral accompa-niment. Since he took the semantically indistinct property of gesture and music as a compositional resource, rather than as a semantically imprecise inconvenience, Gluck carefully placed musical cues in significant parts of his operas, challenging his spectators to work out for each opera which signs stand for what, at what point, under what circumstances, how, and why.

Consequently, a performer's body in Gluck's Paris operas is less about any actors or actresses than about the spectators. The performer's body onstage helps us to become *thinking* interpreters. Whether gesture or music is a more truthful medium was a less pressing question for Gluck than how irreducible each of them is, and how fittingly they reinforce or weaken one another, especially when the success of a production may be contingent upon actors or actresses less skilled than the likes of Garrick and Clairon. Whether stationary or in motion, the body displays the rev-elatory potential of the nonverbal signs of music and gesture and the imperfection of words in human communication. The body spurs spectators to feel characters' torrents of unarticulated thoughts, desires, emotions, and impulses that make up

---

120 "La libre communication des pensées et opinions est un des droits les plus précieux de l'homme; tout citoyen peut donc parler, écrire, imprimer librement, sauf à répondre de l'abus de cette liberté dans les cas déterminés par la loi." http://www.conseil-constitutionnel.fr/conseil-constitutionnel/francais/la-constitution/la-constitution-du-4-octobre-1958/declaration-des-droits-de-l-homme-et-du-citoyen-de-1789.5076.html. Translation taken from Baker, Boyer, and Kirshner, eds, *The Old Regime*, 239.

human consciousness. By making invisible things visible, audible, and thereby perceptible in pantomimes, both Garrick and Gluck found ways, in music and acting,
to enrich the literal meanings of the verbal text. Marmontel might say that Wilson's
production curtails spectators' enjoyment of our interpretations of nonverbal signs
in opera. But this claim, grounded in the utilitarianism of Rousseau, is not as weighty
as Marmontel's more elemental anthropocentric vision: to wit, the pantomime
(whether as a dance or a naturalistic style of acting) helps us develop confidence
in ourselves as thinking subjects interested in – and capable of – comprehending a
broad spectrum of human communication, especially when it comes to detecting
the things that move underneath the observable surface.

CHAPTER FOUR

Things that Walk

O N October 1, 1776 Noverre made a point about liberty in his ballet-pantomime *Apelles et Campaspe, ou La Générosité d'Alexandre* (Paris, Académie Royale de Musique). The plot is about the ancient Greek painter Apelles, who becomes infatuated with Campaspe, one of the favourite mistresses of Alexander the Great, while painting her portrait. Campaspe sits for Apelles, who pictures her variously as the belligerent Pallas, the bucolic Flore, and the enamored Diane who falls in love with Endymion – until he finally decides to paint Campaspe as Venus, the mother of love. Apelles then rushes to the canvas and attempts to paint but he is too aroused to hold his brushes. At one point, the intimacy between the painter and the sitter builds up. Apelles dismisses his attendants, walks towards Campaspe, and lets her know that he loves her. His behaviors touch Campaspe, who promptly falls in love with him, even at the risk of offending Alexander the Great. Here comes Noverre's point: "She prefers *liberty* to grandeur and ... the gift of Apelles's hand will be more valuable to her than Alexander the Great's throne."[1]

Thus Noverre illustrated the process through which Campaspe seeks out liberty for herself in light of Apelles's action. Cahusac explained this impact in the article "Enthusiasm" of the *Encyclopédie* (1755). Enthusiasm is a kind of fury (*fureur*) possessed by a man of genius. During an exquisite performance, superb actors could affect the audience and be affected by their reactions. This reciprocal interaction between actors and their audience was initiated by what Cahusac called "enthusiasm," as mentioned in Chapter Three. "It is enthusiasm that makes one feel; it augments by degrees. It passes from the soul of the actors to that of the spectators, and note that as the spectators are aroused, the performance of the actors becomes more animated." Cahusac's idea of enthusiasm explains the love felt by Apelles and Campaspe: a sentiment is deliberately suppressed by Apelles, revealed nonetheless by his basic reflexes, noticed by a keenly observant Campaspe, and *felt* by her. But Cahusac did not explain why motion is linked to the idea of freedom. To understand

---

1   "Elle préfère la liberté à la grandeur, & ... le don de sa main lui sera plus cher que le trône d'Alexandre." Noverre, *Apelles et Campaspe, ou La Générosité d'Alexandre* (Paris: Delormel, 1776), 12. Four ballet programs of *Apelles et Campaspe* are extant: 1) the 1773 one for Vienna; 2) the 1774 one for Milan; 3) the 1776 one for Paris; and 4) one for London published in *The Works of Monsieur Noverre* (1782). Unless stated otherwise, I refer to the 1776 synopsis. Despite its strong emphasis on performers' movements, this synopsis might not offer an accurate description of a performance. One reviewer was disappointed by the 1774 performance of it in Milan, claiming that the ballet-pantomime was dominated by dances rather than action. See "Lettera a Madame •••• sopra I Balli di *Apelle e Campaspe* e di *Adele*, dati da Mons. Noverre nel Teatro di Milano 1774," in Carmela Lombardi, *Il ballo pantomimo: lettere, saggi e libelli sulla danza (1773–1785)* (Turin: Paravia Scriptorium, 1998), 89–91. On this ballet-pantomime, see Arianna Beatrice Fabbricatore, *La Querelle des Pantomimes*, 235–51.

this link means to place the ideas of motion and action in the history of autonomy. Two key concepts emerge as significant in this chapter: freedom of motion and freedom of action.

MOTION, ACTION, AND AGENCY

What do motion and action mean? Cognitive linguists and philosophers George Lakoff and Mark Johnson claimed in 1998 that "freedom of motion" is a common metaphor for "freedom of action." They provided neither definitions for "motion" and "action," nor explanations for what elements or conditions can make motion or action "free," but they offered suggestive themes for historicist research.[2] Indeed, allusions to free expression are found in Enlightenment writings on pantomime. Dubos, for example, observed in *Réflexions critiques* that ancient actors abandoned themselves to uninhibited personal expressions at particularly emotional moments of a performance: "These places in a dramatic work that the ancients called *Canticas* are typically the most passionate places, because the actor, who believes himself in complete liberty, makes the effort there to offer his most secret and impetuous sentiments that he inhibits or conceals in other scenes."[3] Cahusac noted that movement variety could represent a kind of stylistic freedom that mitigated stylistic uniformity: "It seems that dignity is incompatible with this sweet liberty that alone gives birth to, maintains, and knows how to vary pleasure."[4]

Noverre furthered Cahusac's idea in his *Lettres sur la danse* by mentioning ways for a performer to free themselves from physical or mental restraints. In Letter no.8 Noverre asked actors to free themselves mentally from any preconceived ideas of the roles they were to play, and to reconceive these roles from scratch: "Every actor at the theater must be free. He must not even be hindered from the role and from the character he has to depict."[5] Noverre implied that there was a critical difference between performance and text, and that actors had agency to reconceive a text in their performances. This point is reinforced by Béatrice Didier, who claimed in 2016 that an eighteenth-century pantomime had "a margin of liberty greater than a singer, [who is] subjected more narrowly to rhymes of text and of music."[6] But a movement style – however free it was designed to be – needed to be executed by

2   George Lakoff and Mark Johnson, *Philosophy in the Flesh: The Embodied Mind and Its Challenge to Western Thought* (New York: Basic Books, 1999), 305. On the concept of freedom of action, see Gideon Yaffe, *Liberty Worth the Name: Locke on Free Agency* (Princeton, NJ: Princeton University Press, 2000), 13–20.

3   "Ces endroits d'une pièce dramatique que les anciens appelaient des cantiques, sont ordinairement les endroits les plus passionnés, parce que l'acteur qui se croit dans une entière liberté, y donne l'effort à ses sentiments les plus secrets et les plus impétueux qu'il contraint ou qu'il déguise dans les autres scènes." Dubos, *Réflexions*, 3:178.

4   "Il semble que la dignité soit incompatible avec cette douce liberté, qui seule fait naître, entretient et sait varier le plaisir." Cahusac, *La Danse*, 170.

5   "Tout acteur au théâtre doit être libre: il ne doit pas même recevoir des entraves du rôle & du personnage qu'il a à représenter." Noverre, *Lettres*, 185.

6   Béatrice Didier, "La pantomime à l'Opéra et à l'Opéra Comique dans la deuxième moitié du XVIIIᵉ siècle," in Franck Salaün and Patrick Taïeb, eds, *Musique et Pantomime dans le Neveu de Rameau* (Paris: Hermann, 2016), 189.

a body. In Letter no.12 Noverre demanded that performers prepare their bodies for performance by ridding them of unnecessary muscle tension: "Were we to lay fingers under a restraint, when playing on an instrument; could we expect to have either spirit or brilliance in the execution? – Doubtless no – the perfect and free use of the hand and fingers can only produce that life, sprightliness and precision, which are the essence of the performance."[7]

To understand the relationship between performance and freedom, Noverre identified the factors that might curtail a performer's freedom. Institutionalized customs constituted one factor. As Kathleen Kuzmick Hansell has observed, Noverre freed his idea of ballet-pantomime from the "repressive traditions peculiar to the Paris Opéra" – including the uses of masks, elaborate headdresses, and costumes that restrict dancers' movements – when he imagined his genre of ballet-pantomime as an "offspring of liberty" (*un art enfant de la liberté*).[8] This point is supported by Watelet's definition of "liberty," published in the *Encyclopédie méthodique* on fine arts (*beaux-arts*) (1788): "We understand by this word not only the state opposite of that of slavery, but also the exemption from all subjugations, all fears, which make the situation of the *ingénu* similar, in some respects, to that of the slave."[9] Watelet's definition of liberty is all-encompassing, covering all forms of subjugations and fears. Yet, as discussed in Chapter Three, even the finest actor could not be entirely free from his own physio-psychological condition. Noverre recognized how *little* freedom even the pre-eminent actor David Garrick possessed, despite the fact that he championed a naturalistic style of acting, a style purposefully designed to be free from the wooden, stylized acting style: "You understand, Monsieur, that he [Garrick] is not very free, that his soul is always agitated, that his imagination is constantly working, that he is in a tiring [state of] enthusiasm three quarters of his life, which impairs his health the more he torments himself, and which he internalizes into a sad and wretched situation twenty-four hours before portraying it and freeing himself from it."[10]

Noverre's observations about the unfree Garrick indicate that determinism (*fatalité*) informed his thinking about bodily movement. In general, determinism posits that events are necessarily caused by earlier events and that the principle of causality explains movements of matter (such as atoms) and even human behaviors. In his *L'Homme machine* (1747), Julien Offray de La Mettrie argued that the human

---

7   Noverre, *Lettres*, 322. Translation taken from Burden and Thorp, eds, *The Works of Monsieur Noverre*, 359.

8   On pantomime and freedom, see Kathleen Kuzmick Hansell, *International Encyclopedia of Dance*, ed. Selma Jeanne Cohen, 6 vols. (New York: Oxford University Press, 1998), vol. 4, s.v. "Noverre, Jean-Georges"; Dahms, *Der konservative Revolutionär*, 24–31; Nye, *Mime*, 84–111.

9   "On entend par ce mot non-seulement l'état opposé à celui d'esclavage, mais encore l'exemption de tous les assujettissements, de toutes les craintes, qui rendent la situation de l'ingénu semblable, à quelques égards, à celle de l'esclave." Watelet, s.v. "Liberté."

10 "Vous concevez, Monsieur, qu'il est peu libre; que son âme est toujours agitée; que son imagination travaille sans cesse; qu'il est les trois quarts de sa vie dans un Enthousiasme fatigant qui altère d'autant plus sa santé qu'il se tourmente & qu'il se pénètre d'une situation triste & malheureuse, vingt-quatre heures avant de la peindre & de s'en délivrer." Noverre, *Lettres*, 213.

body works like a machine, observing that inanimate matter, such as the body of a beheaded chicken, a heart of a frog excised from the carcass, or a muscle separated from the body, may twitch on its own for some time before it stops moving. Seeing a body in mechanical terms of cause and effect, action and reaction, La Mettrie saw no essential difference between animals and men. He disagreed that an immaterial soul caused bodily movements, and claimed that his view typified the Enlightenment: "That great chemist [Georg Ernst Stahl] wanted to persuade us that the soul alone was the cause of all our movements; but that is the talk of a fanatic, not a *philosophe*."[11] What La Mettrie meant by a "*philosophe*" in this context, in contradistinction to a "fanatic," was a person who studied science and strived to explain observable effects relative to their causes. In *Système de la nature* (1770), as mentioned in Chapter Three, d'Holbach developed La Mettrie's deterministic thinking by making a distinction between necessity and constraint, claiming that human actions cannot be completely free of necessity, although we can free our actions from *some* constraints.[12]

Thus, eighteenth-century determinists offered a framework for conceptualizing freedom in terms of motion, and this topic has a long history. In *The Nature of Things* (100–50s BC), Lucretius wrote about freedom and motion: "Now by what motion atoms come together to create / Various things, or how these things once formed can dissipate, / And by what force they are compelled, and what freedom of motion / They have to meander through the vasty void, I shall explain, / Just pay close attention" (2.62–67). Hobbes noted in his *Leviathan* (1651) that matter is free when it moves by overcoming external impediments: "Of all living creatures, whilst they are imprisoned, or restrained, with walls, or chains, ... they are not at liberty, to move in such manner, as without those external impediments they would" (2.21.1). Hobbes went on to define what he called "corporal liberty" as "freedom from chains, and prison" (2.21.6). Hobbes's idea of "corporal liberty" was elaborated by Locke, who coined in his *An Essay Concerning Human Understanding* (1690) a new term called "motivity," which means a *will* or the human mental capacity for initiating bodily movements: "The Ideas we have belonging, and peculiar to Spirit, are Thinking, and Will, or *a power of putting Body into motion* by Thought, and, which is consequent to it, Liberty" (2.23.18). But Locke left one question unanswered: what made a being human? British philosopher Samuel Clarke advanced Locke's argument in his Boyle Lectures (1704–05) by differentiating "physical liberty" (i.e., self-moving power) from "moral liberty": "In men, this physical liberty is joined with a sense

---

11   Julien Offray de La Mettrie, *Machine Man and Other Writings*, trans. and ed. Ann Thomson (Cambridge: Cambridge University Press, 1996), 31. See also Ann Thomson, *Bodies of Thought: Science, Religion, and the Soul in the Early Enlightenment* (Oxford: Oxford University Press, 2008), chs. 3 and 6.

12   "Les actions des hommes ne sont jamais libres; elles sont toujours des suites nécessaires de leur tempérament, de leurs idées reçues, des notions vraies ou fausses qu'ils se font du Bonheur, enfin de leurs opinions fortifiées par l'exemple, par l'éducation, par l'expérience journalière" (The actions of men are never free. They are always the necessary results of their temperament, of their received ideas, of the true or false notions they have of happiness, and finally, of their opinions strengthened by example, by education, by daily experience). D'Holbach, *Système de la nature*, 1:228. For a definition of "philosophe," see *Dictionnaire de l'Académie française* (1694), vol. 2, s.v. "Philosophe."

of consciousness of moral good and evil, and is therefore eminently called liberty. In beasts, the same physical liberty of self-moving power is wholly separate from a sense or consciousness or capacity of judging of moral good and evil."[13]

Although Locke and Clarke were British, their writings laid the groundwork for the discourse of liberty in writings of the French Enlightenment. Voltaire, for example, credited Locke in his poem "De la liberté" (1738): "The word Liberty means the power to do what we want. There is not, and there cannot be, any other liberty. This is why Locke defined Power so well."[14] In the article on moral liberty in the *Encyclopédie*, the attributed authors Naigeon and Yvon criticized seventeenth-century determinists such as Hobbes for spreading the view that human beings have no choice but to follow an unalterable sequence of events, that they are no different from "pure automatons," and that their behavior is impelled by external causes "as a clock submits to the movements" engineered by a watchmaker.[15] Naigeon and Yvon disagreed that human behave the same way as matter, arguing instead that individuals who exercise their will possess an inner power, what Clarke called a "power of agency" that could originate a conscious human choice. It is this choice that leads to a decision, which causes action.[16]

To investigate the idea of agency in studies of pantomime, I propose using "freedom of motion" and "freedom of action" as key concepts. "Freedom of motion" is not the same as Hobbes's idea of "corporal liberty" (i.e., freedom from chains and prisons) or Clarke's idea of "physical liberty" (i.e., self-moving power). Rather, "freedom of motion" carries almost the same meaning as Locke's idea of "motivity," which results from the *volition* that "tames the body and represses all the movements with violence."[17] This is a crucial distinction. One who has freedom of motion can choose to move or not move, and does not *need* to move in order to exercise one's agency. A process from unfreedom to freedom would be interpreted by Hobbes as a typical instance of freedom of motion but, according to Locke and Clarke, other processes such as inaction to inaction, or action to inaction, are also examples of freedom of motion, so long as an agent decides not to move or act after weighing available options.

These ideas establish a historicist framework of motion, action, and agency in mid-eighteenth-century France: freedom of motion is not equivalent to freedom of action, and to move is not the same as to act. Freedom of speech (i.e., to speak

13 Samuel Clarke, *The Works of Samuel Clarke*, 4 vols. (New York: Garland, 1978), 4:729.

14 "On entend par ce mot Liberté le pouvoir de faire ce qu'on veut. Il n'y a, et ne peut y avoir d'autre liberté. C'est pourquoi Locke l'a si bien définie Puissance." *CWV*, 17:471. On the reception of Locke's writings in France, see John W. Yolton, *Locke and French Materialism* (Oxford: Clarendon Press, 1991).

15 Naigeon and Yvon [attributed], *Encyclopédie*, vol. 9, s.v. "Liberté [Morale]."

16 On causation, origination, and action, see Ted Honderich, *How Free Are You? The Determinism Problem*, 2nd edn (Oxford: Oxford University Press, 2002), 37–64; on Clarke's idea of freedom, see Jerome B. Schneewind, *The Invention of Autonomy: A History of Modern Moral Philosophy* (New York: Cambridge University Press, 1998), 310–23.

17 "Elle [Cette liberté] dompte les corps, & en réprime avec violence tous les mouvements." Naigeon and Yvon [attributed], *Encyclopédie*, vol. 9, s.v. "Liberté [Morale]."

or not to speak as one wills) can be an example of freedom of action, and one does not need to make any movements when one speaks out. Writers employed different expressions to indicate the idea of freedom of action. For Voltaire, "freedom of action" meant "the power to do what we want" (*le pouvoir de faire ce qu'on veut*), which is tantamount to the expression, "the power to act" (*le pouvoir d'agir*). He made this claim in his *Traité de métaphysique* (1734): "Liberty is only the power to act."[18] The expression "the power to act" became a core idea about human agency in the Enlightenment, an idea that presented an alternative to determinism. According to the article "Moral Liberty" in the *Encyclopédie*, "It is absolutely necessary to recognize a beginning of action, that is, a power to act independent of any previous action, and that this power can be – and indeed is – in man."[19]

That said, although the expression "freedom of action" stresses the word "action," some *philosophes* employed this expression in contexts that had no immediate bearing on bodily movement. In *Discours préliminaire* (1751), d'Alembert explained human agency in terms of freedom to act and to think (*liberté d'agir et de penser*): "It is only the freedom to act and think that is capable of producing great things, and it [the freedom] only needs enlightenment [*lumières*] to preserve itself from excesses."[20] In the article on "natural, moral, divine, and human law," Jaucourt used the expression "freedom to act" in the legal context of rights: "The law can be defined as a rule prescribed by the sovereign to his subjects, either for imposing on them the obligation to do or not do certain things, under the threat of some penalty, or for giving them the freedom to act, or not to act."[21] In his *La Morale universelle* (1776), d'Holbach even drew on the expression "freedom of action" as the equivalent of the whole gamut of human rights: "In the state of society, the rights of men, or the freedom to act, are limited by justice, which shows them that they must only act in a manner consistent with the well-being of society, which is created to interest them because they are its members."[22]

These dissimilar uses of "freedom of action" demonstrate that "freedom of action" was an expression employed in many contexts. For the purposes of this book, these uses – from motion to movement to volition to human rights – could provide conceptual pathways that connect theater with moral philosophy, linking

18 "La liberté est uniquement le pouvoir d'agir." *OCV*, 14:460.

19 "Il faut de toute nécessité reconnaître un commencement d'action, c'est-à-dire un pouvoir d'agir indépendamment d'aucune action précédente, & que ce pouvoir peut être & est effectivement dans l'homme." Naigeon and Yvon [attributed], *Encyclopédie*, vol. 9, s.v. "Liberté [Morale]."

20 "Il n'y a que la liberté d'agir & de penser qui soit capable de produire de grandes choses, & elle n'a besoin que de lumières pour se préserver des excès." D'Alembert, *Discours préliminaire*, xx. [ARTFL]

21 "On peut définir la *loi* une règle prescrite par le souverain à ses sujets, soit pour leur imposer l'obligation de faire, ou de ne pas faire certaines choses, sous la menace de quelque peine, soit pour leur laisser la liberté d'agir, ou de ne pas agir." Jaucourt, *Encyclopédie*, vol. 9, s.v. "Loi [Droit naturel/droit moral/droit divin/droit humain]."

22 "Dans l'état de société les droits des hommes, ou la liberté d'agir, sont limités par la justice, qui leur montre qu'ils ne doivent agir que d'une façon conforme au bien-être de la société, faite pour les intéresser parce qu'ils en sont les membres." D'Holbach, *Œuvres philosophiques*, vol. 5: 1776–1790 (Paris: Coda, 2004), 380.

bodily movements, presented at the theater to the idea of human agency. After all, at around the time Condillac wrote about *langage d'action*, music and dance genres that emphasized actions – Cahusac's *danse en action* to Angiolini's *ballet d'action* to Calzabigi/Gluck's *Orfeo* as an *azione teatrale* – were staged in cities across western Europe. Once these conceptual pathways are in place, "freedom of action" is no longer a suggestive idea coined by Lakoff and Johnson; rather, it becomes a historicist tool bridging the intellectual project of the French Enlightenment and the musical and dance genres in the 1740s to 1760s, which featured "action" as a defining characteristic.

To make "freedom of action" an expression that could explain the phenomenon of pantomime, it is important to treat the expression "freedom of action" and the term "action" independently. Whereas "freedom of action" was sometimes used in legal contexts, "action" had two meanings: pantomime action and dramatic action. In Mallet's article "Action (literature)" of the *Encyclopédie* (1751), "action" was defined as "the entire exterior of an orator – his countenance, his voice, his gesture – which he must match with the subject he is dealing with."[23] To Mallet's mind, action was separate from dramatic action in poetry, for he wrote separate entries for them and made no attempt to discuss them in relation to one another. Yet, contrary to Mallet, Diderot brought action and dramatic action together in his *Entretiens sur le fils naturel* (1757), arguing that pantomime action links closely to dramatic action. A pantomime actor can imitate nature by depicting the quotidian life (*la vie réelle*) in domestic or bourgeois tragedy. Indeed, pantomime action made by a great pantomime such as LUI in Diderot's *Le Neveu de Rameau*, Patrick Salaün argues, externalizes a jumble of feelings, scenes, memories, and musical snippets that LUI experiences internally.[24] But the conflation of action and dramatic action did not last. Diderot's point was challenged by Marmontel, who rethought the definitions of "action" and "dramatic action." Initially, Marmontel followed Diderot's lead, stating in the article "Pantomime (dramatic art)" of the *Supplément à l'Encyclopédie* (1776–77) that it was necessary to employ the art of pantomime at the most passionate moments of a play. Yet, in the article "Action," which he wrote for his *Éléments de littérature* (1787), he asserted that pantomime action should be fundamentally different from dramatic action: "A natural effect of dramatic action is to produce pantomime, but pantomime is not action; and when we say of a play containing much movement, tableaux and acting that there is a lot of action, we make a mistake that can be of consequence."[25]

Marmontel's evolving thinking about pantomime action followed a tradition of dramatic theory in French theater founded upon the Aristotelian three unities (*Poetics* 4.4). In the article "Unity," which he wrote for the *Supplément à*

---

23 "Tout l'extérieur de l'Orateur, de sa contenance, de sa voix, de son geste, qu'il doit assortir au sujet qu'il traite." Mallet, *Encyclopédie*, vol. 1, s.v. "Action [Belles-Lettres]."

24 Diderot, *Œuvres*, 4:1174, 1185. Franck Salaün, "*De la tête aux pieds*: Diderot et les gens de spectacle," *Recherches sur Diderot et sur l'Encyclopédie* 47 (2012), 40–42.

25 "Un effet naturel de l'action dramatique, c'est de produire la pantomime: mais la pantomime n'est pas l'action; & lorsque d'une pièce où il y a beaucoup de mouvements, de tableaux, de jeu de théâtre, on dit qu'il y a beaucoup d'action, on tombe dans une méprise qui peut être de conséquence." Marmontel, *Éléments*, vol. 1., s.v. "Action."

l'Encyclopédie, Marmontel defined "unity of action" in terms of parts and whole, dramatic episodes and dramatic action: "The principal action of a poem must be subordinate to or a result of all the specific actions that are employed as incidents or episodes."[26] On the surface, what was new in 1787 is that Marmontel untangled Diderotian pantomime action from Aristotelian dramatic action, so that he justified speech in French opera. He admitted that pantomime was more accessible than speech because its meanings were more ambiguous, but he insisted that pantomime was only a constituent element of dramatic action: "The spectacle is only a means of poetic eloquence, and although its immediate purpose is to amuse, to please, to move, it is still not its ultimate goal: this goal is to send away the spectator more enlightened, wiser, better, if possible, and at least richer in thoughts and feelings, virtuous."[27]

On a deeper level, Marmontel accepted the place of pantomime in the geneal-ogy of dance and the archaeology of communication, but he also added another dimension by reframing pantomime as a *problem* of dramatic theory, rather than the *solution* to the ossification of *la belle danse* and stylized acting conventions, as Dubos, Cahusac, Jaucourt, Diderot, and others did. In the article "Pantomime" in *Supplément à l'Encyclopédie* (1777), Marmontel categorized pantomime as a dramatic art and defined it as "the language of action, the art of speaking to the eyes, and mute expression." Later in the same article, he argued against substituting pantomime dance for dance at the theater: "There is no reason to want that dance always be pan-tomime."[28] By separating pantomime action from dramatic action, Marmontel pre-sented a post-Diderotian thinking in the 1780s, recognizing characters' expression of their agency without necessarily moving their bodies. The following case studies illustrate the practice and discourse on pantomime in the early 1780s.

A KINETIC FAREWELL

By separating pantomime action from dramatic action, one can notice elements of pantomime in musical works other than operas and ballets. Scholars including Le Guin who work on music and embodiment theorize ways that musicians relate to their *music*-making bodies, but they are yet to explain why it is shocking to see musi-cians make physical movements that have no bearing on the sounds they make. This facet needs attention, especially when this kind of shock adds a theatrical dimension to an otherwise strictly *musical* performance. One of the most discussed examples of musicians' non-music-making action is the Paris premiere of Haydn's symphony H.45 in F-sharp minor (1772). On April 13, 1784 this performance ended the concert

---

26 "L'action principale d'un poème doit être une dépendance, un résultat de toutes les actions particulières qu'on y emploie comme incidents ou épisodes." Marmontel, *Supplément*, vol. 4, s.v. "Unité."

27 "Le spectacle n'est qu'un moyen de l'éloquence poétique; & quoique son objet immédiat soit d'amuser, de plaire, d'émouvoir, ce n'est point encore là sa fin ultérieure: cette fin est de renvoyer le spectateur plus éclairé, plus sage, meilleur, s'il est possible, au moins plus riche de pensées & de sentiments, vertueux." Marmontel, *Éléments*, s.v. "Action."

28 "Il n'y a aucune raison de vouloir que la danse soit toujours pantomime." Marmontel, *Supplément*, vol. 4, s.v. "Pantomime (Art dramatique)."

by having the musicians leave the stage, one after another, *before* the symphony had finished, leaving behind only two violinists to play until the end. The musicians' departure in this performance marked symbolically the end of the occupancy of the Salle des Cent-Suisses, a hall that had housed the Concert Spirituel since its opening in 1725. After this farewell concert the Concert Spirituel was relocated to the Salle des Machines of the Salle du Château des Tuileries, which had been vacant since 1782.[29]

Surprisingly, the Paris premiere of Haydn's "Farewell" symphony was described in Pierre-Jean-Baptiste Nougaret's *Tableau mouvant* (1787) as a pantomime: "The famous Haydn composed ... a symphony of which the last movement is of an extraordinary genre ... At the last [concert of the] Concert Spirituel in the old hall, this symphony was performed with all the pantomime. Only La Houssaye and [Alexandre] Guénin remain in the orchestra to finish the piece."[30] By referring the performance of Haydn's "Farewell" to "pantomime," Nougaret considered panto-mime a *medium* of communication between performers and spectators, not a *genre* of dance that followed generic conventions.

Nougaret's comment deserves particular attention because he was familiar with the discourse and the practice of pantomime. By the time Nougaret published his commentary about Haydn's "Farewell," in 1787, he had been writing about panto-mime for about twenty years. In his *De l'art du théâtre* (1769), he promoted Diderot's idea that a pantomime would enrich the verbal text, not merely enhance a perfor-mance with gesticulation.[31] His suggestion was not always practical, and unsatisfac-tory performances abounded. In *Observations sur les trois derniers Ballets Pantomimes qui ont paru aux italiens & aux François* of 1759, Goudar criticized the *ballet-héroïque La Mort Orphée, ou Les Fêtes de Bacchus* by Auguste Hus (Comédie-Française, June 6, 1759): "Confusion rules there from one end to the other. We would understand nothing of it, if we did not constantly look to find in the livret what a certain attitude means, or what this or that step signifies."[32]

Critics also found it confusing for actors to use gestures extensively while declaiming verses at the spoken theater. In the inaugural issue of the satirical jour-nal *Le Nouveau Spectateur* (1776), edited by Le Fuel de Méricourt, a self-styled

29 See also Constant Pierre, *Histoire du Concert spiritual: 1725–1790* (Paris: Société Française de Musicologie, 1975), 57–58. On musicians' getting up and leaving the hall, see James Webster, *Haydn's "Farewell" Symphony and the Idea of Classical Style: Through-Composition and Cyclic Integration in His Instrumental Music* (New York: Cambridge University Press, 1991), 2, 113–19.

30 Pierre-Jean-Baptiste Nougaret, *Tableau mouvant de Paris, ou Variétés amusantes*, 3 vols. (Paris: Duchesne, 1787), 1:205–207.

31 On pantomime, see Nougaret, *De l'art du théâtre, où il est parlé des différents genres de spectacles, et de la musique adaptée au théâtre*, 2 vols. (Paris: Cailleau, 1769), 1:353–54. On pantomime as a redundant text, see Rougement, *La Vie théâtrale*, 50–51.

32 "La confusion y règne depuis un bout jusqu'à l'autre; on n'y comprendrait rien, si on n'allait chercher à chaque instant dans le petit Livre ce que veut dire une certaine attitude, ou ce que signifie tel ou tel pas." Goudar, *Observations*, 41. For the synopsis, see *La Mort d'Orphée, ou Les Fêtes de Bacchus* (Paris: Delormel, 1759). On Goudar's *Observations*, see Jean-Claude Hauc, *Ange Goudar: Un aventurier des Lumières* (Paris: Honoré Champion, 2004), 86.

philosophe 'showed' the actor Henri-Louis Le Kain's extremely sentimental performance in *Lorédan* (Comédie-Française, 1776). The script was unpublished, but this
Philosophe, a pencil in hand during the performance, *transcribed* Le Kain's extraor-
dinarily sentimental style of declamation when Lorédan just wakes up from a nightmare and finds himself in a prison cell. The beginning of this transcription reads:
" ....?!!!?::? Qu'ai.-.je ... vu??? ... .Ciel!!!!! où..sont::::ces ... é.chaffff.ffauds??? ....."
To offer a critical apparatus for his transcription, this Philosophe wrote in a footnote
what some of these punctuation marks stand for: "Each period is half a second of
silence; every exclamation point is a twirling of eyes toward the sky: at each question
mark he throws his arms from side to side, and he often clenches his fists while biting
his lips. When periods are interlaced with commas, it is the parterre or the boxes that
one stares at."[33] The point of this transcription is not to show that gesture was an
imperfect medium of communication at the theater, but that the concurrent usage
of action and speech might be ineffective. Although Dubos, Rousseau, Diderot, and
others had proposed such usage, the Philosophe showed that "one [medium] always
weakens the other."[34]

   Aside from criticisms about the practicality of pantomime at the theater, the
pantomimic element of Haydn's "Farewell" was received warmly by the Parisians.
According to Nougaret, "The public laughs heartily over the joke [*plaisanterie*]."[35]
No doubt the pantomimic element was one contributing factor of the joke, but
the ingenuity of concert programming was also significant. By the time Haydn's
"Farewell" premiered at the Concert Spirituel, director Joseph Legros, who had
directed the Concert Spirituel since 1777, had introduced works by "foreign" composers to the concert series.[36] From March 25, 1777 to the Easter concert on April
11, 1784, Haydn's symphony was always the opening item whenever it appeared in
a concert. Yet the program of the concert on April 13, 1784 disrupted this tradition:
the concert program followed what William Weber called a "symmetrical" design,
having a sequence of six vocal and instrumental pieces sandwiched between two
symphonies. Rather than beginning the concert with a symphony by Haydn, as had
been the case ever since the Concert Spirituel performed Haydn's symphonies, this
concert opened with a new symphony by the Italian composer Gaetano Brunetti
and *ended* with Haydn's "Farewell." It was a deliberate decision. The program even
specified that it was a symphony "where they leave" (*où l'on s'en va*), suggesting that
musicians performed a kind of "kinetic" farewell to a concert hall. That is, musicians
"said" farewell with their bodily movements: they took off, one after another.

---

33   "Chaque point est une demi-seconde de silence; chaque point d'exclamation est un
      tournoiement d'yeux vers le Ciel: à chaque point d'interrogation on jette ses bras de
      côté & d'autre, & souvent l'on ferme les poings en se mordant les lèvres. Quand il y a
      des points entrelacés de virgules, c'est le Parterre ou les Loges que l'on fixe." *Le Nouveau
      Spectateur* 1 (Paris: Esprit, 1776), 28 n.1.

34   "L'un affaiblit toujours l'autre." *Le Nouveau Spectateur*, 27.

35   "Le Public rit beaucoup de la plaisanterie." Nougaret, *Tableau*, 207.

36   On Legros, see Beverly Wilcox, "The Music Libraries of the Concert Spirituel: Canons,
      Repertories, and Bricolage in Eighteenth-Century Paris," PhD diss., University of
      California at Davis, 2013, 87–94.

This unusual, kinetic kind of farewell was well publicized. The issue of *Journal of Paris* published on the day of the concert of April 13, 1784 announced the circumstantial meaning of Haydn's symphony: "As the last concert at the current concert hall [Salle des Cent-Suisses], this concert will end with a new symphony by Haydn, [which is] analogous to the circumstance."[37] One should note the historical significance of this unconventional programming. After the relocation, Haydn's symphonies resumed to be the opening numbers at the Concert Spirituel whenever they appeared on the program, from April 18, 1784 until the last concert on the Ascension Day of May 13, 1790 at the Panthéon. This programming history shows that Haydn's "Farewell" in Paris had little direct connection to Haydn's experience at Eszterháza, in Hungary. In fact, the well-thought-out and well-received kinetic farewell to the Salle des Cent-Suisses marked the end of a historical phase of institutional history of the Concert Spirituel.[38]

Part of the appeal of Haydn's Paris "Farewell" was that it offered an example of what Hobbes called "corporal liberty," which could be explained by Enlightenment materialism. In his investigation of the "Farewell," James Webster claims that this symphony is overtly programmatic, although no evidence indicates that Haydn used the theme of farewell in his creative process. The nickname "Farewell" came neither from Haydn nor from any eighteenth-century music sources. To offer internal evidence for the claim of being "programmatic," Webster demonstrates tonal and motivic procedures that create a musical journey from instability to stability throughout the symphony, a musical journey that suggests a "psychological progression."[39] What Webster does not address, however, is the linkage between the psychological progression and its physiological effect. This psycho-physiological linkage was theorized by biological materialism in the Enlightenment. D'Holbach claimed in *Système de la nature*: "A body acts and moves by its own energy. Of this kind are the movements of a man who walks, who speaks, who thinks."[40]

But who was doing the thinking? Whereas it was clear that musicians manifest corporal liberty while leaving the stage, it was unclear who exercised freedom of motion and freedom of action. As Locke might have it, a musical *part* is not a *being* that could make choices, and there is no evidence that the musicians who performed that symphony in 1784 participated in a decision process about offering a theatricalized farewell to the hall. The musicians' corporal liberty could suggest Haydn's freedom of action, but there is no hard evidence, as Webster points out, to indicate that Haydn himself came up with the theatrics.[41] At best, the evidence suggests that musicians' corporal liberty in the Paris performance came from director Legros's freedom of action: it was Legros's decision to have musicians leave the stage before

37 *Journal de Paris* (April 13, 1784), 458. See also *Mercure de France* (April 3, 1784), 180.

38 For the program of this concert, see Pierre, *Histoire du Concert Spirituel*, 326. For a list of the foreign composers, see ibid., 175–76. On the symmetrical design of concert programs, see William Weber, *The Great Transformation of Musical Taste: Concert Programming from Haydn to Brahms* (New York: Cambridge University Press, 2008), 45.

39 Webster, *Haydn's "Farewell" Symphony*, 119.

40 D'Holbach, *Système*, 1:49–50.

41 Webster, *Haydn's "Farewell" Symphony*, 2.

the end of the performance; it was Legros who made this choreographed departure symbolically significant; it was Legros who added the visual-kinetic dimension to a musical performance; it was Legros who authorized the pantomimic treatment of this otherwise conventional concert performance; it was Legros who had *Journal de Paris* publicize the unusual concert.

Legros's career path reveals why he privileged the art of pantomime. Before becoming director of the Concert Spirituel, he was the leading haute-contre of the Opéra, who had sung the title role of Gluck's *Orphée* in 1774 and Admète in Gluck's *Alceste* in 1776. He had first-hand experience of the visually stimulating techniques, including pantomime dances and pantomimic acting, that Gluck introduced to his operas. By the time he became director of the Concert Spirituel, Legros probably borrowed the aesthetics of Gluck's opera reform from the Opéra to the Concert Spirituel. In this view, the kinetic farewell was not an accident: it was not intended by Haydn; it was an instance of cultural transferral administered by the director of Concert Spirituel, who transferred the idea of pantomime from Gluckian reform opera to the Paris concert scene. In Enlightenment terms, it was Legros who *spread* the idea of pantomime from the opera house to the concert hall.[42]

FROM *IPERMESTRA* TO *LES DANAÏDES*

Legros's professional experiences illustrate Gluck's enduring impact on Parisian musical culture, even after he left the city. By 1784 Gluck had left Paris for good (in October 1779), but pantomime continued to be used as a dance or a naturalistic style of acting in the operas staged at the Académie Royale de Musique. To be sure, performances of stand-alone *ballet d'action* became established at the Académie Royale de Musique by 1784, but uses of pantomime in French opera persisted.[43] For example, Niccolò Piccinni used two *ballets d'action* (I/vii; II/iii) and a *jeu muet* (II/ii) in his opéra *Diane et Endimion* (premiered at the Académie Royale de Musique on September 7, 1784). The major figure in the post-Gluck era was Salieri, who used pantomimes in all three operas he composed for Paris: *Les Danaïdes* (1784), *Les Horaces* (1786), and *Tarare* (1787).

Eighteenth-century audiences were familiar with the story of the Danaids. In France, composer Charles-Hubert Gervais had staged in 1716 a *tragédie lyrique* called *Hypermnestre* (with re-runs in 1728, 1746, and 1765).[44] *Hypermnestre*, by Théodore de Riupeirous (1664–1706), had been published in 1716, and a new edition of it was published in 1771 by the playwright Antoine-Marin Le Mierre (1733–93). Outside France, Metastasio wrote a libretto called *Ipermestra*, based on Aeschylus's *The Suppliant Maidens*. First performed in Vienna in 1744, with music by Johann Adolf

---

42 Benoît, *Dictionnaire*, s.v. "Concert-Spirituel des Tuileries." Wilcox, "The Music Libraries," 90. On the concept of cultural transfer, see Annegret Fauser and Mark Everist, eds, *Music, Theater, and Cultural Transfer: Paris, 1830–1914* (Chicago: The University of Chicago Press, 2009), 6.

43 On the *ballet d'action* in France in the 1780s, see Ivor Guest, *The Ballet of the Enlightenment: The Establishment of the Ballet d'action in France, 1770–1793* (New York: Dance Books, 1996), chs. 10–15.

44 On Gervais's *Hypermnestre* (1716), see Harris-Warrick, *Dance and Drama*, 336–42.

Hasse, Metastasio's *dramma per musica* was subsequently set to music by twenty-eight composers, including a setting by Gluck for Venice in 1744. Noverre also staged his version of *Ipermestra* as the ballet tragi-pantomime *Hypermnestre ou Les Danaïdes*, with music by Jean-Joseph Rodolphe (also called Johann-Joseph Rudolf), in Stuttgart (1764), Ludwigsburg (1765), Vienna (1769), and Naples (1774).[45]

One of the important aspects of Salieri's *tragédie lyrique Les Danaïdes* is its traceable genealogy. The librettists Du Roullet and Baron Ludwig Theodor von Tschudi stated in the preface to the libretto that they had consulted Calzabigi's *Ipermestra o Le Danaidi* and had borrowed ideas from Noverre's *Hypermnestre*.[46] This piece of information indicates a way to understand *Les Danaïdes* in relation to three genres: Metastasian *dramma per musica*, Gluckian Italian reform opera, and Noverre's ballet tragi-pantomime. Calzabigi began to write this libretto in 1778 at the request of Gluck, who wanted to compose music for *Ipermestra*. Gluck knew this story well. Even though he had composed music for Metastasio's *Ipermestra* thirty years earlier as a *dramma per musica*, evidently he considered setting Calzabigi's libretto on the same subject matter, but this time as an Italian reform opera in a deliberate critique of Metastasio's work. The success of Gluck's *Orphée et Euridice* and *Alceste* at the Opéra might have encouraged him to consider revisiting the subject matter from a different aesthetic. Calzabigi did not mention Metastasio's *Ipermestra* in his *Dissertazione sulle poesie drammatiche del Sig. Abate Pietro Metastasio* (1755), but his version of *Ipermestra* offered what Brown calls a critique of Metastasio's *Ipermestra*.[47] In November 1778 Calzabigi sent the finished libretto of *Ipermestra o le Danaidi* to Gluck, but Gluck did not complete it. Calzabigi then sent it to the castrato and composer Giuseppe Millico, who set it to music in 1783 and performed it in Naples. Millico, who had sung the role of Orfeo in the re-run of Gluck's *Orfeo ed Euridice* in Parma in 1769, shared Calzabigi's reform ideals. Millico did not publish the score of *Ipermestra*, but he praised the simplicity of text, orchestral accompaniment, and the natural, affecting expression of Gluck's reform operas in the preface of his *dramma messo in musica*, called *La pietà d'amore* (Naples, 1782). These biographical links show that Calzabigi and Millico's *Ipermestra* continued the *spirit* of Gluck's operatic reform, although Gluck did not compose its music.

The genealogy indicates that Metastasio's *Ipermestra*, Calzabigi's *Ipermestra o le Danaidi*, and Noverre's *Hypermnestre* formed a traceable cluster of three different genres that informed the genesis of Salieri's *tragédie lyrique Les Danaïdes*. Central to this cluster of works are the principles of Gluckian operatic reform. Other than playing a part in Calzabigi's *Ipermestra*, Gluck helped to facilitate the creation of Tschudi/Du Roullet's *Les Danaïdes*, set to music by Salieri. Gluck refused to

45 On the performance of Hasse's *Ipermestra* in London and its connection to Noverre's career, see Michael Burden, "Regular Meetings: Noverre and Gallini in London, 1756–1795," in Burden and Thorp, eds, *The Works of Monsieur Noverre*, 138.

46 "On nous a communiqué un manuscrit de M. de Calzabiggi [*sic*], Auteur de l'Orphée & de l'Alceste Italiens, dont nous nous sommes beaucoup aidés. Nous avons emprunté quelques idées du Ballet des Danaïdes du célèbre M. Noverre." *Les Danaïdes, tragédie-lyrique en cinq actes* (Paris: Didot, 1784), 2.

47 Bruce Alan Brown, "Calzabigi, Ranieri." *Grove Music Online. Oxford Music Online*, Oxford University Press, www.oxfordmusiconline.com, accessed April 21, 2020.

compose the music of *Les Danaïdes*. He passed the libretto on to Salieri, acknowl-
edging that the younger composer knew of his musical style but doubting his ability to compose the opera. *Les Danaïdes* was initially rejected by the Opéra but, in
response to Emperor Joseph II's letter of recommendation, this was overturned.
Although Gluck was listed with Salieri as a co-composer on the title page of the
livret, he clearly recused himself from this role, as indicated in the score published in
December 1784. The real extent of his contribution to the score may not be known,
but it is evident that Gluck was involved in the genesis and promotion of the opera.[48]

What makes *Les Danaïdes* an important case study in motion, action, and agency
is that Hypermnestre and her sisters could turn into different *types* of being, based
on their cognitive abilities. A comparison of these versions across four genres illustrates a basic point: a human being's humanity is changeable, not fixed. One must
consciously maintain one's humanity, lest one regress into an animalistic human
being. To explain human beings vis-à-vis animalistic beings, one could use Clarke's
dichotomy between man and beast, or a more elaborate theory in Condillac's *Traité
des animaux* (1755), which explains the continuity between human and animal.
Condillac's main concept was the "double self" (*deux moi*) – the self of habit and
that of reflection.[49]

The story of Ipermestra pits filial duty against romantic love, highlighting
Ipermestra, who saves her husband's life by refusing to execute her father's murderous order, in sharp contrast to her sisters, who kill their husbands. Metastasio
emphasized Ipermestra as the only daughter of Danaus, but the versions by Noverre,
Calzabigi, and Du Roullet/Tschudi emphasize Ipermestra in relation to her sisters,
the Danaids. The problem that drives the drama is this: if Ipermestra shares the
same bloodline as her sisters, how come she acts differently from them? This question raises the issue of nature and nurture. The distinction between Ipermestra and
her sisters cannot just be about kin, which is immutable, but also about their *degree*
of humanity, which, to Condillac's mind, is mutable. As the Danaids' humanity is
questionable, they raise the question of the lack of human agency in an extremely
homogeneous environment.

Homogeneity was a much-discussed topic in Enlightenment writings. A common
thought experiment was how ten thousand things of the same kind would act under
the same circumstances. Buffon speculated in his *Histoire naturelle* (1753) that ten
thousand individuals who act like ten thousand automatons or bees share the same
external or internal structure and that they act uniformly.[50] Condillac disagreed. He
questioned the empirical basis of Buffon's idea in *Traité des animaux* (1755), wonder-
ing whether such mechanical uniformity exists at all in nature. While ten thousand

---

48 On the history of the genesis of this opera, see John Rice, *Antonio Salieri and Viennese
    Opera* (Chicago: The University of Chicago Press, 1998), 309–15.

49 On "*deux moi*," see Condillac, *Traité des sensations; traité des animaux* (Paris: Fayard,
    1984), 319, 376.

50 Georges-Louis Leclerc, comte de Buffon, *Histoire naturelle, générale et particulière*, 36
    vols. (Paris: L'Imprimerie royale, 1753), 4:98.

automatons could in theory be manufactured as identical, the same number of bees could not possibly be identical in nature, however well-coordinated they appeared.[51]

In *Traité des animaux* Condillac theorized the differences between humans and animals in terms of instinct and reason. Driven by their needs, animals act on instinct; they develop few abstractions and few general ideas; they have practical knowledge and not theory; and they are unable to analyze complex situations. By contrast, humans act on reason; they identify not only what is good for them, but also truth and beauty; they develop not only practical knowledge, but also theory. Thus Condillac argued that animal has only one self, what he called "the self of habit," but humans possess a "double self" – one of habit and another of reflection – which makes humans more cognitively developed than animals. The self of habit manages the animal faculties of the body (e.g., sight, touch, smell), while the self of reflection monitors non-habitual behaviors. Unlike an animal, which only possesses the self of habit, a human's self of reflection plays a supervisory role by identifying mistakes and correcting them.[52]

Condillac claimed that sharing reflections with fellow humans, using speech, formed the cognitive foundation of a moral and free society governed by laws. "They [humans] *tell* each another everything they feel and everything they do not feel."[53] [emphasis mine] Condillac concluded his *Traité des animaux* by extending the topic from morality to volition. He did not assume that all humans have advanced cognitive functions, because a human is first and foremost an animal, but he claimed that individuals who have agency would employ the advanced cognitive operation of reflection: "The right to choose – liberty – belongs only to reflection. But circumstances control beasts; by contrast, man judges them, he adapts to them, he refuses them, he behaves, he wills, he is free."[54]

Condillac's concept of the "double self" offers an analytical tool for identifying human agency and measuring the *degree* of humanity a human being develops for oneself. Although the Danaids are humans, they allow themselves to regress and behave like animals. Although Hypermestre belongs to the same family as the Danaids, she exercises her moral liberty, thinking and acting like a human. With this concept in place, I now discuss four versions of *Ipermestra* – by Metastasio, by Noverre, by Calzabigi, and by Du Roullet/Tschudi.

---

51 Condillac, *Traité*, 330, 352.

52 Condillac, *Traité*, 375–82.

53 "Ils se dissent les uns aux autres tout ce qu'ils sentent et tout ce qu'ils ne sentent pas." Condillac, *Traité*, 400.

54 "Le droit de choisir, la liberté n'appartenir donc qu'à la réflexion. Mais les circonstances commandent les bêtes: l'homme au contraire les juge, il s'y prête, il s'y refuse, il se conduit lui-même, il veut, il est libre." Condillac, *Traité*, 418. Foucault used the term "conscious freedom" to indicate this type of freedom. See his "The Ethics of the Concern for Self as a Practice of Freedom," in Paul Rabinow, ed., *Ethics: Subjectivity and Truth*, trans. Robert Hurley and others (New York: New Press, 1997), 284.

AN OBEDIENT DAUGHTER

In his *dramma per musica Ipemestra*, Metastasio built a dramatic narrative around human communication. The plot begins with Danaus, king of Argos, who learns from an oracle that he will lose his kingdom and his life at the hands of a son of Aegyptus [Egyptus]. He orders his daughter, Ipermestra, who is about to marry one of Aegyptus's sons, Linceo [Lynceus], to kill her husband on their wedding night. Ipermestra faces a dilemma: should she stay loyal to her father and kill her lover? Or should she betray her father and save her lover's life? Danaus also demands that Ipermestra be loyal to him by keeping his murder plan a secret. Not only is she forbidden to disclose it verbally, but she also may not leak any details using nonverbal signs: "Make sure not to betray / the important secret. / Compose the face, measure the sayings and in need of wrath / then release the brake" (I/i, lines 74–76).[55] In the face of Danaus's command, Ipermestra feels powerless over her words and her behaviors that might come across as perfidious. As she says in an aside in the presence of Linceo, "Oh god! I do not know how to leave, / I do not know how to stay, I do not know how to form words" (I/iii, lines 107–108); in the presence of Linceo and Danao, she says in another aside: "What cruelty! I can / neither speak nor be silent" (I/ix, lines 353–54). Shifting the emphasis from speech to signs, Metastasio built dramatic tension in *Ipermestra* around the problem of communication. Given Danaus's command, the question is not simply: what does Ipermestra do to save her husband? But what does she *end up* doing, relative to what she could do, to save her husband's life without betraying her father?

Without disclosing Danaus's secretive murder plan, Metastasio's Ipermestra behaves in a way that unsettles everybody around her. She becomes a paranoid bride. She does not express joy on her wedding day and avoids eye contact with her fiancé, Linceo. Ipermestra's paranoia upsets Linceo, whose frustration alarms Danaus. Danaus then accuses Ipermestra of perfidy. Feeling affronted, Ipermestra asks Linceo's friend Plisthenes for help, but their encounter fuels Linceo's doubt about Ipermestra's constancy. Meanwhile, having heard of the murder plan from his lover Elpinice, Plisthenes alerts Linceo that Danaus wants Ipermestra to kill him. They revolt against Danaus. Yet here comes an Aristotelian reversal (*Poetics*, 6.3): instead of siding with Linceo and joining the uprising, Ipermestra chooses to be a good daughter by saving her father's life. In the end, Ipermestra's loyalty to *both* her father and her husband shames Danaus, who voluntarily passes his throne to her. The oracle turns out false; this opera is a human drama through and through. No one dies, and virtue triumphs. Ipermestra exercises her freedom of action not because she speaks out (a Hobbesian freedom *from* oppressive silencing), but because she remains silent throughout: she never says anything or makes any signs that betray her father, while leaving secondary characters Plisthenes and Elpinice to foil Danaus's murderous plan. Ipermestra exercises her agency because she refuses to take a side. It is her perceived "passive" behavior that exemplifies her freedom of action.[56]

---

55   "Il gran segreto / guarda di non tradir. Componi il volto, / misura i detti e nel bisogno all'ire / poi sciogli il freno." Metastasio, *Ipermestra*, lines 74–76.

56   On the dramaturgy of Metastasio's *opera seria*, see Feldman, *Opera and Sovereignty*, ch. 6.

A MASS OF KILLERS

It is revealing to compare Metastasio's Italian opera with Noverre's ballet-pantomime on the same topic. Following the convention of the *dramma per musica*, Metastasio did not provide many stage directions for acting, or indicate dance or pantomime, although he did indicate standard cues for singers to exit the stage. In sharp contrast, Noverre used dancers' bodily gestures as a dramatically revealing medium in his ballet-pantomime.

The Danaids are critical to Noverre's ballet because they present a moral standard against which Ipermestra's virtue becomes prominent. Metastasio of course could not bring dozens of characters onstage to represent fifty Danaids and their fifty husbands, since each opera usually consists of some six to eight characters, but he did not even *mention* the Danaids in his libretto. As a result, he eliminated a critical point of reference for understanding Ipermestra. His Ipermestra runs contrary to Aeschylus's *The Suppliant Maidens*, which features the Danaids as animalistic, morally ambiguous beings who become murderous: "Let no murderous plague / come upon this city destroying / without the dance, without lyre; arming Ares, father of tears, and civic violence" (679–82).[57]

While Metastasio emphasized individual characters in his *dramma per musica*, Noverre reduced the number of protagonists, featuring instead the contrasts between protagonists and groups in his *Hypermnestre ou Les Danaïdes* (Stuttgart, 1764). He eliminated the secondary characters of Plisthenes and Elpinice. He staged sharp contrasts between individuals and groups: Hypermnestre [Ipermestra] versus her sisters, Lincée [Lynceus] versus his brothers. He emphasized Hypermnestre, Danaus, and Lincée as individuals by contrasting them with groups (of specters, priests and priestesses, guards, soldiers, officers), furies (i.e., Tisiphone, Alecton, and Mégère), and personifications (i.e., Crime, Betrayal, Perfidy, and Remorse).

Emphasizing crowds of dancers onstage, Noverre staged a mass murder scene, which the story of Danaids demands. His version was not about a problem of communication, as was in Metastasio's version; his version was about a naturalistic rendering of a brutal mass murder. Two years before Noverre staged *Hypermnestre* in Paris, he had used a choreographic technique called "*en cadence*" (in step) in the Naples version to highlight the Danaïdes's collective lack of agency. The word "*cadenza*" means, according to Harris-Warrick and Bruce Alan Brown, "the timing of steps or fitting together of dance and music."[58] This technique was reported by Sara Goudar in 1777, when she claimed that the Danaïdes kill their husbands "in step" (*en cadence*).[59] Choreographer Angiolini also explained this technique in his *Dissertation sur les ballets pantomimes des anciens pour servir de programme au ballet pantomime tragique de Sémiramis* (1765): "All that we do when moving the body and

57 On the moral ambiguity of the Danaids, see David Grene and Richmond Lattimore, eds, *Aeschylus I*, 3rd edn (Chicago: The University of Chicago Press, 2013), 118.

58 On "cadenza," see Harris-Warrick and Brown, *The Grotesque Dancer*, 357.

59 "Quarante-neuf femmes y tuent en cadence quarante-neuf hommes." Sara Goudar, *Œuvres mêlées de Madame Sara Goudar*, 2 vols. (Amsterdam: s.n., 1777), 1:28.

its limbs on a walk that is notated and in step [*en cadence*] is certainly a dance."[60]
Yet, the magnitude is different when a mass of murderers rather than one individual
move *en cadence*. In "Sopra il ballo da osservazioni sopra la musica ed il ballo" (1773),
Ange Goudar discussed the character Brutus, who stabbed Caesar to death onstage
in a ballet, and Brutus's stabbing physical movements were "in step" (*in cadenza*)
with music.[61] This technique synchronizes musical rhythm with the motion of stabbing, and it is this synchronization that creates a calculated and thus chilling effect.
But if Brutus stabbing Caesar to death emphasizes robotic brutality, forty-nine wives
stabbing forty-nine husbands *en cadence* would vastly magnify the brutality of this
mass crime. The significance of this mass murder scene is not simply that the wives
kill their husbands, but that the Danaïdes demonstrate a *collective* relinquishment
of their freedom of action. The Danaïdes voluntarily give up their moral liberty *en
masse*, although they all are born humans.

Surprisingly, as much as Noverre used physical movement (including dance
steps and expressive gestures) as a primary medium in his ballet-pantomime, he
also deployed speech. Contrary to Metastasio's *Ipermestra*, which dramatizes *human*
relationships, Noverre emphasized *spiritual* interventions in his *Hypermnestre*.
According to the synopsis published in 1776, the beginning of the ballet-pantomime
stages an extraordinary scene by employing speech, which is the quintessential
medium that Dubos's conception of pantomime and a ballet-pantomime typically omits. Danaus hears subterranean noise and sees a disembodied hand that
writes characters in fire on the marble wall of his apartment: "Tremble, a son of
Egypt is going to reign in your place."[62] Evidently this disembodied hand indicates a supernatural power. This is an example of what Edward Nye calls "staged
words." Noverre had employed this technique of "staged words" in a nightmare
of *Iphigénie en Tauride*; his pupil Charles Le Picq imagined in his *Castor et Pollux*
a written command sent by gods for Pollux; Angiolini also used the technique of
hand-writing on the wall in *Semiramide*. So did his student Antonio Campioni, in his
version of *Semiramide*. The same idea of spiritual intervention was proposed in an
unperformed adaptation of Metastasio's *Demofoonte* in *Pantomime italienne dramatique mêlée de déclamation et de chant* (1779), where God makes His wish known via
words written in letters of fire: "The order of Apollo / wants that on his altars / we
spill the blood of / an illustrious virgin / on this day every year." The terrified crowd
pleads for clemency; a disembodied voice replies that God's anger will subside once
He receives a sacrifice.[63]

Divine words written by fire and enunciated by a disembodied voice indicate
that Noverre juxtaposed the *supernatural* realm with the *human* one. In the 1807

---

60 "Tout ce qu'on fait en mouvant le corps et ses membres sur une marche notée et en
cadence est certainement une danse." Calzabigi, *Scritti*, 1:158.

61 Ange Goudar, "Sopra il ballo da osservazioni sopra la musica ed il ballo," in Lombardi, *Il
ballo pantomime*, 28.

62 "Tremble, un fils d'Egyptus va régner en ta place." Noverre, *Recueil de Programmes des
Ballets de M. Noverre* (Vienna: Joseph Kurzböck, 1776), synopsis of *Hypermnestre*, 5.

63 "L'ordre d'Apollon / D'une Vierge illustre, / Veut que sur ses autels, / On répande le
sang / Chaque année en ce jour." *Pantomime dramatique ou Essai sur un nouveau genre de
spectacle* (Florence: Jombert, 1779), 11.

synopsis of *Hypermnestre*, Noverre redesigned the scene where the menacing ghost of King Gelanor, whose throne had been usurped by Danaus, appears. Then a disembodied voice resounds: "Tremble, tyrant, death awaits you."[64] Noverre suggested in a footnote added to the 1807 version that a singer declaimed the verse behind the sculptures placed onstage. Nye claims that "staged words" can clarify the narrative, but what takes place in Noverre's *Hypermnestre* is not simply semantic clarification; rather, it is the subjugation of the *human* world of music and gesture to the *supernatural* world of language and speech. The hierarchy of these two worlds brings with it a metaphysics of *presence*. It positions pantomime as a universal language within the supernatural realm, in which language overrules nonverbal signs with semantic precision and clarity. Rather than using pantomime as an alternative to speech, Noverre and Angiolini and their pupils used speech as an exceptional dramatic event without compromising the dominance of dance and gesture, thereby creating a nonverbal *condition* for the *verbal* presence of the supernatural beings. In Noverre's *Hypermnestre*, humans make gestures; God and the ghost speak French. Thus Noverre subjected the supposedly "universal" language of pantomime to the supernatural level. Through writing and speech, this revelatory God asserts his presence to humans and presents the absolute truth, alluding to the first verse of the book of John in the New Testament: "In the beginning was the Word, and the Word was with God, and the Word was God" (1:1). Yet semantic clarity does not guarantee that the oracle is readily understood. In fact, it is the cryptic meaning of a clearly articulated oracle that sustains dramatic tension throughout the ballet-pantomime.[65]

Unlike Metastasio's character Ipermestra, Noverre's Hypermnestre exercises her freedom of action by ignoring Danaus's mandate. Whereas the Danaïdes beg Danaus in vain to spare them from mariticide, Hypermnestre manages to forget (*oublier*) her oaths and Danaus's murderous order, and tells Lincée to escape.[66] How could she *forget* the solemn oaths and something as critical as a king-father's mandate? According to the *Dictionnaire de l'Académie française* (4th edn, 1762), the expression "to forget a duty" means "to fail in one's duty" (*manquer à son devoir*). To forget her oaths, therefore, means that she fails to keep her word. In the Enlightenment, to "forget" something indicated a cognitive aspect. According to the article "Forget" (*oublier*) in the *Encyclopédie*, to forget means to "lose memory" (*perdre la mémoire*) of something. This point brings us to human understanding. In his *Essai sur l'origine des connaissances humaines*, Condillac did not discuss forgetting in particular, but he

---

64 Noverre supplied a footnote for this instance, which reads: "Pour donner à l'action un caractère plus effrayant, un chanteur dérobé par le groupe de sculpture au-devant duquel l'ombre apparait, articule ces mots: *Frémis, tyran, la mort t'attend*." Noverre, *Lettres sur les arts imitateurs en général et sur la danse en particulier*, 2 vols. (Paris: L. Collin, 1807), 2:398 n.1.

65 On this ballet-pantomime, see Bruno Brizi, "Un spunto polemico Calzabigiano: Ipermestra o le Danaidi," in Federico Marri, ed., *La Figura e l'opera di Ranieri de' Calzabigi* (Florence: Leo S. Olschki, 1989), 136–37. On logocentrism, Jacques Derrida, *Of Grammatology*, trans. Gayatri Chakravorty Spivak (Baltimore, MD: The Johns Hopkins University Press, 1997), 3. On staged words, see Nye, *Mime, Music, and Drama*, 95–100.

66 The synopsis reads: "Hipermnestre oublie alors ses serments & les ordres de Danaus; le fer lui échappe de la main, elle se jette aux genoux de son époux, elle les inonde de ses larmes & elle lui recommande la fuite." Noverre, *Recueil*, 15.

discussed memory more generally, including a cognitive operation called "decomposition," which refers to the ability to "subtract from a notion some of the ideas that compose it."[67]

Contrary to Hypermnestre, who can "decompose" Danaus's command, differentiating a command from an act, filial duty from mariticide, the Danaïdes can neither forget their father's command nor bring their self of reflection to supervise their self of habit. Their obedience to a murderous father-king stems from their cognitive *in*capability to develop non-habitual behavior. Their obedience is therefore a symptom of their animality. In Condillac's view, the Danaïdes do not possess a "double self": they commit mariticide and regress to animals because their human selves fail to dominate their animalistic selves, and they *de*-humanize themselves. They succumb to their "animal liberty," the exercise of which "is always in chaos in men, a struggle brought about by passions that are too lively, resulting from the body's bad organization that is either natural or developed from bad habits that have not been repressed."[68] Their degeneration is demonstrated by their cries and gestures, akin to those imagined at the origins of language. As the synopsis describes, "Lincée sees the Danaïdes. Their cries of despair, their distressing voices of repentance, their aimless flight, [and] their frightening gestures chill Lincée's heart. The Danaïdes' ruffled hair, their bloody arms, their physiognomies on which rage leaves its imprint, announce the enormity of their crimes."[69]

In contrast to Metastasio's kinetically un-significative and logocentric *opera seria*, Noverre presented a kinetically stimulating and *differently* logocentric ballet tragic-pantomime. Noverre's version highlights the political impact of freedoms of motion and action. Lincée, wearing funereal attire, is about to be executed, and Hypermnestre awaits his execution. When the lovers see each other, they cannot help but fly to one another. The guards try to hold them back, but the lovers publicly display affection for each other. Their behaviors illustrate the kinetic and spatial aspects of freedom of action by overcoming external and internal impediments to their motion.

Importantly, Hypermnestre and Lincée's motion and action *move* the public, who sympathize with their plight and even overturn the tyrant. Instead of upholding a dichotomy between persuading and convincing, as Batteux, Rousseau, and Diderot did (see Chapter Two), Noverre established a causal relationship between them. The lovers' action *creates* a sympathetic public that becomes not just *persuaded*, on an emotional level, but also *convinced*, on a rational level, that this couple

---

67 Condillac, *Essay*, 45.

68 "L'exercice de la liberté animale … est toujours dans l'homme en désordre, un combat intenté par des passions trop vives qui résultent d'une mauvaise organisation du corps, naturelle ou contractée par de mauvaises habitudes qui n'ont pas été réprimées." François Quesnay [attributed], *Encyclopédie*, vol. 6, s.v. "Évidence."

69 "Lincée aperçoit les Danaïdes. Leurs cris de désespoir, leur accents douloureux poussés par le repentir, leurs courses errantes, leurs gestes effrayantes glacent le cœur de Lincée. Les cheveux hérissés des Danaïdes, leurs bras ensanglantés, leurs physionomies, où la rage est imprimée, annoncent l'énormité de leurs forfaits." Noverre, "Les Danaïdes," 2:404. I follow Sibylle Dahms's catalogue by using the spelling and the title *Hypermestre ou Les Danaïdes*. See her *Der konservative Revolutionär*, 396.

should be innocent. Lincée's supporters then seize on this spontaneous public commotion as an opportunity to launch an uprising against Danaus. Commotion breeds motion and action. The public then protests in the lovers' favor; they destroy the stake; they defeat the guards; they elevate a throne; they remove Lincée's funereal attire and place him on this new throne alongside Hypermnestre, proclaiming him king of Argos. Together, they pledge fidelity to him. By the time Danaus arrives at the scene, he has already lost his throne. Like Metastasio's Ipermestra, Noverre's Hypermnestre safeguards her father. But unlike Metastasio's version, where Ipermestra's virtue shames Danaus, Noverre's version turns Hypermestre's virtue into a catalyst for the final round of conflict. Danaus attempts to kill Hypermnestre with outrage; Lincée rushes to save her, while another officer mortally stabs Danaus, who convulses and dies. The oracle turns out true: Danaus ceases to be king, and Lincée reigns over his kingdom in his stead. Hypermnestre and Lincée's freedom of action, therefore, brings about the tyrant's downfall.[70]

HUMANS VERSUS BACCHANTES

Calzabigi might have gotten to know Noverre's *Hypermnestre, ou Les Danaïdes* when it was performed in Vienna in 1769 and, unlike Metastasio, who made his *Ipermestra* a *dramma per musica* exclusively about *humans*, Calzabigi introduced the supernatural to his *tragedia per musica Ipermestra*, using the deity of Bacchus as an unnatural power that liberates the Danaids. Calzabigi did not employ Bacchus as a character, but he mentioned the deities of Bacchus and Amore, who bless Linceo and Ipermestra's wedding: "I invite you all to inebriate your hearts, / both with Bacchus, and with Love: I await you all." (*Voi tutti invito a inebriarvi il petto, / E di Bacco, e d'Amor: Voi tutti aspetto*) (I/i). It was common to hear about these two deities in Italian opera. Amour was ubiquitous in Italian opera, but Bacchus appeared less frequently and in more specific situations. For example, Bacchus and Amour were mentioned in Monteverdi's lament, "Lasciatemi morire," of his *tragedia in musica Arianna* (1608).[71] A temple dedicated to Bacchus indicates the presence of this deity in Leonardo Leo's version of Metastasio's *Achille in Sciro* (Turin, 1740). A drinking song also suggests Bacchus's presence in Giuseppe Scolari's *dramma per musica La Cascina* (Venice, 1755). Bacchus is called on in the recitative "Bravo poter di Bacco" in Leonardo Vinci's intermezzo *Flacco e Servilia* (Naples, 1727), the recitative "Per Bacco qua i cervelli si perdono" in Pietro Alessandro Guglielmi's *dramma giocoso Le nozze in commedia* (Naples, 1781), and the recitative "Per Bacco il pupilla" in Giovanni Paisiello's *L'amore ingegnoso* (Rome, 1785). Calzabigi followed a convention in invoking these two deities. What was unusual, however, was that Calzabigi brought into play within a single opera the celebratory and destructive aspects of Bacchus.

In *Ipermestra* Calzabigi used the deity of Bacchus primarily as a symbol of revelry that justifies "inoperative" wedding festivities, but the inoperativity (see Chapter

---

70 Noverre, "Les Danaïdes," 2:408–10.

71 On Bacchus and Amore in Monteverdi's *Arianna*, see Tim Carter, *Understanding Italian Opera* (New York: Oxford University Press, 2015), 58.

Three on this term) of these festivities provides a background against which Ipermestra reveals her moral struggle. When the fifty couples celebrate their collective wedding, their choral singing and dancing in Act 3 Scene 1 mark a moment of inoperativity. In three parts, this scene begins and ends with a choral refrain about the joy and vanity of celebration. Each statement of the refrain is followed by a dance (marked "*ballo*" on the libretto). The word "vain" (*vaneggi*) lays bare the superficiality of celebrations, pointing to the middle section of the scene, where Linceo is confounded by Ipermestra's unloving manners, for she refrains from saying anything that Danaus, nearby, might find perfidious. Like Metastasio's Ipermestra, Calzabigi's Ipermestra also refuses to speak with candor in front of Linceo and thus exercises her freedom of action.

In addition to serving as a symbol of revelry, Bacchus plays another role in Calzabigi's *Ipermestra* by transforming the Danaids into bacchantes. In the first two scenes of Act 5, the Danaids appear onstage beating cymbals and shaking Tirsi in acts of fury, singing a refrain as if they were bacchantes liberated by Bacchus: "Evoe! Son of Jupiter / and Semele; / L'Eneo, free / from unknown seas, / from indomitable India. / Winner ..." (*Evoè! Di Giove / Figlio, e di Semele; / Lenèo, Libero; / De' mari incogniti, / Dell' India indomita / Trionfator ...*). Having been freed by Bacchus from unknown locales, these Danaids behave like a mass of non-human bacchantes rather than a community of human beings.[72]

Akin to the bacchantes, the Danaids demonstrate kinetic and spatial freedom, but their unrestrained freedom indicates "corporal liberty" and not freedom of motion, because there is no evidence that they are capable of reflecting upon their behaviors before they take action. When the Danaids murder their husbands, they regress to bacchantes – followers of Bacchus notorious for their preternatural athleticism. In Euripides's *Bacchae*, the bacchae celebrate the Bacchic rites by raising their thyrsi and calling on Bromius, god of ecstatic cries, and rallying beasts: "And all the mountain and the animals joined them in their Bacchic worship – there was nothing that did not move with the running."[73] In Ovid's *Metamorphoses*, the bacchantes display their animal liberty when they butcher Pentheus, King of Thebes, who has insulted Bacchus by calling this androgynous god a "sissyboy." Alone in Mount Cithaeron, Pentheus is terrified by a mass of bacchantes who "rush out after him from every side," none of whom recognizes him as king of Thebes. He is dismembered alive by bacchantes, a group that includes his own mother Agave and his aunt Ino, who think they are slaughtering a boar rather than a man: "She [Agave] tears off his right arm, while Ino in rapture savages the left ... Tossing her hair in frenzy and exulting at the grim sight, Agave tears her son's head from his trunk" (3.926, 930–33). These bacchantes lash out, and they do not reflect upon their conduct. They have brute force, and they do not have conscience. They are driven by the self of habit, and they have no self of reflection. They have a supreme degree of Hobbesian "corporal liberty,"

---

72 Calzabigi discussed the communal aspect of the chorus in his letter to Alfieri of August 20, 1783). See Calzabigi, *Scritti*, 1:205.

73 Euripides, *Bacchae and Other Plays*, trans. James Morwood (Oxford: Oxford University Press, 2008), 49, 64.

but they have neither freedom of motion nor freedom of action. Since they are incapable of caring for others, they are liberated but do not have liberty.[74]

Accordingly, these liberated Danaids are *sub*-human beings, like beasts. Unlike Noverre, who mentioned neither Bacchus nor the bacchantes, Calzabigi invoked Bacchus as the deity whose invisible presence presides over the Danaids, freeing them from some psychic space, liberating them from civil behaviors, and unleashing their animal liberty: "You [Bacchus] ease tigers to the yoke: grape bunches, and vine leaves adorn your crown" (*Tu al giogo agevoli / Le tigri indocile: / Il crin t'adornano / Grappoli, e pampini*, V/ii). The theme of liberation returns in the denouement, when Linceo and his soldiers set Ipermestra free (*Linceo con armati … liberano Ipermestra*, V/vi), but Linceo's liberation of Ipermestra upholds her human agency, whereas Bacchus's liberation of the Danaids destroys theirs. Condillac might say that the Danaids fail to sustain their conscious freedom in the face of an unreasonable command, but Calzabigi called out their animality explicitly. In Calzabigi's libretto, Danaus recognizes the voices of his liberated daughters, but he calls them sub-human monsters (*mostri*): "My dear daughters!" Danaus exclaims and then utters an aside, ("Ah! Tigers!"). (*Mie care figlie! (Ah tigri!)*). Danaus chides himself for being a monster (*un mostro io sono*, V/iii) responsible for reducing his hitherto "human" offspring into animalistic beings.[75]

SIGNS IN SALIERI'S PANTOMIMES

In what ways did Calzabigi's version inform Salieri's *Les Danaïdes*? Calzabigi used the word "ballet" (*ballo*) to mark four occasions: celebrating the wedding, marching to the room after the wedding, reveling after the mass murder, and punishing the Danaids in hell (V/vii). Although Calzabigi never used the word "pantomime," the descriptions of the march and the penal scene indicate that these ballets included pantomimic elements reminiscent of those in Gluck's reform operas.[76] Using Calzabigi's libretto as a reference, Tschudi and Du Roullet employed two designations – dance and pantomime – in their *tragédie lyrique*, staging dances in Acts 1 and 3 (i.e., I/i, I/ii, III/i, III/ii) and three pantomimes (i.e., III/iii, V/iv, V/xi). The linear progression from dances to pantomimes demonstrates that the Danaïdes dance when they are still humans, but they pantomime after they degenerate into animalistic beings.

To understand these dances and pantomimes, one needs to study Salieri's modulations as instituted signs throughout the opera. Already in a G-major "Jouissez du destin propice" (I/i), Salieri uses modulations that indicate the unpredictability of death. In a three-part or "ABA" form, the A section of this andante maestoso

---

74 On the distinction between liberation and liberty, see Foucault, "The Ethics," 282–84, 300.

75 Calzabigi, "Ipermestra o le Danaidi," in *Poesie e prose diverse di Ranieri de' Calsabigi*, 2 vols. (Naples: Onofrin Zambraja, 1793), 1:179–82.

76 Here is the description of the Danaids' march to their rooms: "Si balla; e in ultimo gli Amorini legano gli Sposi, e le Spose colle ghirlande di fiori; e procedendo alcuni con accese fiaccole, li guidano alle loro stanze." Calzabigi, "Ipermestra," 1:162 n.3. For the inferno scene, see ibid., 1:187.

modulates away from G major to the distant keys of B minor (mm.18–21), and to A minor (mm.45–47), when Danaus sings "Often death sneaks in without noise, / and strikes you in the midst of pleasures" (*Sans bruit souvent la Mort se glisse, / Et vous frappe au sein des plaisirs*). Although the home key is G major, the distant tonal areas of mediant minor (B minor) and supertonic minor (A minor) represent a dark undercurrent. Following Section A, Section B elaborates the theme of the unpredictability of death: "Each moment the fatal boat can carry you away without return: / no one knows if Fate / wants to spin the thread of life for another day." (*Chaque instant la fatale barque / Peut vous entraîner sans retour; / Nul de nous ne sait si la Parque / Veut lui filer un autre jour.*) Unlike a typical middle section of a da capo aria that modulates to a closely related key, the middle section modulates from G major to the flat-sixth major of E-flat major (mm.26–29, Example 4.1), suggesting in topographical terms a symbolic *descent* to the Underworld. Under the auspices of Bacchus, these modulations are designed as "arbitrary" or "instituted" signs, whose meanings call for exegesis.

As the dramatic tension mounts, Hypermnestre's perplexing behaviors demand justification. During the wedding festivity, Hypermnestre confronts the "homicide fête" as a celebratory prelude to bloodshed by refusing to drink with Lincée and avoiding eye contact with him. Her avoidance behavior demonstrates a severely limited degree of corporal liberty, but corporal liberty indicating freedom of motion is only one aspect of freedom of action, Locke might say, and whether Hypermnestre speaks or keeps silent indicates another aspect of her freedom of action. In his *Lettre sur les drames-opéra* (1776), Du Roullet theorized about speaking under constraint in an opera: "Once the situation has been brought about, if your characters speak – but only speak exactly of that which their character necessarily inspires, of the situation in which they have been put, and of the passions that must stir them – your scene will have all the perfection to which it is susceptible."[77] To highlight this point, Danaus reminds Hypermnestre of the fatal consequence of her indiscretion: "If you say a word," he forewarns her, "he [Lincée] is dead" (*Si tu dis un mot il est mort*). Similarly, in Act 4 Scene 3, she asks Lincée to leave her, without offering any reasons. She exercises little freedom of *motion*, but her repeated refusals to disclose the secret illustrate her freedom of *action*. Like Metastasio's *Ipermestra*, Tschudi/Du Roullet's *Les Danaïdes* highlights Hypermnestre's avoidance *behavior*, and not her verbal *disclosure* of her father's secret. It is her avoidance behavior that becomes an instituted sign, and this instituted sign is, to Lincée's mind, a cause for concern.

How does a plot that emphasizes signs provide a context for signification in dances and pantomimes? The first pantomime in Act 3 shows the Danaïdes' march to their room after singing a hymn to Bacchus in a *chœur dansé* "L'amour sourit."[78] Composers had used Bacchus in French opera before. What was new here, as mentioned above, was the display of Bacchus's two contrasting attributes – revelry

77 "La situation une fois amenée, si vos personnages disent, mais ne disent exactement que ce que nécessairement doit leur inspirer leur caractère, la situation où vous les avez mis, & les passions qui doivent les agiter, votre scène aura toute la perfection dont elle est susceptible." Du Roullet, "Lettre sur les drames-opéra," in Lesure, *Querelle*, 2:126.

78 On *chœur dansé*, see Cyr, "The Dramatic Role of the Chorus," 105–18; Banducci, "Staging," 5–28.

Example 4.1. Salieri, *Les Danaïdes*, Act 1 Scene 1, Danaus's "Jouissez du destin propice," mm.26–30

and violence – in a single opera.[79] Salieri's D-major setting conceals the murderous undertone disclosed by utterance of the word *vendange* (grape harvest), which invokes not just wine, as was customary, but also the imminent bloodshed: "With him [Bacchus] Amour treads the grape harvest / and causes his passion to sink in the purple wine" (*il foule avec lui la vendange / et fait couler ses feux dans la pourpre du vin*). The word "wine" celebrates a mass wedding and *pre*-celebrates the triumph of mass murder.[80]

To highlight the double senses of celebration, Salieri used in the pantomime the major mode as a general tonal context that includes harmonic mixtures. He set the following pantomime in G major, in 3/4 time, and used the minuet rhythm, all of which are characteristics of inoperative festivities. However, by calling this dance a "pantomime" rather than a "ballet," as Calzabigi did, Salieri suggested that this minuet-derived pantomime does not function as a typical minuet dance that has *real* inoperativity. Instead, Salieri revealed its *false* inoperativity by using harmonic mixture as an instituted sign. He introduced an E-flat in m.18, turning a C-major chord into a C-minor chord (i.e., IV*flat-*$^{6/4}$ chord) (m.18 of Example 4.2). To be sure, the E-flat serves as an upper chromatic neighbor note to D of m.19. This upper chromatic neighbor, which appears to merely "decorate" the note D on a local level, turns out to have structural significance. Salieri also used it again in m.54, where he again highlighted the note E-flat as the upper chromatic neighbor of the dominant, D. This E-flat introduces G minor into the otherwise festive G-major tonal context and spoils the festive mood. Replacing the note E in the IV$^{6/4}$ chord of m.53, the E-flat turns the otherwise common C-major chord into a C-minor chord, or a IV$^{6/4}$ chord into a IV *flat-*$^{6/4}$ chord in G major. A flat-sixth in G major, the note E-flat introduces the minor mode into G major that spoils the festivities. Since the meaning of this minor mode at this instance is non-obvious, it functions as an *instituted* sign.

Salieri used instituted signs to create a dark undertone in various scenes of the opera. Because the meanings of instituted signs are non-obvious, they are suitable for the dynamic of concealment and revelation. This dynamic is at the core of the climax of the opera, which occurs at the end of the recitative "Suivez-moi, Prince" (IV/iv), when the Danaïdes onstage hear the signal to kill their husbands. This signal, absent in Calzabigi's script, is represented not by something attention-grabbing in Salieri's music, such as a *coup d'archet*, but by the tonally ambiguous B-flat major chord that can be heard in the tonal context of this recitative as either a flat-seventh chord in C major or a Neapolitan chord in A minor. Why did Salieri do that? Once again, Salieri used harmonic progression and tonalities as dramatic devices. This tonally ambivalent B-flat major chord functions as an instituted sign rather than a natural sign, whose meaning is known to the Danaïdes but not to their husbands. For Lyncée, this chord is a rare instance of "diegetic" sound (i.e., music heard as sound): "What am I hearing?" (*Qu'entends-je?*) Hypermnestre recognizes that this chord prompts the Danaïdes to kill their husbands and, at this critical moment, she discloses the

79 On Bacchus, see my "Music, Bacchus, and Freedom," in Youn Kim and Sander Gilman, eds, *The Oxford Handbook of Music and the Body* (New York: Oxford University Press, 2019), 161–76.

80 On the relationship between blood and wine, see Mikhail Bakhtin, *Rabelais and His World*, trans. Hélène Iswolsky (Bloomington, IN: Indiana University Press, 1984), 209.

Example 4.2. Salieri, *Les Danaïdes*, Act 3 Scene 3, Pantomime, mm.14–19

forbidden truth to Lyncée in no uncertain terms: "Run! We are slitting the throats of your brothers" (*Fuis! On égorge tes frères*). Hypermnestre's words mark a moment of "recognition," as Aristotle would have it in his *Poetics* (6.4), as she unambiguously betrays her father and tries to save her husband.

Crucially, the tonally ambiguous B-flat major chord accompanies Hypermnestre's act of speaking out. In Salieri's mind, her act is so forceful that it clarifies the tonally ambiguous B-flat major chord. This chord steers away from the C major or A minor of mm.1–9 and resolves, finally, to G minor in m.14. The harmonic progression from B-flat major to G minor turns out to be a very common progression from a major chord to its relative minor chord, precisely when Hypermnestre discloses the truth unambiguously. Thus, this climactic moment discloses the truth, a disclosure that places the tonally ambiguous B-flat major chord firmly in the G-minor tonal context.

Example 4.3. Salieri, *Les Danaïdes*, Act 4 Scene 4, mm.1–14

Hypermnestre's act of speaking out, therefore, disambiguates a tonally ambiguous chord and exemplifies her freedom of action (Example 4.3).

The second pantomime is found in Act 5 Scene 4, which depicts a post-slaughter scene. Danaus congratulates the wives' success in murdering almost all of their husbands but reminds them that Lyncée is still at large. Eager to kill Lyncée, the Danaïdes hunt their final victim. To emphasize the Danaïdes as an undifferentiated

Example 4.3. continued

Example 4.3. continued

mass of murderers who slaughtered an undifferentiated mass of victims, the choreographer Gardel mixed up thirty-two dancers – sixteen brothers and another sixteen
Danaïdes – of different ranks. These de-hierarchized dancers do not signal equality
or a group identity; rather, they represent the Danaïdes's lack of human agency and
their homogeneity. According to *Journal de Paris*, the presentation of de-hierarchized

Example 4.3. continued

dancers created an "absolutely new" effect. Another critic, Bachaumont, evoked the Enlightenment idea of *langage d'action* by complimenting Gardel's choreography, saying that it added greatly to the "truth" (*vérité*) of the pantomime.[81]

81 *Journal de Paris* 118 (April 17, 1784), 517; Bachaumont, *Mémoires secrets*, 25:254.

Example 4.3. continued

Musically speaking, jarring musical elements as instituted signs impart an undertone of unease in the second pantomime within the G-major chorus sung by the Danaïdes: "Gloire! Gloire! Evan Evohé!" (V/iv). The major mode had been used in an "air des bacchantes" in the entrée *Les Bacchanales* of the *ballet-héroïque Les Festes*

Example 4.3. continued

grecques et romaines (1723). What is new in Salieri's setting is that the major mode makes murderous fury *sound like* celebratory festivities. It functions as an accidental sign that creates a sense of déjà vu. Like the "barbarous joy" in Gluck's *Iphigénie en Tauride*, the continuity of festivities and mass murder suggests a perverse delight in animalistic brutality. Against the festal background of mm.1–2, Salieri used three trombones symbolizing death. He composed an un-idiomatic harmonic progression from the tonic chord to the supertonic chord (i.e., I–II) in G major on the word "powerful" (*puissant*) of the line "*Bacchus, ô dieu puissant*" in mm.17–18, using an A-major chord as the secondary dominant – a V/V chord – of G major and moving abruptly away from G major towards the D major of m.20. Salieri carefully avoided parallel octaves and fifths in this unusual harmonic progression by using large melodic leaps and atypical voice leading. The soprano line makes a nosedive of a minor seventh from G to A on the word *puissant*, and the bassoon shoots up an augmented eleventh from G to C-sharp, while the first violin drops a diminished fifth interval from G to C-sharp. The jarring voice-leadings and unprepared harmonic progression away from G major function as instituted signs, indicating Bacchus as a perverse god with uncommon power (Example 4.4).

Example 4.4. Salieri, *Les Danaïdes*, Act 5 Scene 4, Chorus "Gloire! Évan! Evohé!" mm.16–21

Example 4.4. continued

Salieri designed another musically jarring moment as an accidental sign when the chorus declares, in the repeat of the B section, that the Danaïdes no longer possess any humanity. The B section, having first been sung by Plancippe, is repeated by the rest of the Danaïdes in the last section of the chorus. The last verse of this stanza, "they no longer have anything human left" (*Elles n'ont plus rien d'humain*) (mm.44–45), is sung in unison, outlining a simple I–V–I progression formed by an arpeggio of the G-major chord, followed by an un-harmonized implied perfect cadence in G major. The second syllable of this verse "*humain*" (human) falls on the downbeat of m.46, forming an elision with the following A section. The Danaïdes admit that they are humans, although they have been Danaus's daughters, but they have transformed into the non-human bacchantes. The unison at this cadential point is reinforced by the note D-sharp, prolonged by a fermata in m.97 that delays the expected tonic arrival in G major. Thus, the anticipated perfect cadence with the melody D–D–G is replaced by a prolonged chromatic inflection – scale degree 5 to sharp-5 – before reaching the implied cadence in unison. Salieri interrupted the original unison passage with this chromatic interruption before reaching a cadence, extending this unison passage from two measures (mm.44–45) to six measures (mm.95–100). The emphasis on the sharp-dominant, D-sharp in G major, indicates the aberration of the Danaïdes's humanity. Importantly, this D-sharp recalls the penultimate verse of stanza A: "in her hand a blade sparkles" (*Dans sa main le fer étincelle*), where a chromatic melody D–D-sharp–E in the inner voice (mm.26–28) uses the D-sharp to tonicize the following E-minor chord. As the pitch D-sharp – highlighting the word "*main*" (hand) – rhymes with the word "*hu-main*" (human), this combination of a poetic rhyme and the D-sharp as a "musical" rhyme functions as an accidental sign that relates the Danaïdes to the bacchantes (Example 4.5).

The third pantomime marks the penal scene (V/xi), set in Tartary which is reigned over by the Greek god Tartarus, the offspring of Chaos. As the Danaïdes regress to animalistic beings, their mode of communication also degenerates to natural signs akin to those at the origins of language. They lose their ability to speak; they can only move about and scream: "Some of the Danaïdes are chained in groups, tormented by demons, and devoured by serpents; the others, pursued by furies, fill the stage with their movements and their cries. A rain of fire falls perpetually. The whole scene forms a pantomime of the most horrifying kind."[82]

Salieri used pantomimes in *Les Danaïdes* to present the sub-human state of the Danaïdes, presenting their animal liberty, and not human agency. In the article "Liberty (Moral)" in the *Encyclopédie*, the authors mentioned specifically that not all human beings have moral liberty. Mad people, in particular, are not free: "In the insane, the natural movement of their minds is too violent, making their soul their mistress. In this state, the force of the soul is disproportionate to that of the mind that has to carry it."[83] Contrary to the Danaïdes, Hypermnestre exercises her freedom of action not by moving about onstage, but by speaking the truth that she is expressly forbidden to speak of. By highlighting Hypermnestre's verbal revelation as the key moment of dramatic action without making much use of her bodily movement, Salieri dissociated pantomime action from dramatic action, providing examples for Marmontel to theorize dramatic action in the post-Diderotian age.

---

82 "Les Danaïdes sont les unes enchaînées par groupes, tourmentées par les Démons, & dévorées par des serpents; les autres poursuivies par des furies, remplissent le Théâtre de leurs mouvements & de leurs cris, une pluie de feu tombe perpétuellement; le tout forme une Pantomime du genre le plus terrible."*Les Danaïades*, 30.

83 "Dans les fous, le mouvement naturel de leurs esprits est trop violent, pour que leur âme en soit la maîtresse. Dans cet état, la force de l'âme n'a nulle proportion avec celle des esprits qui l'emportent nécessairement." Naigeon and Yvon [attributed], *Encyclopédie*, vol. 9, s.v. "Liberté [Morale]."

Example 4.5. Salieri, *Les Danaïdes*, Act 5 Scene 4, Chorus "Gloire! Évan! Evohé!"
mm.95–101

The important point of Salieri's *tragédie lyrique* is that he used pantomimes not in isolation, but in relation to other dances in *Les Danaïdes*. He used the word "dance" only when the Danaïdes are humans, and the word "pantomime" only when the Danaïdes are sub-humans. Salieri wrote music for the dance in Act 1 and the pantomime in Act 5, saving his most original music for the processional pantomime (III/iv), in which he employed signs that call for musical and dramatic interpretation. He adopted an arch-shaped design, using a high concentration of signs in the middle act, where Hypermnestre exercises her freedom of action while the Danaïdes renounce theirs. The processional pantomime marks the high point of this arch-shape design,

172

Example 4.5. continued

Example 4.6. Salieri, *Les Danaïdes*, Act 5 Scene 4, Chorus "Gloire! Évan! Evohé!" mm.22–34

for it includes a jarring musical sign – the E-flat in G major – that invites audiences to look for a dark undercurrent that runs through the opera. Those who follow this E-flat would notice its origin in a similar Neapolitan relation featuring the motive of D–E flat–D in the dance of Act 3 Scene 2, and would find its enharmonic equivalent – D-sharp – as part of the chromatic line of D–D-sharp–E in Act 5 Scene 4 (mm.26–28 of Example 4.6). What is original about Salieri's arch-shape design is the relation between D and its upper-neighbor note – E-flat or D-sharp – that signals Danaus's murderous scheme during the festivities. In other words, Salieri used signs not just *in* pantomime, but *through* pantomime.

Example 4.6. continued

The sung text underlay reads (in the choral parts, Ch.):

main   le fer ét - in - cel - le   la   mort - sin't l'e' clair de ses yeux.

Example 4.6. continued

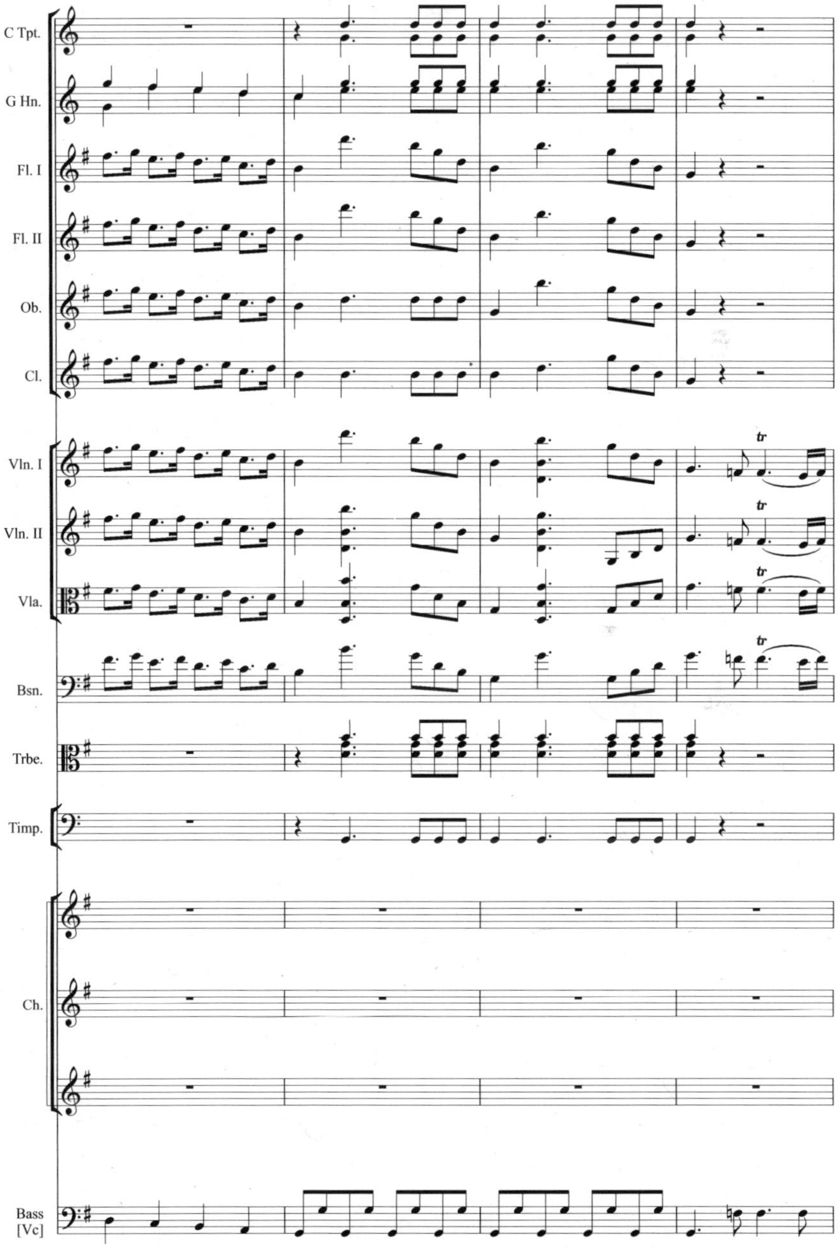

THE ANIMATED STATUE ANIMATES PYGMALION

I have discussed in some detail how Salieri presented the Danaïdes and Hypermnestre as polar opposites, and I wonder: do the audiences identify with the bloodthirsty Danaïdes or the honorable Hypermnestre? One way to answer this question is to think broadly about the relationship between a subject and an object. To this end, I revisit the Pygmalion myth, which shows the transformation of the statue into a real human being. Studies on the Pygmalion stories often focus on the animation of the Statue, which transforms from an object (i.e., a statue) to a thing (i.e., a matter/human fusion) into a human. But this focus often makes us neglect Pygmalion's *own* transformation, which followed from the Statue's animation. In Rameau's *Pygmalion*, Pygmalion admits that he is afraid of being sensitive (*J'ai craint d'être sensible*), and his then-lover Céphise is jealous of his obsession with the Statue: "Pigmalion, is it possible, / that you are insensible / to the love I have for you? / This object keeps you busy: / Can it take away your tenderness from me, / And make you forget ... "[84] He is hardened through the creation of the statue. Ironically, it is the Statue that points out his lack of affection. Soon after the Statue comes alive, she utters to Pygmalion: "Heaven! What an object. My soul is delighted with him!" (*Ciel! Quel objet. Mon âme en est ravie!*) It was common for operatic lovers to address each other as "objects," but it was not at all common for a human being to be called an "object" by a freshly animated statue. At this instance, the word "object" takes on an eerie overtone, raising the possibility of the continuity between selfhood and objecthood, intersubjective and inter-*objective* bond. Its/her utterance objectifies Pygmalion, but this objectification does not last long. Seeing him as her equal, the Statue sheds its previous identity as an object and adopts human subjectivity. She/It recognizes the presence of its soul and says: "my soul is ravished by it [him]" (*Mon âme en est ravie!*). Pygmalion reciprocates her objectification by calling it/her a "likeable object" (*amiable objet*). The central issue of the story is still the animation of the statue, but the animation of the statue also *redefines* the relationship between a human and an object. This story tells the transformation of Pygmalion from the unsentimental to the loving man, as much as it is a story of transforming the Statue from stone to flesh.[85]

Parodies exaggerate Pygmalion's lack of warmth. In Pannard's *opéra-comique en vaudeville Pygmalion, ou La Statue animée*, first performed at the fairground theater at Saint Germain in 1735, Pygmalion turns from an insensible sculptor into a sensible human being. Stone, the artistic medium of Pygmalion's choice, represents his cold personality. As Pygmalion becomes more emotionally invested in the Statue of his creation, he becomes more sensitive.[86] In another parody produced in response to a re-run of Rameau's *Pygmalion* in 1753, Sulpice-Edme Gaubier de Barrault's *Brioché, ou L'Origine des marionnettes* (Théâtre Italien, September 26, 1753), Brioché, who

---

84   "Pigmalion est-il possible, / Que tu sois insensible / Aux feux dont je brûle pour toi? / Cet objet t'occupe sans cesse: / Peut-il m'enlever ta tendresse, Et te faire oublier ... " *Pigmalion* (Paris: Aux dépens de l'Académie, 1748), 2.

85   On interobjectivity, see Brown, *Other Things*, 23, 32.

86   Pannard and Affichard, *Pygmalion, ou La Statue animée*, new edn (1758; repr., Paris: Duchesne, 1773), 3–4.

represents Pygmalion, is excited not over the puppet that has come alive, but over *its* ability to rouse *his* own emotion: "The work of my hands, a puppet, / could therefore inflame me. My madness is complete."[87]

When it comes to sculpture, the Pygmalion story poses a major challenge to sculptors. How could a sculptor represent the process of metamorphosis from a statue to a human being? In his *Salon de 1763*, Diderot wrote about Étienne-Maurice Falconet's marble statuary, which captures the very moment Pygmalion realizes that Galatea is alive: "Life is revealed in her through a light smile that touches her upper lip. What innocence she has! She has her first thought. Her heart is beginning to move on its own, but it will not be long before it palpitates. What hands! What soft-ness of flesh! No, this is not marble."[88] Falconet's Pygmalion, hands off and moving away from the statue he made, detects the statue's life signs with his sight. Falconet's animated statue does not move; Pygmalion moves. Diderot's Pygmalion, by con-trast, shows the doubtful Pygmalion touching his statue in order to examine the life-like object, feeling the motion – flesh, blood, nerves, etc. – that he thinks he detects. The fascinating point is not that Galatea becomes animated, but that the *state* of animation is *spreadable*. The animated Galatea animates Pygmalion in turn, draw-ing Pygmalion close, inviting him to touch her, and making him feel how much of a human being she has become. Diderot's criticism of Falconet's statuary highlights the relation between a subject and an object.

Rousseau shifts his focus from the statue to the sculptor Pygmalion himself. He emphasizes the lack of soul in his *scène lyrique Pygmalion* (1762, premiered 1775). The climax of Rousseau's version arrives when Galatea displays judgment and memory. Galatea moves and walks down the steps. Pygmalion is beside himself. He kneels, lifts his hands, and looks up to heaven. Galatea touches herself and utters her first word "*moi.*" This word is reminiscent of Condillac's statue in *Traité des sensations*. It/she only has the sense of smell when it/she utters the first word. The Statue could not utter this word at the beginning of its existence; it could only say this word *after* it has mustered enough knowledge and judgment of what it is sensing at the present, and after it has acquired the memory of what it has sensed since it was first animated. For Condillac, the animated Statue's first word, "me" (*moi*), is "only the collection of the sensations she experiences, and those of which memory reminds her."[89]

Rousseau's version recalls Condillac's statue and Falconet's statuary. After Galatea utters her first word, Pygmalion loses his conscious self by mechanically repeating the word after her, as if – apart from this echoing her word like a parrot – he is at a loss for words. La Mettrie had discussed in *L'Homme machine* (1747) the risk of mindless echoing as an immediate reaction to a great pantomime performance:

87 "L'ouvrage de mes mains, une Marionnette, / A donc pu m'enflammer; ma folie est complète." Sulpice-Edme Gaubier de Barrault, *Brioché; ou L'Origine des marionnettes, parodie de Pigmalion* (Paris: Duchesne, 1753), 5.

88 "La vie se décèle en elle par un souris léger qui effleure sa lèvre supérieure. Quelle innocence elle a! Elle en est à sa première pensée. Son cœur commence à s'émouvoir; mais il ne tardera pas à lui palpiter. Quelles mains! Quelle mollesse de chair! Non, ce n'est pas du marbre." Diderot, *Œuvres*, 4:286.

89 "Son moi n'est que la collection des sensations qu'elle éprouve, et de celles que la mémoire lui rappelle." Condillac, *Traité*, 56.

"We take everything – gestures, accents, etc. – from those we live with, in the same way as the eyelid blinks under the threat of a blow that is foreseen, or as the body of a spectator *imitates mechanically*, and despite himself, all the movements of a good mime."[90] [emphasis mine] Galatea touches herself again and confirms that she exists, while saying her first complete sentence: "This is me" (*C'est moi*). She then walks a few steps and touches a block of marble in Pygmalion's atelier. She makes a clear distinction between marble and human flesh and comes to a profound realization about the history of her materiality: "This [marble] is no longer me." Her self-knowledge is generated from motion, movement, and then touch. She feels herself, touches herself, and develops a *human* understanding. In his discussion of the sense of touch, Condillac noticed that the statue has to experience one part of her body acting on other parts before uttering the first word.[91] While Condillac stopped short of explaining how this modification takes place, Rousseau believed that sexual arousal gives her the knowledge of herself not only as a *human*, but more specifically as a *woman*. After her recognition of the fundamental material difference between herself and a piece of marble, an amorous exchange, packed with involuntary bodily expressions, takes place between Pygmalion and Galatea, creating a classic episode of Diderotian pantomime and putting the workings of reciprocal animation on full display:

> Pygmalion, in an agitation, in raptures that he can hardly hold back, follows all these movements, listens to her, observes her with a greedy attention that hardly allows him to breathe.

> Galatea approaches him and looks at him. He gets up precipitously, reaches out his arms, and looks at her with ecstasy. She puts a hand on him; he shudders, takes her hand, carries it to his heart, then covers it with ardent kisses."[92]

In his *Pygmalion*, Rousseau translated Cupid's imaginary and innocent desire for Galatea, as depicted in Falconet's statuary, into a display of sexual attraction between a real man and a real woman. Pygmalion's kisses make Galatea not just an object, but specifically his desired *sex* object. Her higher level of self-knowledge comes from the realization of her sexuality, ignited by her creator Pygmalion. She confirms her presence for the third time, sighing and speaking, this time, as a sexually aroused woman: "Ah! Me again." From touching herself repeatedly to knowing that she is being touched and then to recognizing her own sexual arousal, Galatea acquires the self-knowledge of a woman.

The Pygmalion story is remarkable because it shows that anyone – cold or not – *can* become sensitive, emotional, animated, aroused. Benedetto Bonesi, in his *drame lyrique Pygmalion* (Opéra Comique, December 16, 1780), took the implication further by crediting Rousseau for sensitizing his audiences and readers alike. In the dedicatory epistle to a certain Madame la Marquise de M***, Bonesi even related Rousseau to the character Pygmalion: "How many times he [Rousseau] was a happy Pygmalion! How many times he created a soul for so many beings who had only

---

90   La Mettrie, *Machine Man*, 9.

91   Condillac, *Traité*, 89.

92   *CWR*, 10:235.

vegetated until the tears of Julie, the transports of Saint-Preux, the noble impulses of Emile, and the virtues of his Sophie had made them suspect a new existence."[93] The important point here is that Bonesi linked Pygmalion with Rousseau, implying that it was Rousseau who made their readers and audiences responsive to feelings. Since, as Bonesi's logic goes, anyone attuned to Rousseau the Pygmalion could become animated, animation could *spread* from page to stage and beyond.

A contagious performance at the theater should come from actors' enthusiasm. Bonesi's animation scene consists of three phases: first, the Statue comes alive, then she thinks, and, finally, she acquires sensations. Sensations form the basis of ideas, which lead to sentiment, the foundation of happiness. Bonesi is not just interested in the animation of Galatea, but in the ways in which the animation of Galatea transforms Pygmalion from a vegetative state to a sentimental one. Bonesi focused on the animated Galatea as much as the reanimation of Pygmalion, creating a scene where "Pygmalion gathers the first ideas, the first signs of affection from the one he has just animated, and gives her a first kiss."[94] Here, the Pygmalion story displays the origins of life in the physical and the social realms. The animation of Galatea leads to the reanimation of Pygmalion, who in turn offers Galatea a soul. This reciprocal animation between a human/thing and a thing/human illustrates the social impact of corporal liberty, and this idea of reciprocal animation resonates strongly with what Cahusac called the "mutual fire" caused by enthusiasm, warming up the actors and spectators at the theater like a tennis ball, bouncing back and forth between the stage and the parterre.

To what end? What is the point of getting animated at the theater? In his *De la liberté de la musique* (1759), d'Alembert speculated that the concept of freedom of action could be politically transgressive: "All freedoms hold together and are equally dangerous. Freedom of music presupposes freedom to feel, which leads to freedom to think. Freedom to think produces freedom to act. And freedom to act is the destruction of the States." D'Alembert used the Opéra as an example: "Therefore, let us keep the Opéra the way it is, if we have the desire to conserve the royalty. And let's put reins on the license to sing, if we do not want that of speaking to follow it."[95] D'Alembert made the claim in the aftermath of the *Querelle des bouffons*, but his point resonated in the 1770s and 1780s.

Contrary to d'Alembert's speculation, Noverre showed no interest in destroying the States even though he made an explicit case for liberty. In his imaginary world of *Apelles et Campaspe*, Noverre related freedom of action to Condillac's idea of

---

93 "Combien de fois il fut lui-même un Pigmalion heureux! Combien de fois il créa une âme pour tant d'Êtres qui n'avoient fait que végéter jusqu'au moment où les larmes de Julie, les transports de Saint-Preux, les nobles élans d'Émile, & les vertus de sa Sophie leur eurent fait soupçonner une nouvelle existence." Bonesi, *Pigmalion, drame lyrique en un acte et en prose* (Paris: Ballard, 1780), vi.

94 "Pigmalion recueille les premières idées, les premières affections de celle qu'il vient d'animer, & lui donne un premier baiser." Bonesi, *Pigmalion*, ix.

95 *La Querelle des bouffons, texte des pamphlets*, ed. Denise Launay, 3 vols. (Geneva: Minkoff reprints, 1973), 3:397. Translation adapted from Weber, "La musique ancienne," 78.

conscious freedom, but in real life he himself exercised his agency by refusing to use his moral liberty to unsettle the French monarchy. Quite the contrary, he framed the claim of liberty in his ballet as a *product* endorsed rather than suppressed by the monarch. What is remarkable is that Noverre used the dedication to bridge the real world and the imaginary world. The 1776 synopsis of Noverre's *Apelles et Campaspe* includes a dedication to Marie-Antoinette, Queen of France, to whom Noverre taught dancing back in Vienna. Dedication, as theorized by Emily H. Green, indicates exchanges of what Pierre Bourdieu calls symbolic capital in a gift economy. In the dedicatory preface, Noverre thanked Marie-Antoinette for allowing him to stage this work at the Opéra. Importantly, he associated Marie-Antoinette with Alexander the Great *and* himself with Apelles: "In order to paint an [image of] Alexander, one must be an Apelles."[96] This theme of high art as what Bourdieu called "cultural capital" for the powerful patron is at the core of the plot of the ballet-pantomime: in *Apelles et Campaspe* it is Alexander the Great who first asks Campaspe to express diverse attitudes through dance, as he wants to develop Apelles's artistic skills. In this dedication, Noverre aligned the symbolic capital, which was accrued in the *act* of dedication, with the cultural capital, which came from the *content* of his ballet-pantomime. In doing so, he presented his ballet-pantomime as an extension rather than a disruption of *la belle danse* and French theatrical dance. Within his framing, the theme of liberty in the ballet became a marker of Marie-Antoinette's fine taste, not a sign of political threat.

Noverre's claim of stylistic expansion also played a part in the plot. Noverre framed the emergent love affair between Apelles and Campaspe in the context of Roxane's ambition of being queen. He ended the ballet with celebrating the generosity of Alexander the Great, who forgives Campaspe. Generosity, according to the *Encyclopédie*, is a moral virtue that means "a dedication to the interests of others, which sacrifices one's personal benefits."[97] By stressing Alexander the Great's generosity, Noverre showed that a king also had moral liberty, and that not every incident related to the king needed to have a "political" meaning. Campaspe's quest for liberty makes Alexander the Great appear generous, not oppressive. Hence, Noverre's title: *Apelles et Campaspe, ou La Générosité d'Alexandre*.

Tellingly, the celebration of Alexander's generosity was highlighted by music. The composer of the Paris version of *Apelles et Campaspe*, Rodolphe, used a march in D major played by trumpet and horn, a sonority that represents warfare and Alexander the Great, and this march returns at the end of the ballet-pantomime that accompanies the entrance of Alexander the Great and the coronation of Roxane. Within this sharp-leaning outer frame, Rodolphe composed a series of dances in the flat-leaning keys (i.e., F major, B-flat major, E-flat major, C minor, and G minor) that represent the love relationship between Apelles and Campaspe. These two pairs of lovers are neatly differentiated by tonality. *Mercure de France* noted that Noverre presented

---

96 "Pour peindre un Alexandre, il faut être un Apelles." *Apelles et Campaspe*, 2. On dedication and symbolic capital, see Emily H. Green, *Dedicating Music, 1785–1850* (Rochester, NY: University of Rochester Press, 2019), 66–72.

97 "La *générosité* est un dévouement aux intérêts des autres, qui porte à leur sacrifier ses avantages personnels." Stanislas-Catherine, chevalier de Boufflers [attributed], *Encyclopédie*, vol. 7, s.v. "Généreux, Générosité."

two interconnected dramatic actions in one ballet-pantomime: Roxane presents a secondary dramatic action highlighting a noble and imposing monarchy, one that frames the primary action of the amorous relationship of Apelles and Campaspe. This framing device shows that Apelles's free artistic expression is not perceived to unsettle Alexander the Great's reign; instead, it is supported and even *contained* musically and dramatically by the generous Alexander the Great.[98]

Noverre did not consider Marie-Antoinette the only modern paragon of Alexander the Great who could be his patron. He used the claim of liberty as a self-promotional tool. In the 1782 program translated into English, Noverre reinforced the theme of liberty, adding that of equality alongside it. In response to Apelles's involuntary action towards her, Campaspe acknowledges his action with pleasure, telling him that "she prefers liberty to grandeur; that happiness can spring only from equality, and that she has no other wish than to captivate his heart, and freely yield her own."[99] In a re-run of *Apelles et Campaspe* in Lyon in 1787, Noverre evidently realized that he could "sell" – as it were – the symbolic capital that his ballet-pantomime had accrued. He called it "ballet-héroï-pantomime" rather than "ballet-pantomime" on the title page, kept the Paris program the same, but rewrote a dedication to a certain Madame La Marquise d'Ambert, declaring: "By giving me the permission to pay homage to you with my talents, you announce your taste for the Arts ... To dedicate *Apelles et Campaspe* to you is to multiply your image, to offer – as it were – your portrait to your fellow citizens."[100] After Lyons, Noverre continued to sell his ballet-pantomime, ready to repurpose it for another prospective patron. He included this ballet program in the Stockholm manuscript for Gustav III, King of Sweden, in 1791. Perhaps King Gustav III might become his patron. Perhaps he would welcome some symbolic capital (or simply old-fashioned flattery), by being compared to Alexander the Great through his ballet-pantomime.[101]

What is telling about Noverre's self-promotional endeavors is his refusal to make his ballet-pantomime a sign of political threat. He avoided precisely d'Alembert's fear of political subversion that might come from freedom of music or, in his case, music and dance. In his dedication of the synopsis of *Apelles et Campaspe* to Marie Antoinette, he made clear that the connection between reflexes and freedom in the ballet-pantomime was nothing more than a dance style. For this reason, Noverre exercised his *own* freedom of action by separating moral liberty from political liberty. His refusal illustrates the thesis of this chapter: if things can walk, humans can also stay still.

---

98 For this Paris production, Noverre did not use the music composed by Franz Aspelmayer for the 1773 premiere in Vienna. The score composed by Rodolphe is preserved in F-Po, shelf mark Rés. A-240.

99 Burden and Thorp, eds, *The Works of Monsieur Noverre*, 495.

100 "En me donnant la permission de vous faire l'hommage de mes talents, c'est annoncer votre goût pour les Arts ... Vous dédier *Apelles & Campaspe*, c'est multiplier votre image, c'est offrir (pour ainsi dire) votre portrait à vos Concitoyens." Noverre, *Apelles et Campaspe* (Lyon: Mlle Olier, 1787), 3.

101 On this ballet in the Stockholm manuscript of 1791, see Anna Karin Ståhle, "Jean-Georges Noverre Applying for Jobs," in Burden and Thorp, eds, *The Works of Monsieur Noverre*, 161.

CHAPTER FIVE

When Humans Dance like Atoms

O N the title page of *La Littérature renversée, ou L'Art de faire des pièces de théâtre sans paroles* (1775), the anonymous author claimed that the art of performing theatrical works without speech was useful (*utile*) to playwrights. This author was Pierre-Jean-Baptiste Nougaret, a prolific Grub Street writer who published, between 1760 and 1789, some forty-seven books of sundry genres – parodies, poems, elegies, banter, histories, letters, memoirs, odes, tableaux, songs (*chants*), tales, anecdotes, comedies, pantomimes, domestic dramas, operatic libretti, travel literatures, and almanacs/chronicles of spectacles performed at the fairground and the boulevard theaters in Paris. Although he apparently published these works for a wide range of readers, he referenced core Enlightenment ideas in some of them. His point about "useful" pantomime in *La Littérature renversée*, for example, came from Rousseau, for he and his co-author Nicolas-Edme Rétif de La Bretonne had referenced in their *Le Mimographe* (1770) the utility of spectacles that Rousseau had discussed in *Lettre à d'Alembert sur les spectacles* (1758). Yet Nougaret furthered Rousseau's claim by arguing that gesture could at times replace speech not only at the theater, but also in everyday life: if actors who had pronunciation issues – stutterers, those who spoke with a nasal voice, or those from the provinces – could use their bodies as substitutes for their faulty voices, then married couples could also argue silently at home by using gestures.[1]

Whether or not Nougaret believed that gesture could really replace speech in daily settings, his suggestion was grounded in a basic belief – shared by Dubos, Rousseau, Diderot, Condillac, and others – that gestures could function as signs for interpersonal communication, but what was new was that he introduced the theme of equality to the discourse of signification. By calling pantomime a "reversed" literature, Nougaret adopted the theme of reversal pervasive in eighteenth-century culture (e.g., Lesage and Jacques-Philippe d'Orneval's *Le Monde renversé* (1721)) and saw in pantomime a possibility to rethink the hierarchy of theatrical genres. Rather than prioritizing language, he foregrounded gesture; rather than prioritizing script, he foregrounded performance. The elevation of the lowly pantomime to the status of "literature" suggests a literary type of upward mobility, and Nougaret knew for a fact that this goal was achievable. He had been working since 1769 for Nicolas-Médard Audinot, co-director of the Théâtre l'Ambigu-Comique, and this minor troupe performed a group of works – including Nougaret's own spoken comedy *Il*

---

1   On actors with pronunciation issues, see *La Littérature renversée, ou L'Art de faire des pièces de théâtre sans paroles; ouvrage utile aux poètes dramatiques de nos jours* (Berne and Paris: les Débitans de brochures Nouvelles, 1775), 49. For a list of Nougaret's works, see Alexandre Cioranescu, *Bibliographie de la littérature française du dix-huitième siècle*, 3 vols. (Paris: Éditions du Centre national de la recherche scientifique, 1969), 2:1342–45.

n'y a plus d'enfants (1772) – in front of Louis XV at the Château de Choisy on April 8, 1772.[2] Nougaret's lived experience was reinforced by the idea of "natural (or moral) equality," defined by Jaucourt in the *Encyclopédie* as a "natural right" (*droit naturel*), one that was "founded on the constitution of human nature common to *all* men, who are born, grow, survive and die in the same way."[3] [emphasis mine] The logic that links pantomime to the idea of equality goes something like this: if Audinot's troupe could perform for the king, then the minor genres of ambigu-comique and pantomime had some cultural legitimacy; and if the minor genre of pantomime attained the status of literature, then a person of low social rank could step up the social ladder. As Nougaret realized, "These days the smallest *myrmidon* [i.e., a man despised by society] can distinguish himself."[4]

In light of Nougaret's observation, I will explain how the librettist Beaumarchais related the theme of reversal to natural right theory in his only opera *Tarare* (1787, music by Salieri). The theme of reversal in this opera is obvious: it follows the soldier named Tarare, who starts out being oppressed by the tyrant Atar, but ends up being elected by the people as Atar's replacement. As the Genie of Fire observes in the final scene of the opera, "The soldier takes up the throne, and the tyrant is dead" (line 1460). What is less obvious is that Beaumarchais carefully incorporated core concepts of natural right theory in *Tarare*. The connection between reversal and equality is justified explicitly by the Genie of Nature and Fire in the final lines of Beaumarchais's preferred ending of the opera (one without the final divertissement): "Mortal, whoever you are, prince, brama or soldier, / Man! Your greatness on earth does not belong to your station: it is all to your character" (lines 1469–71).[5] In case anyone found the first ending unacceptable due to its lack of final divertissement, Beaumarchais provided an alternative ending (one with a final divertissement) showing the people, led by the second-tier characters (captain of guards Urson and chief of eunuchs Calpigi), who entrust their liberty to Tarare: "King, we put liberty at the feet of your supreme virtue; reign over this people who loves you, by laws and fairness (*équité*)" (lines 1471–74). Beaumarchais claimed that he considered the first ending more "philosophical" than the second one, but he linked the second ending more closely to natural right theory by delineating laws and fairness as the two necessary conditions that guarantee the execution of natural rights: laws

---

2   For a report of the performances at Choisy, see Bachaumont, *Mémoires secrets*, 6:123. On Nougaret, see Michel Faul, *Les Tribulations de Nicolas-Médard Audinot: Fondateur du Théâtre de l'Ambigu-comique* (Lyon: Symétrie, 2013), 51.

3   "L'égalité naturelle ou morale est donc fondée sur la constitution de la nature humaine commune à tous les hommes, qui naissent, croissant, subsistent, & meurent de la même manière." Jaucourt, *Encyclopédie*, vol. 5, s.v. "Égalité naturelle."

4   "[Maintenant] le plus petit *mirmidon* peut s'illustrer." [Pierre-Jean-Baptiste Nougaret,] *La Littérature*, xiv. On social classes, see Sarah Maza, "Bourgeoisie," in William Doyale, ed., *The Oxford Handbook of the Ancien Régime* (Oxford: Oxford University Press, 2012), 127–40.

5   "Mortel, qui que tu soi, prince, brame ou soldat, / Homme! Ta grandeur sur la terre / N'appartient point à ton état: / Elle est toute à ton caractère." Beaumarchais, *Œuvres*, ed. Pierre Henri Larthomas with Jacqueline Larthomas (Paris: Gallimard, 1988), 589.

are the means by which people *return* to the state of natural equality.⁶ As Jaucourt put it in the *Encyclopédie* article "Natural Equality," "In the state of nature, men are born equal, but they do not know how to stay so. Society causes them to lose equality, and they become equal once again only by laws."⁷ Fairness, Jaucourt wrote in a separate article, means "the will (*volonté*) of the prince, formed by the rules of prudence to correct what is found in a law of his state, or in a civil judgment of magistracy established by his orders, when things have been settled differently than the view of the common good would require him in the proposed circumstances."⁸ The source of fairness is natural law, one that makes fairness eternal and inalterable. To support this point, Jaucourt cited almost verbatim the following sentence from letter No.81 of Montesquieu's *Lettres persanes* (1721): "Although we would be free from the yoke of religion, we should not be free from the yoke of fairness."⁹ In addition to emphasizing law and fairness, Beaumarchais highlighted the *people*, who demand Tarare-the-new-sultan to reclaim *their* liberty, which was a core idea in Rousseau's *Discours sur l'origine et les fondements de l'inégalité parmi les hommes* (1755): "For the Magistracy and its Rights being established only upon the fundamental Laws, should they be destroyed the Magistrates would immediately cease to be legitimate, the People would no longer be bound to obey them; and as it would not have been the Magistrate but the Law which had constituted the essence of the State, everyone would return by Right to his Natural freedom (*liberté naturelle*)."¹⁰ The second ending, therefore, makes explicit that the restoration of people's natural liberty should be the principal objective of Tarare's imminent office.

Just as Beaumarchais imparted the ideas of natural equality and liberty in *Tarare*, Salieri also made explicit use of pantomime in *Tarare*, and these two facts together make this opera an excellent case study for exploring music, pantomime, and liberty in pre-Revolutionary France.¹¹ How did Salieri use pantomime, an operatic component that includes copious natural signs? How does the emphasis on natural signs change the relationship between music and text in this opera? What claims did Beaumarchais and Salieri make in *Tarare* about the relationships between natural signs and natural liberty? One set of answers to these questions, I propose, comes

6　Beaumarchais, *Œuvres*, 590.

7　"Dans l'état de nature, les hommes naissent bien dans l'égalité, mais ils n'y sauraient rester; la société la leur fait perdre, & ils ne redeviennent égaux qua par les lois." Jaucourt, *Encyclopédie*, vol. 5, s.v. "Égalité naturelle."

8　"L'équité … est une volonté du prince, disposée par les règles de la prudence à corriger ce qui se trouve dans une loi de son état, ou dans un jugement civil de la magistrature établie par ses ordres, quand les choses y ont été réglées autrement que la vue du bien commun ne le demanderait dans les circonstances proposées." Jaucourt, *Encyclopédie*, vol. 5, s.v. "Équité [Morale/Droit politique]."

9　"Libres que nous serions du joug de la Religion, nous ne devrions pas l'être de celui de l'Équité." Montesquieu, *Lettres persanes*, 2 vols. (Amsterdam: Pierre Brunel, 1721), 2:42.

10　*CWR*, 3:60.

11　On the ballets of *Tarare*, see Mark Darlow, "L'esthétique du tableau dans les ballets de Tarare, version de 1819," in Waeber, ed., *Musique et geste*, 249–64; on Beaumarchais and pantomime, see Jacqueline Waeber, "Beaumarchais et Rousseau: sur quelques aspects de renouveau de la pantomime et du l'avènement du mélodrame," *French Studies of the Eighteenth and Nineteenth Centuries* 8 (2000), 205–24.

from epicurean materialism, disseminated most notably in *De rerum natura* (*On the Nature of Things*) by the Roman poet Titus Lucretius Carus (*c.*97–55 BC). Though rarely discussed in studies of music, *De rerum natura* provides the philosophical context for explaining the concept of "laws of nature" (*lois de la nature*), a concept that in turn elucidates the ideas of "natural law" (*la loi naturelle*) and "natural equality" (*égalité naturelle*) central to natural right theory. To make these connections, I explain in the first part of this chapter how Beaumarchais made *Tarare* a "philosophical" opera, and I explain how Salieri supported Beaumarchais's vision with his music. I then discuss how Nature sanctions reproductive sex and denounces a non-reproductive marriage between an Italian castrato-turned-eunuch and a hypersexual Italian soprano as unnatural, and how Nature denounces language (a medium made up mostly of "conventional" or "instituted" signs) as "impure," in contradistinction to "pure" elements such as gesture and echo (mediums made up of "natural" signs). Using dancers who moved like atoms and *Tarare's* physical gestures as indicators of his moral character, Salieri and Beaumarchais illustrated in *Tarare* that *all* human beings have "natural liberty" (*liberté naturelle*), defined in the *Encyclopédie* as the "right that nature gives to *all* men to dispose of their persons and their assets, in the way they consider most suitable to their happiness, under the restriction that they do so in terms of the natural law, and that they do not abuse it to the detriment of other men."[12]

A PHILOSOPHICAL OPERA

Tarare was the only operatic libretto written by Beaumarchais that was staged at the Académie Royale de Musique, and this libretto includes philosophical ideas central to the Enlightenment. Compared with most French operas in the 1770s and 1780s, *Tarare* had an unusually long gestation. Its genesis probably dates from 1774, when Beaumarchais met Gluck after the performance of *Iphigénie en Aulide* and told him of his admiration for expressing passions through music "without sacrificing the interest of the scene and without stopping the dramatic action." Hearing these remarks, Gluck recognized this man as Beaumarchais, and the two of them planned to collaborate on an opera.[13] A year later Beaumarchais finished the prose version of *Tarare* and had half of it versified. It was accepted in 1784 by the Opéra for performance, the year Salieri staged *Les Danaïdes* at the Opéra, and replaced Gluck as composer for this opera. In the intervening years, Beaumarchais was engaged in a wide range of activities: he premiered *Le Barbier de Séville* at the Comédie-Française on February 23, 1775; he became Louis XVI's secret agent in the summer of 1775, and offered assistance to the American Revolution; he purchased the punches and types invented by John Baskerville in 1779, and used them to publish in 1784 Voltaire's

12   "Liberté naturelle, (Droit naturel.) droit que la nature donne à tous les hommes de disposer de leurs personnes & de leurs biens, de la manière qu'ils jugent la plus convenable à leur Bonheur, sous la restriction qu'ils le fassent dans les termes de la loi naturelle, & qu'ils n'en abusent pas au préjudice des autres hommes." *Encyclopédie*, vol. 9, s.v. "Liberté naturelle."

13   Beaumarchais, *Œuvres complètes de Pierre-Augustin Caron de Beaumarchais*, ed. Gudin de La Brenellerie, 7 vols. (Paris: Léopold Collin, 1809), 7:282.

complete work in the city of Kehl of southwestern Germany; he tried in vain in 1782 to stage at the Opéra his adaptation of Voltaire's 1734 *Samson*, set to music by Rameau; he premiered his *La Folle journée ou Le Mariage de Figaro* on April 27 1784. After the opera was approved by the royal censor Antoine Bret in late 1786, *Tarare* was finally premiered at the Opéra on June 8, 1787. For the first performance Beaumarchais published a hastily produced first edition of the libretto, and issued the amended second and definitive edition two months later, in August, which included a preface entitled *Aux abonnés de l'Opéra qui voudraient aimer l'opéra* ('To the subscribers of the Opéra who would like to love opera').

Beaumarchais's *Aux abonnés* was a crucial text for understanding *Tarare*: in it, Beaumarchais explained why his opera was a product of the intellectual movement of the Enlightenment. There he claimed, "Our age will be cited as one that was deep in science, in philosophy, prolific in discoveries, and full of force and of reason."[14] The reference to the Enlightenment can be gleaned in the Latin quote "Barbarus at ego sum ..." (I am a barbarian) on the title page of the second edition of the libretto. This quote originally came from Ovid's *Tristia* – "Barbarus hic ego sum" – and was quoted by Rousseau for the title page of his *First Discourse* (1750): "Here it is I that am a barbarian, understood by nobody."[15] In the author's foreword (*avertissement*), Beaumarchais introduced his *Aux abonnés* as a "preliminary discourse," which referenced d'Alembert's preliminary discourse for the *Encyclopédie*. Beaumarchais made obvious references to the Enlightenment by showing an acute sense of its being an age of progress. Already in his libretto *Samson* of 1782, based on Voltaire's *Samson* of 1734, Beaumarchais demonstrated a spirit of the Enlightenment: "The love of real talents alone, and the desire to contribute to the progress (*progrès*) of a charming art that experiences the greatest revolution today, have given us the courage to touch the work of the finest genius of our age (*siècle*)."[16] What he meant by "our age" does not mean the decade of the 1780s, but a period that began as far back as the 1680s–1720s, in which writers who participated in the Quarrel of the Ancients and Moderns became aware of the dawn of a new intellectual age called the Enlightenment. In *Aux abonnés*, Beaumarchais kept this spirit alive: "The spirit of the nation seems to be in a happy crisis; a bright and widespread (*répandue*) light (*lumière*) makes everyone feel that everything can be better. We worry; we become restless; we invent, we reform."[17] Crucially, Beaumarchais conceived *Tarare* not simply as a new opera, but a new opera that illustrates a new *way* (*moyen*) for audiences to experience an opera

14   "On citera le nôtre [siècle] comme un siècle profond de science, de philosophie, fécond de découverts, et plein de force et de raison." Beaumarchais, *Œuvres*, 497.

15   Ovid, *Tristia*, 5.10.37. Rousseau quoted Ovid's verse in full: "Barbarus hic ego sum, qui non intellegor ulli." Translation taken from Ovid, *Tristia. Ex Ponto*, trans. Arther Leslie Wheeler, rev. G. P. Goold (Cambridge, MA: Harvard University Press, 1975), 249. On the genesis of *Tarare*, see Beaumarchais, *Œuvres*, 1454–55.

16   Beaumarchais, *Œuvres*, 1437. On *Samson*, see M. Elizabeth C. Bartlet, "Beaumarchais and Voltaire's *Samson*," *Studies in Eighteenth-Century Culture* 11 (1982), 33–47.

17   "L'esprit de la nation semble être dans une crise heureuse; une lumière vive et répandue fait sentir à chacun que tout peut être mieux. On s'inquiète, on s'agite, on invente, on reforme." Beaumarchais, *Œuvres*, 497.

at the Opéra. His goal exemplifies what Edelstein calls a "second-order observation" characteristic of the Enlightenment.[18]

One of the most important features of *Tarare* is that Beaumarchais used a prologue for a "philosophical" frame, complete with a corresponding epilogue that frames the five-act opera proper. At an early stage in the conceptualization of his opera, he jotted down the following idea on a piece of paper, which was discovered in the attic by Beaumarchais's son-in-law, his grandson, and scholar Louis-Léonard de Loménie (best known for *Beaumarchais et son temps* (1856)): "Make a prologue in which nature makes two embryos or two atoms draw lots. Which one will be king and the other slave? Philosophical dissertation on this subject."[19] This fragment forms the basis of the prologue of *Tarare*, when Nature creates shadows (*ombres*) of humans out of atoms: "Cold humans, no yet alive, / atoms lost in space, / let each of your elements get closer and take its place, / following order, gravity / and all immutable laws / Let the eternal dispenser / impose on your fellow beings. / Humans not yet alive, / Appear alive in my eyes" (lines 40–49). The two embryos or atoms turn out to be Atar and Tarare, and Beaumarchais made Tarare Atar's successor. In evoking atoms and gravity (*la pesanteur*), Beaumarchais explicitly adopted the epicurean topic called "atomism," which, according to Yvon and Johann Heinrich Samuel Formey, referred to a "very ancient corpuscular physics" made known by Pierre Gassendi, Michel de Montaigne, Isaac Newton, and others, who were entranced by Lucretius's didactic poem (what Jaucourt called *poème philosophique*) *On the Nature of Things*. As Yvon and Formey claimed, "There is no better way to get a complete idea of atomism than to read the famous poem by Lucretius."[20]

By evoking atomism and thus Lucretius's *On the Nature of Things*, Beaumarchais used atomist matter theory to illustrate the idea of "natural equality." Atoms are separate and equal, and their movements follow laws of nature. These themes resonate strongly with the language of the first paragraph of the American Declaration of Independence of July 4, 1776: "When in the Course of human events, it becomes necessary for one people to dissolve the political bands which have connected them with another, and to assume among the powers of the earth, the separate and equal station to which the *Laws of Nature* and of *Nature's God* entitle them, a decent respect to the opinions of mankind requires that they should declare the causes which impel them to the separation."[21] [emphasis mine] The Declaration had been

18 Beaumarchais, *Œuvres*, 510. On "second-order observation," see Edelstein, *The Enlightenment*, 45.

19 "Faire un prologue où la nature fait tirer au sort deux embryons, ou deux atomes. Lequel sera roi, et l'autre esclave? Dissertation philosophique à ce sujet." Beaumarchais, *Notes et Réflexions*, intro. Gérard Bauër ([Paris]: Hachette, 1961), 90.

20 Abbé Claude Yvon and Jean-Henri-Samuel Formey, *Encyclopédie*, vol. 1, s.v. "Atomisme."

21 "Declaration of Independence: A Transcription," https://www.archives.gov/founding-docs/declaration-transcript; on the military supplies, see Streeter Bass, "Beaumarchais and the American Revolution," *Studies in Intelligence* 14, no.1 (1970), 8, article unclassified and approved for release by Central Intelligence Agency, United States of America, on 18 April 2005; on Beaumarchais and the American Revolution, see Harlow Giles Unger, *Improbable Patriot: The Secret History of Monsieur Beaumarchais, the French Playwright*

signed in Congress by representatives of thirteen states of America about a month after Beaumarchais received one million livres from the French Treasury, on June 10, 1776, to sell military supplies to the Americans – muskets, powder, tents, ammunitions, plus shoes, wool stockings, blankets, buttons, buckles, needles, thread, pocket knives for soldiers, in addition to lots of silk and wool for uniforms. Beaumarchais acknowledged the Declaration on August 18 1776. In a letter to the Congress of the newly established United States of America (*Provinces unies d'Amérique*), he expressed his respect for the "brave nation that defends so well her liberty" and notified them of the establishment of his company in Europe that would ship them all of their needs in support of their "honorable war."[22] In *Tarare* Beaumarchais personified nature as a female figure in the way that Lucretius personified nature as Venus; he evoked Lucretius's Venus who uses her strong libido as the life force of all things: "Life-stirring Venus, Mother of Aeneas and of Rome, / Pleasure of men and gods, you make all things beneath the dome / Of sliding constellations teem, you throng the fruited earth / And the ship-freighted sea – for every species comes to birth / Conceived through you, and rises forth and gazes on the light."[23]

According to his library's inventory, Beaumarchais owned a copy of Lucretius's *De rerum natura*, in its original Latin, printed in Birmingham in 1772 by the English typographer-printer John Baskerville. Beaumarchais himself did not need to read the poem in French, but there was a demand for French translations.[24] After *De rerum natura* was rediscovered by Poggio Bracciolini in 1417, Michel de Marolles published a French translation in 1650 and published the second edition in 1659. In 1685 Jacques Parrain des Coutures published a new French translation in Paris, which was reprinted in Lyons in 1695, and again in Paris in 1708. In 1768 a free prose translation with a *discours préliminaire* by a certain Lagrange, tutor of d'Holbach's children, was published in Paris and Amsterdam. In 1788, the year after *Tarare* premiered with success in Paris, Antoine Le Blanc de Guillet published a translation in verse, complete with a *discours préliminaire*. In the *discours préliminaire* to his 1768 translation of Lucretius's poem, Lagrange called this poem "reckless" (*téméraire*), but he crowned Lucretius a "profound and sublime" philosopher: "No philosopher … has ever spoken about the gods with more audacity. Not only does Lucretius deny their providence, but he asserts that they are not the designers and conservators of the universe."[25]

---

who Saved the American Revolution (Hanover, NH: University Press of New England, 2011).

22 Beaumarchais, *Correspondance*, ed. Brian N. Morton, 3 vols. (Paris: Nizet, 1969), 2:241–42.

23 Lucretius, *The Nature of Things*, trans. A. E. Stallings (London: Penguin, 2007), 1.1–5.

24 Donald C. Spinelli, *L'inventaire après décès de Beaumarchais* (Paris: H. Champion, 1997), 96.

25 "Aucun philosophe…n'a jamais parlé des Dieux avec plus d'audace: non seulement Lucrèce nie leur providence; mais il assure qu'ils ne sont pas les créateurs & les conservateurs de l'univers." Lagrange, *Traduction libre de Lucrèce*, 2 vols. (Paris and Amsterdam: Châtelain, 1768), 1:i–ii. On Poggio Bracciolini and the reception of *De rerum natura*, see Stephen Greenblatt, *The Swerve: How the World became Modern* (New York: Norton, 2011).

On the Nature of Things was considered an insightful but a controversial book after it was rediscovered in the early fifteenth century, but it provides the very philosophical context for Beaumarchais and Salieri to think deeply about motion in nature and, in practical terms, the presentation of motion through pantomime in an opera. Lucretius's main thesis is that matter is made of indivisible units called atoms, "building blocks of all things," (book 1, line 51), indestructible particles (book 1, line 234). Atoms are "separate," but are "always part of something else, primal and indivisible" (book 1, lines 604–605); atoms are always in "agitated motion" (book 1, line 341). Since the fate of two atoms is the main idea of the opera and since matter in motion is one of the core ideas in Lucretius's philosophical poem, how did Salieri bring together the idea of atoms in motion and the practice of pantomime in *Tarare*?

THE SPECTACLE OF NATURE

Let's take a moment to review how Gluck used pantomime. In Gluck's Paris operas, as discussed in Chapter Three, Gluck consistently used a short recitative to introduce a pantomime dance. This technique ensures a logical connection between pantomime and its adjacent components: the sung text in recitatives makes the ensuing pantomimes meaningful by projecting semantically suggestive and emotionally expressive content onto them. In some cases, most notably the dagger scene in Gluck's version of *Armide*, Gluck inserted orchestral musical segments between words of a verse, creating evocative musical segments that suggest a singer's naturalistic style of acting, and contemporary writers associated these segments with the term "pantomime." In these cases Gluck did not ascribe semantic and emotional meanings to music and dance, as he did in the recitative-pantomime sequences, but he supplied highly suggestive orchestral musical segments for actors and actresses.

Salieri adopted Gluck's techniques in all three of his French operas *Les Danaïdes* (1784), *Les Horaces* (1786), and *Tarare* (1787), each of which includes one pantomime dance. In *Les Danaïdes*, as discussed in Chapter Four, the librettists Du Roullet and Tschudi indicated pantomime in the penultimate scene, using bodily movements and cries to represent the Danaïdes, who express themselves as sub-human bacchantes: "Some of the Danaïdes are chained by groups, tormented by demons, and devoured by serpents; the others, chased by the furies, fill up the stage with their movements and their cries. A rain of fire falls endlessly; the whole forms a pantomime of the most terrifying type."[26] In *Les Horaces* (1786) Salieri used a pantomime in the second intermède (i.e., between Acts Two and Three) to present soldiers' revolt: "A crowd of soldiers of the two armies leave their ranks. They rush to separate the champions who persist in fighting, despite the efforts of their leaders to hold them."[27] Compared with these two pantomimes, Salieri used the pantomime dance in the prologue of *Tarare* to depict not movements made by human bodies, but movements of air. As Beaumarchais wrote, "The overture makes a violent noise in the [musical] airs, a terrifying shock of all the elements. The curtain, while raising,

---

26 *Les Danaïdes*, 50. On this scene, see John A. Rice, "The Staging of Salieri's *Les Danaïdes* as Seen by a Cellist in the Orchestra," *Cambridge Opera Journal* 26, no.1 (2014), 79–80.

27 *Les Horaces, tragédie-lyrique, en trois actes, mêlée avec intermèdes* (Paris: Ballard, 1786), 35. On *Les Horaces*, see Adolphe Jullien, *La Cour et l'Opéra* (Paris: Didier, 1878), 201–13.

shows only some clouds that swirl, tear apart, and reveal the unbridled gusts of wind; they form, while whirling, dances of the most violent turbulence."[28]

Since there is only one pantomime in each opera, the meanings of a pantomime are context driven, relative to other dances of the opera. What the pantomime of wind in *Tarare* stands for depends upon the two sections of sarabande that occur in the third scene of the prologue, the European fête (III/iv) that consists of what Beaumarchais called "figured dance" (*danse figurée*, or *la danse simple* that impart dramatic action), and the general end-of-the-opera divertissement celebrating the coronation of Tarare in Beaumarchais's second ending.

As the only pantomime dance in the opera, the pantomime of the wind in the prologue illustrates atoms' movement in nature. The overture begins at night. Salieri sustains the tonic chord of C major for eight measures with scalar runs played by the violins in unison to depict stasis, and this stasis is presented in music by harmonic, motivic, rhythmic means. This beginning is followed by a pantomime dance that depicts wind (*Pantomime, les Vents*), in C minor. In a common mimetic technique, Salieri used bursts of ascending scalar runs to depict turbulence, but designed an uncommon transition from the pantomime to the prologue. The pantomime ends with a diminished seventh chord on C-sharp, a chord remotely related to C major or C minor, which shows no hint of tonal direction. The diminished seventh chord leads directly, without a cadence, to Nature's entrance in the first scene of the prologue, a technique recalling Gluck's, in *Iphigénie en Tauride*. To maximize voice-leading efficiency, Salieri makes the note B-flat – one of chord tones of the diminished seventh chord on C-sharp – descend a half step to A. This note A, in the first measure of the first scene of the prologue, instantly turns the tonally unstable diminished seventh chord into the dominant seventh chord of D minor, providing a clear tonal goal that leads to the tonicization of D minor in m.6 (Example 5.1). The arrival of Nature, therefore, brings *tonal* order to end the turbulence. Hence, she sings: "It is enough to disturb the universe; / Furious winds, stop shaking up the air and the wave. It is enough. Take your chains back: May the gentle breeze alone reign over the world."[29]

Asking dancers to move like atoms that form the turbulence, Salieri and Beaumarchais used the pantomime dance to visualize wind. Wind, as defined by Formey in the *Encyclopédie*, is "a perceptible turbulence in the air, by which a considerable quantity of air is pushed from one place to another."[30] Numerous composers had used music to depict such natural phenomena as breeze, waves, wind, rain, snow, storm, thunder, and lightning. Rameau, for example, published the keyboard piece *Les Tourbillons* that depicts whirlwind (RCT 3, *c.*1724), but an eighteenth-century opera composer could illustrate the *movement* of air through dance. This is a distinct advantage, for Lucretius emphasized that atoms "cannot be seen" (book 1, line 269). This is also a distinct advantage in the context of the Enlightenment that

---

28 Beaumarchais, *Œuvres*, 513.

29 "C'est assez troubler l'univers; Vents furieux, cessez d'agiter l'air et l'onde. C'est assez, reprenez vos fers: Que le seul zéphyr règne au monde." Beaumarchais, *Œuvres*, 514.

30 "VENT, s.m. (*Phys.*) une agitation sensible dans l'air, par laquelle une quantité considérable d'air est poussée d'un lieu dans un autre." Jean-Henri-Samuel Formey, *Encyclopédie*, vol. 17, s.v. "Vent."

Example 5.1. Salieri, *Tarare*, Prologue Ouverture, mm.106–112, and Prologue Scene 1, "C'est assez troubler l'univers," mm.1–9

placed emphasis – symbolic, metaphoric, linguistic – on the idea of illumination.[31] In *Système de la nature* (1770), for example, d'Holbach emphasized the sense of sight in the process of perceiving causal relation: "As soon as we see a cause take effect, we regard its effects as natural."[32] That is to say, it is insufficient for audiences to know that wind is formed by movement of air or to hear representations of wind in music; it is mandatory for wind to be *seen* as movement of air.

31 See Darrin M. McMahon, "Illuminating the Enlightenment: Public Lighting Practices in the Siècles des Lumières," *Past & Present* 240, no.1 (2018), 119–59.

32 "Dès que nous voyons une cause agir nous regardons ses effets comme naturels." D'Holbach, *Système de la nature*, 1:76.

Example 5.1. continued

Example 5.1. continued

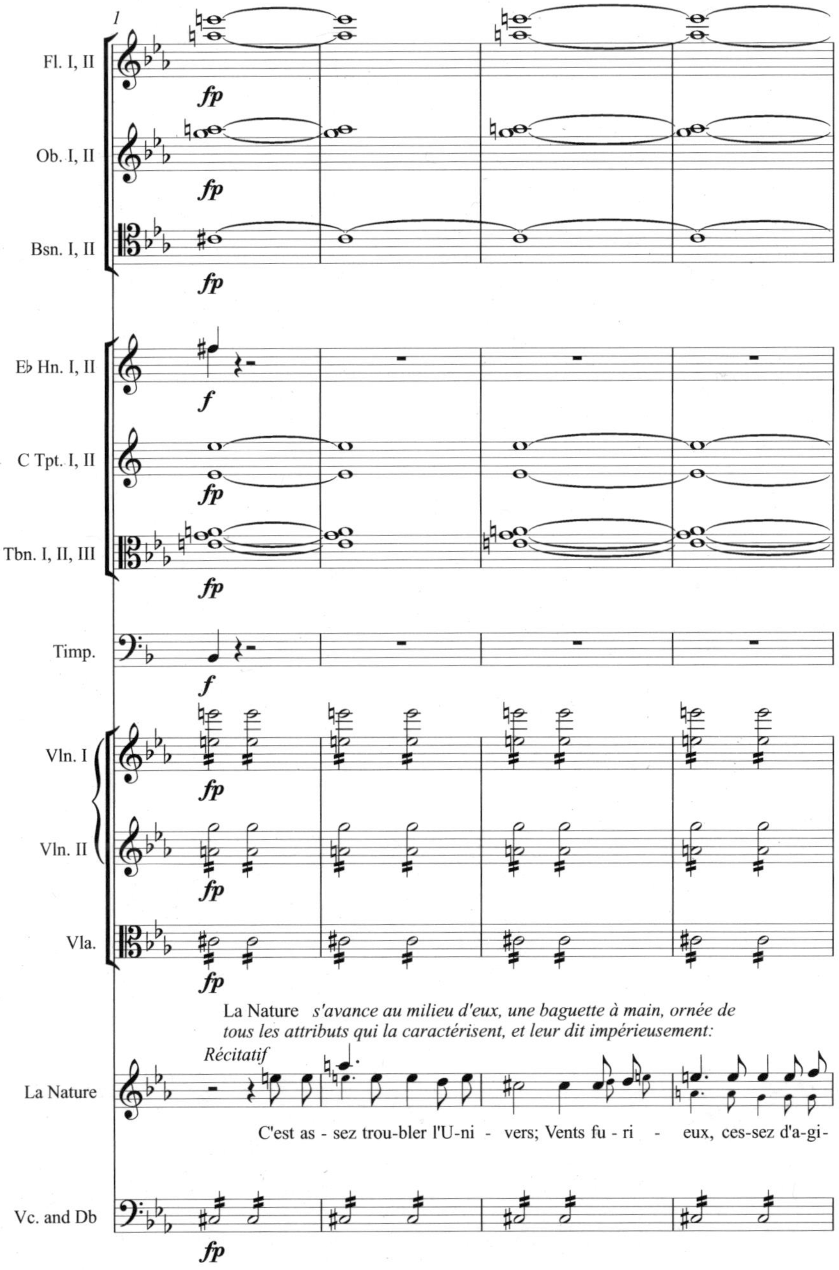

Example 5.1. continued

Example 5.1. continued

Note that the visualized wind does not impart a narrative or any human emotions in the pantomime dance, as Dubos would like to see; instead, this visualization removes human agency from this pantomime, *de*-humanizing this pantomime dance and paring down biological materialism to the more basic version of Lucretian materialism. By having dancers move like wind, Salieri brought onstage atoms that move mechanically in accordance with inviolable laws of nature, what Lucretius called "the laws of fate" (book 2, line 254). Rather than presenting atoms that move like a dance, Salieri presented his pantomime dancers who move like atoms. The physical movements of atoms – whirling, twirling, and swirling of clouds, gusts of wind, and the most violent turbulence – make what Lagrange called the "spectacle of nature."[33]

PURE AND IMPURE ELEMENTS

What makes Salieri's pantomime dance remarkable is not the use of pantomime as a dance, but the philosophical rationale that justified it. In the first scene of the prologue, Nature admits that she uses the "purest elements" (line 34) to create the most powerful people of an empire, but she regrets that their language is far from pure: "It is their language, we must well smile at it: a noble pride makes them almost sure of it. But see how nature spills them by thousands, without choice and without moderation" (lines 36–39). She then casts a spell and creates shadows of human beings, as mentioned above. By pointing out language as an "impure" element, Nature implies that language is composed of instituted signs and that movements of atoms in space function as natural signs – signs that obey *her* laws, what d'Alembert called "laws of nature" (*lois de la nature*).[34]

The polarity of pure and impure elements is significant to *Tarare*, for it establishes the relationship between natural and instituted signs in music and poetry that constituted the conceptual foundation for mid-century Italian opera reform and Gluck's Paris operas. In *Aux abonnés* Beaumarchais claimed that "it is not about the art of singing, the talent of modulating well, or the combination of sounds. It is not about music in itself that I want to speak to you: it is the *action* of poetry on music, and the *reaction* of the latter on poetry at the theater that matters to me, relative to the works in which these two arts come together."[35] Beaumarchais's Newtonian language recalls the entry "laws of nature" in the *Encyclopédie*, written by d'Alembert: "reaction is always contrary and equal to action."[36] Already at the opening of the opera, the pantomime of the wind does not simply illustrate a mimetic dance *style* akin to the motion of air in a cyclone, but this style is *theorized* by Nature and explained further by Beaumarchais in *Aux abonnés* to follow laws of nature. By connecting music/poetry to natural/instituted signs, Beaumarchais not only aligned Gluckian reform operatic principles with the Enlightenment theories of the origins of language, but he aligned these two facets with Lucretian materialism.

---

33   Lagrange, "Discours préliminaire," *Traduction libre de Lucrèce*, vii.

34   On "laws of movement" and "laws of nature," see d'Alembert, *Encyclopédie*, vol. 11, s.v. "Nature, lois de la."

35   Beaumarchais, *Œuvres*, 497.

36   "La réaction est toujours contraire & égale à l'action." D'Alembert, *Encyclopédie*, vol. 11, s.v. "Nature, lois de la."

That said, while Beaumarchais and Salieri used pantomime dance as a representation of atoms in motion, they did not revert to the Dubosian opposition of pantomime and *la belle danse*; instead, Beaumarchais dismantled this simple opposition by finding fault with excessive repetition. In the preface to *Le Barbier de Séville* called "Lettre modérée sur la chute et la critique du 'Barbier de Séville'," published in late July of 1775, Beaumarchais used what he called "the elevated dance" (*la danse élévée*) performed by the dancers Gaetano Appolino Balthasar Vestris and Dauberval at the Opéra to denounce repetitive music: "Hey! Go, then, music. Why always repeat? Are you not slow enough? Instead of narrating briskly, you keep repeating! Instead of depicting the passion, you cling to words!"[37] Beaumarchais was inspired by the *pas de caractère* in Vestris and d'Auberval for gestural variety and expressivity, just as Diderot admired in his *Éloge de Richardson* (1762) the distinct expressions of the forty characters in Samuel Richardson's *History of Sir Charles Grandison*. Beaumarchais wrote: "See how the superb Vestris or the proud d'Auberval performs a *pas de caractère*. He does not yet dance but, from as far away as it appears, his free and casual bearing already makes the spectators look up ... When the musician repeats his phrases twenty times and makes his movements monotonous, the dancer varies his endlessly."[38] Beaumarchais's remarks about *la danse élévée* extended Noverre's point of ballet-pantomime as "an offspring of liberty." What he recognized was not the synchronization of music and dance, but the *need* for composers to learn from expressive dancers by capturing the gestural nuances in expressive style of dancing with music. Beaumarchais urged composers to sing in the way that the dancer dances so that audiences will have "melodramas (*mélodrames*) instead of operas."[39] Some twelve years after he published his "Lettre modérée", Beaumarchais in his *Aux abonnés* reiterated almost word for word the same criticism of repetitive music ("Instead of narrating briskly, you keep repeating! Instead of depicting passions, you cling idly to words!"), in a clear act of self-referencing.

By criticizing repetitive music, Beaumarchais shifted the discourse of pantomime from the polarity between pantomime and *la belle danse* to one between pantomimic dance made of non-repetitive bodily movements and dance types made of repetitive dance steps. Taking what he called *la danse élévée* as the pinnacle of dancing, one comparable to *mélodrame*, Beaumarchais in effect reinforced Dubos's emphasis on dancers' expressive bodies. To be sure, he did not address how "pure" *la danse élévée* was, but he nonetheless found *la danse élévée* more expressive – and thus *purer* – than other standardized dance types. If anything, he considered the pantomime of wind the only type of dance that Nature considers completely pure.

---

37 "Eh! Va donc, musique! Pourquoi toujours répéter? N'es-tu pas assez lente? Au lieu de narrer vivement, tu rabâches! Au lieu de peindre la passion, tu t'accroches aux mots!" Beaumarchais, *Œuvres*, 286.

38 "Voyez le superbe Vestris ou le fier d'Auberval engager un pas de caractère. Il ne danse pas encore; mais, d'aussi loin qu'il paraît, son port libre et dégagé fait déjà lever la tête aux spectateurs ... Pendant que le musicien redit vingt fois ses phrases et monotone ses mouvements, le danseur varier les siens à l'infini." Beaumarchais, *Œuvres*, 286. For Diderot's admiration for individualized expressions, see Diderot, *Œuvres*, 4:162.

39 "Compositeurs! Chantez comme il danse, et nous aurons, au lieu d'opéras, des mélodrames!" Beaumarchais, *Œuvres*, 287.

VIRTUOUS INACTION

With Beaumarchais declaring his preference for *melodrama*, Beaumarchais and Salieri justified their use of the Gluckian technique of suggestive orchestral accompaniment that mimics movements, including visible movements such as physical gestures or invisible movements such as palpitations. His vision was fueled by the great eighteenth-century English actor, Garrick, and his wife. Beaumarchais himself met the Garrick couple in London. In a letter dated July 23 1774 Beaumarchais told Garrick that he was inspired by Madame Garrick's "delicate and highly expressive smiles" (*les sourires fins et pleins d'expression*) and that he would like to make good use of these types of bodily expressions in his *Le Barbier de Séville* (to be premiered the following year).[40] In *Tarare* two scenes illustrate this technique. The more obvious scene is the one in which Tarare disguises as a mute (IV/vi), where Salieri uses music to disclose his unspoken thoughts. The less obvious scene is the story-telling scene (III/ii), where Ulson recounts an offstage combat between Tarare and Altamort in front of Atar (III/ii). In both cases, Tarare exercises restraint, illustrating his character. We will discuss each instance in turn.

The mute scene is one of the rare episodes in *Tarare* that illustrates Tarare's agency. Having been rejected by Tarare's wife Astasie, the vindictive Atar would like to see her "tied up by an old negro and humiliated through a hundred cries" (lines 1065–66). Atar has Calpigi send the "basest of mutes of the seraglio" to be the "new husband" for Astasie, without knowing that Calpigi would send Astasie's husband Tarare disguised as that mute. After hearing about this plan, Astasie decides to avoid the encounter and to disguise her maidservant Spinette to look like herself. The mute scene takes place in Astasie's apartment, when Tarare (in the guise of an anonymous black mute slave) expects to see Astasie but sees instead a woman he does not recognize (Spinette disguised as Astasie). Contrary to Atar's expectation, this mute/Tarare remains a few steps away from Spinette/Astasie. Salieri uses three orchestral segments to present this encounter, all built upon a melody of small-range, short motifs separated by eighth rests, soft dynamics, and an unadventurous I–V–I harmonic progression tonicizing D major and G major. Salieri uses music to highlight Tarare's cautious inaction, which is interpreted by Spinette/Astasie as an expression of his "respect" for her (Example 5.2). She observes that the mute "does not have the fierce appearance of other monsters of these premises" (lines 1168–69), and she concludes: "Mute, your respect touches me, I am reading your love in your eyes: a tender vow from your mouth could not express it better to me" (lines 1170–74). The uneventful encounter between Tarare/mute and Spinette/Astasie may be anticlimactic to Atar, but Tarare/mute's inaction before Spinette/Astasie is testimony to his agency.

Another example also illustrates Tarare's inaction. As reported by Urson, Tarare's duel with Altamort illustrates Tarare's character. Immediately before the fight, Tarare declares his rule: "Let's decide the fate of the vanquished, my law ... is death" (lines 726–27). During this combat Tarare injures Altamort, but he decides not to exercise his "right of war" (*droit de la guerre*, line 754), described by Montesquieu

---

40 David Garrick, *The Private Correspondence of David Garrick*, ed. James Boaden, 2 vols. (London: Colborn and Bentley, 1832), 2: 609.

Example 5.2. Salieri, *Tarare*, Act 4 Scene 6, "Comme il est laid," mm.1–15

Example 5.2. continued

in *De l'esprit des loix* (1748) as "the right to kill."[41] Tarare rationalizes his decision, saying: "Fear nothing, superb Altamort: / Between us the war is over. If the right of giving death is that of granting life, I spare your life willingly. Mourn your perfidy for a long time" (lines 755–60).

    Salieri set Ulson's account to an accompanied recitative that has a melodramatic effect. After singing a segment of one to three verses, Ulson pauses, leaving the orchestral accompaniment to illustrate through music the content of what he has just sung. For example, the verse "Tarare is the first one who arrives at the meeting place" is followed by stately music; another verse "Tarare comes converse with us" is followed by an ascending triadic melody with double-dotted rhythm, which suggests

41   "Ils [Les auteurs de notre droit public] ont supposé dans les conquérants un droit, je ne sais quel, de tuer." Montesquieu, *De l'Esprit des loix*, 2:20. [ARTFL]

Tarare's acknowledgement of the soldiers who come to support him. The sung text projects semantic meanings onto the ensuing musical segment, and the musical segment draws semantic meanings from the text that has just been sung. Poetry and music, therefore, form an action-and-reaction pair in Newtonian terms. Poetry acts; music reacts. The recitative works like a scroll, where key semantic meanings of a verse are identified and localized by music, and audiences are prompted by the text-then-music sequence to focus on the moment-to-moment unfolding of events in Ulson's account. The narrative is, therefore, in the present tense; the orchestral accompaniment translates events into music, and slows down the narrative pace, all the while narrowing the narrative field and giving it a sense of urgency. Hence, this narrative exemplifies a melodramatic moment in the opera.

How does Salieri illustrate through music the *exact* moments when Tarare develops mercy for his enemy? Tarare spares Altamort's life twice. In the first instance, Altamort wards off the first blow, but gets hit by the next one. Tarare slices off his crest with his scimitar and sends it flying. Salieri depicts these movements by using descending sixteenth scalar runs to depict the blow, followed by ascending runs for the flying motion. Salieri's music slows time down; events appear to happen in slow motion: steel sparkles; the helmet is broken; black blood streams down. Apparently, someone is injured, but who? Altamort or Tarare? At this moment, Salieri tightens the narrative pace by synchronizing music with text. "God!" Altamort screams, accompanied by a loud E-flat major chord on the second beat of the quadruple time music in m.58, which makes a syncopation: "I am injured!" Tarare attacks Altamort again, this time right on his head. A strong C^7 chord in m.60 (i.e., dominant seventh chord in F major) paints the word "plumb" (*plomb*), again on the second beat that repeats the syncopated rhythm. This C^7 chord as the dominant seventh lasts for three beats, and resolves to an F-major chord on the downbeat of m.61. Tarare gets ready to strike again, but he hesitates. This time Salieri uses a D^7 chord in m.62. Coming after the C^7 chord that resolves to F, the D^7 chord gives the impression of being the beginning of a harmonic sequence that would resolve to G major. Yet Salieri disrupts the expected resolution. Instead of prolonging this D^7 chord for three beats, Salieri sustains it four times longer, for twelve beats (or three full measures, mm.62–64) – a long duration that intensifies the need for harmonic resolution. The resolution to the G-minor chord does happen, in m.65, but it comes after Atar realizes that Altamort must have lost the combat (Example 5.3). This twelve-beat harmonic suspense demonstrates the time it takes for Tarare to develop compassion for his injured opponent: he is ready to finish him off, but he spares his life.

After he pardons Altamort's life for the first time, the combat resumes that leads to another chance to kill Altamort. Blinded by his blood, Altamort fidgets; he wobbles. Tarare, bent down on the saddle, spurs his horse forward. Salieri uses scalar ascending and descending runs in E major to depict the horse. Tarare dismounts from the horse, accompanied by a sixteenth broken-chord figuration outlining a C-major chord, in m.75, and runs towards Altamort. The bass moves step-by-step upwards from C through F, in mm. 77–78, from the dominant to the tonic chord of F major. Then it stays there for five full measures (mm.78–82) without moving toward any harmonic goal or even indicating a tonal direction, all the while "everyone, their hearts frozen, shudders with the horrifying *droit de la guerre* ..." (lines 751–53).

Example 5.3. Salieri, *Tarare*, Act 3 Scene 2, "Avant que ma fête commence," mm. 57–65

Example 5.3. continued

Example 5.4. Salieri, *Tarare*, Act 3 Scene 2, "Avant que ma fête commence," mm. 75–84

Eventually Ulson finishes off his sentence, with "by the holy and sublime effort of a noble enemy." Salieri makes this moment suspenseful with a harmonic and tonal stasis, which forms a musical and psychological plateau where everyone holds their breath, waiting for Ulson to declare that Tarare exercises his right to kill Altamort. To highlight this moment, Salieri uses the first inversion of a D⁷ chord that resolves to G minor, in mm.83–84, using two notes – A and C – as pivot notes between the F-major chord and the D⁷ chord. What is crucial is that Salieri uses these pivot notes

Example 5.4. continued

to make F major veer abruptly and yet efficiently toward the remote key of G minor. Once again, Tarare decides not to kill Altamort (Example 5.4).

In these scenes Tarare illustrates his character repeatedly and consistently through inaction: he shows no desire to violate Spinette although he is expected to do so, and he refrains twice from killing his enemy after defeating him in a combat. Salieri captures these moments in his music by creating suspense through surprisingly cautious musical materials for a potentially racy scene: delayed harmonic resolution, harmonic stasis, and modulations to remote tonal regions nimbly via pivot notes (rather than pivot chords). Unlike Gluck, who had a penchant for depicting unspoken competing thoughts, Salieri does not make Tarare weigh competing thoughts; rather, his music illustrates his inaction – thoughtful suspension of visible action – until he figures out his next move. It is Tarare's considered inaction that demonstrates his moral liberty; it is his repeated acts of mercy that demonstrate a behavioral pattern, and it is this pattern that demonstrates his moral character, defined in the *Encyclopédie* as "the habitual disposition of the soul."[42]

PROLOGUE AND EPILOGUE

Tarare's demonstrated moral liberty illustrates the concept of natural liberty, and Beaumarchais made this critical connection in the prologue and epilogue of the opera. Unlike most French operas performed in the second half of the eighteenth century, the opera *Tarare* has a prologue and a corresponding epilogue that frame the five-act opera proper. Why did Beaumarchais use them?

As shown in his unpublished notes, Beaumarchais intended to reinvent rather than to rehabilitate the Quinaultian type of prologue for the Enlightenment. Harris-Warrick has observed that almost all French operas from 1669 to 1749 had a prologue, but the convention gradually went out of fashion after mid-century; Rameau's *Zoroastre* (1749) was the first lyric tragedy without a prologue that premiered at the Académie Royale de Musique. This fact does not, however, mean that all prologues ceased to be performed onstage after 1749. *Les Trois Âges de l'opéra* (Devismes/Grétry, April 27, 1778), for example, was performed as a prologue to the one-act *pastorale-héroïque, La Fête de flore* (Saint Marc/Trial; Opéra, June 18, 1771). Criticisms of the prologue came from librettist Marmontel. In the preface to the livret of Rameau's *pastorale-héroïque Acante et Céphise* (November 1751), which celebrated the birth of one of Louis XV's grandsons, Louis-Joseph Xavier, Marmontel criticized the prologue as a distraction, for it diverted audiences' interest and attention away from the drama. He proposed using the *music* in the overture of *Acante et Céphise* to express the encomium and public celebration commonly found in the prologue, to the extent that music can do.[43] Rameau thus marked on this score "wishes of the nation" (*vœux de la nation*) at the beginning of the overture, followed by a section called fireworks (*feu d'artifice*), and a concluding "fanfare." Laudation conventionally concentrated in the prologue is redistributed throughout *Acante et Céphise*, from the overture through the concluding chorus "Vive la race de nos rois, / C'est la source de notre gloire" (Long live the race of our kings, / This is the source of our glory).[44]

If the prologue gradually went out of fashion after 1749, then it was odd for Beaumarchais to write a prologue and a corresponding epilogue for *Tarare* in 1787. No evidence shows that Beaumarchais *meant* to revive the Quinaultian type of operatic prologue, but he might have borrowed ideas from non-operatic prologues, such as Samuel Johnson and David Garrick's *Prologue and Epilogue* (London, 1747). In

---

42 "Caractère, en Morale, est la disposition habituelle de l'âme." *Encyclopédie*, vol. 2, s.v. "Caractère [Morale]."

43 "Pour tenir lieu de Prologue on a essayé de peindre dans l'ouverture, *autant qu'il est possible à la Musique*, les vœux de la Nation, & les réjouissances publiques, à la nouvelle de la naissance du Prince." *Acante et Céphise, ou La Sympathie, pastorale héroïque, à l'occasion de la naissance de Monseigneur Le Duc de Bourgogne* (Paris: Delormel, 1751), 8.

44 Harris-Warrick, "Le prologue de Lully à Rameau," 209–10.

the prologue declaimed by Garrick himself at the opening of the theater in Drury Lane in 1747, Garrick noted that Nature reversed the decline of tragedy with "pantomime and song" after having identified folly and wit in *Faustus*.⁴⁵ Garrick also wrote an epilogue for an imitation of Voltaire's *L'Ecossaise* (1760) called *The English Merchant* (Drury Lane, 1766) by George Colman the Elder. Beaumarchais might have known of this fact, for Voltaire mentioned it in the entry "Ana, anecdotes" of his *Questions sur l'Encyclopédie* (1770–74), which was published in the city of Kehl with funding supplied by Beaumarchais himself.⁴⁶

Beaumarchais might have used the prologue in *Tarare* to discuss nature and the creation of a social order, and it is helpful to place his prologue-epilogue in the tradition of the *opéra-ballet Les Éléments* (1721) and Rameau's *ballet-héroïque Zaïs* (libretto by Cahusac, 1748), both of which include a prologue about the creation of the world. *Les Éléments* was based on epicureanism. Written by Pierre-Charles Roy and set to music by Destouches and Delalande, it was the third ballet performed by Louis XV on December 22, 1721, at the theater of the Palais des Tuileries. Contrary to the ballets by Campra, which aimed at subverting royal propaganda, *Les Éléments* celebrated Louis XV's pending reign (due to begin in 1723). In a prefatory poem called "Terpsichore to the King," librettist Roy praised the young Louis XV for rejuvenating France and its high arts and for dancing in front of the public, hoping that Louis XV would continue his great-grandfather Louis XIV's interest in military conquests.⁴⁷

Les Éléments stages primordial chaos in the prologue that evokes the epicurean rather than the Christian theory of the beginning of the world. The theme of primordial chaos appears to take the book of Genesis of the Bible as its source: "In the beginning, God created the heaven and the earth. And the earth was without form, and void; and darkness was upon the face of the deep. And the Spirit of God moved upon the face of the waters."⁴⁸ Indeed, Jean-Féry Rebel composed an orchestral work *Les Éléments* (1737), in which a section that depicts "chaos" repeats seven times during the overture with decreasing intensity, and this structure references the seven-day period of creation described in the book of Genesis. Yet, as Roy specified in the preface to the 1721 livret, his idea of generative chaos did not come from the book of Genesis, but from book four of Virgil's *Eclogues* (37 BC) and book six of his *Aeneid* (19 BC), both of which disseminate epicurean ideas. Here is a summary of

45　Samuel Johnson and David Garrick, *Prologue and Epilogue, Spoken at the Opening of the Theatre in Drury Lane* (London: E. Cave, 1747), 5–6.

46　For the epilogue, see George Colman, *The English Merchant, a Comedy* (London: Becket and De Hondt, 1767), 70–73.

47　"Le Grand ROY, dont le Ciel commence en Toy l'image, En adoptant mes Jeux, en consacra l'usage: Et Ceux qui sur la Scène avaient suivi ses pas, Le suivirent bientôt dans l'ardeur des combats." *Les Élémens, troisième ballet dansé par le Roy, dans son palais des Tuilleries, Le Lundy vingt-deuxième jour de Décembre 1721* (Paris: Ballard, 1721), iv. On Louis XV as continuing Louis XIV's legacy as a dancer onstage, see Mary Grace Swift, "The Three Ballets of the Young Sun," *Dance Chronicle* 3, no. 4 (1979–80), 370. On the theater where *Les Éléments* premiered, see Barbara Coeyman, "Theatres for Opera and Ballet during the Reigns of Louis XIV and Louis XV," *Early Music* 18, no.1 (1990), 27.

48　Gen. 1:1–2 (King James Version).

Roy's prologue: a mass of clouds, rocks, and water is motionless and suspended in the air, and fire leaks out of a volcano. Fate (*Le Destin*) sorts out this chaos: he makes fire erupt from the volcano; he separates clouds in the sky from water on earth; he makes trees covered by fruits and flowers grow out of the earth. As Roy claimed in the preface to the livret, "The elements are born from chaos. We knew the moment of their birth. Following the example of Virgil, we believed we can announce from the beginning of the world the destinies of A PRINCE, who must make them happy."[49]

After Fate's act of creation, genies representing the four elements – air, fire, water, and earth – come to offer their praises for the organized chaos. These four elements were discussed by the ancient Greek poet Empedocles (*c.*492–432 BC), whose epicurean poem *On Nature* was used by Lucretius as a model for his *On the Nature of Things*. Lucretius wrote: "The elements of things – the folk who yoke together air with fire, and earth with water, and those people who suppose that everything out of this elemental foursome grows: that is, out of wind and rain and earth and fire. Of these, standing in the forefront is the great Empedocles" (book 1, lines 713–16). Roy featured the four elements, but he did not mention atoms; instead, he designed Roman gods that represent each element: the element of air is represented by Queen of heaven and wife of Jupiter, Juno, by King of wind Aeolus, by Sun, and Dawn; the element of fire is represented by Goddess of the hearth-fire Vesta, God of terrestrial fire and by metalworking Vulcan, and blacksmiths; the element of water is represented by Neptune, by the sea nymph and mother of Achilles, Thetis, and the sirens; and the element of earth is represented by the goddess of fertility and of the mountains Cybele, by goddess of agriculture Ceres, god of wine Bacchus, goddess of fruits Pomona, and goddess of flowers and spring Flora. These four elements become the subjects of the four *entrées* of this opéra-ballet. Compared with *Tarare*, in which Beaumarchais explicitly mentioned atomism, Roy never mentioned atoms, and his treatment of the four elements indicated a *pre*-Enlightenment conception of epicureanism. The rupture is obvious when one reads the discussion of the four elements in Enlightenment writings. According to the article "atomism" by the abbé Yvon and Formey, Empedocles claimed that "the nature of all bodies came only from the mixture and separation of particles, and although he accepted the four elements, he claimed that these elements were themselves composed of atoms or corpuscles."[50] Likewise, d'Alembert considered the theory of four elements outdated, as he wrote in the article "Elements (Physics)" of the *Encyclopédie* that the theory of the four elements devised by the "ancients" had been "abandoned."[51]

Nevertheless, Roy's epicurean prologue is not entirely out of date, for its emphasis on Love (*Amour*) brings forth a main point of Lucretian materialism. Not everyone

---

49 "Les ÉLÉMENS sont nés du Chaos; l'on a saisi le moment de leur naissance: Et à l'exemple de Virgile, on a cru pouvoir annoncer dès le commencement du monde, les destinées d'UN PRINCE qui en doit faire le bonheur." *Les Élémens*, v.

50 "Empédocle, Pythagoricien, disait ... que la nature de tous les corps ne venait que du mélange & de la séparation des particules; & quoiqu'il admît les quatre éléments, il prétendait que ces éléments étaient eux-mêmes composés d'atomes ou de corpuscules." Yvon and Formey, *Encyclopédie*, vol. 1, s.v. "Atomisme."

51 On the prologue, Beaumarchais, *Œuvres*, 505; d'Alembert, *Encyclopédie*, vol. 5, s.v. "Élémens [Physique]."

is happy with the creation of four elements. Venus complains that her son Love feels neglected by this act of creation. Since elements destroy the harmony of primordial chaos, Love should be the only force that binds these disparate elements together. Fate predicts that "after one hundred famous kings in history, he will come from among mortals to fulfill desires, but he must call to mind the memory of heroes, and, leaving to your son the empire of pleasures, he will want only that of glory."[52] Venus asks Fate to show her the image of the mortal who resembles her son, Love, and thus Fate introduces a person who does not need to be named: "See which subjects I will create for him, and without naming him to you, you will know their master." At this instant, according to the livret, Louis XV and members of his court appear at the back of the stage, and he is welcomed by Venus and the chorus as "a master of the universe" (*un Maître à l'Univers*).[53] The staging makes clear that it was Louis XV who should remember the greatness of his ancestors; it was Louis XV who resembled Love; it was Louis XV who was the unnamed power center; and it was Louis XV, as master of the universe, who could make the elements bring him military and marine victories. Venus's followers dance a sarabande, followed by another dance in 6/8 time marked "lively" (*gay*). The sarabande represents Love, as it is a type of dance that, according to the 1727 edition of Furetière's *Dictionnaire universel*, "consists of light-hearted and amorous movement."[54] Hence Venus justifies Love and pleasures: "Imagine making use of your leisure pastimes. The reason of this beautiful age is the choosing of pleasures. May Love reign over your amusements. Come, follow in his steps. If this god is not present, your games have few charms."[55]

Why should we care about these works? While most new operas composed after 1749 did not include a prologue, revivals of operas with a prologue and writings about the topic kept it relevant to French culture in the second half of the eighteenth century. At the Opéra the ballet *Les Éléments* was performed in 1725 and had re-runs in 1734 and 1742. It was performed 106 times from 1767 through 1777, and its last *entrée*, "Earth," was performed as a stand-alone section forty-two times between 1769 and 1781. The overture of Rameau's *Zaïs* (1748) depicts primordial chaos and was performed a total of seventy times from 1761 through 1770. The performance histories of these works (and sections of them) show that they were a part of the cultural memory through the 1770s and early 1780s. Besides, Marmontel discussed the prologue in *Supplément à l'Encyclopédie* (1776–77). There, Marmontel identified two

---

52 "Après cent Rois célèbres dans l'Histoire, il viendra des Mortels accomplir les désirs; Mais il doit des Héros rappeler la mémoire, Et laissant à ton Fils l'Empire des plaisirs, il ne voudra que celui de la gloire." *Les Éléments*, 4.

53 The stage direction read: "Le fonds du Théâtre s'ouvre, LE ROY paraît avec sa Cour." *Les Élémens*, 4.

54 "Elle a un mouvement gai & amoureux." Antoine Furetière, *Dictionnaire universel*, new edn corrected and augmented by Henri Basnage de Beauval and Jean Baptiste Brutel de la Rivière, 4 vols. (La Haye: Pierre Husson, 1727), vol. 4, s.v. "Sarabande." On a history of this term, see Daniel Devoto, "La folle sarabande (II)," *Revue de musicologie* 46 (122), 169 n.1.

55 "Songez à faire usage de vos loisirs, La raison du bel âge, c'est le choix des plaisirs: Qu'Amour règne en vos fêtes, Venez, suivez ses pas; Si ce Dieu n'en est pas, Vos jeux ont peu d'appas." *Les Élémens*, 79–80.

main types of prologues in French lyric theater. The first type was used in Quinault's *tragédies en musiques* (i.e., *Cadmus et Hermione, Alceste, Persée, Proserpine, Persée, Phaëton, Armide, Amadis*), and Marmontel called this type obsolete: "These prologues no longer take place, and ...no one hardly dares to read them, persuaded, as we are, that they are only full of dull praises and of unctuous short airs."[56] The second type of prologue provides a common theme for independent entrées of opéra-ballet. Marmontel cited chaos in the prologue of the ballet *Les Éléments* as an example: "The time has come. Stop, sad chaos. / Appear, elements. / Gods, go prescribe them movement and rest. / Hold every imprisoned one in its empire. / Flow, waves, flow; fly, rapid fire. / Veil tinged blue by the air, embrace nature. / Earth gives birth to fruit. Cover yourself with verdure. / Arise, mortals, to obey the Gods."[57]

Marmontel reprinted the article "Prologue" in his *Éléments de littérature* of 1787, and this reprint brought the discourse of prologue to the period of pre-Revolutionary France. Yet this reprint does not indicate the continuity of the legacy of prologue; by contrast, the reprint indicates change. On the one hand, this reprint supported Georgia Cowart's point that the libertine aesthetics initiated in the Regency laid the aesthetic foundation for the idea of liberty in the Enlightenment.[58] On the other hand, Marmontel mentioned the prologue not to affirm its cultural legacy, but to call it "old." Marmontel's dismissal of the prologue as antiquated demonstrates that what Baker called the linguistic "invention" of the Old Regime operated in tandem with the disappearance of the prologue as a cultural practice.[59] Marmontel used the prologue to describe a general change between the Regency and pre-Revolutionary France, but this change raises an issue: it does not help to explain the prologue-epilogue pair in Beaumarchais's *Tarare*. Why did Beaumarchais use the prologue, the function of which is magnified by a matching epilogue, in an age when the Quinaultian prologue was explicitly framed as "old"? What was Beaumarchais thinking?

NATURE AS A FERTILE WOMAN

No evidence suggests that Beaumarchais wanted to reinstate the Quinaultian style of prologue, but the content of the prologue and epilogue provides internal evidence of other functions in the opera. Beaumarchais was thinking about organizing the operatic plot topically and structurally, framing the five-act orientalist opera with a non-ethnic-specific, universalist prologue-epilogue pair; he was also thinking about defining what is "natural" and "unnatural" in the prologue and the epilogue,

---

56 "Ces *prologues* n'ont plus lieu, & ... personne ne s'avise guère de les lire, persuadé, comme on l'est, qu'ils ne sont pleins que de fades louanges, & de petits airs doucereux." Marmontel, s.v. "Prologue."

57 "Les tems sont arrivés: cessez triste chaos: / Paraissez éléments: Dieux, allez leur prescrire, / Le mouvement & le repos. / Tenez les enfermés chacun dans son empire. / Coulez, ondes, coulez; volez, rapides feux; / Voile azuré des airs, embrassez la nature, / Terre enfante des fruits, couvre-toi de verdure; / Naissez, mortels, pour obéir aux Dieux." Marmontel, s.v. "Prologue."

58 Georgia J. Cowart, *The Triumph of Pleasure: Louis XIV & the Politics of Spectacle* (Chicago: The University of Chicago Press, 2008), xviii.

59 Keith Michael Baker, *Inventing the French Revolution: Essays on the French Political Culture in the Eighteenth Century* (Cambridge: Cambridge University Press, 1990), 16–18.

establishing in the outer frame of the opera the core ideas of natural right theory in an attempt to criticize tyranny as unnatural. The key to explaining the meanings of the prologue-epilogue frame is the personification of Nature.

One of the groundbreaking designs in the prologue and epilogue of *Tarare* is the use of Nature as a personified character. Sung by a soprano, Nature, or the Genie of the Reproduction of Beings, sexualizes nature, and she brings together the acts of creation and procreation. Just as Venus needs Mars in Lucretius's *On the Nature of Things*, Nature needs a sexual partner for procreation, and this need creates a dramatic reason to evoke biological materialism. In Scene Two, Fire, who represents the sun, comes onstage. His entrance makes night turn into day, a breeze replaces unbridled wind, and order regulates chaos. The exchanges between Nature and Fire demonstrate their relationship as sexual. Fire admires Nature for establishing "a superb system" (line 12) on earth, and Nature asks Fire to animate the beings that she has created: "Fervent genie from the fiery sphere, through which mine is animated, offer my work some moments" (lines 13–15). This prologue deploys the libertine theme in *Les Éléments*: that love is *the* element that brings disparate elements together. Beaumarchais presented in *Tarare* the creation of human beings in two distinct stages. Nature performs the first stage of creation, one that follows Newtonian laws. Nature casts a spell and creates "cold humans" (line 40) from the atoms dispersed in space. She creates shadows (*ombres*), or "disembodied souls," who need to be animated by her lover Fire for the second stage of creation.

This two-stage creation shows that all beings are born free when Nature creates them. While the point may be self-evident, it illustrates the crux of the idea of natural liberty as understood during the Enlightenment. In the article "Natural Liberty" of the *Encyclopédie*, the anonymous author defined this term as the primary state that man acquires by nature, and went on to define what it means for humans to be "born free": "They are not subject to the power of a master, and no one has a right of ownership over them."[60] In the first stage of creation, the shadows created by Nature are in a liminal state, yet they have the capacity to be sensitive to music that arouses their sexual desire.[61] These shadows perform some "slow and cold dances, showing in them the liveliest emotion of what they feel, see, and hear."[62] Remarkably, Salieri set these "slow and cold dances" as a multi-sectional dance song featuring the sarabande: an instrumental introduction that uses the sarabande dance rhythm (mm.1–9), followed by a sarabande sung by the chorus (mm.10–29), a contrasting section sung by soloists and a duet with little connection to the sarabande (mm.30–41), and a return to the choral sarabande (mm.42–55). Salieri's use of the sarabande deserves explanation. In general, the sarabande, according to Diderot (discussed in Chapter Two), was a type of non-significative dance – he did not see that dances with an established path such as the sarabande had much meaning worthy of discussion. The remarkable point is that Salieri did not follow Diderot's characterization: he found the sarabande meaningful and, in this instance, he highlighted the sarabande's

---

60   *Encyclopédie*, vol. 9, s.v. "Liberté naturalle."

61   On the liminal state, see Victor Turner, *The Ritual Process: Structure and Anti-Structure* (New York: Aldine, 1969; repr., 2008), 94–96.

62   "[Une foule d'ombres] forme des danses lentes et froides, en marquant la plus vive émotion de ce qu'elles sentent, voient et entendent." Beaumarchais, *Œuvres*, 515.

affective meaning, using it to temporarily halt the forward momentum of the drama, making the plot inoperative, Bloechl might say, and allowing audiences to shift their attention from the dramatic action to the affective content. The sarabande does not impart any narrative content, but Salieri used it to recall the sarabande as a symbol of Love in *Les Éléménts*. The dancers become increasingly sensuous during their dances, which lead to a choral number built upon the sarabande dance rhythm, in which the shadows describe their state of arousal: "What unknown charm attracts us? / Our hearts are fulfilled by it. / With a vague pleasure I sigh; I want to express it, I cannot" (lines 50–53). The chorus ends up pointing out the reciprocity of sensuousness and sensuality that each choral member feels: "While enjoying, I feel that I am desiring; while desiring, I feel that I am enjoying" (lines 54–55). The author of the *Encyclopédie* article "Natural Liberty" stated that natural liberty allows human beings in their pristine condition the "power to do what seems good to them"; in the case of *Tarare*, the first thing these freshly created shadows do is to connect with their sensuality through music and dance.[63]

The reciprocity of jouissance and desire explicates the relationship between sex and knowledge. In the article "Jouissance" of the *Encyclopédie*, Diderot defined this term as the enjoyment of knowing as much as feeling the advantages of possessing something sensually stimulating. Enjoying a lush garden built by a sovereign, for example, may enthrall sensible beings and cause jouissance; indulging in physical pleasure and having the knowledge of that pleasure also cause jouissance. Jouissance comes specifically from sexual intercourse between sensible human beings, and not between human beings and beasts or other lifeless beings. Diderot did not deny that these non-human beings may give a man some pleasure during sexual intercourse, but he claimed that whatever sensual pleasure one might get from these alternative kinds of copulation would be qualitatively different from jouissance, which helps one obtain knowledge and discernment through copulation.

According to Diderot, the greatest purpose of nature is to reproduce offspring and it is nature that originates jouissance. During copulation it is nature that makes members of both sexes aware of her plan. "They feel a vague and melancholic restlessness, an alarming state mixed with pleasure and pain ... All other needs are suspended. The heart palpitates; body parts twitch; voluptuous images enter one's mind; torrents of senses flow into the nerves, irritating them, and will yield to a new sense laying siege which declares itself and torments. Vision is blurred, and delirium is born; reason must serve instinct, and nature is satisfied." The important point for Diderot is that reproductive sex is the only type of sex authorized by nature: "That is the way these things happened at the beginning of the world and that still happen at the back of the den of an adult savage."[64]

---

63 "En vertu de cet état, tous les hommes tiennent de la nature même, le pouvoir de faire ce que bon leur semble." *Encyclopédie*, vol. 9, s.v. "Liberté naturelle."

64 "Une inquiétude vague & mélancholique les avertit du moment; leur état est mêlé de peine & de plaisir ... le sentiment de tout autre besoin est suspendu; le coeur palpite; les membres trésaillent; des images voluptueuses errent dans le cerveau; des torrents d'esprits coulent dans les nerfs, les irritent, & vont se rendre au siège d'un nouveau sens qui se déclare & qui tourmente. La vue se trouble, le délire naît; la raison esclave de l'instinct se borne à le servir, & la nature est satisfaite ... C'est ainsi que les choses

In the second stage, Fire finishes the process of creation that Nature has initiated. He realizes that the shadows are too content with their natural liberty to desire power and status, which, to his mind, is a problem. The shadow of Altamort, who would become the general of the tyrant Atar's army, says: "We do not ask for [anything]; we are" (line 68). Fire asks who among the shadows would want to be a leader. The shadow of Urson, who would become the captain of the tyrant Atar's guards, shows indifference to power: "Who wanted it? What does it matter to us?" (line 70) None of the shadows created by Nature has any desire for power; this lack of desire despite their state of natural equality is interpreted by Fire not as a sign of innate virtue, but of profound ignorance. He complains that the shadows are "cold, without passions, without tastes" (line 71). Fire's criticism makes Nature admit that her creations are half made – they must be animated by her sex partner: "Ah! I have formed them without you. / Brilliant Sun, in vain Nature is fecund / without a ray of your sacred fire, my work is dead, and its purpose lost" (lines 73–76).

The cosmology presented in the prologue makes a case for Lucretian materialism. Addressing love as a sentiment that must be realized by copulation, Fire credits the exclusive biological process that creates sensible beings: "Glory to the eternal Wisdom, / Who, while creating immortal love, / Wanted that, through its sole intoxication, / The sensible being would see the light of day. / Ah! If my ardent and pure flame / had not ignited your womb, / Sterile lover of Nature, / I had been trained without purpose" (lines 77–84).

The overt celebration of heterosexual intercourse ran against eighteenth-century Catholic doctrine. Diderot wrote an article "Voluptuous" for the *Encyclopédie*, one of Diderot's forty-six articles modified by the publisher André-François Le Breton before it was published. Diderot originally defined a voluptuous person as one who loves sensual pleasures. He complained about the overly stringent, Augustinian Catholic view of associating all sorts of pleasures with suffering, of denying the bodily pleasures that God creates for humans, of dismissing too quickly signs of divine generosity such as delicious wines and exquisite fruits, and of believing that bodily pleasures were little other than temptations. After Diderot approved the page proofs, Le Breton crossed out two words – "preach us" – of the following quote, which in effect eliminated Diderot's explicit reproach to the Catholic censure of sexuality: "Those who ~~preach us~~ teach I don't know which austere doctrine that would afflict the sensibility of organs we have received from nature, which wished the preservation of species, including our own, still to be an object of pleasure."[65] The censored article reveals counter-clerical content. Diderot did not claim that he denied God, but he denounced the denial of bodily pleasures preached by Catholic priests, exposing the tension between epicurean celebration of bodily pleasure and Catholicism.

---

se passaient à la naissance du monde, & qu'elles se passent encore au fond de l'antre du sauvage adulte." Diderot [attributed], *Encyclopédie*, vol. 8, s.v. "Jouissance [Grammaire/ Morale]."

65 "Ceux qui ~~nous prêchent~~ enseignent je ne sais quelle doctrine austère qui nous affligerait sur la sensibilité d'organes que nous avons reçue de la nature qui voulait que la conservation de l'espèce & la nôtre fussent encore un objet de plaisirs." Diderot, *Encyclopédie*, vol. "18," s.v. "Voluptueux."

Diderot's epicurean celebration of bodily pleasure as a justification for reproductive sex is reinforced by d'Holbach's criticism of celibacy. In *Le Christianisme dévoilé* (1756, published in 1766), d'Holbach criticized the Catholic reframing of celibacy as "voluntary castration." Evoking epicureanism, d'Holbach wrote, "Nature, or the author of nature, invites human beings to multiply by the appeal of pleasure"; taking procreation as natural, d'Holbach found it difficult to comprehend why celibacy was considered by Catholicism as a "state of perfection," a celibacy "which depopulates the society, which contradicts nature, which invites debauchery, which makes men isolated, and which can be advantageous only to the odious politics of the priests of some Christian factions, who make it their duty to separate themselves from their co-citizens, to form a fatal body, which drags on forever without descendents."[66]

The epicurean thinking in the Enlightenment illustrates the significance of Nature in *Tarare*. Nature anthropomorphizes nature, and her commands become nature's laws, some of which are physical laws of nature theorized by Newton. Importantly, the technique of using personified Nature to introduce laws of nature is used by Lucretius: "And just as children shudder at everything at black of night, / So sometimes things we are afraid of in the broad daylight / Are only bugbears as tots dread in a darkened room, / And therefore we must scatter this terror of the mind, this gloom, / Not by the illumination of the sun and his bright rays, / But by observing Nature's laws and looking on her face" (book 2, lines 55–61). Yet, as dictators of laws of nature, Nature also determines the boundaries of the "natural" and denounces the "unnatural." Lucretius wrote that Earth, the Great Mother, "creator of our bodies" (book 2, line 599), is revered by Phrygians, who violently "made her priests eunuchs to illustrate that those who would degrade / The Mother's power, ungrateful to their parents, had no right / To bring descendants forth unto the boundaries of Light" (book 2, lines 615–17). The denunciation of eunuchs in Lucretius's *On the Nature of Things* is central to *Tarare*: in the prologue and epilogue, Nature talks to all shadows except those of Arthénée (great priest of Brama) and Calpigi. While the fact that Nature ignores Arthénée is consistent with the theme of counter-clericalism in the opera, it is striking that Nature ignores the castrato-turned-eunuch Calpigi while she and Fire interact extensively with Calpigi's future wife Spinette. To be sure, Nature might ignore Calpigi because he is also a Christian, but her lack of interest in him comes from a deeper concern: she does not recognize him as a being that she has created. In other words, Nature pays no attention to a castrato/eunuch because she does not consider him natural. Between a naturally hypersexual woman and a non-reproductive man, Nature favors the natural woman and disregards the artificially modified man.

---

66   "Voilà les vues qu'il s'efforce de traverser, en proposant, comme un état de perfection, un célibat qui dépeuple la société, qui contredit la nature, qui invite à la débauche, qui rend les hommes isolés, et qui ne peut être avantageux qu'à la politique odieuse des prêtres de quelques sectes chrétiennes, qui se font un devoir de se séparer de leurs concitoyens, pour former un corps fatal, qui s'éternise sans postérité." D'Holbach, *Le Christianisme dévoilé, ou Examen des principes et des effets de la religion Chrétienne* (London [i.e., Nancy]: [s.n.], 1756 [i.e., 1766]), 196–97. [ARTFL] On the publication history of this book, see Jeroom Vercruysse, *Bibliographie descriptive des écrits du Baron d'Holbach* (Paris: Lettres modernes, 1971), year 1756, A1.

THE UNNATURAL CASTRATO AND HIS WIFE

The coupling of Nature to Fire sets up a heteronormative framework that casts the love between Tarare and Astasie as natural but spotlights the non-reproductive marriage between Spinette and Calpigi as unnatural. In scene three of the prologue, the shadow of Spinette is already more sexual than all other shadows, even though she is still disembodied. Fire tells her that her looks will cause a hundred debates, implying that she is naturally flirtatious. And her shadow replies ardently: "I would want ... I would want ... I would want to submit to everything"; her reply makes Fire exclaim, "oh, Nature!" (lines 91–92). Given her hypersexual nature, what happens when Spinette marries a castrato Calpigi, who cannot copulate, not to mention procreate?

The Italian couple is crucial to the opera by serving as the western 'Others', the agents of change in the seraglio in which the chain of command and customs follow a fixed hierarchy. As a couple from the West, they "de-exoticize" the opera, Ralph Locke might say, and introduce Enlightenment values by exercising their agency and their moral liberty.[67] The first act begins with a fight between the tyrant Atar and Calpigi. Atar wants to kidnap the wife of his soldier Tarare, but Calpigi reminds him that this act is unethical because Tarare had saved his life. In a private setting Calpigi and Atar maintain an interdependent and mutually wounding relationship, which, according to Sarah C. Maza, is fundamental to the master-and-servant relationship in eighteenth-century France.[68] Yet in the next scene Calpigi pays lip service to Atar in the presence of others. The opening scenes show that Calpigi is obedient to Atar in public but undermines his power in private. He is alternately the rational person from the West cognizant enough to label Atar in the second half of the opera a "ferocious tyrant" (line 708) and an "inhuman despot" (line 1254). Calpigi is the character who dares disobey Atar in private, in as much as one who serves as a submissive eunuch can, and has to execute unreasonable demands such as having a festivity ready at a day's notice. Calpigi stages a "European celebration" (*une fête européanne*) (line 785) for "entertaining" (*amuser*) Atar's "adored" queen, Astasie, who cries onstage (*son mouchoir sur les yeux*) throughout this "celebration." Excelling at the double roles he plays, Calpigi exercises his agency well beyond the confines of the seraglio by becoming an all-knowing performer, developing a liaison with the audiences in the opera house during the performance. When Atar makes Tarare promise to surrender his wife, Calpigi thinks out loud, in an aside unheard by characters onstage, but speaks directly to the audience through the invisible fourth wall: "Good Lord! I am serving a dreadful man" (line 395). His little asides throughout the opera turn his audiences at the opera house into his knowing cohorts. By letting the audiences know that he overtly supports the monarch and covertly dismisses him, Calpigi divides the audiences' attention into two layers, one following the happenings onstage, another listening for his unspeakable criticisms of the happenings. By inviting audiences to side with his private, *real* opinions while allowing them to witness his public, *contrived* flattery, Calpigi maintains a calculated,

---

67 On music and the exoticizing process, see, for example, Ralph P. Locke, *Music and the Exotic from the Renaissance to Mozart* (New York: Cambridge University Press, 2015), 24.

68 Sarah C. Maza, *Servants and Masters in Eighteenth-Century France: The Uses of Loyalty* (Princeton, NJ: Princeton University Press, 1984), esp. chs. 4 and 7.

appropriate, and professional relationship with his tyrannical boss. Calpigi exerts his western impact on the seraglio, acting rationally and purposefully with supreme fluency, masterminding events onstage, and manipulating audiences' interpretation of these events in real time.

Equipped with an ability to navigate various fixed positions in the seraglio, Calpigi emerges as the most intriguing, the most resourceful, and the most trustworthy character in the opera precisely because of his complicated background. As an erstwhile castrato who was trained to use his voice, he discloses, in an autobiographical barcarolle (III/iv) that concludes the only divertissement specifically called the "European fête" of the opera: "I was born in Ferrara; / there, through medical treatment by a greedy father / My song was made very embellished. Alas! *povero Calpigi*" (lines 863–66; mm.931–39 of Example 5.5). Singing these verses in

Example 5.5. Salieri, *Tarare*, Act 3 Scene 4, "Peuple léger," mm.929–39

Example 5.5. continued

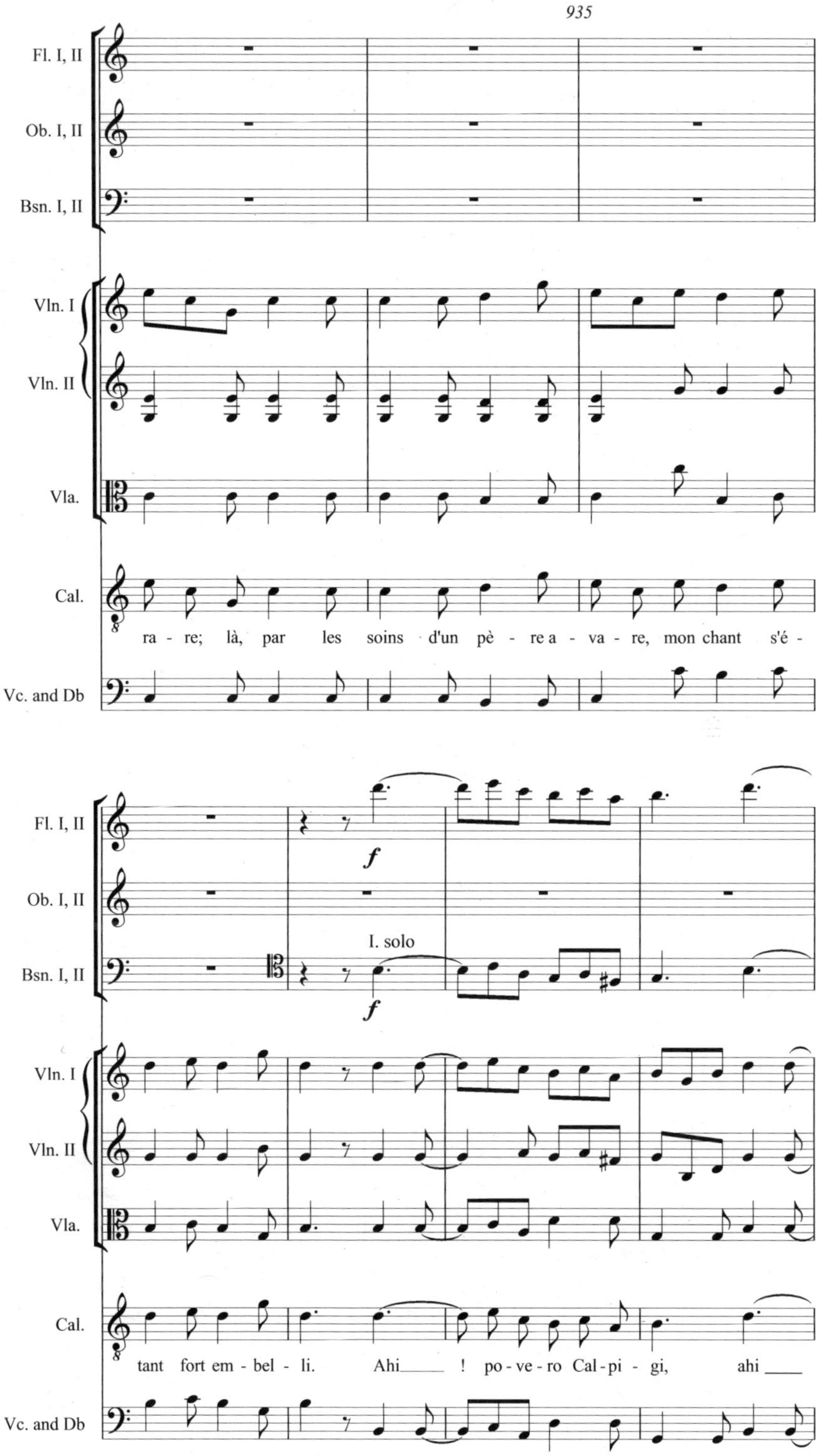

French in the first person and then pitying himself in Italian in the third person, Calpigi discloses his identity as an Italian castrato, halfway through the opera. Yet Calpigi's only aria fails to showcase him as a practicing castrato singer: he does not demonstrate any embellishment, any lengthy melisma, or any vocal pyrotechnics expected of an Italian castrato; rather, he performs like a *retired* castrato who knows how to sing, but is no longer able to dazzle audiences with much of the vocal pyrotechnics that he must have mastered. He complains about his unhappy marriage to a hypersexual Italian soprano; he regrets being a "simulacrum husband" (line 873); he protests living as an asexual person at home as if he were "a zero" (line 877). Yet his complaints take a turn. He celebrates the career that his extraordinary voice has brought about. As a boy he was involuntarily castrated; as an adult he enjoys the social distinction his voice has brought him: "After leaving the conservatory, I became the premier singer in the Neapolitan monarch's choir. Ah! *Bravo, caro Calpigi*" (lines 867–70). Bouncing between shame and pride, self-deprecation and self-congratulation, a disabled husband and an able singer, Calpigi shows how he negotiates his complex identity.

Interestingly, his fractured identity unsettles the strophic form of the barcarolle and, by extension, even the power structure in the seraglio. Immediately before he sings the barcarolle, Calpigi strategizes in an aside to "mix a name in it that will get us through the night" (line 862). He does insert the name – Tarare – into the fifth and last couplet of the barcarolle, when he recalls that Tarare saved him from the pirate who had captured him and Spinette: "Soon, through Libya, / Egypt, Isthmus, and Arabia, / He [the pirate] was going to sell us to Sophi [king of Persia]; Alas! Poor Calpigi! / We are taken, says the Barbarian. Who picked us up? It was Tarare …" (lines 896–900). As soon as Calpigi utters Tarare's name, Astasie, everyone – even Atar himself – repeats this name in succession (lines 900–901). Their responses amplify the effect. The utterances of this name provoke Atar, who disperses the crowd onstage, bringing Calpigi's otherwise accessible and strophic barcarolle to an end without a proper cadential ending. Yet this unfinished barcarolle provides the favorable chaos for Tarare himself to sneak into the seraglio. After this incident, Calpigi becomes more outwardly rebellious. When Urson wants to capture the mute man (Tarare in disguise) who is supposed to have sexually violated Astasie, Calpigi discloses that the mute is in fact Tarare (lines 1235–36). Calpigi plays an instrumental role in the climax of the opera, when Atar, knowing that he has lost the support of his subjects, asks the soldiers and eunuchs in the seraglio a point-blank question: "Defenders of the seraglio, am I still your king?" One eunuch answers, "Yes!" But Calpigi counters by saying, "No!" His answer is repeated by all soldiers and the people. Immediately, Calpigi offers a solution and points at Tarare, saying: "It is he." His nomination is immediately rejected by Tarare himself, who says, "Never!" But Calpigi leads the soldiers and the people to reinforce this nomination, saying: "It is you!" In addition to being persuasive, Calpigi demonstrates supreme interpretive skills. In response to Atar's last words ("Death is less harsh to my eyes … / than reigning by you [Tarare] over this odious people" (lines 1416–17)), Calpigi offers in public a critical interpretation of them: "A single word repairs all the wrongs of his reign: he leaves the throne to Tarare" (lines 1418–19). Once again, Calpigi manages to persuade everybody, including Tarare himself, to welcome Tarare as the future king. All these incidents show that Calpigi, as the erstwhile Italian castrato, serves as an unsettling chief eunuch in the closed quarter of Atar's seraglio, *and* as an enabling agent who masterfully punctures Atar's tyrannical domain. He prevents anarchy immediately after the tyrant's death and puts in place a well-deserved king who continues the sovereignty.[69]

The use of an Italian castrato as an operatic character evokes rounds of age-old debates about the merits of Italian and French music, and about the reception of Italian castrato in France. Italian music had a long reputation for bending what French composers considered their established compositional rules. The French bass viol player André Maugars, for example, observed in *Response faite à un curieux sur le sentiment de la musique d'Italie* (1639) that Italian sacred music has more art, science, variety, and license than French sacred music.[70] In Lully's *Ballet de la raillerie* (1659) Musique française criticizes Musique italienne for her extravagant songs with lengthy coloraturas and strong emotions. Musique italienne counters by attacking Musique française's sad and languid manner.[71]

The dramatic meaning of Calpigi's barcarolle recalls the tradition of Italian music at the Opéra that symbolized liberty in French music, especially in the genre of the *opéra-ballet* that was influenced by Théâtre Italien. *La Fête des barquerolles* was the first entrée of *Les Fêtes vénitiennes* (1710). In the entrée "Les Devins de la place Saint Marc" of *Les Fêtes vénitiennes* by Antoine Danchet with music by Campra, the French cavalier Léandre speaks to the young Venetian girl Zélie at the Saint Mark Square of Venice: "I know how to force a rebellious heart to commit its liberty to me."[72] Yet the meanings of liberation changed in mid-century. In "De la liberté de la musique" (1759), d'Alembert contrasted Italian and French musical styles and linked liberty to Italian lyric comedies. Reflecting upon the *Querelle des bouffons*, d'Alembert believed that Italian music such as the intermède allowed composers the freedom to explore a variety of musical styles: "The only genre of music that did not lose anything in Italy, that was perhaps even perfected there, is the burlesque and comic genre. The liberties it permits [and] the varieties to which it is susceptible leave the genius of composers more at its ease."[73]

---

69 On the socially disabled, see Katherine Crawford, "Desiring Castrates, or How to Create Disabled Social Subjects," *Journal for Early Modern Cultural Studies* 16, no.2 (2016), 64. On the idea of order emergence, see Jonathan Sheehan and Dror Wahrman, *Invisible Hands: Self-Organization in the Eighteenth Century* (Chicago: The University of Chicago Press, 2015), 9.

70 "Je trouve en premier lieu, que leurs compositions de Chappelle ont beaucoup plus d'art, de science, & de variété que les nôtres; mais aussi elles ont plus de licence." André Maugars, *Response faite à un curieux sur le sentiment de la musique d'Italie*, intro. trans. and notes by H. Wiley Hitchcock (Geneva: Minkoff, 1993), 20.

71 Georgia Cowart, *The Origins of Modern Music Criticism: French and Italian Music, 1600–1750* (Ann Arbor, MI: UMI, 1981), 9, 16.

72 "Je sais contraindre un cœur rebelle / à m'engager sa liberté." *Les Festes vénitiennes, ballet représenté par l'Académie royale de musique* (Paris: Delormel, 1750), 17. On *La Fête des barquerolles*, see Harris-Warrick, *Dance and Drama*, 255.

73 "Le seul genre de Musique qui n'ait rien perdu en Italie, qui peut-être même s'y est perfectionné, c'est le genre burlesque & comique; les libertés qu'il permet, la variété dont il est susceptible, laissent le génie des compositeurs plus à son aise." D'Alembert,

Music aside, Italian actors who performed Italian plays in France were known to perform with more freedom than French actors. In the section on pantomime in *De la poésie dramatique* (1758), Diderot claimed that the acting style of Italian performers came across as original and easy; their performance was not filled with the insipid speech and absurd intrigue characteristic of French plays; they often forgot about the presence of the spectators; their degree of absorption in their performance paradoxically drew spectators' attention to their performance. It would take Diderot years to articulate this paradox fully in his *Paradoxe sur le comédien*, published in Grimm's *Correspondance littéraire* in 1770; but already in *De la poésie dramatique* (1758), Diderot expressed a preference for the madness (*ivresse*) in Italian acting: "What especially makes them [French actors] symmetrical, stiff, and numb is that they perform from [the principle of] imitation, that they have another theater and other actors in view. What are they doing, then? They arrange themselves in a circle; they enter the stage with counted and measured steps; they seek applause; they get out of the action; they address the parterre; they speak to it, and they become sullen and false."[74] Believing that pantomime was a vehicle of truth, Diderot argued that "gesture must often be written in place of speech."[75]

In the context of what Italian music and acting style meant in France, the Italian elements in *Tarare* – Calpigi and Spinette as Italian singers and Calpigi's barcarolle – are loaded with meanings in this French orientalist opera. What matters in this opera is not how "Italian" it was, but how the unnatural marriage of the unnatural Italian married couple, Calpigi and Spinette, created a *natural* and thus legitimate cause for separation, and how this natural desire for freedom from an unnatural marriage generated enabling *conditions* for the liberation of Astasie. What made Calpigi a particularly colorful figure was that he is more three-dimensional than in accounts of a castrato or a eunuch circulated in the eighteenth century. In *Traité des eunuques* (1707), lawyer (*avocat*) Charles Ancillon argued eloquently against allowing eunuchs (including castratos) to get married, even though eunuchs might be more liable to the crime of lubricity than "perfect men" precisely because they were incapable of making women pregnant, and even though eunuchs were "sought out" by corrupted women" (*les femmes débauchées*) because they could give these women the "pleasure of marriage" without posing risks.[76] In the legal world, the idea that a eunuch could get married was considered a joke. Lawyer Jacques-Pierre Brissot (1754–93) remembered having purchased a law degree in Reims and found it unbelievable that the examiners there asked him at the examination if eunuchs could get married. After Brissot paid some five to six hundred livres for this slapstick comedy (*pantalonnade*), he returned to Paris and presented himself at the *Parlement*

"De la liberté de la musique," in *La Querelle des bouffons, texte des pamphlets*, with intro., commentaries, and index by Denise Launay, 3 vols. (Geneva: Minkoff, 1973), 3:415.

74   "Ce qui surtout les symétrise, les empèse et les engourdit, c'est qu'ils jouent d'imitation; qu'ils ont un autre théâtre et d'autres acteurs en vue. Que font-ils donc? Ils s'arrangent en rond; ils arrivent à pas comptés et mesurés; ils quêtent des applaudissements, ils sortent de l'action; ils s'adressent au parterre; ils lui parlent, et ils deviennent maussades et faux." Diderot, *Œuvres*, 4:1336.

75   "Le geste doit s'écrire souvent à la place du discours." Diderot, *Œuvres*, 4:1337.

76   Charles Ancillon, *Traité des eunuques* (s.l.: s.n., 1707), 158–64.

and became a lawyer.[77] These negative accounts of the castrato notwithstanding, Beaumarchais designed Calpigi in *Tarare* as an unnatural character from Italy who plays an essential role in uprooting tyranny.[78]

UNNATURAL ECHO AND ECHOLALIA

The opposition of a natural woman and an unnatural man resonates with the binary opposition of pure and impure elements in nature. Asked by Fire if she uses the purest elements to create the powerful and the great men of an empire, Nature criticizes their language as unnatural, as mentioned earlier in this chapter. Thus, Nature makes a Dubosian distinction between natural and conventional signs. She does not dismiss language, but she makes a basic point that language is made by man, not by her.

Nature's understanding of language as impure is shown in the word "Tarare" as a perverse type of name for a person, not to mention a hero who would be elected sultan by the people. In *Aux abonnés* Beaumarchais explains that the word Tarare is the title of his opera but is not its theme. The word "Tarare," as in the expression "*Tarare pompon*," entered the French lexicon in *Curiositez françoises, pour supplement aux dictionaires* (1640); it means that "one does not care about anything, that one mocks the warnings of others." The word "tarare" is also onomatopoeic, explained in *Dictionnaire françois* (1680) as a representation of "the sound of the trumpet."[79] This colloquial interjection expresses an instant remark of disagreement, contradiction, opposition, dismissal, and distrust; and this word should, according to John Rice, be translated into English as "nonsense," or cognates such as rubbish, garbage, crap, bull, or bullshit.[80] Mentions of this word in French printed texts peaked around 1700, because the tune "Tarare, pon pon" was used at the Théâtre Italien, and scripts that consist of this colloquial expression were published at around that time. For example, the script of Evaristo Gherardi's comedy *Les Souffleurs*, published by Jacques Dentand in *Le Théâtre italien* (1695), consists of an exchange between Octavio and Arlequin. Octavio plays an air on the guitar, an air that prompts Arlequin to sing an echo of its refrain "Tarare, pon pon."[81] This tune was printed in the second volume of *Les Parodies du Nouveau théâtre italien* (1738), and Barthélemy-Christophe Fagan's *opéra-comique La Fausse ridicule* (1744). Tarare was also used as a colloquial

---

77 Jacques-Pierre Brissot de Warville, *Mémoires de Brissot*, intro. M. de Lescure (Paris: Didot, 1877), 170–71; Bell, *Lawyers and Citizens*, 34.

78 On the castrato as an exemplary lover, see Julia Prest, "In Chapel, On Stage, and in the Bedroom: French Responses to the Italian Castrato," *Seventeenth-Century French Studies* 32, no.2 (2010), 160.

79 "C'est un mot qui sert à dénoter qu'on ne se soucie de rien, que l'on se mocque [*sic*] des avertissements d'autrui." Antoine Oudin, *Curiositez françoises, pour supplément aux dictionaires* (Paris: Sommaville, 1640), s.v. "Tarare." "Tarare. Mot imaginé pour représenter le son de la trompette." Pierre Richelet, *Dictionnaire françois: contenant les mots et les choses* (Geneva: Widerhold, 1680), s.v. "Tarare."

80 John A. Rice, *Antonio Salieri and Viennese Opera* (Chicago: The University of Chicago Press, 1998), 392.

81 The longitudinal word-use-frequency is obtained in the beta version of *Dictionnaire vivant de la langue française* (DVLF) [ARTFL, accessed May 6, 2019].

interjection in spoken comedy such as Fagan's *comédies Le Rendez-vous* and *L'Amitié rivale*, published in 1760.[82]

The onomatopoeic origin of the word "tarare" draws attention to the repetitive, echoic property of its sound (i.e., ta-ra-re), and its echoic property alone became a resource at the theater. In *Les Souffleurs* Arlequin complains about break-ins by some thieves. The poet Octavio cannot see Arlequin, but he interprets Arlequin's complaints as rumors. Because he is a poet, he rhymes the word rumors (*rumeurs*) with murmur (*un murmure*). He asks Arlequin to speak and claims that he is leaving (*je me retire*). Arlequin remains hidden and replies by repeating the last syllable of Octavio's line "*tire, tire, tire, tire, tire, tire.*" Now Octavio interprets Arlequin's reply as an echo and thinks that only an echo – which should obey natural law – and he, himself, are in the house. (*Nul n'est donc en ces lieux qu'un écho seul, seul & moi*). Arlequin repeats his last words as if he were creating an echo: "*et moi, & moi, moi, moi, moi,*" but in fact his echo could work as a reply, which means that he – an agent in addition to the echo he makes – is *also* in the house. This double response – as a mechanical echo devoid of agency and as a thoughtful reply revealing agency – makes this moment witty; but what makes it really comical is that Octavio fails to recognize the double nature of Arlequin's echo and, with that, he fails to notice another person in the house despite Arlequin's full disclosure of his presence. Octavio thinks aloud about what he can do to attract the person who enchants him (*Que puis-je faire écho pour plaire à qui m'echante?*) Arlequin responds by repeating the last syllable ("*chante*") of Octavio's word "*enchante,*" transforming the verb "to enchant" into "to sing": "*Chante, chante, chante, chante.*" Octavio follows Arlequin's echoes by playing with the verb "*chanter.*" Octavio asks if one can sing when one is desperate (*Peut-on chanter hélas, quand on est aux-abois [?]*), and Arlequin replies by repeating mechanically the last syllable "*-bois.*" Octavio keeps pressing and exclaims what his fate will be in the empire of love! (*Quel sera donc mon sort dans l'amoureux Empire!*) – to which Arlequin once again offers a modified echo, repeating the last syllable of the word "*em-pire*" and turning it into the expression "*pire en pire*" (worse and worse). Octavio then invites Arlequin to sing with him and complains that love is a rascal (*un fripon*): "*Pour chanter avec moi qu'amour est un fripon.*" Arlequin mechanically echoes the last syllable of the word *fripon* mechanically: "*pon, pon.*" This response prompts Octavio to speak to his guitar: "Finish your chords my faithful guitar" (*Apprêtez vos accords ma fidèle guitare*). Finally, Arlequin transforms the last syllable of the word "*-tare*" into "*tarare*" and sings the well-known refrain "*tarare, tarare ponpon, tarare ponpon,*" bringing the two rhymes (i.e., -*pon* and -*are*) in one refrain. Arlequin leaves the stage while remarking: "Sir, echo is going to make you sleepy," rhyming "*echo*" with "*dodo*" (*Monsieur l'echo va faire dodo*).[83]

Gherardi's clever uses of the echo anticipate a similar scene in a *comédie mêlée d'ariettes* called *Fleur d'Épine*, which was staged in 1776 when Beaumarchais was

---

82   Evaristo Gherardi, "Les Souffleurs," in *Le Théâtre italien* (Genève: Jacques Dentand, 1695), 10; Barthélemy-Christophe Fagan, *Théâtre de M. Fagan et autres œuvres du même auteur*, 4 vols. (Paris: Duchesne, 1760), 1:47, 275; 4:149.

83   Gherardi, "Les Souffleurs," 8–10. The expression "faire dodo" is a *mot d'enfant*, which means "to sleep." See Philibert-Joseph Le Roux, *Dictionnaire comique, satyrique, critique, burlesque, libre, et proverbial*, 2 vols. (Pampelune, s.n.: 1786), vol. 1, s.v. "Dodo."

versifying *Tarare*. Beaumarchais claimed in *Aux abonnés* that he borrowed the echo idea from a story by Anthony Hamilton. Hamilton's story – according to Pierre Henri Larthomas and Jacqueline Larthomas who published the 1988 edition of Beaumarchais's *Œuvres* – is called *Histoire de Fleur-d'Épine* (1730) and features a prince called "Tarare."[84] Beaumarchais criticized Hamilton for underestimating the echoic property of the word Tarare as a dramatic resource. The Larthomas edition states that the story and the opera have nothing in common other than the name "Tarare," but does not mention the story's adaptation as a genre with spoken dialogues and singing called *comédie mêlée d'ariettes*. In this adaptation, which premiered at the Théâtre Italien on August 22, 1776, *Fleur-d'Épine* included a "duet echo" (*duo en écho*) so ingenious that it was praised by *Mercure de France*.[85]

In *Fleur-d'Épine* two treatments of the word "Tarare" recall those in Gherardi's *Les Souffleurs*. In the first instance, echo is explained as echolalia. The mean-spirited female fairy Dentue (played by the actor Michu of the Théâtre Italien *en travestie*) announces that she is to marry Tarare. In the presence of her parents and a group of "ridiculous" figures, including dwarfs, giants, lame people, and hunchback people, Dentue sings an ariette: "My husband is charming; he is a Prince, really; his appearance is attractive; his height is elegant. I present to you this lover. His is a rare merit; he is called Tarare."[86] The word "Tarare" as a pun, indicating a name and an interjection (i.e., nonsense), transforms the sentimental buildup into a moment of absurdity, and the impromptu chorus amplifies the absurd effect with echoes – "*Tarare, Tarare, Tarare*" – without realizing the absurdity of using the word "tarare" as the name for a prince.[87] Fleur d'Épine and Tarare do not find their response celebratory; they find it noisy, and they consider echo as echolalia: "O heaven! What a din! There is not a crow, not a single starling, not a bird, not an echo that does not say Tarare."[88]

In the second instance, the librettist Claude-Henri de Fusée de Voisenon presents the opposite of the chorus's mechanical echo by having Tarare offer a type of echo so unnatural that it seems to have agency. Dentue's son, Dentillon, thinks of ideas to tame his future wife, Fleur-d'Épine, through intimidation. Tarare, who is in love with Fleur-d'Épine, is hiding somewhere onstage, and supplies some fictitious echoes to counter Dentillon's ideas. Voisenon designed an imaginative *duo en écho* for this scene, with Tarare echoing Dentillon's lines as if they were singing a duet. When Dentillon claims that Fleur-d'Épine is beautiful (*Que Fleur-d'Épine est belle*), Tarare offers a natural, mechanical echo by saying "*belle*." But this echo also

---

84 Beaumarchais, *Œuvres*, 1461 n.3 (for p.504).

85 "Il y a de la gaieté dans cette pièce, quelquefois un peu force par les jeux de mots. La musique en est agréable; plusieurs morceaux ont été fort applaudis, tels qu'un écho en dialogue intrigue." *Mercure de France* (September 1776), 163.

86 "Mon Époux est charmant. Il est Prince vraiment, / Sa mine est séduisante, / Sa taille est élégante, / Je vous présente / Cet Amant. / C'est un mérite rare; On le nomme Tarare." *Fleur d'Épine, comédie en deux actes, mêlées d'ariettes* (Paris: Duchesne, 1776), 23.

87 Marmontel, *Supplément à l'Encyclopédie*, vol. 2, s.v. "Chœur."

88 "O Ciel! / Quel tintamarre! / Il n'est pas un corbeau, / Pas un seul étourneau, / Pas un oiseau / Pas un écho / qui ne dise Tarare." *Fleur d'Épine*, 24. On echo and echolalia, see Daniel Heller-Roazen, *Echolalia: On the Forgetting of Language* (New York: Zone Books, 2008), 34.

works as a semantically viable response that affirms Dentillon's exclamation. What is truly ingenious is that Tarare exercises his agency, omitting his echoes whenever he disagrees with Dentillon. He refrains from offering an echo after Dentillon says "when I will have received her faith" (*Lorsque j'aurai reçu sa foi*). Yet when Dentillon asks himself which of the two of them – Dentillon or Fleur-d'Épine – must be disloyal (*Qui des deux doit être infidèle?*), Tarare offers a modified echo by omitting the consonant "d" of the last syllable, changing the syllable "-*dèle*" into the word "*elle*," which means "her." Dentillon follows up with another question: "Who could play with me?" (*Qui pourrait se jouer à moi?*), to which Tarare replies, "me" (*moi*), a reply that serves *both* as a mechanical echo and a sensible response. Dentillon responds as if he were having a conversation with an unnatural type of echo that has agency: "I will prevent her escaping. Is marriage instead of happiness therefore a trap?" (*J'empêcherai qu'elle n'échappe. Le mariage en lieu d'être un Bonheur est donc une attrape?*) Tarare echoes the last word "*attrape*" (trap) and gives Dentillon the answer he asks for. Dentillon then says, "but I will control her by terror" (*Mais je la contiendrai par la terreur*), to which Tarare offers neither a response nor a repetition, but a judgment, transforming his echo "terror" (*terreur*) into the word "error" (*erreur*). Tarare's echoes are different from the mechanical ones in *Les Souffleurs*, for they are not mechanical echoes that follow the laws of nature, ones that make listeners drowsy; rather, they are thoughtful replies. The echoes are not just echolalia; they must not come from nature: "Let's go. Let's go. The echo over here does not make common sense" (*Allons, allons, cet écho-là n'a pas le sens commun*).[89]

These examples demonstrate that the word "tarare" brings with it a logic of negation, but the sound of this word – *ta-ra-re* – imitates the sound of a trumpet and, therefore, the utterance of the interjection "tarare" brings forth the semantic meaning of negation and the sonic effect of amplification. Since Beaumarchais knew Hamilton's story *Fleur-d'Épine*, and probably the 1776 *opéra-comique*, how did he use the properties of unnatural echo and echolalia in *Tarare*?

A HERO NAMED "NONSENSE"

Beaumarchais wanted the word "tarare" to create a logic of negation that produces comical situations in *Tarare*. In *Aux abonnés* he explained that he used this clichéd word as a name to introduce some coquetry to the opera; to throw in some error; to show his audiences that he Beaumarchais was a jovial man; to invite his audience to laugh at his opera or himself. It was fun, he believed, when he took a refrain "*tarare pompon*," popular in comedy, and had it set to an opera for the Opéra, which was the premier cultural institution in France. In the spirit of reversal, he wanted to see what would happen if he gave this opera a proverbial title. The utterance of the name of Tarare "excited astonishment in the audiences, which caused them to repeat it to everybody as soon as it was pronounced."[90] Beaumarchais used the technique of amplification, which he called a "quirk" (*bizarrerie*) to design dramatic transitions

---

89 *Fleur d'Épine*, 34.

90 "Le nom de Tarare excitait un étonnement dans les auditeurs, qui le faisait répéter à tout le monde aussitôt qu'on le prononçait." Beaumarchais, *Œuvres*, 504.

in the opera. As he explained in *Aux abonnés*, the *person* "Tarare," though respected by the people, is unbearable to the despot Atar, and "this name is not pronounced in front of him without infuriating him, and without causing great change to the characters' situation."[91] Using the word "tarare" as both the name of a person and a colloquial interjection, Beaumarchais employed the double meaning of this word to comic ends.

By design, then, utterances of the word "Tarare" in the prologue create dramatic situations that are at once delightful and sentimental. In the prologue, Nature tells the shadow of Astasie, "Tarare will obtain your faith" (line 99); Astasie, moved by Nature's assignment, exclaims while placing a hand on her chest, "Tarare!" (line 100) The comic effect comes from the double meaning of the word "tarare." While it is fine that Tarare, as the name of Astasie's future husband, will obtain her faith, it makes no sense whatsoever to say that *nonsense* will obtain her faith. The ridiculousness is reinforced when Astasie is completely oblivious to the semantic meaning of this word and becomes emotional – she acts as if she were touched by the name, with "her hand on chest" – at the prospect of falling in love with some nonsense. To further emphasize the ridiculousness, Fire remarks that the name "Tarare" makes her blush (line 102). The double meaning of the word mocks the culture of sentimentality.[92]

Another kind of utterance of the word "Tarare" in the prologue makes claims about natural rights. Nature criticizes her lover, Fire, for making Atar despot of Asia who reigns in the seraglio of Ormus while limiting the career prospects of Tarare: "You have made him [Tarare] soldier, but do not go further; / This is Tarare [name/ nonsense]. Soon you will be the witness of their future difference" (lines 134–36). By uttering the line "this is Tarare" (*C'est Tarare*), Nature introduces "Tarare" as a person; but by uttering the line "this is tarare," Nature censures Fire's limited vision as incompatible with natural law. According to Jaucourt's article "Natural, law" in the *Encyclopédie*, a "natural law" (*la loi naturelle*) is a law that God imposes on *all* human beings: "Natural laws are so named because they derive uniquely from the constitution of our being before societies were established. The law, which by impressing on us the idea of a creator draws us toward him, is the first of the natural laws by dint of its importance, but not [first] in the order of his [the creator's] laws."[93] Thus, Nature's objection to Fire makes clear that her opinion carries authority; her objection also emphasizes the idea of universality – that is, the applicability to all human beings (*tous les hommes*) – as central to the concepts of "natural law," "natural equality," and

---

91 "On ne prononce point son nom [Tarare] devant lui [Atar] sans le mettre en fureur et sans qu'il arrive un grand changement dans la situation des personnages." Beaumarchais, *Œuvres*, 504.

92 On the sentimental and the anti-sentimental, see Stefano Castelvecchi, *Sentimental Opera: Questions of Genre in the Age of Bourgeois Drama* (Cambridge: Cambridge University Press, 2013), 188–209.

93 "Les lois naturelles sont ainsi nommées parce qu'elles dérivent uniquement de la constitution de notre être avant l'établissement des sociétés. La loi, qui en imprimant dans nous-mêmes l'idée d'un créateur, nous porte vers lui, est la première des lois naturelles par son importance, mais non pas dans l'ordre de ses lois." Jaucourt, *Encyclopédie*, vol. 11, s.v. "Naturelle, loi."

"natural liberty" of natural right theory. In *Tarare*, whatever Nature utters carries the weight of natural laws. For example, right after Nature criticizes Fire for trying to limit a soldier's achievement, Nature commands the shadows of Atar and Tarare to embrace one another, a command that stems from *her* principle of natural equality: "Children, hug each other: equal by nature, / How far you will be in society! From the proud grandeur to humble poverty, / this immense gap is from now on yours; / unless from Brama the mighty goodness, / by a premeditated decree, brings you closer to one another, / for the example of kings and humanity" (lines 137–44). To Nature's mind, Atar and Tarare are as equal as the atoms who form the turbulence. Nature, therefore, serves as much as a creator of all human beings as a progenitor of natural right theory.

The opera *Tarare* is loaded with Enlightenment ideas, and small wonder that Beaumarchais claimed in the preface that he had devised a new "way" of appealing to audiences at the Opéra. In fact, however, none of the components in *Tarare* was entirely new. All French operas used dance, and an increasing number of them in the second half of the eighteenth century employed pantomime as a type of dance – in some cases as a naturalistic style of acting. What was new to *Tarare* was how Salieri employed pantomimes and dances within the framework of Lucretian materialism. This novelty came from Beaumarchais's philosophical prologue-epilogue framework, which illustrated how Nature creates laws of nature. Within this framework, language becomes an impure element; physical movements that obey immovable natural laws are self-explanatory; heterosexual sex between Nature and Fire becomes the source of all life; non-reproductive coupling becomes unnatural; the belief in divine provenance is replaced by the theory of atomism; a tyrant becomes replaceable; a soldier becomes the king-elect. The opera differentiates a tyrant from a king, as defined in the article "King (political government)" in the *Encyclopédie*: "A king stops the arm of the oppressor; he overthrows [*renverse*] tyranny ... He must govern the peoples according to the laws of the state, just as God governs the world according to the laws of nature."[94] Within this framework, an old world can be refreshed, and a new world can return it to its origin where human beings rediscover their natural liberty. And *this* point is new to French opera.

Despite the claim of natural liberty, Beaumarchais kept the sovereignty of Ormus in *Tarare* intact. In his opera, human beings strive for their natural liberty after realizing that they have been ruled by a tyrant. Their attempt does not mean that Beaumarchais toppled the sovereignty of that closed world, nor does it mean that Beaumarchais used the opera to make a claim of "political liberty," explained by Jaucourt in the *Encyclopédie* as a kind of political right, grounded in good civil and political laws, that citizens enjoyed. He discussed another type of political right – that of a state, which was formed by laws that ensure proper distribution of legislative power, the executive power that deals with people's rights, and another executive

---

94   "Il [Un roi] arrête le bras de l'oppresseur: il renverse la tyrannie ... Il doit les [les peuples] gouverner selon les lois de l'état, comme Dieu gouverne le monde selon les lois de la nature." *Encyclopédie*, vol. 14, s.v. "Roi [Gouvernement politique]."

power that deals with civil rights.[95] What Beaumarchais did was to show how a tyrant is replaced by a king who demonstrates character, despite his humble origin. In the spirit of renewal rather than destruction, Beaumarchais showed onstage Nougaret's 1775 idea of reversed literature; he drew ideas from Lucretius's *On the Nature of Things* that were at once bold and elusive, but highly suggestive in the political context of pre-Revolutionary France in 1787 – at a time when French audiences no longer thought about George III of the United Kingdom, as Beaumarchais had done when beginning work on the opera in the mid-1770s. Whichever "tyrant" one might relate Atar to, Beaumarchais and Salieri made clear in *Tarare* that a tyrant can be replaced and a tyrannical regime can be renewed, when humans believe that they *all* can dance like atoms.

95 Jaucourt, *Encyclopédie*, vol. 9, s.v. "Liberté politique."

Epilogue

I began writing this book by asking myself a series of why-not questions: if Noverre linked pantomime to liberty, why not figure out how his thinking correlated with the discourse on liberty? If Gluck used ballet-pantomime in his French operas, why not survey a history of operas in pre-Revolutionary France that included the element of pantomime? If Garrick and Gluck made a case for a natural style of human expression, why not figure out why the social circle hosted by d'Holbach welcomed Garrick when he was in Paris? If the *philosophes* – Condillac, Rousseau, and Diderot – thought deeply about signs, why not trace their thinking to Dubos, who wrote extensively about signs and pantomime in his *Réflexions critiques*? If Dubos was an important figure in the discourse on signs, why not use his ideas as the foundation of an argument, working outward toward the music/dance/theater culture in France? If the discourse on pantomime was a phenomenon in the intellectual movement of the Enlightenment, why not investigate its impact on the early years of the French Revolution, when Article 11 of the *Déclaration des droits de l'homme et du citoyen de 1789* explicitly protected freedom of communication?

My answers to these why-not questions have shaped this book, which brings together aesthetics, music history, and intellectual history. Consequently I have discovered that, on the most basic level, pantomime was a designation, one that indicated a dance style. This style had long been used in French opera, as Harris-Warrick has demonstrated, without the designation of "pantomime." But the consistent uses of this designation in the eighteenth century – in operas as well as in writings about dance, theater, and opera – signaled a kind of revival of ancient Roman pantomime in modern theater, which, as Edelstein argues, was a key characteristic of the Enlightenment. My argument is that pantomime was not simply a style in music and dance history; rather, writers including Dubos, d'Alembert, Condillac, Rousseau, Diderot, Jaucourt, and Marmontel built a critical framework that placed the cultural phenomenon of pantomime within the intellectual movement known as the Enlightenment. Using the *Système figuré* in the *Encyclopédie* as a visual illustration of this critical framework, I identified four conceptual axes that shaped the pantomime as an Enlightenment phenomenon: 1) the genealogy of dance (i.e., *la belle danse* and ancient Roman pantomime), 2) the archaeology of human communication (i.e., language, gesture, and signs), 3) the hierarchy of fine arts (i.e., *bas comique* and opera), and 4) materialist ideas of movement (i.e., motion and action).

The Enlightenment context has allowed me to explain composers' uses of signs in a repertory that has not been examined in a book-length study. In 2001 historian Rosenfeld investigated the meanings of signs in the French Revolution. In 2005 Waeber wrote a survey of the melodrama – a genre featuring the interplay of language, text, and music – which stemmed from Rousseau's *scène lyrique Pygmalion*. In 2006 Le Guin asked what it means for a cellist to play Luigi Boccherini's cello repertory, and theorized what it means for a performer to "embody" another per-former. In 2011 theater historian Nye placed the development of *ballet d'action* within a broader intellectual history and devoted one chapter to music. In 2012 Stephen Rumph used signs as historicist tools to explain Mozart's compositions. In 2017 Lockhart examined reception of French Enlightenment thoughts in Italian opera from 1770 to 1830.

Building upon this body of literature, I explain in *Music, Pantomime, and Freedom in Enlightenment France* how the leading composers active in eighteenth-century France – notably Rameau, Rousseau, Gluck, and Salieri – used signs in and through pantomime for their compositions. For this reason, this book contributes to the growing field of study that Le Guin calls "carnal musicology."

Emphasis on the Enlightenment also enables me to explain the relationships between pantomime and types of liberty, especially moral liberty. In *De la poésie dramatique* (1758), Diderot made a clear connection between pantomime and lib-erty: "In the performances of Italian works, our Italian actors perform with more liberty than our French actors ... We find in their action something original and easy that pleases me and would please everyone, without the insipid speeches and the absurd intrigue that distort it."[1] Diderot's observations of the Italian style of acting manifested during the French Revolution, although the theme of liberty was not explicitly evoked. At the Théâtre de Monsieur the Italian buffoon Luigi Raffanelli was described in 1789 as an actor who knew "how, with great skill, to take advantage of music to make his pantomime livelier and more salient."[2]

Other sources indicated new conceptions of the meanings of language and ges-ture around 1789. In a published *drame* called *Mort de Mme. Noblesse*, dated July 14, 1790, which was the first anniversary of the Fall of the Bastille, the dying Madame Noblesse convulses uncontrollably with an ulcerated tongue. Her physical condi-tion and her incapacity to speak symbolize the decline of polite bearing and lan-guage.[3] On the other hand, gesture and silence were taken to be weak forms of human expression, suitable only for the oppressed in the Old Regime, when tyrants reigned supreme. In the *Code national, dédié aux États généraux* (1788), the anony-mous author wrote, "Silence is the favorite means of the tyrant, and the end he pro-poses. To his eyes a look is usually suspect, a gesture often an error, a word always a crime, and the stupidest forgetting of oneself the only quality he values."[4] At the

---

1   "Dans les pièces italiennes, nos comédiens italiens jouent avec plus de liberté que nos comédiens français ... On trouve dans leur action je ne sais quoi d'original et d'aisé, qui me plait et qui plairait à tout le monde, sans les insipides discours et l'intrigue absurde qui le défigurent." Diderot, *Œuvres*, 4:1336.

2   "Le sieur Raffanelli ... sait, avec beaucoup d'adresse, tirer parti de la musique pour rendre sa pantomime plus vive & plus saillante." *L'Année littéraire* 4, no.22 (June 3, 1789), 90. On Raffanelli, see Andrea Fabiano, *Histoire de l'opéra italien en France (1752–1815): Héros et héroïnes d'un roman théâtral* (Paris: CNRS, 2006), 119–22.

3   *Mort de Mme. Noblesse, drame* (s.l.: s.n., July 14, 1790), 9, 14. US-Cn, Case FRC 5644.

4   "Le silence est le moyen favori du tyran, & la fin qu'il se propose. A ses yeux un regard est ordinairement suspect, un geste souvent une faute, une parole toujours un crime, & l'oubli le plus stupide de soi-même, la seule qualité dont il fasse cas." *Code national, dédié aux États généraux* (Geneva: s.n., 1788), 201. US-Cn, Case FRC 15032.

same time, speaking out was valued as a political act. The lyrics of vaudeville "Liberté à tout homme de parler, d'écrire et d'imprimer ses pensées" (1792) read: "Now in this empire / We can do everything and say everything, / print everything, write everything, / because we have decreed it."[5] The idea of freedom of communication remained a topic of discussion after the 1789 *Déclaration*. For example, a draft of the constitution presented at the Convention nationale on June 24, 1793 proposed this article: "The right to manifest one's thought and opinions, either by means of the press, *or in any other way*, the right to assemble peacefully, the free exercise of worship, cannot be prohibited."[6] [emphasis mine]

These sources indicate that the Enlightenment argument for pantomime as a means of human expression was still considered valid to some extent during the Revolution. The young guard, who on the morning of January 21, 1793, while screaming, displayed Louis XVI's severed head to the spectators, barely exercised his right of freedom of communication, although such theatrics were considered by *philosophes* in pre-Revolutionary France as natural, universal, truthful, and intelligible. Using the designation of "pantomime" in their compositions, generations of composers in eighteenth-century France had provided copious examples for actors and actresses to express themselves through their bodies. Their compositions contributed to the history of freedom of *expression* before the political concept of freedom of *communication* was born.

5   "A présent dans cet empire / On peut tout faire et tout dire, / Tout imprimer, tout écrire, / Car nous l'avons décrété." François Marchant, *La Constitution en vaudevilles* (Paris: Les Libraires royalistes, [1792]), 23. US-Cn, Case FRC 22023.

6   "Le droit de manifester sa pensée & ses opinions, soit par la voie de la presse, soit de toute autre manière, le droit de s'assembler paisiblement, le libre exercice des cultes, ne peuvent être interdits." *Acte constitutionnel, précédé de la Déclaration des droits de l'homme et du citoyen* (Saumur: D. M. Degout, 1793), 4. US-CN, FRC 2125.

Select Bibliography

PRE-1800 SOURCES

Acte constitutionnel, précédé de la Déclaration des droits de l'homme et du citoyen (Saumur: D. M. Degout, 1793).

Alembert, Jean Le Rond d', *Preliminary Discourse to the Encyclopedia of Diderot*, trans. with intro. by Richard N. Schwab (Chicago: The University of Chicago Press, 1995).

Algarotti, Francesco, *Essai sur l'Opéra, traduit de l'italien du comte Algarotti* (Paris: Ruault, 1773).

Amusements du cœur et de l'esprit, Les, 4 (January 1739; 4th edn, 1742).

Ancillon, Charles, *Traité des eunuques* (s.l.: s.n., 1707).

Année littéraire, L', 4, no.22 (June 3, 1789).

Aubignac, François-Hédelin, *La Pratique du théâtre* (Paris: Antoine de Sommaville, 1657).

Autreau, Jacques, *Œuvres de Monsieur Autreau*, 4 vols. (Paris: Briasson, 1749).

Bachaumont, Louis Petit de, *Mémoires secrets pour servir à l'histoire de la république des lettres en France*, 36 vols. (London: Adamsohn, 1777–89).

Bacon, Francis, *Advancement of Learning and Noveum Organum*, rev. edn (New York: Co-operative, 1900).

Batteux, Charles, *The Fine Arts Reduced to a Single Principle*, trans. James O. Young (Oxford: Oxford University Press, 2015).

Beaumarchais, Pierre Augustin Caron de, *Correspondance*, ed. Brian N. Morton, 3 vols. (Paris : Nizet, 1969)

—— , *Notes et Réflexions*, intro. Gérard Bauër ([Paris]: Hachette, 1961).

—— , *Œuvres*, ed. Pierre Henri Larthomas with the collaboration of Jacqueline Larthomas (Paris: Gallimard, 1988).

—— , *Œuvres complètes de Pierre-Augustin Caron de Beaumarchais*, ed. Gudin de La Brenellerie, 7 vols. (Paris: Léopold Collin, 1809).

Bonesi, Benedetto, *Pygmalion, drame lyrique en un acte et en prose* (Paris: Ballard, 1780).

Bonnet, Jacques, *Histoire générale de la danse sacrée et profane* (Paris: D'Houry fils, 1723).

Boulenger de Rivery, Claude-François-Félix, *Recherches historiques et critiques sur quelques spectacles* (Paris: Jacque Merigot fils, 1751).

Brissot de Warville, Jacques-Pierre, *Mémoires de Brissot*, intro. M. de Lescure (Paris: Didot, 1877).

Cahusac, Louis de, *La Danse ancienne et moderne ou Traité historique de la danse*, ed. Nathalie Lecomte, Laura Naudeix, and Jean-Noël Laurenti (Paris: Éditions Desjonquères, 2004).

Calzabigi, Ranieri de, *Scritti teatrali e letterari*, ed. Anna Laura Bellina, 2 vols. (Rome: Salerno, 1994).

— , and Alessandro Ercole Pepoli, *Poesie e prose diverse di Ranieri de' Calsabigi*, 2 vols. (Naples: Presso Onofrin Zambraja, 1793).

Chabanon, Michel-Paul-Guy de, *Observations sur la musique et principalement sur la métaphysique de l'art* (Paris: Pissot, 1779).

Chambers, Ephraim, *Cyclopædia, or, an Universal Dictionary of Arts and Sciences*, 2 vols. (London: J. J. Knapton and others, 1728).

Clarke, Samuel, *The Works of Samuel Clarke*, 4 vols. (New York: Garland, 1978).

Code national, dédié aux États généraux (Geneva: s.n., 1788).

Collé, Charles, *Journal et mémoires de Charles Collé*, 3 vols. (Paris: Didot, 1868).

Colman, George, *The English Merchant, a Comedy* (London: Becket and De Hondt, 1767).

Condillac, Étienne Bonnot de, *Essai sur l'origine des connaissances humaines*, ed. Aliènor Bertrand (Paris: Vrin, 2002).

— , *Essay on the Origin of Human Knowledge*, trans. Hans Aarsleff (Cambridge: Cambridge University Press, 2001).

— , *Lettres inédites à Gabriel Cramer*, ed. Georges Le Roy (Paris: Presses universitaires de France, 1953).

— , *La Logique, ou Les Premiers Développements de l'art de penser* (Paris: L'Esprit, 1780).

— , *Traité des sensations; traité des animaux* (Paris: Fayard, 1984).

Cook, William, *The Elements of Dramatic Criticism* (London: Kearsly, 1775).

Coyer, Gabriel-François, *Découverte de la pierre philosophale. L'année merveilleuse avec un supplément* (Pegu: s.n., 1748).

Davies, Thomas, *Memoirs of the Life of David Garrick*, 2 vols. (London: Printed for the author, 1780).

Desboulmiers, Jean, *Histoire de l'opéra comique*, 2 vols. (Paris: Deladoué, 1770).

Diderot, Denis, *Œuvres*, ed. Laurent Versini, 5 vols. (Paris: Laffont, 1994–97).

— , *Œuvres complètes de Diderot*, ed. Jules Assézat, 20 vols. (Paris: Garnier frères, 1875–77).

Dubos, Jean-Baptiste, *Réflexions critiques sur la poésie et sur la peinture*, 2 vols. (Paris: Mariette, 1719).

— , *Réflexions critiques sur la poésie et sur la peinture*, 3 vols. (Paris: Mariette, 1733).

Edgeworth de Firmont, Henry Essex, *Mémoires de M. l'abbé Edgeworth de Firmont: dernier confesseur de Louis XVI*, compiled by C. Sneyd Edgeworth and trans. from English by Edmund Burke (Paris: Gide, 1815).

Engel, Johann Jakob, *Ideen zur einer Mimik* (Berlin: s.n., 1785); adapted as *Practical Illustrations of Rhetorical Gesture and Action*, trans. Henry Siddons (London: Richards Phillips, 1822).

Essai sur les hiéroglyphes des égyptiens, 2 vols. (Paris: Hippolyte-Louis Guerin, 1744).

Euripides, *Bacchae and Other Plays*, trans. James Morwood (Oxford: Oxford University Press, 2008).

Fagan, Barthélemy-Christophe, *Théâtre de M. Fagan et autres œuvres du même auteur*, 4 vols. (Paris: Duchesne, 1760).

Furetière, Antoine, *Dictionnaire universel*, 3 vols. (La Haye and Rotterdam: Arnout & Reinier Leers, 1690).

— , *Dictionnaire universel*, new edn, corrected and augmented by Henri Basnage de Beauval and Jean Baptiste Brutel de la Rivière, 4 vols. (La Haye: Pierre Husson, 1727).

Garrick, David, *An Essay on Acting* (London: Bickerton, 1744).

— , *The Private Correspondence of David Garrick*, ed. James Boaden, 2 vols. (London: Colborn and Bentley, 1832).

Gaubier de Barrault, Sulpice-Edme, *Brioché; ou L'Origine des marionnettes, parodie de Pigmalion* (Paris: Duchesne, 1753).

Goudar, Ange, *De Venise: Remarques sur la musique et la danse* (Venice: Palese, 1773).

— , *Observations sur les trois derniers ballets pantomimes qui ont paru aux Italiens & aux François* ([Paris: Nicolas-Bonaventure Duchesne], 1759).

Goudar, Sara, *Œuvres mêlées de Madame Sara Goudar*, 2 vols. (Amsterdam: s.n., 1777).

Grimm, Friedrich Melchior, *Correspondance littéraire, philosophique et critique*, 16 vols. (Paris: Garnier frères, 1877–82).

Hobbes, Thomas, *Leviathan*, ed. John Charles Addison Gaskin (Oxford: Oxford University Press, 1996).

Holbach, Paul Henri Thiry, baron d', *Le Christianisme dévoilé, ou Examen des principes et des effets de la religion Chrétienne* (London [i.e., Nancy]: [s.n.], 1756 [i.e., 1766]).

— , *La Morale universelle* (Amsterdam: M. M. Rey, 1776).

— , *Œuvres philosophiques*, vol. 5: 1776–1790 (Paris: Coda, 2004).

— , *Système de la nature*, 2 vols. (Paris: Fayard, 1990).

— , *Système social ou principes naturels de la morale et de la politique* (Paris: Fayard, 1994).

Hume, David, *An Enquiry Concerning Human Understanding*, ed. Peter Millican (Oxford: Oxford University Press, 2007).

— , *A Treatise of Human Nature*, ed. David Fate Norton and May J. Norton, 2 vols. (Oxford: Clarendon Press, 2007).

Johnson, Samuel, and David Garrick, *Prologue and Epilogue, Spoken at the Opening of the Theatre in Drury Lane* (London: E. Cave, 1747).

Journal de musique 237 (August 24, 1788).

Journal des beaux-arts et des sciences (September 1774).

L'Aulnaye, François-Henri-Stanislas de, *De la saltation théâtrale ou Recherches sur l'origine, les progrès et les effets de la pantomime chez les Anciens* (Paris: Barrois l'ainé, 1790).

La Dixmerie, Nicolas Bricaire de, *Les Deux Âges du goût et du génie français* (La Haye and Paris: Lacombe, 1769).

La Fontaine, Jean de, *Œuvres diverses* (Paris: Gallimard, 1942).

La Mettrie, Julien Offray de, *Machine Man and Other Writings*, trans. and ed. Ann Thomson (Cambridge: Cambridge University Press, 1996).

Lagrange, *Traduction libre de Lucrèce*, 2 vols. (Paris and Amsterdam: Châtelain, 1768).

Le Roux, Philibert-Joseph, *Dictionnaire comique, satyrique, critique, burlesque, libre, et proverbial*, 2 vols. (Pampelune [Paris]: s.n.: 1786).

Leclerc, Georges-Louis, comte de Buffon, *Histoire naturelle, générale et particulière*, 36 vols. (Paris: L'Imprimerie royale, 1753).

Leibniz, Gottfried Wilhelm, Freiherr von, *Essais de Théodicée* [1710] (Paris: Aubier, 1962).

Lesage, Alain-René, *Histoire de Gil Blas de Santillane*, ed. Roger Laufer (Paris: Garnier-Flammarion, 1977).

Lessing, Gotthold Ephraim, *Theatralische Bibliothek*, vol. 3 (Berlin: Christian Frederick Voss, 1755).

Lettre écrite à un ami sur les danseurs de corde, et sur les pantomimes qui ont paru autrefois chez les Grecs & chez les Romains, & à Paris en 1738 (Paris: Valleyre, 1739).

Locke, John, *An Essay Concerning Human Understanding*, ed. Pauline Phemister (Oxford: Oxford University Press, 2008).

Lucretius, *The Nature of Things*, trans. A. E. Stallings (London: Penguin, 2007).

Mably, Gabriel Bonnet de, *Lettres à Mme la marquise de P*** sur l'opéra* (1741; repr. New York: AMS Press, 1978).

Mainbray, *Les Dupes ou Rien n'est difficile en amour* (Paris: [De Lormel], 1740).

Marchant, François, *La Constitution en vaudevilles* (Paris: Les Libraires royalistes, [1792]).

Marmontel, Jean-François, *Éléments de littérature*, 6 vols. (Paris: Chez Née de la Rochelle, 1787).

— — , *Poétique française* (Paris: Lesclapart, 1763).

Mattheson, Johann, *Abhandlung von den Pantomimen, historisch und critisch ausgeführt* (Hamburg: Carl Samuel Geissler, 1749).

Maugars, André, *Réponse faite à un curieux sur le sentiment de la musique d'Italie*, intro., trans., and notes by H. Wiley Hitchcock (Geneva: Minkoff, 1993).

Mémoires pour server à l'histoire de la Révolution opérée dans la Musique par M. le Chevalier Gluck (Naples and Paris: s.n., 1781).

Menestrier, Claude-François, *Des Ballets anciens et modernes selon les règles du théâtre* (Paris: René Guignard, 1682).

Mercure, Le, June and July 1721.

Mercure de France [various issues between 1739 and 1784].

Montesquieu, Charles de Secondat, baron de, *De l'Esprit des loix*, ed. J. Brethe de la Gressaye, 4 vols. (Paris: Les Belles lettres, 1950–61).

— — , *Lettres persanes*, 2 vols. (Amsterdam: Pierre Brunel, 1721).

— — , *My Thoughts (Mes pensées)*, trans. and ed. Henry C. Clark (Indianapolis, IN: Liberty Fund, 2012).

Morize, André, *L'Apologie du luxe au XVIIIe siècle et "Le Mondain" de Voltaire: étude critique sur "Le Mondain" et ses sources* (Paris: s.n., 1909; Geneva: Slatkine, 1970).

La Mort d'Orphée, ou Les Fêtes de Bacchus (Paris: Delormel, 1759).

Mort de Mme. Noblesse, drame (s.l.: s.n., July 14, 1790).

Nemeitz, Joachim Christoph, *Séjour de Paris* (Leiden, Amsterdam: Jean van Aboude, 1727).

Nougaret, Pierre-Jean-Baptiste, *De l'art du théâtre, où il est parlé des différents genres de spectacles, et de la musique adaptée au théâtre*, 2 vols. (Paris: Cailleau, 1769).

––, *La Littérature renversée, ou L'Art de faire des pièces de théâtre sans paroles; ouvrage utile aux poètes dramatiques de nos jours* (Berne and Paris: les Débitans de brochures Nouvelles, 1775).

––, *Tableau mouvant de Paris, ou Variétés amusantes*, 3 vols. (Paris: Duchesne, 1787).

Nouveau Mercure, Le, January 1718

Nouveau Spectateur, Le 1 (Paris: Esprit, 1776).

Noverre, Jean-Georges, *Apelles et Campaspe* (Lyon: Mlle. Olier, 1787).

––, *Lettres sur la danse, et sur les ballets* (Lyon: Delaroche, 1760).

––, *Lettres sur la danse, sur les ballets et les arts*, 4 vols. (St Petersburg: Jean Charles Schnoor, 1803).

––, *Lettres sur les arts imitateurs en général et sur la danse en particulier*, 2 vols. (Paris: L. Collin, 1807).

––, *Recueil de Programmes des Ballets de M. Noverre* (Vienna: Joseph Kurzböck, 1776).

Ovid, *Tristia. Ex Ponto*, trans. Arther Leslie Wheeler, rev. G. P. Goold (Cambridge, MA: Harvard University Press, 1975).

Pannard, Charles-François, and Thomas Laffichard, *Pygmalion, ou La Statue animée*, new edn (1758; repr. Paris: Duchesne, 1773).

Pantomime dramatique ou Essai sur un nouveau genre de spectacle (Florence: Jombert, 1779).

Parfaict, Claude, and François Parfaict, *Dictionnaire des théâtres de Paris*, 7 vols. (Paris: Lambert, 1756; Paris: Rozet, 1767).

––, *Mémoires pour servir à l'histoire des spectacles de la foire*, 2 vols. (Paris: Briasson, 1743).

Perroquet, Le, Mélange de diverses pièces intéressantes pour l'esprit et pour le cœur, 2 vols. (Frankfurt: François Varrentrapp, 1742).

Piron, Alexis, *Œuvres complètes d'Alexis Piron*, pubd by Rigoley de Juvigny, 7 vols. (Paris: Lambert, 1776).

Pygmalion (Paris: Aux dépens de l'Académie, 1748).

Querelle des bouffons, La, texte des pamphlets, with intro., commentaries, and index by Denise Launay, 3 vols. (Geneva: Minkoff, 1973).

Rameau, Jean-Philippe, *The Complete Theoretical Writings of Jean-Philippe Rameau*, ed. Erwin R. Jacobi, 6 vols. (Rome: American Institute of Musicology, 1967–72).

Recueil des comédies et ballets représentés sur le théâtre des petits Appartements.

Richelet, Pierre, *Dictionnaire français: contenant les mots et les choses* (Geneva: Widerhold, 1680).

Rollin, Charles, *Histoire ancienne des Égyptiens, des Carthaginois, des Assyriens, des Babyloniens, des Mèdes, et des Perses, des Macédoniens, des Grecs*, 5 vols. (Paris: Estienne, 1740).

Rousseau, Jean-Jacques, *The Major Political Writings of Jean-Jacques Rousseau: The Two Discourses and the Social Contract*, trans. and ed. John T. Scott (Chicago: The University of Chicago Press, 2012).

Rousseau, Pierre, *L'Année merveilleuse* (Paris: Cailleau, 1748).

Sallé, Claude, *Histoire de l'Académie Royale des Inscriptions et Belles Lettres*, 19 vols. (Paris: L'Imprimerie royale, 1718–81).

Scudéry, Georges de, *L'Apologie du théâtre* (Paris: Courbé, 1639).

Servandoni, Jean Nicolas, *Lettre au sujet du spectacle des aventures d'Ulysse* (Paris: Prault fils, 1741).

Sorel, Charles, *La Bibliothèque française* (Paris: Compagnie des Libraries du Palais, 1664).

Supplément au Roman comique, ou Mémoires pour servir à la vie de Jean Monnet, 2 vols. (London: s.n., 1772).

Théâtre italien, Le (Geneva: Jacques Dentand, 1695).

Tribut de la toilette, Le, 2 vols. (Paris: Madame Boivin, [between 1747 and 1753]).

Weaver, John, *An Essay towards an History of Dancing* (London: J. Tonson, 1712).

—— , *A History of Mimes and Pantomimes* (London: J. Roberts, 1728).

POST-1800 SOURCES

Aarsleff, Hans, "Philosophy of Language," in Knud Haakonssen, ed., *Cambridge History of Eighteenth-Century Philosophy,* 2 vols. (Cambridge: Cambridge University Press, 2006), 451–95.

Agamben, Giorgio, *Homo Sacer: Sovereign Power and Bare Life,* trans. Daniel Heller-Roazen (Stanford, CA: Stanford University Press, 1998).

—— , *Nudities,* trans. David Kishik and Stefan Pedatella (Stanford, CA: Stanford University Press, 2011).

Austin, Jong Langsaw, *How to Do Things with Words* (Cambridge, MA: Harvard University Press, 1962).

Baker, Keith Michael, *Inventing the French Revolution: Essays on the French Political Culture in the Eighteenth Century* (Cambridge: Cambridge University Press, 1990).

—— , John W. Boyer, and Julius Kirshner, eds, *The Old Regime and the French Revolution* (Chicago: The University of Chicago Press, 1987).

Bakhtin, Mikhail, *Rabelais and His World,* trans. Hélène Iswolsky (Bloomington, IN: Indiana University Press, 1984).

Banducci, Antonia L., "Staging and Its Dramatic Effect in French Baroque Opera: Evidence from Prompt Notes," *Eighteenth-Century Music* 1 (2004), 5–28.

Barnett, Dene, *The Art of Gesture: The Practices and Principles of 18th-Century Acting* (Heidelberg: Carl Winter, 1987).

Bartlet, M. Elizabeth C., "Beaumarchais and Voltaire's *Samson," Studies in Eighteenth-Century Culture* 11 (1982), 33–47.

Bass, Streeter, "Beaumarchais and the American Revolution," *Studies in Intelligence* 14, no.1 (1970), 1–18.

Baud-Bovy, Samuel, "De l'*Armide* de Lully à l'*Armide* de Gluck: Un siècle de récitatif à la française," in Jean-Jacques Eigeldinger, ed., *Jean-Jacques Rousseau et la musique* (Neuchâtel: Baconnière, 1988), 63–76.

Bell, David A., *Lawyers and Citizens: The Making of a Political Elite in Old Regime France* (New York: Oxford University Press, 1994).

Benoit, Marcelle, ed., *Dictionnaire de la musique en France aux XVIIe et XVIIIe siècles* (Paris: Fayard, 1992).

Berchtold, Jacques, Christophe Martin, and Yannick Seite, eds, *Rousseau et le spectacle* (Paris: Armand Colin, 2014).

Bergman, Gösta M., "La Grande mode des pantomimes à Paris vers 1740 et les spectacles d'optique de Servandoni," *Theatre Research/Recherches Théâtrales* 2, no.1 (1960), 71–81.

Betzwieser, Thomas, "*Le chœur et son double*. Glucks Konzept der szenischen Chor-Bewegung und seine Umsetzung auf der aktuellen Opernbühne," in Nicola Gess, ed., *Barocktheater Heute* (Bielefeld: Transcript Verlag, 2008), 49–61.

−−, "Musical Setting and Scenic Movement: Chorus and *Chœur dansé* in Eighteenth-Century Parisian Opéra," *Cambridge Opera Journal* 12, no.1 (2000), 1–28.

−−, ed., *Von Gluck zu Berlioz: Die französische Oper zwischen Antikenrezeption und Monumentalität* (Würzburg: Königshausen & Neumann, 2015).

Bloechl, Olivia, "On Not Being Alone: Rousseauean Thoughts on a Relational Ethics of Music," *Journal of American Musicological Society* 66, no.1 (2013), 261–65.

−−, *Opera and the Political Imaginary in Old Regime France* (Chicago: The University of Chicago Press, 2017).

Bouissou, Sylvie, *Jean-Philippe Rameau: Musicien des Lumières* (Paris: Fayard, 2014).

−−, Pascal Denécheau, and France Marchal-Ninosque, eds, *Dictionnaire de l'Opéra de Paris sous l'Ancien Régime (1669–1791)*, 4 vols. (Paris: Classiques Garnier, 2019–20).

Brandenburg, Daniel, and Martina Hochreiter, eds, *Gluck auf dem Theater: Kongressbericht Nürnberg 7.–10. März 2008*, Gluck-Studien 6 (Kassel: Bärenreiter, 2011).

Brillaud, Jérôme, "If You Please! Theater, Verisimilitude, and Freedom in the Letter to d'Alembert," in Christie McDonald and Stanley Hoffmann, eds, *Rousseau and Freedom* (Cambridge: Cambridge University Press, 2010), 77–91.

Brizi, Bruno, "Un spunto polemico Calzabigiano: Ipermestra o le Danaidi," in Federico Marri, ed., *La Figura e l'opera di Ranieri de' Calzabigi* (Florence: Leo S. Olschki, 1989), 119–46.

Brown, Bill, *Other Things* (Chicago: The University of Chicago Press, 2015).

Brown, Bruce Alan, *Gluck and the French Theatre in Vienna* (Oxford: Clarendon, 1991).

Burden, Michael, and Jennifer Thorp, eds, *The Works of Monsieur Noverre Translated from the French* (Hillsdale, NY: Pendragon Press, 2014).

Buschmeier, Gabriele, "Glucks *Armide*-monologue, Lully und die 'Philosophes,'" in Axel Beer and Laurenz Lütteken, eds, *Festschrift Klaus Hortschansky zum 60. Geburtstag* (Tutzing: H. Schneider, 1995), 167–80.

Carter, Tim, *Understanding Italian Opera* (New York: Oxford University Press, 2015).

Castelvecchi, Stefano, *Sentimental Opera: Questions of Genre in the Age of Bourgeois Drama* (Cambridge: Cambridge University Press, 2013).

Charlton, David, "New Light on the *Bouffons* in Paris (1752–1754)," *Eighteenth-Century Music* 11, no.1 (2014), 31–54.

−−, *Opera in the Age of Rousseau: Music, Confrontation, Realism* (Cambridge: Cambridge University Press, 2015).

−−, "Storms, Sacrifices: The 'Melodrama Model' in Opera," in David Charlton, ed., *French Opera, 1730–1830: Meaning and Media*, X:1–61 (Ashgate, Aldershot: 2000).

—— , ed., *French Opera, 1730–1830: Meaning and Media*, X:1–61 (Ashgate, Aldershot: 2000).

Christensen, Thomas, *Rameau and Musical Thought in the Enlightenment* (New York: Cambridge University Press, 1993).

Cioranescu, Alexandre. *Bibliographie de la littérature française du dix-huitième siècle*. 3 vols. Paris: Éditions du Centre national de la recherche scientifique, 1969.

Coeyman, Barbara, "Theatres for Opera and Ballet during the Reigns of Louis XIV and Louis XV," *Early Music* 18, no.1 (1990), 22–37.

Cohen, Selma Jeanne, ed., *International Encyclopedia of Dance*, 6 vols. (New York: Oxford University Press, 1998).

Cowart, Georgia J., *The Origins of Modern Music Criticism: French and Italian Music, 1600–1750* (Ann Arbor, MI: UMI, 1981).

—— , *The Triumph of Pleasure: Louis XIV & the Politics of Spectacle* (Chicago: The University of Chicago Press, 2008).

Crawford, Katherine, "Desiring Castrates, or How to Create Disabled Social Subjects," *Journal for Early Modern Cultural Studies* 16, no.2 (2016), 59–90.

Croll, Gerhard, "'Apollo non in macchina.' Zur Scena ultima der Wiener *Alcester*," in Daniel Brandenburg and Martina Hochreiter, eds, *Gluck auf dem Theater: Kongressbericht Nürnberg 7.–10. März 2008, Gluck-Studien* 6 (Kassel: Bärenreiter, 2011), 55–60.

—— , and Renate Croll, *Gluck: Sein Leben. Seine Musik* (Kassel: Bärenreiter, 2014).

Cyr, Mary, "The Dramatic Role of the Chorus," in Thomas Bauman and Marita Petzholdt McClymonds, eds, *Opera and the Enlightenment* (New York: Cambridge University Press, 1995), 105–18.

Dahms, Sibylle, *Der konservative Revolutionär: Jean Georges Noverre und die Ballettreform des 18. Jahrhunderts* (Munich: Epodium, 2010).

Dällenbach, Lucien, *The Mirror of the Text*, trans. Jeremy Whiteley with Emma Hughes (Chicago: The University of Chicago Press, 1989).

Darlow, Mark , *Dissonance in the Republic of Letters: The Querelle des Gluckistes et des Piccinnistes* (Oxford: Legenda, 2013).

—— , "L'esthétique du tableau dans les ballets de Tarare, version de 1819," in Jacqueline Waeber, ed., *Musique et geste en France de Lully à la Révolution: Études sur la musique, le théâtre et la danse* (Bern: Peter Lang, 2009), 249–64.

—— , "*Nihil per saltum*: Chiaroscuro in Eighteenth-Century Lyric Theatre," in Sarah Hibberd and Richard Wrigley, eds, *Art, Theatre, and Opera in Paris, 1750–1850: Exchanges and Tensions* (Farnham: Ashgate, 2014), 37–52.

Darnton, Robert, *The Great Cat Massacre and other Episodes in French Cultural History* (New York: Basic Books, 1984).

—— , "The High Enlightenment and the Low-life of Literature in Pre-Revolutionary France," *Past and Present* 51, no.1 (1971), 81–115.

Daston, Lorraine, "Attention and the Values of Nature in the Enlightenment," in Lorraine Daston and Fernando Vidal, eds, *The Moral Authority of Nature* (Chicago: The University of Chicago Press, 2004), 100–126.

Davies, James Q., *Romantic Anatomies of Performance* (Berkeley, CA: University of California Press, 2014).

Démoris, René, "*Narcisse*: ou comment l'auteur se donne en spectacle," in Jacques Berchtold, Christophe Martin, and Yannick Seite, eds, *Rousseau et le spectacle* (Paris: Armand Colin, 2014), 100.

Denoiresterres, Gustave, *Gluck et Piccinni: 1774–1800*, 2nd edn (Paris: Didier, 1875).

Derrida, Jacques, *Of Grammatology*, trans. Gayatri Chakravorty Spivak (Baltimore, MD: The Johns Hopkins University Press, 1997).

— , *Voice and Phenomenon: Introduction to the Problem of the Sign in Husserl's Phenomenology*, trans. Leonard Lawlor (Evanston, IL: Northwestern University Press, 2011).

Devoto, Daniel, "La Folle sarabande (II)," *Revue de musicologie* 46 (122), 145–80.

Didier, Béatrice, *La Musique des lumières* (Paris: Presses Universitaires de France, 1985).

— , "La pantomime à l'Opéra et à l'Opéra Comique dans la deuxième moitié du XVIIIe siècle," in Franck Salaün and Patrick Taïeb, eds, *Musique et Pantomime dans le Neveu de Rameau* (Paris: Hermann, 2016), 175–90.

Dill, Charles, "Rameau Reading Lully: Meaning and System in Rameau's Recitative Tradition," *Cambridge Opera Journal* 6, no.1 (1994), 1–17.

— , "Rameau's Imaginary Monsters: Knowledge, Theory and Chromaticism in *Hippolyte et Aricie*," *Journal of the American Musicological Society* 55, no.3 (2002), 456–58.

Doran, Robert, *The Theory of the Sublime from Longinus to Kant* (New York: Cambridge University Press, 2015).

Dratwicki, Benoît, "Lully d'un siècle à l'autre, du modèle au mythe (1754–1774)," in Agnès Terrier and Alexandre Dratwicki, eds, *L'Invention des genres lyriques français et leur redécouverte au XIXe siècle* (Lyon: Symétrie, 2010), 309–46.

Edelstein, Dan, *The Enlightenment: A Genealogy* (Chicago: The University of Chicago Press, 2010).

— , ed., *The Super-Enlightenment: Daring to Know Too Much* (Oxford: Voltaire Foundation, 2010).

— , Robert Morrissey, and Glenn Roe, "To Quote or not to Quote: Citing Strategies in the *Encyclopédie*," *Journal of the History of Ideas* 74, no.2 (April 2013), 213–36.

Elias, Norbert, *The Civilizing Process*, trans. Edmund Jephcott, rev. edn ed. by Eric Dunning, Johan Goudsblom, and Stephen Mennell (Oxford: Blackwell, 2000).

Fabbricatore, Arianna Beatrice, *La Querelle des Pantomimes: Danse, culture et société dans l'Europe des Lumières* (Rennes: Presses universitaires de Rennes, 2017).

Fabiano, Andrea, *Histoire de l'opéra italien en France (1752–1815): Héros et héroïnes d'un roman théâtral* (Paris: CNRS, 2006).

Faul, Michel, *Les Tribulations de Nicolas-Médard Audinot: Fondateur du Théâtre de l'Ambigu-comique* (Lyon: Symétrie, 2013).

Fauser, Annegret, and Mark Everist, eds, *Music, Theater, and Cultural Transfer: Paris, 1830–1914* (Chicago: The University of Chicago Press, 2009).

Feldman, Martha, *The Castrato: Reflections on Natures and Kinds* (Berkeley, CA: University of California Press, 2015).

— , *Opera and Sovereignty: Transforming Myths in Eighteenth-Century Italy* (Chicago: The University of Chicago Press, 2007).

Foster, Susan Leigh, *Choreography & Narrative: Ballet's Staging of Story and Desire* (Bloomington, IN: Indiana University Press, 1998).

Foucault, Michel, "The Ethics of the Concern for Self as a Practice of Freedom," in Paul Rabinsow, ed., *Ethics: Subjectivity and Truth*, trans. Robert Hurley and others (New York: New Press, 1997), 281–307.

――, *Madness and Civilization: A History of Insanity in the Age of Reason*, trans. Richard Howard (New York: Vintage, 1988).

―― , *The Politics of Truth*, ed. Sylvère Lotringer and Lysa Hochroth (Los Angeles: Semiotext(e), 2007).

Frazer, Michael L., *The Enlightenment of Sympathy: Justice and the Moral Sentiments in the Eighteenth Century and Today* (New York: Oxford University Press, 2010).

Fuller, David, "Of Portraits, 'Sapho,' and Couperin: Titles and Characters in French Instrumental Music of the High Baroque," *Music and Letters* 78, no.2 (1997), 149–74.

Fumaroli, Marc, *Histoire de la rhétorique dans l'Europe modern (1450–1950)* (Paris: Presses universitaires de France, 1999).

Garsten, Bryan, *Saving Persuasion: A Defense of Rhetoric and Judgment* (Cambridge, MA: Harvard University Press, 2006).

Gastoué, Armand, "Gossec et Gluck à Opéra de Paris: Le ballet final d'*Iphigénie en Tauride*," *Revue de musicologie* 16, no.54 (May 1935), 87–99.

Gebauer, Gunter, and Christoph Wuff, *Mimesis: Culture-Art-Society*, trans. Don Reneau (Berkeley, CA: University of California Press, 1992).

Girdlestone, Cuthbert, *Jean-Philippe Rameau: His Life and Work*, intro. Philip Gossett (1957; repr., Mineola, NY: Dover, 2014).

Goodden, Angelica, *Actio and Persuasion: Dramatic Performance in Eighteenth-Century France* (Oxford: Clarendon, 1986).

Gordon, Mel, *Lazzi: The Comic Routines of the Commedia dell'arte* (New York: Performing Arts Journal Publications, 1983).

Goulbourne, Russell, *Voltaire Comic Dramatist* (Oxford: Voltaire Foundation, 2006).

Green, Emily H., *Dedicating Music, 1785–1850* (Rochester, NY: University of Rochester Press, 2019).

Green, Robert A., "Aristophanes, Rameau and *Platée*," *Cambridge Opera Journal* 23, nos.1–2 (2012), 1–26.

Grene, David, and Richmond Lattimore, eds, *Aeschylus I*, 3rd edn (Chicago: The University of Chicago Press, 2013).

Guest, Ivor, *The Ballet of the Enlightenment: The Establishment of the Ballet d'action in France, 1770–1793* (New York: Dance Books, 1996).

Gullstam, Maria and Michael O'Dea, eds, *Rousseau on Stage: Playwright, Musician, Spectator* (Oxford: Voltaire Foundation, 2017).

HaCohen, Ruth, "The Music of Sympathy in the Arts of the Baroque; or, the Use of Difference to Overcome Indifference." *Poetics Today* 22, no.3 (2001), 607–50.

Halliwell, Stephan, *The Aesthetics of Mimesis: Ancient Texts and Modern Problems* (Princeton, NJ: Princeton University Press, 2002).

Hansell, Kathleen Kuzmick, "Theatrical Ballet and Italian Opera," in Lorenzo Bianconi and Giorgio Pestelli, eds, *Opera on Stage*, trans. Kate Singleton (Chicago: The University of Chicago Press, 2002), 177–295.

Harris, Ellen T., "Silence as Sounds: Handel's Sublime Pauses," *Journal of Musicology* 22 (2005), 521–58.

Harris, Joseph, *Inventing the Spectator: Subjectivity and the Theatrical Experience in Early Modern France* (Oxford: Oxford University Press, 2014).

Harris-Warrick, Rebecca, "Ballet, Pantomime, and the Sung Word in the Operas of Rameau," in Cliff Eisen, ed., *Coll'astuzia, col giudizio: Essays in Honor of Neal Zaslaw* (Ann Arbor, MI: Steglein, 2009), 31–61.

—, *Dance and Drama in French Baroque Opera: A History* (New York: Cambridge University Press, 2016).

—, "*Le Prologue de Lully à Rameaui*," in Michel Noiray and Solveig Serre, eds, *Le Répertoire de l'opéra de Paris (1671–2009): Analyse et interprétation* (Paris: École des Chartes, 2010), 199–211.

—, "'Toute danse doit exprimer, peindre …': Finding the Drama in the Operatic Divertissement," *Basler Jahrbuch für historische Musikpraxis* 23 (1999), 187–210.

—, and Bruce Alan Brown, eds, *The Grotesque Dancer on the Eighteenth-Century Stage: Gennaro Magri and His World* (Madison, WI: The University of Wisconsin Press, 2005).

—, and Carol G. Marsh, *Musical Theatre at the Court of Louis XIV: Le Mariage de la grosse Cathos* (Cambridge: Cambridge University Press, 1994).

Heartz, Daniel, *From Garrick to Gluck: Essays on Opera in the Age of Enlightenment*, ed. John A. Rice (Hillsdale, NY: Pendragon, 2004).

—, *Haydn, Mozart, and the Viennese School* (New York: Norton, 1995).

—, *Music in European Capitals: The Galant Style, 1720–1780* (New York: Norton, 2003).

Heller-Roazen, Daniel, *Echolalia: On the Forgetting of Language* (New York: Zone Books, 2008).

Hobson, Marian, *The Object of Art: The Theory of Illusion in Eighteenth-Century France* (New York: Cambridge University Press, 1982).

Honderich, Ted, *How Free Are You? The Determinism Problem*, 2nd edn (Oxford: Oxford University Press, 2002).

Howard, Patricia, *Gluck: An Eighteenth-Century Portrait in Letters and Documents* (Oxford: Clarendon, 1995).

Isherwood, Robert, "The Conciliatory Partisan of Musical Liberty: Jean Le Rond d'Alembert, 1717–1783," in Georgia Cowart, ed., *French Musical Thought, 1600–1800* (Ann Arbor, MI: UMI Research Press, 1989), 95–120.

Jay, Martin, *Downcast Eyes: The Denigration of Vision in Twentieth-Century French Thought* (Berkeley, CA: University of California Press, 1993).

Joly, Jacques, *Les Fêtes théâtrales de Métastase à la cour de Vienne (1731–1767)* (Clermont-Ferrand: Faculté des Lettres et Sciences Humaines de Clermont-Ferrand II, 1978).

Jullien, Adolphe, *La Comédie à la cour* (Paris: Firmin-Didot, 1885).

—, *La Cour et l'Opéra sous Louis XVI* (Paris: Didier, 1878).

── , *Histoire du théâtre de Madame de Pompadour dit Théâtre des petits cabinets* (Paris: Baur, 1874).

Kantorowicz, Ernst H., *The King's Two Bodies: A Study in Mediaeval Political Theology* (Princeton, NJ: Princeton University Press, 1957).

Kasunic, David, "Rousseau's Cat," *Journal of the American Musicological Society* 66, no.1 (2013), 266–70.

Kintzler, Catherine, "La Danse, modèle d'intelligibilité dans l'opéra français de l'âge classique," *Ateliers* 11 (1997), 71–80.

── , *Poétique de l'opéra français de Corneille à Rousseau*, 2nd edn (Paris: Minerve, 2006).

Kors, Alan Charles, *D'Holbach's Coterie: An Enlightenment in Paris* (Princeton, NJ: Princeton University Press, 1976).

La Salvia, Adrian, "Zwischen Klassik und Romantik: Traum-Szenen im französischen Musiktheater," in Thomas Betzwieser, ed., *Von Gluck zu Berlioz: Die französische Oper zwischen Antikenrezeption und Monumentalität* (Würzburg: Königshausen & Neumann, 2015), 87–109.

Lagrave, Henri, "La Pantomime à la foire, au Théâtre-Italien et aux Boulevards (1700–1789). Première approche: historique du genre," *Romantische Zeitschrift für Literaturgeschichte* 3–4 (1979), 408–30.

Lakoff, George, and Mark Johnson, *Philosophy in the Flesh: The Embodied Mind and Its Challenge to Western Thought* (New York: Basic Books, 1999).

Lalonger, Edith, and Jonathan Williams, "Music, Dance, and Narrative in Rameau's *Zaïs*: Bringing the Immortal back to Life," *Dance Research* 33, no.2 (2015), 212–26.

Lancelot, Francine, *La Belle Dance: catalogue raisonné fait en l'An 1995* (Paris: Van Dieren 1996).

Law, Hedy, "Harpocrates at Work: How the God of Silence Protected Eighteenth-Century French Iconoclasts," in Patricia Hall, ed., *Oxford Handbook of Music and Censorship*, (New York: Oxford University Press, 2017), 153–74.

── , "Music, Bacchus, and Freedom," in Youn Kim and Sander L. Gilman, eds, *Oxford Handbook of Music and the Body* (New York: Oxford University Press, 2019), 161–76.

── , "'*Tout, dans ses charmes, est dangereux*': Gesture and Seduction in Grétry's *Céphale et Procris* (1773)," *Cambridge Opera Journal* 20/3 (2010), 241–68.

Le Guin, Elisabeth, *Boccherini's Body: An Essay in Carnal Musicology* (Berkeley, CA: University of California Press, 2005).

Legrand, Raphaëlle, "Louis de Cahusac et Jean-Philippe Rameau: Geste, danse et musique," *Les Cahiers du CIREM* 26–27 (1992–93), 31–40.

── , and Nicole Wild, *Regards sur l'opéra-comique: Trois siècles de vie théâtrale* (Paris: CNRS, 2002).

Lespinard, Bernadette, "De l'adaptation des airs de danse aux situations dramatiques dans les opéras de Rameau: Esquisse d'une typologie," in Jérôme de la Gorce, ed., *Jean-Philippe Rameau: Colloque internationale* (Paris: Champion, 1987), 445–99.

Lesure, François, *Querelle des gluckistes et les piccinnistes* (Geneva: Minkoff, 1984).

Levin, David, *Unsettling Opera: Staging Mozart, Verdi, Wagner, and Zemlinsky* (Chicago: The University of Chicago Press, 2007).

Locke, Ralph P., *Music and the Exotic from the Renaissance to Mozart* (New York: Cambridge University Press, 2015).

Lockhart, Ellen, *Animation, Plasticity, and Music in Italy, 1770–1830* (Berkeley, CA: University of California Press, 2017).

Lombardi, Carmela, *Il ballo pantomimo: lettere, saggi e libelli sulla danza (1773–1785)* (Turin: Paravia Scriptorium, 1998).

Loughridge, Deirdre, "Who Measured the Wind and Made the Fingers Move," *Journal of the American Musicological Society* 66, no.1 (2013), 270–75.

McDonald, Christie, and Stanley Hoffmann, eds, *Rousseau and Freedom* (Cambridge: Cambridge University Press, 2010).

McMahon, Darrin M., "Illuminating the Enlightenment: Public Lighting Practices in the Siècles des Lumières," *Past & Present* 240, no.1 (2018), 119–59.

Marshall, David, "Rousseau's Pygmalion and the Theatre of Autobiography," in Maria Gullstam and Michael O'Dea, eds, *Rousseau on Stage: Playwright, Musician, Spectator* (Oxford: Voltaire Foundation, 2017), 157–75.

Martin, Isabelle, *Le Théâtre de la Foire: des tréteaux aux boulevards* (Oxford: Voltaire Foundation, 2002).

Martina, Alessandra, *Orfeo/Orphée: Storia della trasmissione e della recezione* (Turin: De Sono, 1995).

Masson, Paul-Marie, "Lullistes et Ramistes, 1733–1752," *L'Année musicale* 1 (1911), 187–211.

—— , *L'Opéra de Rameau* (Paris: Henri Laurens, 1930).

Maza, Sarah C., "Bourgeoisie," in William Doyale, ed., *The Oxford Handbook of the Ancien Régime* (Oxford: Oxford University Press, 2012), 127–40.

—— , *Servants and Masters in Eighteenth-Century France: The Uses of Loyalty* (Princeton, NJ: Princeton University Press, 1984).

Montenoy, Charles Palissot de, *Œuvres complètes*, 6 vols. (Paris: Collin, 1809).

Mulvey, Laura, *Visual and Other Pleasures*, 2nd edn (New York: Palgrave Macmillan, 2009).

Naudeix, Laura, *Dramaturgie de la tragédie en musique (1673–1764)* (Paris: Honoré Champion, 2004).

Noiray, Michel, *Vocabulaire de la musique de l'époque classique* (Paris: Minerve, 2005).

Norman, Buford, *Touched by the Graces: The Libretti of Philippe Quinault in the Context of French Classicism* (Birmingham, AL: Summa, 2001).

Nye, Edward, *Mime, Music, and Drama on the Eighteenth-Century Stage: The Ballet d'action* (Cambridge: Cambridge University Press, 2012).

O'Dea, Michael, "Rousseau's Ghost: *Le Devin du village* at the Paris Opera, 1770–1779," in Maria Gullstam and Michael O'Dea, eds, *Rousseau on Stage: Playwright, Musician, Spectator* (Oxford: Voltaire Foundation, 2017), 209–25.

Philippi, Daniela, "'Gluck les distribua derrière les coulisses:' Zum Einsatz der Chöre in Glucks *Alceste*," in Ursula Kramer and Wolfgang Birtel, eds, *Chöre und chorisches Singen* (Mainz: Are, 2009), 139–53.

Pierre, Constant, *Histoire du Concert spirituel: 1725–1790* (Paris: Société française de musicologie, 1975).

Prest, Julia, "In Chapel, On Stage, and in the Bedroom: French Responses to the Italian Castrato," *Seventeenth-Century French Studies* 32, no.2 (2010), 152–64.

Primavesi, Patrick, "The Dramaturgy of Rousseau's *Lettre à d'Alembert* and Its Importance for Modern Theatre," in Maria Gullstam and Michael O'Dea, eds, *Rousseau on Stage: Playwright, Musician, Spectator* (Oxford: Voltaire Foundation, 2017), 21–75.

Ravel, Jeffrey, *The Contested Parterre: Public Theater and French Political Culture 1680–1791* (Ithaca, NY: Cornell University Press, 1999).

Rex, Walter E., "Sexual Metamorphoses on the Stage in Mid-Eighteenth-Century Paris: The Theatrical Background of Rousseau's *Narcisse*," *Studies on Voltaire and the Eighteenth Century* 278 (1990), 265–76.

Rice, John A., *Antonio Salieri and Viennese Opera* (Chicago: The University of Chicago Press, 1998).

—— , "The Staging of Salieri's *Les Danaïdes* as Seen by a Cellist in the Orchestra," *Cambridge Opera Journal* 26, no.1 (2014), 65–82.

Rizzoni, Nathalie, "Le Geste éloquent: la pantomime en France au XVIIIᵉ siècle," in Jacqueline Waeber, ed., *Musique et geste en France de Lully à la Révolution: Études sur la musique, le théâtre et la danse* (Bern: Peter Lang, 2009), 129–48.

—— , "Un Représentant pittoresque de Terpsichore: Le maître à danser dans le théâtre français de la première moitié du XVIIIᵉ siècle," in Alain Montandon, ed., *Sociopoétique de la danse* (Paris: Anthropos, 2012), 207–22.

Roach, Joseph R., *The Player's Passion: Studies in the Science of Acting* (Ann Arbor, MI: University of Michigan Press, 1985).

Roche, Daniel, *France in the Enlightenment*, trans. Arthur Goldhammer (Cambridge, MA: Harvard University Press, 1998).

Rosenfeld, Sophia, *Common Sense: A Political History* (Cambridge, MA: Harvard University Press, 2011).

—— , *A Revolution in Language: The Problem of Signs in Late Eighteenth-Century France* (Stanford, CA: Stanford University Press, 2001).

Rosow, Lois, "How Eighteenth-Century Parisians Heard Lully's Operas: The Case of *Armide*'s Fourth Act," in John Hajdu Heyer, ed., *Jean-Baptiste Lully and the Music of the French Baroque: Essays in Honor of James R. Anthony* (Cambridge: Cambridge University Press, 1989), 213–37.

—— , "Opera in Paris from Campra to Rameau," in Simon P. Keefe, ed., *Cambridge History of Eighteenth-Century Music* (Cambridge: Cambridge University Press, 2009), 272–94.

—— , "Performing a Choral Dialogue by Lully," *Early Music* 15, no.3 (1987), 325–35.

Rougement, Martine de, *Le Vie théâtrale en France au XVIIIe siècle* (Paris: Champion, 2001).

Rumph, Stephen, *Mozart and Enlightenment Semiotics* (Berkeley, CA: University of California Press, 2012).

Rushton, Julian, "'Iphigénie en Tauride:' The Operas of Gluck and Piccinni," *Music & Letters* 53, no.4 (1972), 411–30.

Russo, Elena, *Styles of Enlightenment: Taste, Politics, and Authorship in Eighteenth-Century France* (Baltimore, MD: The Johns Hopkins University Press, 2007).

Sadler, Graham, "Rameau, Piron, and the Parisian Fair Theatres," *Soundings: A Music Journal* (1974), 13–29.

–– , and Shirley Thompson, "The Italian Roots of Marc-Antoine Charpentier's Chromatic Harmony," in Anne-Madeline Goulet and Gesa zur Nieden, eds, *Europäische Musiker in Venedig, Rom und Neapel, 1650–1750* (Kassel: Bärenreiter, 2015), 546–70.

Sahlins, Marshall, *What Kinship Is – And Is Not* (Chicago: The University of Chicago Press, 2013).

Sajous-d'Oria, Michèle, "*Alceste* selon Servandoni ou *Le Triomphe de l'amour conjugal*: spectacle orné de machines et animé d'acteurs pantomimes," in Daniel Brandenburg and Martina Hochreiter, eds, *Gluck auf dem Theater: Kongressbericht Nürnberg 7.–10. März 2008, Gluck-Studien* 6 (Kassel: Bärenreiter, 2011), 61–70.

Salaün, Franck, "*De la tête aux pieds*: Diderot et les gens de spectacle," *Recherches sur Diderot et sur l'Encyclopédie* 47 (2012), 25–42.

–– , "L'imagination au défi: la grande pantomime du *Neveu de Rameau*," in Franck Salaün and Patrick Taïeb, eds, *Musique et Pantomime dans le Neveu de Rameau* (Paris: Hermann, 2016), 227–50.

–– , and Patrick Taïeb, eds, *Musique et Pantomime dans le Neveu de Rameau* (Paris: Hermann, 2016).

Sawkins, Lionel, "Voltaire, Rameau, Rousseau: A Fresh Look at *La Princesse de Navarre* at its Revival in Bordeaux in 1763," *Studies on Voltaire and the Eighteenth Century* 265 (1989), 1334–40.

Schneewind, Jerome B., *The Invention of Autonomy: A History of Modern Moral Philosophy* (New York: Cambridge University Press, 1998).

Semmens, Richard, *Studies in the English Pantomime, 1712–1733* (Hillsdale, NY: Pendragon, 2016).

Sermain, Jean-Paul, "Le Spectacle de La Nouvelle Héloïse," in Jacques Berchtold, Christophe Martin, and Yannick Seite, eds, *Rousseau et le spectacle* (Paris: Armand Colin, 2014), 227–36.

Sheehan, Jonathan, and Dror Wahrman, *Invisible Hands: Self-Organization in the Eighteenth Century* (Chicago: The University of Chicago Press, 2015).

Spinelli, Donald C., *L'Inventaire après décès de Beaumarchais* (Paris: H. Champion, 1997).

Starobinski, Jean, *Jean-Jacques Rousseau: Transparency and Obstruction*, trans. Arthur Goldhammer with intro. by Robert Morrissey (Chicago: The University of Chicago Press, 1988).

Strong, Tracy B., "Music, the Passions, and Political Freedom in Rousseau," in Christie McDonald and Stanley Hoffmann, eds, *Rousseau and Freedom* (Cambridge: Cambridge University Press, 2010), 94–102.

Swift, Mary Grace, "The Three Ballets of the Young Sun," *Dance Chronicle* 3, no. 4 (1979–80), 361–72.

Thomas, Downing A., *Aesthetics of Opera in the Ancien Régime, 1647–1785* (New York: Cambridge University Press, 2002).

–– , *Music and the Origins of Language: Theories from the French Enlightenment* (Cambridge: Cambridge University Press, 1995).

—, "Rameau's *Platée* Returns: A Case of Double Identity in the *Querelle des bouffons*," *Cambridge Opera Journal* 18, no.1 (2006), 1–19.

Thomson, Ann, *Bodies of Thought: Science, Religion, and the Soul in the Early Enlightenment* (Oxford: Oxford University Press, 2008).

Tomlinson, Gary, *Metaphysical Song: An Essay on Opera* (Princeton, NJ: Princeton University Press, 1999).

Trousson, Raymond and Frédéric S. Eigeldinger, eds, *Dictionnaire de Jean-Jacques Rousseau* (Paris: Honoré Champion, 2006).

Turner, Victor, *The Ritual Process: Structure and Anti-Structure* (New York: Aldine, 1969; repr. 2008).

Unger, Harlow Giles, *Improbable Patriot: The Secret History of Monsieur Beaumarchais, the French Playwright who Saved the American Revolution* (Hanover, NH: University Press of New England, 2011).

Van Kley, Dale K., *The French Idea of Freedom: The Old Regime and the Declaration of Rights of 1789* (Stanford, CA: Stanford University Press, 1994).

Vechten, Carl Van, "Notes on Gluck's *Armide*," *The Musical Quarterly* 3, no.4 (1917), 539–47.

Vendrix, Philippe, "La Notion de révolution dans les écrits théoriques concernant la musique avant 1789," *International Review of the Aesthetics and Sociology of Music* 21, no.1 (1990), 71–78.

Verba, Cynthia, *Dramatic Expression in Rameau's Tragédie en musique: Between Tradition and Enlightenment* (New York: Cambridge University Press, 2013).

—, *Music and the French Enlightenment: Rameau and the Philosophes in Dialogue*, 2nd edn (New York: Oxford University Press, 2016).

Vercruysse, Jeroom, *Bibliographie descriptive des écrits du Baron d'Holbach* (Paris: Lettres modernes, 1971).

Waeber, Jacqueline, "Beaumarchais et Rousseau: sur quelques aspects de renouveau de la pantomime et du l'avènement du mélodrame," *French Studies of the Eighteenth and Nineteenth Centuries* 8 (2000), 205–24.

—, "'Cette horrible innovation': The First Version of the Recitative Parts of Rousseau's 'Le Devin du village,'" *Music & Letters* 82, no.2 (2001), 177–213.

—, "Décor et pantomimes du Devin du village: Une étude didascalique," *Annales de la Société Jean-Jacques Rousseau* 45 (2003), 131–65.

—, "'Le Devin de la foire'? Pantomime et jeu muet dans *Le Devin du village*," in Jacques Berchtold, Christophe Martin, and Yannick Seite, eds, *Rousseau et le spectacle*, edited by Jacques Berchtold, Christophe Martin, and Yannick Seite (Paris: Armand Colin, 2014), 105–30.

—, "'Le devin de la Foire?' Revaluating the Pantomime in Rousseau's *Devin du village*," in Jacqueline Waeber, ed., *Musique et geste en France de Lully à la Révolution: Études sur la musique, le théâtre et la danse* (Bern: Peter Lang, 2009), 149–72.

—, *En Musique dans le texte: Le mélodrame, de Rousseau à Schoenberg* (Paris: Van Dieren, 2005).

—, "Jean-Jacques Rousseau's 'Unité de mélodie,'" *Journal of the American Musicological Society* 62, no.1 (2009), 79–143.

—, ed., *Musique et geste en France de Lully à la Révolution: Études sur la musique, le théâtre et la danse* (Bern: Peter Lang, 2009).

—— , "Rousseau on Music: A Case of Nature vs. Nurture," in Eve Grace and Christopher Kelly, eds, *The Rousseauian Mind* (London: Routledge, 2019), 297–307.

—— , "Rousseau's 'Pygmalion' and the Limits of (Operatic) Expression," in Maria Gullstam and Michael O'Dea, eds, *Rousseau on Stage: Playwright, Musician, Spectator* (Oxford: Voltaire Foundation, 2017), 103–18.

Weber, William, *The Great Transformation of Musical Taste: Concert Programming from Haydn to Brahms* (New York: Cambridge University Press, 2008).

—— , "Learned and General Musical Taste in Eighteenth-Century France," *Past & Present* 89 (1980), 58–85.

Webster, James, *Haydn's "Farewell" Symphony and the Idea of Classical Style: Through-Composition and Cyclic Integration in His Instrumental Music* (New York: Cambridge University Press, 1991).

Wilcox, Beverly, "The Music Libraries of the Concert Spirituel: Canons, Repertories, and Bricolage in Eighteenth-Century Paris," PhD diss., University of California at Davis, 2013.

Winter, Marian Hannah, *The Pre-Romantic Ballet* (Brooklyn: Dance Horizons, 1974).

Wokler, Robert, *Rousseau, the Age of Enlightenment, and Their Legacies*, ed. Bryan Garsten (Princeton, NJ: Princeton University Press, 2012).

Yaffe, Gideon, *Liberty Worth the Name: Locke on Free Agency* (Princeton, NJ: Princeton University Press, 2000).

Yeo, Richard, "Classifying the Sciences," in Roy Porter, ed., *The Cambridge History of Science, vol.4: Eighteenth-Century Science* (Cambridge: Cambridge University Press, 2003), 249–63.

Yolton, John W., *Locke and French Materialism* (Oxford: Clarendon Press, 1991).

Index